Tcl 8.5 Network Programming

Build network-aware applications using Tcl, a powerful
dynamic programming language

Wojciech Kocjan

Piotr Beltowski

BIRMINGHAM - MUMBAI

Tcl 8.5 Network Programming

First published: July 2010

Production Reference: 1250610

Published by Packt Publishing Ltd.
32 Lincoln Road
Olton
Birmingham, B27 6PA, UK.

ISBN 978-1-849510-96-7

www.packtpub.com

Cover Image by Parag Kadam (paragvkadam@gmail.com)

Credits

Authors
Wojciech Kocjan
Piotr Beltowski

Reviewers
Hemang Lavana
Dmitry V.Tishakov

Acquisition Editor
Douglas Paterson

Development Editor
Mehul Shetty

Technical Editors
Charumathi Sankaran
Rupal J

Indexer
Hemangini Bari

Editorial Team Leader
Aanchal Kumar

Project Team Leader
Lata Basantani

Project Coordinator
Joel Goveya

Proofreaders
Lesley Harrison
Aaron Nash

Graphics
Geetanjali Sawant

Production Coordinators
Aparna S. Bhagat
Arvindkumar Gupta

Cover Work
Aparna S. Bhagat

About the Authors

Wojciech Kocjan is a programmer having ten years of experience with Tcl. His past experience includes both open source projects, involvement in commercial/government projects, as well as working for international corporations.

Over the years, Wojciech has contributed and created multiple open source projects related to Tcl. He is also the author of *Learning Nagios 3.0, Packt Publishing* and multiple publications on IT related subjects.

> I'd like to thank my wife Joanna and my son Kacper for all the help and support during the writing of this book.

Piotr Beltowski is an IT and software engineer, and co-author of several US patents and publications. He has a master of Science in Telecommunications, and his technical experience includes various aspects of telecommunications, such as designing IP networks or implementing support of network protocols. Piotr's experience as Level 3 customer support lead makes him focused on finding simple solutions to complex technical issues.

His professional career includes working in international corporations such as IBM and Ericsson (as a contractor).

> I would like to thank all my family and friends, especially Kasia and Monika for all the help and support they gave me during the writing of this book.

About the Reviewers

Hemang Lavana is the lead architect of Cisco's central test automation infrastructure group that designs and develops Tcl and Eclipse-based tools. He has over twelve years of architecture and design experience in developing high performance, robust, and scalable products focusing on modularity and extensibility.

After graduating from the prestigious Indian Institute of Technology, Bombay, Hemang earned a Ph.D. in Computer Engineering from North Carolina State University. He has published several papers and articles in various conferences on asynchronous, distributed and collaborative software for workflow automation. He is also the author of the award winning software WebWiseTclTk.

Dmitry V.Tishakov was born in 1971 in Sevastopol (Russia, Crimea). He received higher technical education at the Sevastopol device-building institute till 1994. In 2007, he completed his education from the Sevastopol Humanitarian University. He is a qualified engineer (Systems Engineering), psychologist, and photographer.

Dmitry was engaged in the system engineering of physical experiments automation, the automated "information gathering and processing" systems for atomic power stations, and hardware-software training systems.

Besides having operational experience as a system administrator and a system integrator, he also has operational experience in several areas, such as TV (the Independent TV-broadcasting company, Kaliningrad, Russia), software development, and the electro-technical industry. Since 2004, he has been working in the Tavrida Electric industrial group (`http://www.tavrida.com`), which is on one of leaders in the world of the electro-technical industry. Here he was involved in working out the automated quality testing and monitoring systems for industrial controllers.

I would like to thank Graham Ellis, Well House Consultant (Melksham, Wiltshire) for his answers to my questions when I started learning Tcl/Tk technology several years ago.

Table of Contents

Preface

Tcl or **Tool Command Language** is a very powerful, but easy-to-learn dynamic programming language, suitable for a very wide range of uses. Tcl is a mature yet evolving language used by developers, from one man shops to large corporations. .

It is commonly used for rapid prototyping, scripted applications, GUIs, and testing. Tcl is used on embedded-system platforms, both in its full form and in several other small-footprinted versions. Tcl is also used for CGI scripting and as the scripting language for the Eggdrop bot.

Tcl is popularly used today in many automated test harnesses, both for software and hardware, and has a loyal following in the Network Testing and SQA communities. According to the Tcl website, many have called it the "best-kept secret in the software industry". It is used for rapid development, truly cross-platform GUIs, flexible integration, elegant networking model, great I18N and thread support—all that and it's easy to learn and easy to deploy!

This book will delve into the network programming capabilities of Tcl: one of the best-kept secrets of the software industry.

What this book covers

Chapter 1, Introducing Tcl serves as a quick introduction to the Tcl world. It explains what the Tcl is, how to install it and start using it. It presents some tools for making development easy, such as Eclipse and Komodo. It describes Tcl language basics, such as language syntax, data types, and the important commands. This and the following chapters build a solid base for Tcl programming.

Chapter 2, Advanced Tcl Features focuses on advanced topics. More common commands are introduced. The reader learns how to handle time, namespaces, and use Tcl as an object-oriented programming language. A large part of the chapter is dedicated to file I/O operations. The reader also learns how to create Tcl packages or modules. Event loop and various types of events are also discussed. Threads are introduced in the end.

Chapter 3, Tcl Standalone Binaries teaches you how to break free from the constraint of having the Tcl interpreter installed, and how to build portable, standalone executable applications written in Tcl. You will also learn about the Metakit database concepts and its usage.

Chapter 4, Troubleshooting Tcl Applications focuses on topics related to "fixing" the applications. First, the reader learns how to introduce, configure, and apply logging information to the code. Later, the available tools and ways of debugging both local and remote applications are presented.

Chapter 5, Data Storage discusses topics such as text data storage and processing. Some of these include working with SQL databases (both remote systems such as MySQL and Postgresql, and local ones like SQLite), processing XML data (parsing and generation), handling plaintext data while focusing on common encoding issues.

Chapter 6, Networking in Tcl presents basic information about the TCP/UDP networking abilities of Tcl, from both the client and server sides. Core concepts and commands are discussed extensively along with examples.

Chapter 7, Using Common Internet Services teaches you how to send e-mails from Tcl, build e-mails containing HTML and various kinds of messages. It discusses how to retrieve, parse, and process e-mail messages, and also covers how to get data over HTTP, read RSS feeds, and upload and download files over FTP.

Chapter 8, Using Additional Internet Services introduces the reader to additional Internet protocols: querying information using DNS and querying the current date and time over an NTP service. It also discusses LDAP and how to use it to query information about user registries and how to authorize users. It describes the comm protocol, which can be used to communicate between local and remote Tcl applications. It presents how the protocol can be used and how the comm commands can be made secure.

Chapter 9, Learning SNMP describes SNMP (Simple Network Management Protocol) and its use for management of multiple types of devices – such as routers, switches, modems, and servers. It introduces the reader to how data is structured in SNMP by describing MIB (Management Information Base). It describes Scotty package, which provides SNMP functionality to Tcl. Step-by-step instructions are given for retrieving information and retrieving notifications from devices. It also describes how Tcl can be used to create custom SNMP agents using the Scotty package. This chapter also describes ICMP-related features; performing ping and trace routes.

Chapter 10, Web Programming in Tcl introduces Tclhttpd: a Tcl-based web server that can be used standalone and embedded in other applications. Using it for providing static files and web applications is described in detail. Built-in templating system is shown as well. This chapter also gives information on other subjects, using CGI scripts, handling specific types of files from Tcl, authorizing requests, and creating custom template systems.

Chapter 11, TclHttpd in Client-Server Applications provides details on creating HTTP-based client-server applications. It gives the reader a good understanding of how such applications are created, by providing a step-by-step example of building such an application. It also discusses building the client and the server as standalone binaries and providing automatic updates of the client. This example is then extended to show how modules can be added to allow additional code to be deployed to clients on demand.

Chapter 12, SOAP and XML-RPC covers creating and using web services from Tcl. It describes how to invoke methods over XML-RPC, along with an example of how this can be done to automatically add blog posts. SOAP is also described. This chapter shows how to create an SOAP-based web service and how such services can be used from within Tcl.

Chapter 13, SSL and Security focuses on the security aspects of network programming. It shows the reader how to secure communications and ensure that applications or users can authenticate remote systems. Step-by-step instructions are given on how to create a public key infrastructure and securely transfer keys to systems in the network. The chapter also introduces the reader to Tcl's safe interpreter feature and how it can be used to create a role-based security model for running unsecure Tcl code.

What you need for this book

The book is written so that both experienced and novice Tclers can find useful information inside. It starts with a quick introduction to Tcl and its networking support for those who are less familiar with them.

Authors focus on showing practical, yet simple examples for each module and command described so that the reader understands how to use them when solving the real life problems. The examples given are useful programs that try to solve real-world needs. All sample programs are clear and concise, yet nothing essential is left out and the programming style focuses on readability rather than on stylistic rigor or efficiency.

Who this book is for

This book is for Tcl developers who have basic knowledge of network programming concepts, who want to add networking capabilities to their applications. Working knowledge of Tcl and basic experience of network protocols will be useful. The reader should be familiar with basic concepts used in modern networking—keywords such as TCP, HTTP, or XML should not be a mystery. The book does not require advanced knowledge of Tcl – the first few chapters will swiftly introduce the readers into it, allowing them to refresh the information or gain a quick overview of the Tcl language abilities.

Conventions

In this book, you will find a number of styles of text that distinguish between different kinds of information. Here are some examples of these styles, and an explanation of their meaning.

Code words in text are shown as follows: "Calculations in Tcl are done by using a separate command called expr "

A block of code is set as follows:

```
proc createDict {} {
    set value [dict create]
    dict set value firstValue 1
    dict set value otherValue 2
    return $value
}
```

When we wish to draw your attention to a particular part of a code block, the relevant lines or items are set in bold:

```
% puts [clock format [clock scan "12:45 +3 hours"]]
Tue Sep 22 15:45:00 CEST 2009
```

Any command-line input or output is written as follows:

```
set rows [mk::select myTag.people]

printRows myTag.people $rows
```

New terms and **important words** are shown in bold. Words that you see on the screen, in menus or dialog boxes for example, appear in the text like this: "After a successful installation, we can go to the **Administrative Tools** folder and run the **Services** applet.".

Warnings or important notes appear in a box like this.

 Tips and tricks appear like this.

Reader feedback

Feedback from our readers is always welcome. Let us know what you think about this book—what you liked or may have disliked. Reader feedback is important for us to develop titles that you really get the most out of.

To send us general feedback, simply send an e-mail to feedback@packtpub.com, and mention the book title via the subject of your message.

If there is a book that you need and would like to see us publish, please send us a note in the **SUGGEST A TITLE** form on www.packtpub.com or e-mail suggest@packtpub.com.

If there is a topic that you have expertise in and you are interested in either writing or contributing to a book on, see our author guide on www.packtpub.com/authors.

Customer support

Now that you are the proud owner of a Packt book, we have a number of things to help you to get the most from your purchase.

Downloading the example code for the book

You can download the example code files for all Packt books you have purchased from your account at http://www.PacktPub.com. If you purchased this book elsewhere, you can visit http://www.PacktPub.com/support and register to have the files e-mailed directly to you.

Errata

Although we have taken every care to ensure the accuracy of our content, mistakes do happen. If you find a mistake in one of our books—maybe a mistake in the text or the code—we would be grateful if you would report this to us. By doing so, you can save other readers from frustration and help us improve subsequent versions of this book. If you find any errata, please report them by visiting `http://www.packtpub.com/support`, selecting your book, clicking on the **let us know** link, and entering the details of your errata. Once your errata are verified, your submission will be accepted and the errata will be uploaded on our website, or added to any list of existing errata, under the Errata section of that title. Any existing errata can be viewed by selecting your title from `http://www.packtpub.com/support`.

Piracy

Piracy of copyright material on the Internet is an ongoing problem across all media. At Packt, we take the protection of our copyright and licenses very seriously. If you come across any illegal copies of our works, in any form, on the Internet, please provide us with the location address or website name immediately so that we can pursue a remedy.

Please contact us at `copyright@packtpub.com` with a link to the suspected pirated material.

We appreciate your help in protecting our authors, and our ability to bring you valuable content.

Questions

You can contact us at `questions@packtpub.com` if you are having a problem with any aspect of the book, and we will do our best to address it.

1
Introducing Tcl

The purpose of this chapter is to refresh your memory with some basic and fundamental information about Tcl—what it is, what it is not, and why it was created. It is not intended to make you learn Tcl from scratch or to replace or duplicate the official Tcl documentation—there are a lot of sources, both online and printed. However, it is to briefly summarize facts and allow the reader to easily "tune in" to the topic of the book. If you are new to Tcl, after going through this chapter, you will have an overview of the language and its basics, and it would be a good idea to experiment with it, create your own scripts, and study sophisticated options for the described commands before proceeding to further reading. If you are an experienced Tcl programmer, you can probably skip this chapter.

This chapter discusses the origins of Tcl language—the fundamental idea behind its creation, why it was created, and what kind of problems it addresses. It presents Tcl concepts, describes the possibilities Tcl offers, and explains flexibility that comes from a choice of extensions available for use. We also learn about the license agreement it is distributed under and who is involved in this undertaking.

The chapter also talks about a range of enterprise-level platforms supported by Tcl. Its strength comes from the portability it offers. We briefly describe how to obtain a ready-to-use distribution to start your adventure with Tcl, along with its installation on both Windows and Unix environments.

We also describe the tools you can use to develop your own code. To start doing this, nothing more than a plaintext editor is required. However, you will save lots of time and frustration by using an **Integrated Development Environment (IDE)**. Both **Eclipse** and **Komodo** are discussed, along with installation and configuration tips, and the creation and execution of your first script.

After that, we come to Tcl's syntax, giving you the basics of reading the code and creating your first scripts. Once you have read this, you will be able to understand the structure of the code, identify its blocks and particular instructions. You will also get familiar with the basic data types and flow control structures offered by the language.

What is Tcl/Tk

Basically, Tcl is yet another scripting language. It was created by Professor John K. Ousterhout in 1988. Why would someone bother to create their own language? John and his students created a set of tools for designing integrated circuits at the University of California at Berkeley. Many of these tools had their own dedicated command languages, allowing interaction with the user. As the primary focus was on the tools, the command languages were often weakly designed, with odd syntax. With the passing of time, the team realized they were missing an easy-to-use, simple, and embeddable common command language that would allow various tools to have a unified command syntax, and it was only a matter of time before Tcl came into existence.

Consider building a complex application similar to the task of building a house. All you need are bricks of different shapes and functionality, and some kind of substance such as filler or glue to keep it all together. This filler is Tcl, and the bricks are components exposed as commands. What more, you can use bricks (components) provided by someone else (like factory), or you can create your own sophisticated bricks that will do whatever you need them to do, and all these bricks are still joined by the same substance—Tcl! Therefore, an application should be considered as a set of components / modules / "bricks" of different characteristics and purposes, each exposed as a command with standardized syntax and a Tcl script that joins them all. Now when creating your program, you do not have to 'reinvent the wheel' by implementing another to learn the error-prone command language—you can simply embed Tcl inside it. Tcl strongly supports and forces componentization of your application. It allows you to configure and control every application module so that it fits your needs.

Tcl is a scripting language with a UNIX-shell like syntax, where all operations are commands. Yes, let's say that again—it's all about the commands here. Everything in Tcl is a command. It comes with a set of built-in commands that implement basic ideas that every programming language simply has to have, namely variables, flow control, or procedures. But this is where the magic begins, as you will see later in the second chapter, the flexibility of Tcl allows us to easily extend it with object-oriented programming concepts.

Tcl is supported on a wide range of platforms, including Microsoft Windows, Mac OS, Linux, Solaris, HP-UX, AIX and others. You can get a full list of supported platforms at: `http://www.tcl.tk/software/tcltk/platforms.html`

Tcl is a dynamic scripting language—this means the source code you write using Tcl is not compiled in to binary file that may be executed on its own. On the contrary, it is stored 'as is'—in form of a set of instructions (commands) written in one or more plaintext files, interpreted at runtime by the Tcl interpreter. The interpreter is nothing more than a normal binary application that can understand and process scripts it is provided with. A support for a specific platform means that there is an interpreter for this platform.

Each running Tcl interpreter should be considered as a separate virtual machine having its own internal state that is consequently modified by subsequent commands read from standard input. The commands can also be read from the file, so you can execute your existing script, which will eventually lead the virtual interpreted machine to a new state and then interact with it dynamically.

It is possible to use Tcl entirely in an interactive manner by entering commands manually instead of executing an earlier created script. In order to do this, you simply run the interpreter and enter commands via the simple, standard shell—after the prompt (by default it is % character). This ability adds great flexibility into both experimenting with and rapidly developing the code. This shell application is commonly called `tclsh`, but for example, *in* case of the ActiveTcl distribution (described later in this chapter), the name `tclsh85` is used to reflect Tcl version it supports. The following screenshot illustrates the shell's start as well as the execution of some basic commands:

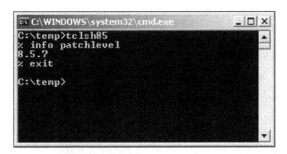

The Tcl command `info patchlevel` returns Tcl's version information and `exit` terminates the interactive interpreter shell.

As Tcl scripts are nothing more than plaintext files, you do not need any special tools to develop them. All you need is a text editor with which you can create or modify Tcl files. If `tclsh` is executed with the filename, the shell is not shown, and the interpreter executes the script that is read from that file. The following screenshot illustrates this:

```
C:\WINDOWS\system32\cmd.exe                         _|□|×|
C:\temp>dir /B
main.tcl

C:\temp>type main.tcl
# my first Tcl script
puts "Hello World one more time!"

C:\temp>tclsh85 main.tcl
Hello World one more time!

C:\temp>
```

The script file called `main.tcl` constitutes the entire script in this example. Its content is the very much used "Hello World" example:

```
#my first Tcl script
puts "Hello World one more time!"
```

The first line demonstrates how comments are made in Tcl—it starts with the # character, and the second line contains the command `put` with the string attribute enclosed within quotation marks. This command will send the provided string to standard output.

To execute it, we pass the file to Tcl interpreter `tclsh85`.

Along with `tclsh` comes another application called `wish`, which basically has the same functionality. The main difference is that it preloads the Tk package and, in case of MS Windows, creates a separate window-based shell rather than using the system console.

Early implementations of Tcl interpreters were internally based on string representation of executed script that resulted in sluggish execution and poor speed. In later versions, a "just-in-time" compiler was added, which converts the Tcl script, on the fly, into the **byte code language** (BCL) internal representation—a concept used in languages such as Java. Such a byte code representation of the script is next executed by the interpreter, which significantly improves its performance. It is also possible to save compiled script for future usage, with the typical extension `.tbc`. The main benefit to using bytecode files is that the source code is hidden—it does not give any real performance improvements.

Based on what we discussed till now, any Tcl program consists of one or more scripts plus an interpreter. Such a form allows easy and rapid development, meaning that you simply need to modify one of your scripts with text editor, but it also has its own drawbacks. It is much easier to distribute your program as a standalone, ready-to-execute binary file. Distribution of Tcl source files would be really awkward—for example, you may be not able to install the interpreter because of your system administrator's policy. Besides, how many times have you wanted to try out some interesting Java application only to get angry when you realized that to run it, you have to download dozens of megabytes and install Java virtual machine? If you consider this a "not so elegant" solution and are in favor of standalone applications, here is the good news—it is possible to pack all your scripts along with the interpreter into one binary, executable file that is not different from "normal" applications! We will discuss this in more detail in *Chapter 3*. It is quite possible that you are already an unknowing user of such applications, as there are a number of these available, for example, an excellent MP3 player called *SnackAmp* (`http://snackamp.sourceforge.net`) or the encrypted passwords vault *Password Gorilla* (`http://www.fpx.de/fp/Software/Gorilla/`).

Tcl language is a standard example of an open source idea. The BSD-style license gives you all the freedom of usage; you can use and modify it in any way you want—also, commercial usage is permitted (detailed license is available at `http://www.tcl.tk/software/tcltk/license.html`). Both Tcl and Tk are maintained by a world-wide community lead by the group of experts composing Tcl Core Team. Anyone can propose improvements by using the **Tcl Improvement Proposal (TIP)** feature and sending the proposal to TCT. The community's central site is the Tcl Developer Xchange (`http://www.tcl.tk/`), which serves as a primary source of Tcl-related information.

One of the most significant contributors is a Canadian Software Company called **ActiveState**, which specializes in dynamic languages. It provides its own distribution of Tcl called *ActiveTcl* and also offers various development tools (both of these are discussed later in this chapter).

Across this book, we will present Tcl in its latest available version, which is 8.5 at the time of writing this book. However, majority of information is valid for the version 8.4 and the previous versions. To sum it all up, Tcl is a mature scripting language with a lot of extensions coming from the open source community, and it allows you to quickly develop multi-platform command-line or GUI-based applications.

Extensions

The great flexibility of Tcl comes from its ability to extend the available set of commands known to the interpreter by adding additional extensions, that is, Tcl packages. Packages can be written in pure Tcl, making them platform-independent, or in native code like C/C++, which is then compiled for a specific target platform. It is possible that a package will consist of both of these. There are a lot of packages available on the Internet, both free of use and commercial. A good place to start is **Tcllib — Tcl Standard Library**. This is a set of extensions written in pure Tcl, available at `http://tcllib.sourceforge.net/`. Soon you will notice that we will use various packages from this repository for the examples in this book.

What's more interesting is that if you find out that nobody created an extension you would like to use, you will be able to create your own one and share it with the community.

Tk

One of the extensions this chapter will cover is Tk, which was developed by John Osterhout. Tk is a cross-platform GUI framework, which provides the same functions for Tcl as AWT and Swing do for Java. In other words, it is a library that contains a set of typical basic elements (widgets) such as buttons, frames, a canvas, menus, and so on. Tk widgets are flexible in terms of their customization options; almost every aspect may be defined at time of creation or modified later. One of its features is a native "look and feel", which simply means that Tcl/Tk graphical applications do not differ significantly from other native applications in terms of the look and usage. As over the years, Tk appearance started to fall behind the looks of modern operating systems, a number of extensions were created. Also worth mentioning is the Tile Widget Set (`http://tktable.sourceforge.net/tile/`), which brings re-implementation of some Tk core widget, as well as addition of a few new widgets. Tile is also an engine that allows the usage of themes. According to the Tile documentation:

> *A theme is a collection of elements and styles that determine the look and feel of the widget set.*

Tile has been incorporated into Tk core functionality in version 8.5, which means it is now available in all Tcl/Tk distributions. Although many Tk widgets have corresponding newer Tile equivalents, they can coexist in one application and the developer has the freedom of choice as to which version to use.

As an example, have a look at the following screenshot of SnackAmp that illustrates Tcl's possibilities in the field of GUI applications:

Tk became so popular that it is no longer Tcl-specific. It is now possible to use it in other scripting languages like Perl or Python.

Installation

Source releases for Tcl/Tk along with configuration, compilation, and installation instructions are available at `http://www.tcl.tk/software/tcltk/download.html`, so everyone can compile the interpreter for themselves. Typically, you don't want to waste your time doing this, especially when someone has done it before, and the fastest and easiest way is to get precompiled binaries for your platform. Among the various distributions of Tcl, ActiveTcl is considered as one of the best. It is available at ActiveState's site `http://www.activestate.com/activetcl/`. Not only does it contain Tcl and Tk, but it also offers a large number of extensions. The unique strength of the ActiveTcl distribution is that it covers a wide range of enterprise-level operating systems by offering binaries for Windows, Linux, Mac OS X, Solaris, and HP-UX. In this chapter, we will focus on installation under Windows XP and Ubuntu Linux. As almost every Linux distribution comes with its own set of Tcl binaries, users of these systems usually have more choices.

At the time of writing this book, the latest stable release of ActiveTcl is 8.5.7.0.

Windows

In the case of Microsoft Windows, ActiveTcl is substantially the only choice. Installation is simple; the installer is distributed in the form of an executable file (named as something like `ActiveTcl8.5.7.0.290198-win32-ix86-threaded.exe`). Once you download and run it, you will be presented with a graphical installation wizard similar to the one shown in the following screenshot:

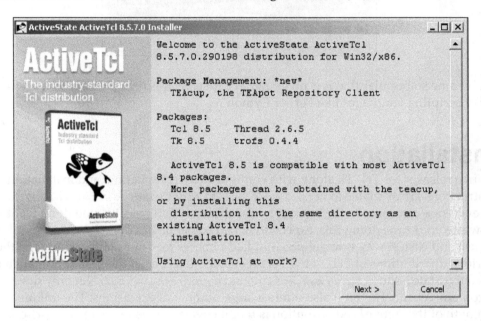

On subsequent screens, you will be presented with a detailed ActiveTcl License. You will also be able to specify installation directory — associate the application with the `.tcl` extension and configure some of the other details. For the rest of this chapter, we will assume that Tcl is installed in the `C:\Tcl` directory.

The installer updates system variable PATH with the path to the directory where Tcl binaries are located, that is `C:\Tcl\bin`. It allows you to execute commands like `tclsh85.exe` anywhere, without specifying the directory's full path. Note that, as usual, you are advised against using a path containing whitespaces.

Unix-like systems

We will consider Unix-compatible systems using Ubuntu 9.04 Linux as a popular, easy-to-get example. In the case of these systems, you have more choices than you do with Windows. One of the choices you have is to install ActiveTcl (there is a good chance it supports your platform), another is to search for a precompiled Tcl distribution. Ubuntu, for example, comes with a significant number of optional packages of additional software prepared by the community. Among them are of course binary compilations of Tcl. It is possible that your system already has the Tcl distribution installed, but even if not, it is extremely easy to install it, because Ubuntu will be able to suggest what packages should be installed based on the commands that these packages provide for the system. The following is a screenshot of such a situation:

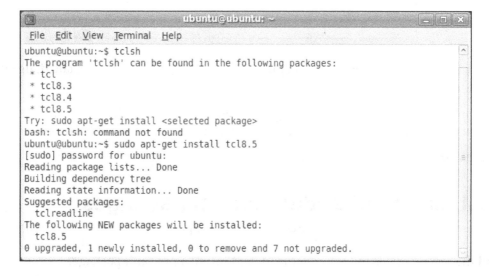

The user wants to execute the `tclsh` command to get Tcl interactive shell. The package that provides this command is not yet installed, and the system informs the user what packages are available. In this case, we have decided to choose `tcl8.5` and install it using the command-line command as follows:

```
sudo apt-get install tcl8.5
```

Once installed, you can run the `tclsh` command to get the interactive Tcl shell as follows:

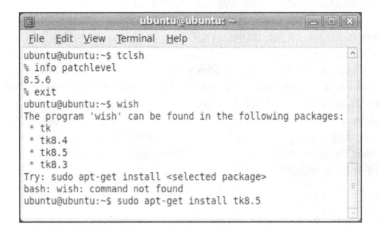

To verify the detailed version of Tcl interpreter which you have just installed, use the `info patchlevel` command.

Tk comes in a separate Ubuntu package. You will be notified of this if you attempt to run an application that requires it, for example `wish`. Similarly, it can be installed with:

```
% sudo apt-get install tk8.5.
```

Installation of additional Tcl packages

Just like core Tcl installation, extensions, that is Tcl packages, can also be installed in two ways: the first is to get the source code of an extension and build (compile) it, and the second one is to find, download, and install a pre-built package.

In order to be able to use the extension in your script, it must be available for the interpreter. There are several locations where Tcl can search for it, and these locations are kept in the special Tcl variable called `auto_path`. You can learn its value by starting the Tcl shell and executing the following command:

```
puts $auto_path
```

The `puts` command prints the content of the specified variable to standard output. In the case of Windows, the output appears as:

```
Command Prompt - tclsh85                                        _ □ ×
C:\Documents and Settings\Administrator>tclsh85
% puts $auto_path
C:/Tcl/lib/tcl8.5 C:/Tcl/lib c:/tcl/lib/teapot/package/win32-ix86/lib c:/tcl/lib
/teapot/package/tcl/lib
% _
```

Now that you know this, you can put the packages you require under the `C:\Tcl\lib` location to make them available for the interpreter. The concept of the `$auto_path` variable and other packages will be described in more detail in the next chapter.

ActiveTcl comes with a handy utility called **Teacup**. This utility allows for easy installation of prebuilt Tcl extensions from external remote repositories called Tcl Extension Archives. These archives, also known as **Teapot**, are centrally managed sites. Currently, there is one public Teapot maintained by ActiveState. By using Teacup, you can install the package you need into your local repository and then use it in your scripts. It will automatically solve dependencies, localize package(s), and download and install them.

Additional tools

In these days of rapid application development, using plaintext editors like `notepad` or `vi` can be really inconvenient and time consuming. Luckily, there is far better alternative — an **Integrated Development Environment** (**IDE**). IDEs are tools that allow efficient code creation and editing, support testing your code from within the editor, and usually also offer debugging capabilities.

At the time of writing this book, there are two IDEs worth mentioning: Eclipse and Komodo. Both support syntax highlighting and coloring, auto completion, creating launch configurations, managing projects and dependencies, and have many other useful features.

Eclipse

It is hardly possible that you have not heard about Eclipse nowadays. An open source IDE supporting a wide variety of languages, extensible with plugins is considered as one of the best programming environments, and it is all free. Due to the fact that Eclipse was developed in Java, the CPU/memory requirements may be slightly higher than in case of native applications, but in return, it is available for the Windows, Linux, and Mac platforms.

First you have to install the **Java Runtime Environment** (JRE), we strongly suggest installing latest version available (at the moment it is version 6 Update 17), you can get it from `http://java.com`. We will discuss Eclipse Classic 3.5.0 available for download at `http://www.eclipse.org/downloads/`. The installation process is simple—just download and unzip the file to a location of your choice and run `eclipse.exe`. The full description of Eclipse is out of scope of this book, we will present only the necessary steps to get it running for Tcl development purposes.

By default, Eclipse supports only Java development, so we have to install an additional extension called the **Dynamic Languages Toolkit (DLTK)** for Tcl support. In order to do this it, you have to navigate to the **Help | Install New Software...** menu. A new window will show up, as shown in the following screenshot:

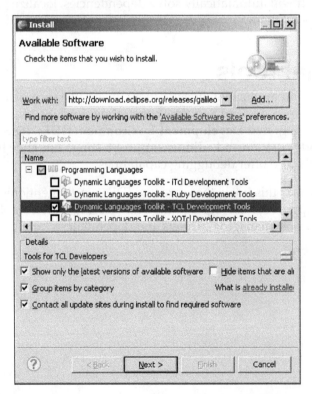

First, select the **Galileo** site from the list at the top. Eclipse will download a list of all available extensions from this site; this may take a while. Once the list is visible, expand **Programming Languages** and select **Dynamic Languages Toolkit – TCL Development Tools**. Once you click on **Next**, Eclipse will automatically resolve dependencies and select all the necessary plugins to install. In this case, it will choose to install the DLTK Core and **Eclipse Modelling Framework (EMF)** extensions, as shown in the following screenshot:

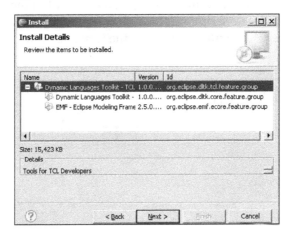

Following this, Eclipse will download and install all the necessary files, and ask you to restart. Once it is done, you have to configure installed Tcl interpreters. Eclipse requires at least one interpreter in order to be able to run scripts. To configure it, navigate to **Window | Preferences** to open the preferences dialog, and then go to **Tcl | Interpreters**. Click the **Add...** button on this pane, and then **Browse...** and navigate to the interpreter binary, which is installed at `C:\Tcl\bin\tclsh85.exe`. Once done, you should have configured the default interpreter like here, as shown in the following screenshot:

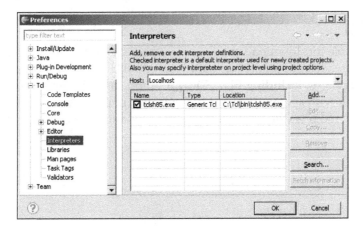

Now you have your Eclipse fully configured to create and run Tcl scripts! To get a taste of working with Eclipse, let's create the same Hello World example. Navigate to **File | New | Project...** and choose **Tcl Project** from the **Tcl** category and then create a project named **TclHelloWorld**—it will be shown in the Script Explorer view (by default, on the left of the Eclipse window). The next step is to right-click on the project name in this view and select **Tcl File**, and name it main.tcl. As a template, select **Tcl File**. Eclipse will create the file with a specific header that we will explain later. Add the puts command to that script, just as you did in the previous example. Now it is time to execute the script—right-click on it and select **Run As | Tcl Script**. The output of this execution will be visible in the Console view. The following screen illustrates it:

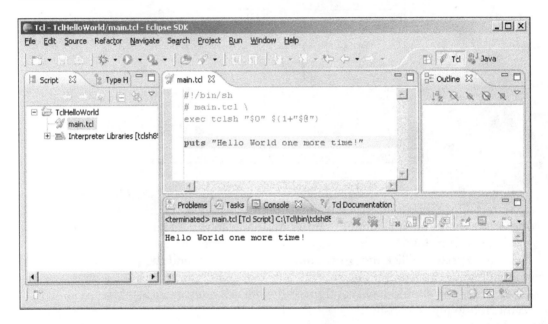

Komodo

Komodo, available for download at http://www.activestate.com/komodo, comes in two flavors: free Komodo Edit and paid Komodo IDE. Both support a wide range of scripting languages, including PHP, Ruby, Python, and of course Tcl. The first one is a simple editor with syntax checking and coloring, and also Project Management abilities. The second one extends the offered functionality as it comes with a debugger.

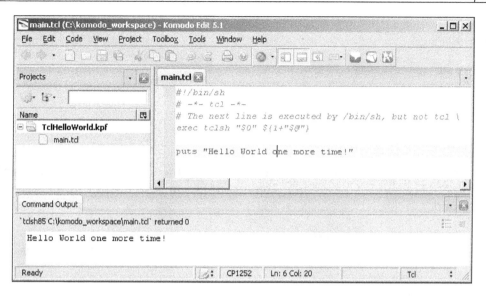

Similar to Eclipse, you can create a project (using **File | New | New Project...**) and a file inside it (right-click on project name in the left pane and select **Add | New file...**). The new file is created based on a language-specific template, which comes with the universal header described later in this chapter.

To run the script, navigate to **Tools | Run Command...** and enter `tclsh85 %F` in the Run dialog, and then click on the **Run** button.

tkcon – an alternate Tcl shell

If you find the standard Tcl shell too primitive, you must definitely have a look at **tkcon** — a standard console replacement with many useful features including a command history and syntax highlighting. What is even more interesting is that it is implemented as another Tcl package, and therefore it is perfectly possible to embed tkcon in to your Tcl application. The following is a screenshot of tkcon console, with the `puts $auto_path` command's output:

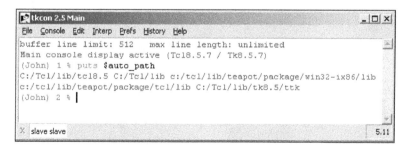

Tkcon is, by default, included in the ActiveTcl distribution. To install it on Ubuntu, enter:

```
% sudo apt-get install tkcon .
```

In order to run it, simply execute the command tkcon.

Tcl syntax

Tcl scripts are nothing more than plaintext files saved with 16-bit Unicode encoding. Such a script consists of one or more commands that are executed by the interpreter at runtime.

Each line of the script (with exceptions described as follows) consists of the command and zero or more command arguments, all separated by whitespaces (spaces or tabs).

If the line starts with the # character, it is considered to be a comment and not processed by the interpreter.

If the line ends with the \ (backslash) character, the next line is considered to be a continuation of current one. This is useful for breaking long lines and improving the readability of the code.

You can also join separate commands using ;, as shown in the following example:

```
puts "one"; puts "two"
```

Tcl commands documentation syntax

The comprehensive documentation for Tcl 8.5 is located at http://www.tcl.tk/doc/. This section does not intend to replace or compete with it, but to briefly introduce Tcl's grammar and rules. Therefore, we strongly recommend reading the documentation, especially the descriptions of the main commands.

Running the script

Let's revisit the main.tcl script which was introduced earlier in this chapter:

```
#my first Tcl script
puts "Hello World one more time!"
```

The first line is the comment. The second line has the `puts` command with one parameter — the text string — in quotations marks. As we mentioned previously, you can run the script with:

```
tclsh main.tcl
```

However, in some cases, it would be far more comfortable to run it as a standalone program. On Windows, you can associate the `.tcl` extension with the Tcl interpreter to achieve this. On Unix, the script will look like:

```
#!/usr/bin/tclsh
#my first Tcl script
puts "Hello World one more time!"
```

The first line starts with the `#!` sequence, often referred to as *shebang*. The presence of these two characters at the very beginning of the executable file informs the system's program loader that the file is a script and also specifies the interpreter which should be used to run it. In this case, the first line issues an instruction to Unix shell, specifying that the script should be interpreted by `/usr/bin/tclsh`. As the `#` character itself is often a comment marker, the line will be ignored by the interpreter. However, it is not a good idea to hardcode the path, because it may be different for other systems, thus making our code not non-portable. A better solution is:

```
#!/bin/sh
#my first Tcl script \
exec tclsh "$0" $@"
puts "Hello World one more time!"
```

In this case, the script is interpreted by standard `sh` shell. This shell is unable to run Tcl commands, but it will run the `exec` command perfectly, effectively launching `tclsh`, passing the script name and other arguments (if any). The trick is that we do not want the Tcl interpreter to process the `exec` command, as it was intended for `sh` only. In order to avoid this problem, the previous line ends with `\`, so both the second and third lines of that script are treated like comments by the interpreter.

Recently, also another solution has gained popularity, that is:

```
#!/usr/bin/env tclsh
#my first Tcl script
puts "Hello World one more time!"
```

The `env` command searches for `tclsh` using system PATH variable and executes it, therefore, no direct path to it is required.

Running commands directly in the tclsh interpreter

In the case of "one-liner" examples, we can also easily enter them directly into the Tcl shell — you will recognize them by the % prompt character. It is worth mentioning that the shell offers hints about the syntax of any command. This is extremely useful if you don't quite remember the required arguments or their order:

```
% puts
wrong # args: should be "puts ?-nonewline? ?channelId? string"
```

The syntax of such a hint is commonly used throughout the Tcl documentation. Question marks indicate optional arguments (in this example, -nonewline or channelId are both optional).

Variables

As with any other language, Tcl allows us to define variables. Let's consider the following example:

```
set myVariable "someValue"
puts $myVariable
```

The first command set creates a variable named myVariable and sets its value to somevalue. The second command, that is puts, prints the variable's value on the screen. myVariable is the variable name and the $ operator is used to get its value. When the interpreter starts processing the second line, it will first substitute all the variable values, so the line will effectively be puts "someValue", and then it will execute it. This will result in the following output:

```
someValue
```

To delete a variable, use the unset command:

```
% unset myVariable
% puts $MyVariable
can't read "MyVariable": no such variable
```

Grouping

In an earlier example, we used "" to group *Hello world one more time!* into one single argument. Without it, we would get a syntactical error, as each word would be treated as separate argument for the `puts` command:

```
% puts Hello world one more time!
wrong # args: should be "puts ?-nonewline? ?channelId? string"
```

It is also worth mentioning that whitespaces could be also escaped using the \ character, as shown in the following example:

```
% puts Hello\ world\ one\ more\ time!
Hello world one more time!
```

If the argument consists of only one word, grouping is not necessary, but it's still possible.

The text inside quotation marks is processed before being passed to the command. What this it means is that all references to variables are replaced with the variable's values, for example:

```
% set var World; puts "Hello $var"
Hello World
```

The substitution gets complicated if you don't want to have any whitespace between the variable's value and the text that follows. In this case, you can end the variable name with '\' or put it into { }, as in the following example:

```
% set var World; puts "Hello $vars!"
can't read "vars": no such variable
% puts "Hello $var\s!"
Hello Worlds!
% puts "Hello ${var}s!"
Hello Worlds!
```

The third option is the preferred one because of its readability.

Grouping is also possible with curly braces, that is, { }. The difference is that text inside the quotation marks is evaluated, and the text inside { } is not, consider the following:

```
% set var World; puts {Hello $var}
Hello $var
```

In the second case, $var was not substituted with its real value World, because it was inside { }.

One more unique feature of curly braces is that they allow multiple lines inside them. In the code:

```
% puts {Hello
World!}
Hello
World!
```

The new line character that terminates the first line is not processed, and therefore, it also breaks the output into two lines. Of course, it is legal to also use \:

```
% puts {Hello\
World!}
Hello World!
```

Nesting commands

The ability to execute commands wouldn't be very valuable if there wasn't some way to provide the result of one command to another. In Tcl, we can use [] to execute a command and capture its return value:

```
% set var [info patchlevel]; puts "Current patchlevel is: $var"
Current patchlevel is: 8.5.6
```

In this example, the output of the info patchlevel command is used as the value for the var variable. It is also perfectly possible to use [] inside quotation marks, as its content will be processed by the interpreter:

```
% puts "Current patchlevel is: [info patchlevel]"
Current patchlevel is: 8.5.6
```

Data types

Basically, every variable in Tcl can be considered as a string. The internal representation of such a variable depends on its execution state (see *Chapter 2, Advanced Tcl features* for more details). Being a dynamic language, Tcl converts the value of a variable to a suitable type at runtime. Let's consider the following example:

```
% set x "2"; expr $x + 3
5
% set x "text"; expr $x + 3
invalid bareword "text"
in expression "text + 3";
```

We introduce the new Tcl command `expr` that allows arithmetic operations. In this example, the string `"2"` is converted to an integer by `expr` and it returns correct value, but the string `text` causes an error, because it cannot be converted.

To operate on strings, the `string` command is extremely useful. The convention of this command is that it accepts a subcommand name as the first argument. For example, if we assume that `str` is a *Hello World!* string, in order to get its length, you can use:

```
% string length $str
12
```

Also, in order to reverse it, use:

```
% string reverse $str
!dlroW olleH
```

The `String match` command can be used to verify if the given string matches the *pattern*. The pattern is basically another string, but apart from normal characters, some special sequences can be also used:

Sequence	Interpretation
?	Matches any, exactly one character
*	Matches 0 or more of any of the characters
[chars]	Matches exactly one character, only that specified inside [] brackets. It is possible to use the [a-z] syntax to match all characters in this range, in this case from 'a' to 'z
\	Allows escaping of any of the special characters, such as ?, *, [or] and treats them as normal characters to be match with

The command returns 1 if the string is successfully matched and it returns 0 otherwise:

```
% set str aStringToMatch
% string match *ToMatch $str
1
% string match ?StringToMatch $str
1
% string match {[a-c]StringToMatch} $str
1
% string match {[b-c]StringToMatch} $str
0
```

Note that in the last two cases, this pattern is put into curly braces to prevent the interpreter from considering the content of the [] braces as a command to be executed.

Describing every string subcommand is beyond the scope of this chapter, the details can be found in the manual at http://www.tcl.tk/man/tcl8.5/TclCmd/string.htm.

It is worth mentioning at this point that depending on the context, the variable's value may be treated as a text string, a number, or a logical value, just as we will see in the following examples.

More than pure strings, Tcl introduces the concept of two interesting data types — lists and arrays (hashmaps).

Lists

A Tcl list holds an ordered sequence of elements such as strings, other lists, and other variables. To create a list, you can use the `list` command:

```
set myList [list element1 element2 element3]
```

In this example, we create a list using three elements, separated with whitespaces, and assign the list to the `myList` variable.

What is interesting is that there is no straight demarcation between the list and the string, and therefore, the following code also creates a list:

```
set myList "element1 element2 element3"
```

Curly braces are also possible here. The conclusion is that every string may be considered as a list. The advantage of using the `list` command is that it takes care of correct formatting, adding braces and backslashes when necessary. Consider either of the following two commands:

```
set myList "one two {another list here}"
set myList {one two {another list here}}
```

They will create a list in which the third element will be another list consisting of elements specified in curly braces. The same effect can be achieved using the `list` command:

```
set myList [list one two [list another list here]]
```

From the user's point of view, a list is both a string and a list, because there is no visible difference:

```
% puts $myList
one two {another list here}
```

As you can see, the `list` command added the { } braces at the correct points.

So why even bother with lists? Lists allow you to organize and structure your data, and the benefits of using them are that Tcl offers a set of commands that operates on lists. Lists tend to be extremely useful in typical scripts, therefore, we will briefly review the possible operations on them.

To get the number of elements in your list, use `llength`. This command takes one parameter, that is, the list. The output is the number of elements in the list.

```
% llength [list one two three]
3
```

The command `lindex` retrieves an element from a list. In basic usage, it takes the list and the index of the element as arguments. Just as in other programming languages, indexes start from zero in Tcl.

```
% set myList [list one two three]; lindex $myList 0
one
```

We can also specify the index as the special keyword `end`, which indicates the last element. For example:

```
% set myList [list one two three]; lindex $myList end
three
```

We can also specify `end-<n>`, which indicates the nth element from the end. The value `end-0` is the same as the `end` value; the value `end-1` specifies the last but one item and so on. For example:

```
% set myList [list one two three]; lindex $myList end-1
two
```

If the retrieved element is another list, `lindex` also has the ability to retrieve its element by providing additional indexes:

```
% set myList [list one two [list another list here]]; lindex $myList
2 0
another
```

In this example, the third element (its index value is 2) of `myList` is, in turn, another embedded list, and we retrieve its first element—string `another`—by specifying an additional index value to `lindex`— 0.

The `lrange` command returns a subset of the original list. It accepts the list as the first argument followed by the index of the first and last items that should be included in the new list. Both the first and last elements are included in the resulting list. The index can be in the form of an integer or in the `end` or `end-<n>` forms.

This command returns a new list consisting of elements that is the start to end indexes:

```
% set myList {1 2 3 4 5}; puts [lrange $myList 1 3]
2 3 4
```

In this case, `1` is the starting index and `2` the ending one, so the returned list consists of the second and third elements of the original list.

We can use the `lappend` command to add one or more elements to an existing list. It accepts the variable name of the list, followed by any number of elements to be added to the list. The command inserts new elements at the end of the specified variable and does not return the new list—instead, it is automatically set as the new value of the specified variable.

For example:

```
% set myList {one two}; lappend myList 3 4; puts $myList
one two 3 4
```

This command can also be used to create new lists if the variable passed as the first argument does not exist.

The `linsert` command can be used to insert one or more elements into a list at the specified index. Unlike `lappend`, it takes the value of the list as its first argument, followed by the index to insert elements at and any number of elements to insert. For example:

```
% set myList {1 5}; set myList [linsert $myList 1 2 3 4]; puts
$myList
1 2 3 4 5
```

As for any other list-related command, the index can be in the form of an integer or in the `end` or `end-<n>` forms.

The `lset` command allows you to replace the values of elements with new ones. It accepts a variable name, and one or more indexes, followed by the new value to set. The changed list is stored back in the variable specified as the first argument.

For example, we can specify a single index to modify the nth element of a list:

```
% set myList {1 2 3}; lset myList 1 0; puts $myList
1 0 3
```

Similar to `lindex`, this command can access and modify elements of sub-lists. For example:

```
% set myList [list one two [list another list here]]; lsert myList
end 0 new; puts $mylist
One two {new list here}
```

The `lreplace` command is also similar to it, but allows replacing a set of elements. It accepts the list as the first argument, the start and end indexes to replace, and the new items to insert instead of the specified elements. The command removes elements between start and end inclusively and inserts new items in their place. Like `linsert`, it does not alter an existing list, but returns a new one. For example:

```
% set myList {1 2 3 4 5}; puts [lreplace $myList 1 3 0 0]
1 0 0 5
```

In case you don't specify new replacement items, the command will only remove elements within a range:

```
% set myList {1 2 3 4 5}; puts [lreplace $myList 1 3]
1 5
```

The `lsort` command can be used to sort lists in Tcl. For example:

```
% set myList {5 1 3 4 2}; puts [lsort $myList]
1 2 3 4 5
```

It is also possible to modify the sorting order by specifying additional options, for example `-decreasing`:

```
% set myList {5 1 3 4 2}; puts [lsort -decreasing $myList]
5 4 3 2 1
```

By default, the elements are compared as text values—therefore, when sorting 9, 10, 11, and, 2, the result would be 10, 11, 2, and 9. The following switches allow us to define how elements are compared, which affects the output of the sorting operation:

Switch	Description	Example
-ascii	Compares elements as text; this is the default if no switch has been specified	List: {a b c 9 10 11 2} Sorted: {2 9 10 11 a b c}
-integer	Compares elements as integer values	List: {9 10 11 2} Sorted: {2 9 10 11}
-real	Compares elements as floating point values	List: {11.0 2.0 9 1.2 1} Sorted: {1 1.2 2.0 9 11.0}
-dictionary	Compares elements using dictionary-style comparison; see the following paragraph for more details	List: { Di beta al Beta} Sorted: {al Beta beta Di}

Dictionary-based sorting is similar to text-based comparison, except that character case is ignored here. An exception is when both the elements are the same, in that case, the uppercase elements are put before lowercase elements. If strings contain numbers, they are compared as integers, not characters. For example, when sorting 9, 10, 11, and 2 using the -dictionary switch, the result would be 2, 9, 10, and 11.

We can also tell lsort to use all elements in the list as sub-lists and compare them only using specified elements of these sub-lists, by using the -index option. The value for the option can be a single index or a list of indexes, where each element of the index list indicates an index in a sub-list. For example:

```
puts [lsort -integer -index 1 {{Alpha 2} {Beta 1} {Gamma 3}}]
{Beta 1} {Alpha 2} {Gamma 3}
```

Another option is to use your own custom implementation of the comparison algorithm. To do so, you have to define a command that accepts two arguments (items from the list that is being sorted) and returns the integer value by complying to the following rules:

- The value is **negative** when the first argument is considered to be lower than the second

- The value is 0 when both arguments are considered equal

- The value is a **positive** value when the first argument is higher than the second one

It is illustrated in the following example:

```
proc compareStrings {s1 s2} {
   return [expr {[string length $s1] - [string length $s2]}]
}

set animals [list snake crocodile monkey cat]

puts "default: [lsort $animals]"
puts "custom:  [lsort -command compareStrings $animals]"
```

We have the `animals` list that contains some animal names. The default implementation will sort it in the alphabetical order, but we will be able to define our own implementation in the form of the `compareString` procedure, which will sort it in the order of the word's length:

```
default: cat crocodile monkey snake
custom:  cat snake monkey crocodile
```

An interesting property of the `lsort` command is that when two elements are considered as the same, their order in the output is the same as the order in which they were taken as inputs. This can be used to sort lists of lists using multiple orders. We need to sort the list by each element we want it to be sorted using, but in the reverse order.

For example, we can sort a list where each element is a sub-list consisting of first name, last name, and age. If we want to order it by the last name and the decreasing order of age for the same last names, we need to sort it by age first and later by the last name:

```
set list {{John Doe 32} {Joe Smith 29} {Jane Doe 35}}
set list [lsort -integer -decreasing -index 2 $list]
puts [lsort -dictionary -index 1 $temp]
```

The result of this sort would be:

```
{John Doe 32} {Jane Doe 35} {Joe Smith 29}
```

You can search through your list to find the element(s) that match your pattern using `lsearch`:

```
% set myList {zero one two three}; puts [lsearch $myList three]
3
```

This command looks for the element three in myList, and returns the index of the first occurrence of the searched element — 3 (or -1 if element is not found). It will be able to accept options such as:

- -glob — specifies that a pattern is in the glob-style (similar to file mask, see the string match command's description for details: http://www.tcl.tk/man/tcl8.5/TclCmd/string.htm)

- -regexp — similar to the previous option, but the pattern is compliant with the regular expression's syntax (http://www.tcl.tk/man/tcl8.5/TclCmd/re_syntax.htm)

- -inline — the command will return the value of the element found instead of the index

- -all — the command will return a list of all matching occurrences, instead of just the first one

These options can be combined together; for your convenience, here is an example of their usage:

```
set myList {zero one two three}

puts "First match (glob)   : \
   [lsearch -glob $myList *t*] -> \
   [lsearch -inline -glob $myList *t*]"
puts "First match (regexp): \
   [lsearch -regexp $myList e$] -> \
   [lsearch -inline -regexp $myList e$]"
puts "All matches (glob)   : \
   [lsearch -all -glob $myList *t*] -> \
   [lsearch -all -inline -glob $myList *t*]"
puts "All matches (regexp): \
   [lsearch -all -regexp $myList e$] -> \
   [lsearch -all -inline -regexp $myList e$]"
```

The expression *t* will match any string containing the letter t and the regular expression e$ will match any string that ends with the letter e.

The output will be:

```
First match (glob)   :  2 ->  two
First match (regexp):  1 ->  one
All matches (glob)   :  2 3 ->  two three
All matches (regexp):  1 3 ->  one three
```

The command `lassign` allows you to assign values from the list to different variables on a single line. For example:

```
lassign {1 2 3} a b c
```

The effect of this command is equal to the execution of the following:

```
set a 1
set b 2
set c 3
```

The first argument is a list, and the consecutive arguments are names of the variables. If there are more variables than list elements, the remaining elements will be set to empty strings.

Arrays

Another important data type for storing a set of values is an array. In Tcl, arrays are essentially associative maps, because any string value is permitted as an array key (index). Consider the following example:

```
set myArray(key1) element1
set myArray(key2) element2
set myArray(3) element3
```

After looking at the first line, the interpreter knows that the `myArray` variable will be an array, because of presence of the `()` braces. Inside these braces, the array key `key1` is written, and it is mapped to the string `element1`. We have three keys overall—`key1`, `key2`, and `3` (note that the last one is different from the first two, but still valid)—that point to three values: `element1`, `element2`, and `element3` respectively. The key name can contain any character, and also spaces (of course, with the correct syntax, for example, by using the *Esc* key with a backslash).

To manipulate array variables, use the `array` command with the appropriate operator and arguments. The most common operations are:

The command `array exists` returns the value `1` only when the variable passed as an argument exists and is an array:

```
% array exists myArray
1
% array exists fictionalArray
0
```

Otherwise, the command will return 0.

We can use the `array unset` command to delete an array:

```
% array exists myArray
1
% array unset myArray; array exists myArray
0
```

We can also delete a specified key or keys by specifying the pattern to match the keys that we want to delete as follows:

```
array unset myArray prefix,*
```

This will delete all the elements of an array that starts with `prefix,`.

You can convert an array into a list using `array get`:

```
% array get myArray
index1 element1 index2 element2 3 element3
```

The list it returns consists of **name-value pairs**. This means that for each element in the array, this command returns its name as an element followed by its value as another element.

We can also use `array get` to get specific elements of an array, by adding a pattern to match keys, similar to `array unset`. For example:

```
array get myArray prefix,*
```

This will return information only for keys starting with `prefix,`.

To reverse this operation and set one or more keys in an array from the name-value pairs, we can use `array set` command:

```
% array set anotherArray "1 first 2 second"
% array exists anotherArray
1
```

If you want to get a list of key names existing in a particular array, the `array names` command comes handy:

```
% array names myArray
index1 index2 3
```

Similarly, we can get only a subset of names by running:

```
array names myArray prefix,*
```

This will return only the keys which start with `prefix,`.

array size

`array size` returns the number of key-value mappings:

```
% array size myArray
3
```

Although arrays are popular and commonly used, there are some drawbacks to using them. They are not Tcl objects on their own, but rather a collection of variables, a way in which a particular variable name can store zero or more key-value relations:

```
set myarray(somekey) "my value"
```

If we set an array key with the previous command, `myarray` is not a variable by itself, but rather each key and value pair is stored as a Tcl object. From the programming perspective, this has little impact. However, once you set an array, you cannot pass it as a variable; for example:

```
set myarray(somekey) "my value"
return $myarray
```

The preceding code will raise an error (we will present `return` later in this chapter). However, it is okay to reference it via the variable name in commands such as `upvar`, `variable`, which are explained later throughout *Chapter 2*.

Also, only one dimensional arrays are supported—so the syntax like `myArray(1)(2)` is incorrect. This can be bypassed by using some specific key name convention, for example with the '.' or ':' characters:

```
set my3DArray(0.0.0) element1
set my3DArray(0.0.1) element2
set my3DArray(1.0.1) element3
```

Effectively, `my3DArray` can be treated as a three-dimensional array, with indexes separated by the character (or string) of your choice.

Dictionaries

To address the previously mentioned drawbacks of arrays, a new data type was introduced, which is quickly gaining acceptance and popularity among Tcl developers—**dictionary**. Dictionaries are somewhat similar to arrays in that they keep mapping between key and value, but a dictionary is treated as an object. Dictionaries can also be truly multi-dimensional. The other difference is that dictionaries are significantly faster than arrays.

The new command `dict` was introduced to operate on dictionaries. The command is natively present in Tcl 8.5, but it can be also used in Tcl 8.4 by adding the `dict` package.

To create a dictionary, use the `dict create` command with the equal number of arguments; alternately, keys and values:

```
set myDict [dict create key1 value1 key2 value2 key3 value3]
```

The previous line creates a dictionary with three mappings and stores it in the `myDict` variable.

This command also allows us to create multi-level dictionaries:

```
set a [dict create 1 [dict create 2 [dict create 3 value]]]
```

Here, in dictionary a, the key 1 is mapped to other dictionary which has key 2 mapped to the third dictionary, wherein key 3 is mapped to `value`.

To access the mapped value, you can use the `dict get` command:

```
% dict get $myDict key2
value2
% dict get $a 1 2 3
value
```

The second command's invocation in this example demonstrates how to access a third-level variable.

These are only the basics, there are also many other operations available for dictionaries, these can be compared to the operations for arrays described earlier, because their concepts are similar. For the complete documentation of the `dict` command, you can refer to `http://www.tcl.tk/man/tcl8.5/TclCmd/dict.htm`.

Mathematical expressions—expr

There is a separate command called `expr` that handles all mathematical and logical operations. The command accepts an expression to evaluate. An interesting detail is that this expression can be passed as one argument, or as unlimited number of arguments. The following calls to `expr` will return the same result:

```
expr "3 + 7 * 2"
expr 3 + 7 * 2
expr {3 + 7 * 2}
expr 3+7*2
```

All the preceding operations return the value 17 as the result.

In case of logical expressions, values of arguments, such as 1 (or any other numeric non-zero value), true, TRUE, yes or YES are considered as logical true, and 0, false, FALSE, no, and NO as logical false. The following is an example of a logical AND (the && operator) and OR (the operator || operator):

```
% expr yes && no
0
% expr yes || no
1
```

Flow control and loop instructions

Like almost any other language, Tcl has a set of commands — conditional and iterational — to control the flow of the program.

Flow control

The first one is the command if:

```
set condition 1
if {$condition} {
        puts "condition is true"
} else {
        puts "condition is false"
}
```

Depending on the boolean value of the condition variable, the first or the second part of the command is executed. In this case, the output is:

```
condition is true
```

Note that the entire if command call could be written in one line:

if {$condition} {puts "condition is true"} else {puts "condition is false"}

The first argument is an expression representing a logical condition. The value is evaluated in the same way as in case of the expr command.

It is possible to skip else and the second script body, or to add more conditions by using elseif with another condition, and a script to execute in case the condition is true.

The second command `switch` allows us to decide what action should be taken based on the value passed; for example, consider the following example code:

```
set value second
switch $value {
    first {puts "first value"}
    second {puts "second value"}
    default {puts "some other value"}
}
```

As the value of `value` variable is `second`, the second script body is passed to the Tcl interpreter, resulting in the output **second value** on the screen.

It is possible to skip the `default` section. Also, more than one acceptable value separated by the – character may be defined for each of the sections:

```
switch $value {
    1 - 1st - first {puts "first value"}
    2 - 2nd - second {puts "second value"}
    default {puts "some other value"}
}
```

The values 1, 1st, or first will all match with the first section.

Finally, it is possible to use patterns that we have used with `string match` command to match the appropriate section, by specifying the –glob option with the `switch` command:

```
switch -glob $value {
    *st {puts "first value"}
    *nd {puts "second value"}
    default {puts "some other value"}
}
```

In this case, both the values `second` and `2nd` would match with the second option.

Loops

Tcl offers three commands that allow the *iterational* execution of code: `for`, `while`, and `foreach`.

The following example presents the usage of the `for` command:

```
for {set x 1} {$x < 4} {incr x} {puts "$x execution"}
```

The first argument is a code snippet executed at the beginning of the loop (in this example, it defines the counter variable x and initializes it with value 1). The second one is a condition that is checked to be logically true before each loop (if the counter is smaller than 4) and the third is the condition which is evaluated after each loop—in most cases, to increase the counter (for example, using the command incr). The last part of the statement is the body of the loop. The output of the example is:

```
Command Prompt - tclsh85                                    _ |□| x
C:\Documents and Settings\Administrator>tclsh85
% for {set x 1} {$x < 4} {incr x} {puts "$x execution"}
1 execution
2 execution
3 execution
%
```

The while command operates in a similar fashion, with the exception that the condition is evaluated after each loop, not before, and there is neither a start nor "after each loop" code section present. The equivalent of the previous example code written with while is:

```
set x 0
while {$x < 3} {incr x; puts "$x execution"}
```

The last command is foreach. The idea behind this command is to pass one (or more) lists, and the loop's body is executed for every element of the list:

```
Command Prompt - tclsh85                                    _ |□| x
C:\Documents and Settings\Administrator>tclsh85
% foreach word "one two three" {puts "the following word is: $word"}
the following word is: one
the following word is: two
the following word is: three
%
```

The following example shows using two lists at the same time. In every loop, consecutive elements from both lists are assigned to the variables amount and item:

```
Command Prompt - tclsh85                                    _ |□| x
C:\Documents and Settings\Administrator>tclsh85
% foreach amount "one two three" item "dog chickens bottles" {puts "$amount $item"}
one dog
two chickens
three bottles
%
```

What is interesting here is that the lists are not required to be of the same length. If one of them is shorter, the empty value is used instead of using missing elements.

`foreach` also allows us to fetch multiple variables in one shot—for example, to put all data in a three-column table in HTML, it's just as easy as:

```
foreach {c1 c2 c3} $data {
    append html "<tr><td>$c1</td><td>$c2</td><td>$c3</td></tr>"
}
```

Here `$data` is a list.

It is possible to control the flow of loops with the commands `break` and `continue`. Using the first one will cause the loop to exit permanently, even when the end condition is not met. The second command causes the skipping of the current loop and the immediate start of the next one, or the end of the loop if the command that was skipped was the last one.

Defining your own commands

Up until this moment, we have been using only commands delivered by 'someone'. It is time to create our own command for the first time:

```
proc myCommand {name} {
    return "Hello $name, have a nice day!"
}
```

We use the `proc` command to define a new command (procedure) called `myCommand`. `proc` accepts three arguments: the procedure name, a list of arguments for this procedure, and its body. Note that just like any other argument, these have to be separated by whitespaces. In this case, `myCommand` accepts only one argument—`name`. The implementation is simple, because the command returns some greetings as its execution result. You can use this command in the same way as the others:

```
Command Prompt - tclsh85                                    _ □ ×
C:\Documents and Settings\Administrator>tclsh85
% proc myCommand {name} {
        return "Hello $name, have a nice day!"
}
% puts [myCommand John]
Hello John, have a nice day!
%
```

Summary

Tcl is a mature language and it is easy to use. It covers a wide range of domains, ranging from task automation to fully-featured GUI applications. Its syntax is a bit different from other languages, but once mastered, it becomes clear and logical. The wide set of available extensions along with the ability to define your own commands means there are virtually no limits in terms of extending the capabilities it offers. This fact combined with its support for various platforms makes Tcl a truly swiss-army-knife equivalent among programming languages. Often considered as 'just' another scripting language, trifled and underestimated, Tcl may really surprise you with its abilities and potential.

In this chapter, we have learned:

- The origins, concepts, and possibilities provided by the Tcl language
- Which platforms it supports, and how to get and install the Tcl interpreter
- About some of the tools available to ease the development of Tcl code
- The syntax and fundamental commands of the language

Having read this chapter, you are now ready to continue to the next one, which will teach you some more advanced Tcl features. Not only will you learn about the many technical details of the interpreter itself, but you will also become familiar with file operations, the packaging system, event loops, and threads.

2

Advanced Tcl Features

Now that we know Tcl basics a lot better, it is time to learn some of Tcl's more advanced functionality. This chapter focuses on some aspects of Tcl that will be needed for the chapters that follow throughout the book.

This chapter talks about how Tcl works internally, what we need to be aware of and how we can leverage it to our needs. It introduces in detail how Tcl evaluates code, substitutes variables, and evaluates embedded commands. It also talks about the different types of variables and how they can be used within our code.

We also describe how to work with files in Tcl. This chapter covers how to read and write files, and introduces the concept of channels within Tcl and how different types of channels work. We also show how to copy, rename, and delete files and directories, get information about them, and how to learn about platform-specific issues.

After that, you will see how the Tcl packaging system works and how we can extend it and create reusable packages. It mentions the package system, which is how Tcl has been doing things for a long time. It also introduces us to the Tcl modules concept, which was included in Tcl 8.5 and changes the way some of the packages are built and found on a system.

We also dive into the idea of the event loop, one of Tcl's most powerful features — what it is, the different types of events, how Tcl receives them, and how to use them in our applications. We learn about file events, timer events, and scheduling periodic jobs.

This chapter also gives us a good idea of how threads can be used from within Tcl. It talks about how we can create child threads, communicate with them, and share information between threads. It also shows some examples of how we can use Tcl threads to implement a system where a child thread performs data manipulation, while the main thread is responsible for data management.

Tcl features

The previous chapter introduced the basics of the Tcl language. We learned the basics of strings, lists, dictionaries, and integer and floating-point numbers. This section introduces some of the more advanced Tcl features— working with the time and date, data, namespaces, and stack frames.

Learning some of these features is required if you wish to understand and use Tcl and its features in a better way—especially meta programming, which can be used to create our own syntax and alter a program's flow control. This is one of Tcl's powerful features.

Working with time and date

When writing applications in Tcl, we'll often need to work in the context of date and time. One example is reading a file's access time, another one calculating how much time is left until, for example, next Sunday at 4 AM. Tcl uses the Unix timestamp for all date and time manipulations. This is a common approach which assumes that all dates and times are specified as a number of seconds since midnight on the 1st January 1970 GMT. This is similar to how most operating systems track time. An interesting fact is that regardless of which time zone you are currently in, the actual number of seconds is the same everywhere. The only thing that changes is that when it gets converted to actual time and date, the local time zone is then taken into account.

The Tcl command `clock` can be used for the majority of date and time related operations. Finding out the current time is done using the `clock seconds` command, which returns a Unix timestamp value. Taking this value at various times can be used to calculate how many seconds have passed, for example:

```
% set earlier [clock seconds]
1253652955
% set now [clock seconds]
1253652998
% expr {$now - $earlier}
43
```

The timestamp idea, although simple and elegant, is not clear when it comes to interpreting the value. The date and time can be converted to a more readable form by using the `clock format` command, which takes a timestamp as the first argument and formats it as a string. The command also accepts several options, including `-gmt`, requiring a Boolean value as argument, which allows it to work with a GMT time and date. We can also specify the format in which the date and/or time should be presented. The format string may include various tokens that will be replaced to appropriate values, some of them are:

Format	Description	Example
%Y	4 digit year	2009
%m	Number of months	09
%d	Number of days	22
%H	Number of hours	20
%M	Number of minutes	56
%S	Number of seconds	38

All formatting possibilities and other options can be found on the `clock` command's manual page at:
http://www.tcl.tk/man/tcl8.5/TclCmd/clock.htm

For example, this is how the same timestamp can be printed out in different ways:

```
% puts [clock format $now]
Tue Sep 22 22:56:38 CEST 2009
% puts [clock format $now -format "%Y-%m-%d - %H:%M"]
2009-09-22 22:56
% puts [clock format $now -gmt 1]
Tue Sep 22 20:56:38 GMT 2009
```

Tcl can also do the opposite—read a textual representation of a date and convert it to a timestamp. This can be done using the `clock scan` command, which accepts and automatically detects many different types of date and time specification. Text can also specify only a date or only time, in which case it is scanned. For example:

```
% puts [clock scan "Tue Sep 22 22:56:38 CEST 2009"]
1253652998
% puts [clock scan "2009-09-22 22:56:38"]
1253652998
```

By default, clock scan parses text basing on the current date and time—so if the text contains only a time, today's date will be used. By adding the `-base` option, we can specify what timestamp should be taken as the base timestamp for our operations. For example, scanning just a time can produce different results with different bases:

```
% puts [clock format [clock scan "12:40"]]
Tue Sep 22 12:40:00 CEST 2009
% set base [clock scan {2009-10-01}]
% puts [clock format $base]
Thu Oct 01 00:00:00 CEST 2009
% puts [clock format [clock scan "12:40" -base $base]]
Thu Oct 01 12:40:00 CEST 2009
```

Besides parsing actual date and time values, `clock scan` is also able to parse and understand an argument that specifies a difference in time, in which case it is based on the current or provided date and time. The syntax is `<number> <units>`. For example:

```
% puts [clock format [clock seconds]]
Tue Sep 22 22:56:38 CEST 2009
% puts [clock format [clock scan "1 hour -15 minutes"]]
Tue Sep 22 23:41:38 CEST 2009
% puts [clock format [clock scan "45 minutes"]]
Tue Sep 22 23:41:38 CEST 2009
```

Note the flexibility of the input format, we specified the 45 minute interval in various ways here. The `clock scan` command can also do parsing according to the format in which a given date and time is specified:

```
% puts [clock scan "20090922225638" -format "%Y%m%d%H%M%S"]
1253652998
```

It is also possible to combine multiple date and time specifications, in which case Tcl will parse each part individually and combine the results based on the order of the statements. For example, we can pass an arbitrary value and then a difference:

```
% puts [clock format [clock scan "12:45 +3 hours"]]
Tue Sep 22 15:45:00 CEST 2009
```

Using `clock scan` for parsing user input allows us to create a powerful mechanism for scheduling, or providing when certain operations can be performed.

An interesting feature of Tcl's date and time handling is the ability to handle the stardate notation that was used in the Star Trek movies and series. We can use %Q formatting to print out the stardate. For example:

```
% puts [clock format [clock seconds] -format %Q]
Stardate 63723.9
```

We can also reverse this operation by running:

```
% puts [clock format [clock scan "Stardate 63723.9"]]
Mon Sep 21 21:36:00 CEST 2009
```

Stardates are calculated from 1946-01-01, each year incrementing the date by 1000, the day of year is then divided by number of days in a year (for example, Dec 31st 1946 maps to value of 997). Current time of day is then divided by the entire day's duration and added as value between 0 and 1 — for example, noon is specified as 0.5.

Even though this is an interesting gadget in Tcl, it is not a good idea to store a date or time in this way.

For more details on the clock command, please see the corresponding manual page at: http://www.tcl.tk/man/tcl8.5/TclCmd/clock.htm

Tcl data types

As seen in the previous chapter, Tcl provides only a few data types and every data type can be converted to or from a fundamental type, that is, a string. This approach is geared towards the dynamic typing concept where the programming language does not perform strict type checking, therefore, not limiting the way an application manipulates its data. Having a small subset of data types and conforming to a common approach throughout many Tcl extensions helps in achieving this goal.

In essence, Tcl offers the following object types:

- String / binary data: It consists of zero or more bytes or Unicode characters and can store any data.

- Integer value: An integer, stored as either 32 bit or 64 bit, depending on needs; starting with Tcl 8.5, it can store integer numbers of any size, which can be used in many algorithms and/or encryption code; examples, for example *12, 7321322*.

- Floating point value: A floating point value, stored as double-precision internally; for example: *3.14159265*.

- List: It consists of zero or more Tcl objects, and can always be converted from and to a string, accessed via large number of list-related commands; for example: {element0 {sublist {item with spaces}}}.

- Dictionary: It allows us to store zero or more key-value relations, where a key can have only one value, where the value can be any valid Tcl object (including a Tcl list), accessed via dict command and its subcommands.

Arrays are not first-class objects in Tcl, and therefore, are not mentioned in the list. First class objects are data that can be passed directly. They can be used in commands such as set and return.

Arrays themselves are not such objects — they can be passed by their names using a command such as upvar, but it is not possible to return an array — for example, the following will not work:

```
proc createArray {} {
    set value(firstValue) 1
    set value(otherValue) 2
    return $value
}
```

This command will fail with the error that the variable value is an array. Dictionaries can be used as first-class objects which work in the same way as arrays — storing key-value information that can be set and retrieved in a fast way. Dictionaries can be passed between procedures, for example:

```
proc createDict {} {
    set value [dict create]
    dict set value firstValue 1
    dict set value otherValue 2
    return $value
}
```

Each data type can be represented as a string and each type can be compared with any other type, although sometimes, internally, they are converted to strings when comparing values of different types.

Lists and dictionaries work in such a way that each element they keep is another object of a different data type, for example, a list contains zero or more elements of any data type, this is similar for dictionaries where each value is an object of specified data types. It is also true for arrays, where each element of an array is also any data type.

For binary, string, integer, and floating-point values storing a value of particular type and manipulating it is done through commands to manipulate strings and/or binary data.

Internally, Tcl stores data in the most efficient way and converts it as needed. When programming in Tcl, we don't need to know how data is currently stored. All operations will convert data as needed—converting a string to integer, a list, dictionary, or whatever is needed.

If a conversion to the required data type is not possible, an error is thrown—for example, when converting some text to integer, an error will be thrown because it's not an integer value. Otherwise, all conversions are done without us knowing about it.

For example, we can set a variable by running:

```
set variable 12345678
```

When run, it will set the value of the variable to 12345678, which most probably will be stored as a string. Following that, we can run:

```
incr variable
```

At this point, Tcl will convert this to an integer and increment the value, using integers for internal calculations. Next, when we do the following:

```
puts $variable
```

Tcl will print the value of 12345679, but will keep an integer representation of the value internally.

Similarly, strings are converted to lists whenever list operations are performed, such as invoking commands llength, lindex, or any other command that operates on lists.

Calculations in Tcl are done by using a separate command called expr. Due to how Tcl syntax is defined, it would be difficult to allow users to specify calculations in readable way.

Expressions passed to expr are written in ways similar to any other programming language such as C or Python. They should always be passed as a single argument, enclosed in braces. Variables and commands inside the expression will be substituted. For example:

```
% set somevar 12 ; puts [expr {4 + $somevar * 13}]
160
```

Evaluation of expressions is done so that priorities of various operands are taken into account, for example, multiplication being done before addition, as shown in the previous example.

More details about expr command, acceptable expressions and operands can be found in its manual page at:
http://www.tcl.tk/man/tcl8.5/TclCmd/expr.htm

One of the most interesting aspects of Tcl is how commands are built and evaluated. The main principle of the language is that at evaluation time, all commands are built as lists, with the exception that newline characters and semi-colons are treated as command separators. This means that we can build commands as lists and they can be evaluated using the eval command, which then returns result from the command. For example:

```
set mycommand [list clock]
lappend mycommand format
lappend mycommand [clock seconds]
lappend mycommand -format "%Y-%m-%d %H:%M:%S"
puts [eval $mycommand]
```

The preceding code will cause the current date and time to be printed to the standard output. One thing worth noting is that in this example the result from clock seconds is appended to the list during building of the command, so running puts [eval $mycommand] at different times will always print out the time and date from when the mycommand variable was built.

In the preceding example, the command clock second is evaluated only once, but the clock format is run each time eval $mycommand is invoked. For example, when running:

```
set value 0
set mycommand [list incr]
lappend mycommand value
puts [eval $mycommand]
puts [eval $mycommand]
```

The script will invoke the incr value command each time eval $mycommand is run. The output from the script will be as follows:

```
1
2
```

The `eval` command can be used to evaluate lists or commands. For lists, it evaluates a list as single command, where the first element is the command name and each element of the list. If the specified argument is not a list, it evaluates it as one or more Tcl commands from it—similar to how the `source` command loads a script.

One of the major benefits of using lists to build commands is that any Tcl code can easily build other Tcl code. A simple example can be building one invocation of a command with all arguments specified either as result of other operations, for example, invoking `file delete` with result from `glob` command, which returns a list of files as a list.

The following command will fail:

```
file delete [glob /path/*] [glob /other/path/*]
```

Tcl will pass all files in /path as a single argument and all files in /other/path as the second argument. If the files /path/file1 and /path/file2 were present, an error that file /path/file1/path/file2 could not be deleted will be thrown.

In this case, instead of iterating over a list and deleting a single item at a time, we can do:

```
set command {file delete}
set command [concat $command [glob /path/*]]
set command [concat $command [glob /other/path/*]]
eval $command
```

As we can see, this method can also be used to add multiple results in a single command invocation. This can be used, for example, to perform batch operations for something such as storage systems, where such an approach results in better performance.

Tcl 8.5 also introduces another way of adding results from a command, that is, as multiple arguments to another command. If a command placed in brackets is preceded by {*} statement, its result is added to results as a list, where each element is added as another argument. In all other cases, results' commands in brackets are passed as a single argument. For this particular example, we can simply run:

```
file delete {*}[glob /path/*] {*}[glob /other/path/*]
```

This will also cause the command to get all results from both invocations of the `glob` command as multiple arguments.

Global, namespace, and local variables

As with any other languages, Tcl has several types of variables — global, local or namespace variables. **Global** variables are the ones that are defined and accessible at the global stack frame, for example, when the Tcl interpreter loads main script. They can also be made accessible from any place using the `global` command, passing as arguments one or more global variable names that should be made available.
For example:

```
proc printValue {} {
    global somevalue
    puts "somevalue=$somevalue"
}
set somevalue 1
printValue
```

Local variables are variables that are used within a procedure and are only available for code in this procedure and for this particular invocation of a procedure. The following example will not work as expected, because the variable used is local:

```
proc addItem {item} {
    lappend items $item
    puts "All items: $items"
}
addItem "Item1"
addItem "Item2"
```

For both invocations of `addItem`, it will only print out the currently added item for all items in the list, because the `items` variable is local and Tcl does not keep track of it across invocations.

Namespaces in Tcl make it possible to keep commands, variables, and any other metadata within a namespace context. All namespaces have separate commands and variables, which allow us to create reusable code that will not interfere with code in different namespaces.

This can be used to keep libraries or pieces of our code separated so that they do not interfere with each other. For example, if all the multiple pieces of our application define a command called `addItem`, there will be a collision and one of them will overwrite the other one. Keeping each part of the application or reusable components in separate namespaces makes it possible to resolve such conflicts, such as `queue::addItem`. Namespace names are separated by double colons; in previous case, the namespace is called `queue` and `addItem` is a command within that namespace.

Namespaces are created by invoking the namespace `eval` command, which creates a namespace if it does not exist yet and can be used to evaluate code within that namespace. For example:

```
namespace eval queue {}
```

A namespace variable can be made accessible to procedures inside this namespace by using the `variable` command, specifying a variable name as the only argument. This is similar to the `global` command, which makes a global variable available in a procedure, but the variable is specific to the namespace that current command is created in.

Converting the previous example to namespaces we get:

```
proc queue::addItem {item} {
    variable items
    lappend items $item
    puts "All items: $items"
}
queue::addItem "Item1"
queue::addItem "Item2"
```

This example will now work correctly, because the variable `items` is now a namespace variable in the `queue` namespace. It is also possible to access the variable outside of the namespace itself by using a fully qualified name for the variable—for example, we can add the following at the end of previous example:

```
puts "All items after adding: $::queue::items"
```

This will correctly print both items added to the queue. We have used `::queue` for a namespace name as adding `::` indicates that we mean the namespace queue within the global namespace. As namespaces can be nested, it is safer to specify the namespace names as fully qualified names.

Global variables in this context are variables bound to global namespace. Therefore, they can always be accessed in the same form as variables for any other queue. In order to access the global variable `somevalue`, we can refer to it as `::somevalue`. For example:

```
proc printValue {} {
    puts "somevalue=$::somevalue"
}
set somevalue 1
printValue
```

Similar to first example in this section, it will write `somevalue=1` to standard output.

In addition to this, TclOO objects have their own per-instance variables that can be accessed from within TclOO objects. This subject is described in more detail in the next section.

Stack frames

The **stack frame** is the context in which current Tcl code is evaluated, and it defines what variables are available, the namespace in which code is evaluated, and many other things. When Tcl loads the main script, that script is evaluated in the global stack frame, which is stack frame 0. Whenever a command is invoked, it creates a new stack frame for this command. For example:

```
proc proc1 {} {
    proc2 "world!"
}
proc proc2 {text} {
    puts "Hello $text"
}
proc1
```

The main code is evaluated in stack frame 0, proc1 is evaluated in stack frame 1, and proc2 is evaluated in stack frame 2. This mechanism handles values such as local variables, which are bound to specific stack frame.

When running inside proc2, this is how stack frame would appear:

Stack frame	Command
0 (global)	proc1
1	proc2 "world!"
2	puts "hello world!"

The following table is a list of all stack frames and what commands they are running at the time when the puts command is invoked. The variable text, which is an argument to proc2 is available in stack frame 1. The puts command is invoked using this variable, so the actual command is run using contents of this variable.

Stack frames are created only for invocations of procedures, object methods, and other operations that require local variables — operations such as iterations with for, foreach, or while commands are performed within the same frame stack.

It is possible to evaluate commands or use variables from different stack frames using upvar and uplevel commands. The first command allows us to map a variable from a different stack frame as the local one in the current stack frame.

The commands `upvar` and `uplevel` are used for many different purposes, from referencing variables by their names to creating new control structures. In these cases, we need to use variables from the previous stack frame.

For example, if we were to write a simple command called `forsequence` that takes a variable name, and the minimum and maximum values, we would use it as follows:

```
forsequence i 1 20 {
    puts "I=$i"
}
```

We could implement the command so that the command which is provided as the last argument is evaluated in previous stack frame as follows:

```
proc forsequence {varname min max command} {
    upvar $varname var
    for {set var $min} {$var <= $max} {incr $var} {
        uplevel 1 $command
    }
}
```

The `uplevel` command allows us to run any command in a different stack frame. For both commands, the first argument can a specify level or how many levels up the operation should be done. If no argument is specified, it defaults to 1 level up. The argument can be:

- A number; in which case it specifies the number of stack frames up in the stack.

- A number prefixed by # character; in which case the number specifies the stack frame.

For example, while being in the `proc2` stack frame (stack frame 2), #1 indicates the stack frame (stack frame 1) of `proc1`, and 2 would indicate the global stack frame (stack frame 0 – 2 levels up).

The `upvar` command requires us to specify one or more pairs of variable names, where the first variable name is the variable name in other stack frame context and the second variable name is the variable name for the local stack frame context.

The following is an example of using `upvar` to work on variables from different stack frames:

```
proc proc1 {} {
    set othervalue 1
    proc2
}
proc proc2 {} {
    upvar 2 somevalue sv
    upvar #1 othervalue ov
    puts "sv=$sv ov=$ov"
}
set somevalue 12
proc1
```

This would cause `sv=12 ov=1` to be written to standard output, as `proc2` is able to access variables from other stack frames.

Another example can be writing a command that extends the Tcl's `incr` command. If the variable is already set, it is incremented by the specified number; otherwise, the variable is set to the default value. For example:

```
proc incrOrSet {variable increment defaultValue} {
    upvar 1 $variable var
    if {[info exists var]} {
        incr var $increment
    } else {
        set var $defaultValue
    }
}
```

The preceding example first maps the variable whose name is specified as the first argument (variable) to the local variable `var`. It then checks if that variable exists, referencing it as the local variable `var`. If it exists, it is incremented by a specified number; otherwise it is set to the default value.

The `uplevel` command allows us to evaluate commands in different stack frames. This can be used for various reasons — from running commands in the caller's stack frame to creating new control structures entirely in Tcl.

All arguments are concatenated as a command to be evaluated, although, it is recommended to pass the command as one argument. For example:

```
proc proc1 {} {
    set value 1
    proc2
}

proc proc2 {} {
    uplevel 1 {puts "Value=$value"}
}

proc1
```

This will cause `Value=1` to be printed out as the `puts` statement is evaluated within the stack frame of `proc1`, even though it is within `proc2`.

A more practical example can be creating a procedure that runs code only if certain flags are enabled:

```
proc runIf {constraint command} {
    global allconstraints
    if {$constraint in $allconstraints} {
        uplevel 1 $command
    }
}
```

The preceding example will run the command specified as the second argument if the constraint specified by first variable is set. Constraints are checked against the global variable `allconstraints` — the operator `in` returns true if the value of `$constraint` is in the `$allconstraints` list.

For instance, the following example would check whether the platform the code is running on is win32 and load the registry package if this is true:

```
runIf platform-win32 {
    package require registry
}
```

While this example simplifies this a bit, the same approach is used in Tcl's test suite package called `tcltest` — constraints specify whether a certain test is to be run or not and whether it is used to skip tests in specific cases or not, for the platform that the test suite is running on.

While the same thing could be accomplished with a simple `if` command in this case, this example also applies to more complex scenarios. Creating custom commands to implement flow control and optional execution, which is similar to the `if` command can be used to optimize Tcl performance. For example, we can define the following procedure:

```
proc debugCode {code} {
    uplevel 1 $code
}
```

We can then add debug statements as follows:

```
proc sampleCommand {} {
    set value [calculateValue]
    debugCode { puts "Value = $value" }
    return $value
}
```

For production code, we can disable running such code by defining the procedure as empty and accepting any arguments — for example:

```
proc debugCode {args} {}
```

In this case, when running our code in a test environment, we'll receive information about the value on standard output. When running this code in production nothing will be printed out. Tcl optimizes this so that production code will automatically skip `debugCode` statements while testing code will evaluate them. This is in turn much faster than using an `if` command directly. This mechanism is used by Tcl logging packages which are described in more detail in *Chapter 4*.

Both `upvar` and `uplevel` operate within the namespace of the stack frame that we are referring to. For example, if our current function is within the namespace `myexample::ns2` and the previous stack frame was in the `myexample` namespace, referencing one level up would cause names to be looked up from the `myexample` namespace. For example:

```
namespace eval myexample {}
namespace eval myexample::ns2 {}

proc myexample::testproc {} {
    return [ns2::testproc]
}

proc myexample::ns2::testproc {} {
    variable localvar
    upvar 1 ns2::localvar referencedvar
    set referencedvar "This was set as referenced"
```

```
        return $localvar
    }

    puts [myexample::testproc]
```

This script will output the text "**This was set as referenced**" text since upvar
referenced the myexample::ns2::localvar variable and localvar was mapped to
the exact same variable. The uplevel command works in a similar way, if our code
were to invoke uplevel with the command set ns2::localvar "Something", then
the same variable would be modified.

Usually upvar and uplevel are used to work in the context of the previous stack
frame and/or reference variables by the names by which they were accessible in the
other stack frames, but it is possible to use upvar to map any variable to any other
variable name. It is often used for creating state data as an array, passing the array
name to different functions, and using upvar to reference it under a different name.
For example:

```
    namespace eval myqueue {}

    set myqueue::queueid 0

    # function to create a myqueue instance
    proc myqueue::create {} {
        variable queueid
        # initialize unique identifier
        set id ::myqueue::[incr queueid]

        # map variable to access our data as local variable d
        upvar #0 $id d

        set d(items) {}
        set d(itemcount) 0

        return $id
    }

    proc myqueue::add {id item} {
        # map variable to access our data as local variable d
        upvar #0 $id d

        lappend d(items) $item
        incr d(itemcount)

    }

    proc myqueue::get {id item} {
        # map variable to access our data as local variable d
        upvar #0 $id d
```

```
        # throw an error if no data currently exists
        if {$d(itemcount) == 0} {
            error "No items currently in queue"
        }

        # get and remove first item from queue
        set item [lindex $d(items) 0]
        set d(items) [lrange $d(items) 1 end]
        incr d(itemcount) -1

        return $item
}

# sample usage - add 2 items to queue and retrieve them
set id [myqueue::create]
myqueue::add $id item1
myqueue::add $id item2

puts [myqueue::get $id]
puts [myqueue::get $id]
```

The output from this example would be as follows:

item1

item2

The example above shows how upvar is commonly used to achieve a lightweight mechanism for keeping data across invocations and making it possible to reuse it. The example is trivial (and can be implemented simply by using a list, without identifiers and arrays), but it shows how this mechanism can be used for keeping data.

Object-oriented programming

Object-oriented programming has been a feature Tcl offered for several years with additional packages. This was possible due to the fact that Tcl syntax is easily extendable. Those packages include Incr Tcl, which is available from http://incrtcl.sourceforge.net/itcl/, XOTcl available from http://media.wu-wien.ac.at/ and Snit which can be obtained from http://www.wjduquette.com/snit/.

However, with the release of version 8.5, Tcl now comes with an object-oriented programming functionality included called **TclOO**. When Tcl 8.6 is out, TclOO will soon be part of core language. In Tcl 8.5 it is an extension to the language, but leverages 8.5 extensions to support it.

This is a set of additions that allows us to build a class hierarchy on its own. TclOO is designed so that it is possible to build wrappers so that it works the same as Incr Tcl, XOTcl, or Snit. So, for those of you that use any OO extension, it might be the right time to switch. For those of you that don't know any OO system yet, start with TclOO if your applications need to work on Tcl 8.5 and newer.

One of major features that TclOO offers is multiple inheritance. This means that a class can inherit from more than one class. For example, a class that implements a network server for queuing data would inherit classes for supporting queues and classes for network connectivity. TclOO also allows multiple classes to derive from same base classes.

In addition to inheritance, TclOO also supports mixins. For classes they work similar in a way to inheritance, but mixins can also be applied to individual objects. Mixins can be added and removed dynamically. This means that we can add all methods and functions of a class on the fly to an object. Mixins are explained in more detail later in the chapter.

TclOO also offers method forwarding — this means that a method of an object can be forwarded to a different command, passed to an object as any method for that object, or as a specified method for that object.

If you are familiar with object-oriented programming in languages such as C++ or Java, Tcl's object-oriented system is different from it.

As Tcl is a dynamic language, TclOO is more dynamic and offers more features that are common for scripting languages, but which compiled languages usually lack. TclOO offers features such as modifying definitions per-object, for example adding method forwarding, mixins, or changing method definition for a specific instance of an object. Examples of how this can be done can be found later in this chapter.

Tcl does not offer features such as defining interfaces or virtual classes, which are used commonly in technologies such as Java, C++, and .NET. In Tcl world, creating an interface simply means defining set of methods and parameters they accept. Implementing a class that has all the methods is sufficient. The object itself does not even need to be written in TclOO. After that, any code can use this class/object by invoking the defined interface. This approach is in sync with Tcl's dynamic design.

Class definition

Let's start by creating a simple counter class that will allow incrementing, getting the current counter, and resetting it:

```
oo::class create counter {
    constructor {} {
        my Resetcounter
    }

    method Resetcounter {} {
        # map variable "c" as local variable and set to 0
        my variable c
        set c 0
    }

    method increment {} {
        # map variable "c" as local variable and increment
        my variable c
        incr c
    }

    method getvalue {} {
        # return current value
        my variable c
        return $c
    }
}
```

We start by creating new class called `counter`. Then we define a constructor, which invokes the method `Resetcounter` to set the counter to 0. The command `my` is used to invoke methods for the current instance of an object. Also, the command `my variable` can be used to map an object specific variable as local variable, so `my variable c` means that the object-specific variable `c` becomes available for a specified method.

The `increment` method increases the value of the counter and `getvalue` returns it. We can now create an instance of this class by invoking `<className>` `new`. It creates a new object instance and returns its unique identifier, which is also a command name using which we can run methods of this object. For example, to create two counters and increment them, we can do the following:

```
set c1 [counter new]
set c2 [counter new]
$c1 increment
$c2 increment
$c1 increment
puts [$c1 getvalue]
```

This will create two `counter` instances and store their identifiers/commands in variables c1 and c2. We then increment c1 twice and c2 once. The result is 2 being printed out. In order to delete both objects, we can simply invoke the built-in `destroy` method:

```
$c1 destroy
$c2 destroy
```

The following diagram shows how public methods are mapped to the `counter` class. Items in bold indicate public methods while those in italics indicate private methods; the arrows indicate the path in which each method is looked up:

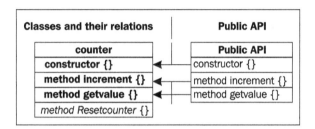

In this case, all public methods are simply mapped to counter class. Method `Resetcounter` is not public and, therefore, is not available from public API.

Besides creating a whole class along with its definition, it is also possible to define parts of a class independently using `oo::define` command. It needs an existing class name as the first argument and either an additional definition as one argument or a definition inlined as multiple arguments. For example, we can define a `setvalue` method in two ways, one option is:

```
oo::define counter {
    method setvalue {value} {
        my variable c
        set c $value
    }
}
```

And the other possibility is:

```
oo::define counter method setvalue {value} {
    my variable c
    set c $value
}
```

Inheritance

We can create classes that inherit from other classes — for example, if we want to make a counter that also resets its count after being read, we can do this:

```
oo::class create resetablecounter {
    # declare class we inherit from
    superclass counter
    method getvalue {} {
        # get result from our counter class
        set result [next]
        my Resetcounter
        return $result
    }
}
```

This causes our class to inherit everything from the counter class — in TclOO this means that counter is a superclass to resetablecounter. We also override the getvalue method. We use the next command, which calls commands from the superclass and is discussed in more detail later in this chapter. Next we run the Resetcounter method to reset the counter. We are invoking the superclass to get and reset the actual value so that if the implementation of the counter class changes, we will still be able to use the underlying implementation.

We can see how methods are inherited from the counter class in the following diagram:

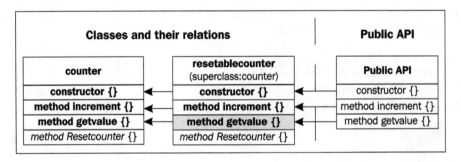

The object constructor and increment method are mapped to the counter class. The method getvalue is created in the resetablecounter class and, therefore, its implementation in the counter is not invoked automatically. However, our code invoked the next command to explicitly invoke getvalue from the counter class.

At this point, it is worth mentioning that the concept by which variables in TclOO work differs from the concepts of object-oriented programming from C++ or Java. Variables are set up at each object level and are not differentiated or protected by the class that created them. This way our `resetablecounter` class can access data from the `counter` class. On the other hand, there is no explicit need to create variables and they can be added on the fly. When destroying an object, all its variables are deleted.

TclOO also introduces a mechanism for invoking commands from within the object and from external code. By default, all methods are accessible from both inside of an object (by invoking `my <methodName>`) and from outside of an object (by invoking `$c1 <methodName>` for our example). This can be changed by adding `unexport` or `export` to class definition. For example, we can create a class that doesn't allow the `increment` method to be invoked from outside of object methods by doing:

```
oo::class create timedcounter {
    superclass counter

    constructor {} {
        # here we should set up some timer event to increment
        # the counter periodically
    }

    unexport increment
}
```

Often our classes will inherit from multiple base classes. In this case, we need to specify more than one `superclass`. In this case all methods are looked up in all base classes along with all their direct and indirect base classes. If a method is implemented by multiple classes, then the order in which classes are specified determines which one is run. However, the command `next` will look into other base classes as well, so one base class can retrieve information from other base classes. For example:

```
oo::class create testclass {
    method getvalue {} {
        puts "In testclass"
        next
    }
}

oo::class create testcounter {
    superclass testclass counter
}
```

In this case, running `getvalue` from `testcounter` class will cause `In testclass` to be printed to standard output and the method would return current value. Internally, TclOO will cause `getvalue` from `testclass` to be invoked, which then invokes the method from the `counter` class using `next` command.

The `next` command can also be used for methods that accept parameters. In this case, we need to run `next` with parameters that are expected by the base class, which can be different than currently accepted arguments. For example, assuming our `counter` class already has a `setcounter` method that accepts the new value as an argument, we can override it to write new value and run the implementation from the base class in the following way:

```
oo::class create othercounter {
    superclass counter
    method setvalue {value} {
        puts "Setting value to $value"
        next $value
    }
}
```

Object definitions

TclOO works in such a way that both classes and objects can define and/or override methods by using the `oo::objdefine` command. It accepts an object name and the definition that should be added.

For example, in order to add additional code to the `getvalue` method of only a specified instance of a class, we can do the following:

```
oo::objdefine $c1 {
    method getvalue {} {
        puts "Hello world from getvalue for this object only"
        next
    }
}
```

We are using the `next` command, because from the TclOO perspective, an object-specific implementation of a method is treated in the same way as though a subclass would override a particular method, so `next` invokes the same method within the class for this object.

Using mixins

Mixins in TclOO work in a way similar to inheritance. When our class mixes in another class, all methods available from that class are also available from within our class. The main difference is that when our class inherits a base class, methods from our class override methods in the base class. Mixins work in the opposite way — methods from a mixin override methods from our class so that mixins can interact with our class.

For example, we can build a mixin that caches results based on arguments:

```
oo::class create cache {
    method perform {args} {
        my variable cachedata

        # key for caching data,
        #for now we assume it's all arguments
        set key $args

        # if we don't know the results yet, run actual method
        if {![info exists cachedata($key)]} {
            set cachedata($key) [next {*}$args]
        }

        return $cachedata($key)
    }
}
```

This mixin is generic enough, so it can cache any class that performs calculations when the `perform` method is invoked. Now we can define our class that will use the `cache` mixin to increase performance:

```
oo::class create complexcalculation {
    # use caching mechanism
    mixin cache

    method perform {a b} {
        # simulate long running calculations
        # by waiting for 0.5 second
        after 500
        return [expr {$a + $b}]
    }
}
```

The following shows how cache and `complexcalculation` classes are related:

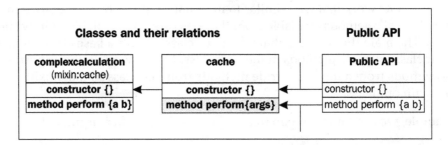

In this case, even though the `complexcalculation` class refers to cache, from method lookup perspective, the implementation in cache class has higher priority. Therefore, invoking `perform` actually calls the method from the cache class. Implementation in cache calls `perform` from `complexcalculation` using `next` command.

Our class definition specifies a list of mixins that should be included for each instance of an object. In this case, it contains only one mixin – our `cache` class. When invoking `perform` method, calculations will take 0.5 second to perform due to delay, first time it is invoked with specific arguments. Next time the mixin will simply return a cached value without our method actually being implemented.

Another difference is that mixins can be applied to an individual object, while inheritance needs to be carried out for the entire class. For example, our `complexcalculation` class might be implemented without the `mixin cache` statement in the class definition and later on we can do the following to apply caching to only specific objects.

This way we can enable caching by invoking the `oo::objdefine $object mixin cache` command – it sets mixins to our `cache` class. Invoking the `oo::objdefine $object mixin` command will disable caching by setting no mixins for this object. Note that even if a class definition specifies a list of mixins, we can explicitly disable it – for example, disable cache on specific instances for debugging purposes. This gives more flexibility than static inheritance.

Forwarding methods

Method forwarding is a feature that allows specifying that a method of a class will be forwarded to another command, another object or a specific method in an object. While forwards can easily be implemented as methods, this takes the burden of maintaining and passing arguments correctly off the developer of this class.

Let's assume we have a class called `eventhandler` that allows a generic set of operations, such as adding and removing a command to be run when something occurs. If we inherit this class in our code, we could only have one type of event. So it makes more sense to create one or more objects and forward all calls to these objects. For example:

```
oo::class create messagingserver {
    # forward method log to
    # mainlogger command in global namespace
    forward log ::mainlogger
    constructor {} {
        # create forwarded method when user
        # connects and disconnects from our server
        oo::objdefine [self] forward \
            userconnected [eventhandler new]
        oo::objdefine [self] forward \
            userdisconnected [eventhandler new]
    }

    destructor {
        # delete event handler objects
        userconnected destroy
        userdisconnected destroy
    }
}
```

This causes our class to have the method `log` which forwards it to the `mainlogger` command – outside of object definition and common for all instances of an object. This can be defined for the entire class because forwarding is done in the same way for all objects.

It will also cause the methods `userconnected` and `userdisconnected` to forward all parameters to that object – meaning that the first parameter will be the method to invoke for that object and all remaining arguments will be passed as arguments to that method.

As we need to create an object instance, we need to do that from inside the constructor – as objects are created with unique identifier for each instance of `messagingserver` instance, we need to perform this for each object separately and from within our constructor. The `self` command returns the current object identifier so that we can invoke `oo::objdefine` to add method forwarding definition from a constructor.

The following diagram shows how each of publicly available methods maps to other objects and procedures:

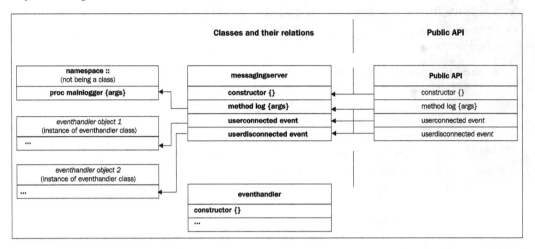

The `method log` actually invokes the `mainlogger` command from the `::` namespace. `userconnected` and the `userdisconnected` methods invoke methods from other objects.

Additional information

While some of the approaches might seem different from known solutions (such as objects in C++, Java, or Python), mechanisms in TclOO offer much more flexibility to the developer. As one of key Tcl aspects is that it is a dynamic language, its object-oriented programming syntax also offers similar flexibility.

TclOO also offers a feature called filters, which control and filter method invocations. It can be used to achieve highly advanced features such as caching and aspect programming. While this topic is beyond the scope of this book, we recommend readers doing advanced object-oriented programming in Tcl investigate this feature, and in particular, read the `http://wiki.tcl.tk/20308` page, which shows how to extend the `oo::class` to add aspects.

More information about TclOO features can be found in the following Tcl manual pages:

- `http://www.tcl.tk/man/tcl8.6/TclCmd/my.htm`
- `http://www.tcl.tk/man/tcl8.6/TclCmd/object.htm`
- `http://www.tcl.tk/man/tcl8.6/TclCmd/next.htm`
- `http://www.tcl.tk/man/tcl8.6/TclCmd/define.htm`
- `http://www.tcl.tk/man/tcl8.6/TclCmd/class.htm`

Accessing files

Tcl allows us to read from and write to files by using channels. A channel can be an open file, but it can also be a network socket, a pipe, or any other channel type. Depending on the type of the channel, it can support reading from it, writing to it, or both.

Tcl comes with three default channels — stdin, stdout, and stderr. These channels correspond to the standard input, standard output, and standard error channels of operating systems. Standard input can be used to read information from the user, standard output should be used to write information to user, and standard error is used to write errors. Depending on how our application is run, these channels can be redirected from/to files.

In the case of Microsoft Windows and applications using the GUI version of Tcl, invoked using the wish or tclkit commands, standard channels are not available. This is because graphical applications in Microsoft Windows do not have standard consoles. In such cases, an equivalent of these channels is created that allows interacting with the user from Tk console window. For example:

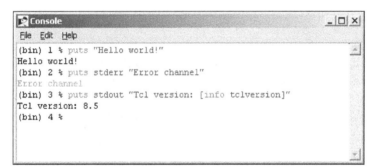

The puts command in this form is described in more detail later in this section.

Reading and writing files

The open command can be used in order to open a file for reading and/or writing. It can be invoked either with just the filename, the filename and the open mode as well as filename, open mode and permissions, when creating a new file. Permissions are ignored on Microsoft Windows systems and default to 0666 if they are not specified on all other systems. Permissions are combined with the mask set up for current process, usually set by the umask system command. This is similar to how all file creation operations work on Unix systems. The open command returns the name of the newly opened channel — it can be used for all commands that operate on channels.

The open mode is a string specifying the access mode, defaulting to r if it is not specified. Mode r opens the file for reading only. Mode r+ opens file for reading and writing; the file must already exist. The w mode opens the file for writing only, truncating it if the file already exists, and creating it if it does not exist. The w+ mode opens the file in same mode as w mode, but allows both reading and writing. The a mode opens the file for writing only, setting the current pointer in file to end if the file already exists, and creating the file if it does not exist. The a+ mode opens the file in same mode as a mode, but allows both reading and writing.

The following table summarizes each of the modes, which operations are permitted, and any additional activity that takes place:

Mode	Readable	Writable	Initial position	Must exist	Is truncated
r	Yes	No	Beginning of file	Yes	No
r+	Yes	Yes	Beginning of file	Yes	No
w	No	Yes	Beginning of file	No	Yes
w+	Yes	Yes	Beginning of file	No	Yes
a	No	Yes	End of file	No	No
a+	Yes	Yes	End of file	No	No

The columns "Readable" and "Writable" describe which operations can be performed on a file. "Initial position" specifies whether the initial position after opening the file is its beginning or end. "Must exist" specifies whether the file has to exist at the point when open command is called. "Is truncated" specifies whether a file is created as an empty file if it already exists when open command is called.

The open command can also be used to run external processes. In this case, the first argument should be command name prefixed by a pipe character (|). An additional argument might specify the open mode, otherwise Tcl will open the application in read-only mode. For example:

```
set chan [open "|route"]
while {![eof $chan]} {
    gets $chan line
    puts "Route information: > $line <"
}
close $chan
```

The commands gets and eof used to read information are described in more detail later in this chapter.

They can be used to parse information from external commands as well as to interact with a text-based application or command. In order to write to an application, we need to pass `r+` as the mode to the `open` command. Then we can use `gets` to read a channel and use `puts` to write to it.

In many cases, it is enough to use `exec` command, which allows running processes and reading their output. It accepts `system` command and its parameters as arguments to the command. By default, `exec` returns standard output as result of the command and if anything is written to standard error, `exec` throws an error with this data. For example, we can rework the preceding example to a simpler one by using `exec`:

```
foreach line [split [exec "route"] \n] {
    puts "Route information: > $line <"
}
```

The `split` command converts output to a list of lines that the `route` system command writes to standard output.

The `exec` as well as `open` commands are used for running a system command; streaming one command to another command handles majority of shell-like syntax for redirecting and conditional execution. For example, we can redirect input, output, or error streams and can redirect them in a way similar to shell commands. The following example runs `ifconfig` and `grep` to return only lines with IP addresses, which can then be parsed.

```
set text [exec /sbin/ifconfig 2>/dev/null | grep "inet addr"]
```

The `exec` command also throws an error if a child exits with non-zero code. For example, we can try to run the command route with invalid parameters:

```
exec false
```

On Unix systems, the `false` command always exits with code 1. This command would cause an error child process that is exited abnormally to be thrown.

Please see `http://www.tcl.tk/man/tcl8.5/TclCmd/exec.htm` for more details on the use of the `exec` command and flow control.

Reading from a channel can be done either by using `gets` or `read` command. The first command reads a single line from a channel and can be invoked with only the channel name, in which case it returns string read from the channel. It can also be invoked with the channel name and variable name, in which case it reads a line, and that string is written to specified variable and a returns number of bytes read. The `read` command can be used to either read all remaining data, if invoked with channel name only, or the specified number of bytes, if invoked with a channel name and number of bytes.

Writing to a channel can be performed using `puts` command. The command can be invoked with only one argument, which causes the specified argument to be printed to standard output. It can also be invoked with a channel name and a second argument, which causes the second argument to be written to the channel. Specifying the `-nonewline` option as the first argument causes `puts` not to append a newline character at the end, which is done by default.

Often, a `puts` command only adds data to a buffer associated with a channel and writes actual data to disk if the buffer is full. If a write should be performed immediately, the `flush` command can be used. This command is invoked with the channel name as its only argument. Invoking the command will cause all buffers to be written. Buffering is discussed more in the section focusing on the `fconfigure` command.

An example usage for `flush` is to make sure data is sent to a channel. For example, in order to make sure text is written to standard output, we can do the following:

```
puts -nonewline "Enter your first name: "
flush stdout
gets stdin firstName
```

This command will print out **Enter your first name:** and then read user's input from standard input. As standard output is configured to buffer data, the text would not be printed without first invoking `flush stdout`.

In order to move to the current location in a file, we can use the `seek` command. This command accepts a channel as the first argument, followed by the position we want to move to. Optionally, we can also specify the origin of the offset. It can be either `start`, `current` or `end`; if skipped, it defaults to `start`. In first case, the position indicates an offset from the beginning of a file. The `current` position is relative to the current position in the file and `end` means that offset is relative to end of the file. This makes sense only if the position is a non-positive number.

The `eof` command is used to verify if end of the file has been reached for a channel. This is usually checked inside a `while` statement, to iterate until EOF has been reached. All channels opened by `open` command as well as all other channels in Tcl need to be closed with a `close` command.

```
set chan [open "/tmp/myfile" w]
puts $chan "Tcl version: [info tclversion]"
puts -nonewline $chan "Additional line"
puts $chan " of text"
close $chan

set chan [open "/tmp/myfile" r]
while {![eof $chan]} {
```

```
        gets $chan line
        puts "Line: > $line <"
    }
    close $chan
```

The result would be as follows:

Tcl version: 8.5

Additional line of text

Tcl channels also are configurable, which means that they have standard and non-standard options that we can get or set. Typical functions include file encoding, newline handling, the *End of File* character, buffering, and blocking mode versus non-blocking mode. Non-standard options vary depending on the type of the channel — serial ports, network connections, and other channels have options specific to their type.

Configuring channel options

You can get and set all options using the fconfigure command. If this command is run with only a channel name, it returns a list of all options along with their values. Running fconfigure with a channel and option name returns this option's current value, and passing both the name and new value causes the option's value to be set to what we specified.

One of the most commonly used options is whether a channel is blocking or non-blocking, which is set by the option -blocking and its value is a Boolean value. A blocking channel causes each attempt to read more data than currently available to block until that data is available — for example, a gets command will return only after an entire line can be read. A non-blocking channel returns as much data as is currently available and does not wait for more. By default, channels are in blocking mode, so -blocking is set to 1.

Tcl channels work in such a way that each channel has an output buffer. It is used when writing data to a channel and depending on configuration, data can either be buffered or written to disk. Option -buffering specifies type of buffering that will be done for this channel. If the value is full, then Tcl will always buffer data and only write when its internal buffer is full. If it is set to line, Tcl will write data to the channel after each newline character. Setting it to none will always cause Tcl to write data to channel. By default, all channels have -buffering set to full, except for standard input, standard output, and standard error channels, which are set to line, line, and none respectively.

We can also set the size of the buffer that Tcl will use with the -buffersize option. It specifies the maximum number of bytes that Tcl should use for the internal output buffer. It is also affected by the -buffering option, which determines when Tcl writes data to the channel.

Tcl channels offer native translation of newline characters and different encodings. A channel can be configured as binary file or any encoding that Tcl handles and various modes for handling newline characters. By default, channels are configured to use system native encoding (which is determined depending on operating system and environment) and use native newline translation (*CR LF* on Windows, *LF* on Unix).

The -translation option defines how newline translation is done and/or whether a file is in binary mode. It can be one of the following values:

Translation mode	Description
lf	ASCII character 10
cr	ASCII character 13
crlf	ASCII characters 13 followed by 10
auto	Automatic detection (for input only)
binary	Binary translation of all data

The binary option tells Tcl that it should ignore any translation (including encoding handling) and treat a channel as binary.

It is also possible to specify a list of two elements, where the first element means how newlines are read and the second one determines how newlines are written — for example, {auto crlf} means that reading is determined automatically, but CR and LF is always used for writing. This translation value is the default for Tcl on Microsoft Windows.

In addition to this, the option -encoding allows us to specify the encoding used for reading and writing to a channel. For example, in order to read a channel in UTF-8, we need to configure the channel to use utf-8 encoding. To work with file in UCS-2, we need to specify encoding unicode. Available encoding names can be retrieved using the encoding names command, which is explained in more detail in *Chapter 5*.

You can modify both the -translation and -encoding options as you are reading a file – so it is possible to read the first line of an XML file with utf-8 encoding and see whether it contains encoding information. If it does, we can change the encoding and read the remaining part of the file with the correct encoding. For example:

```
# open a file and read its first line
set chan [open "/path/to/file.xml" r]
fconfigure $chan -translation auto -encoding utf-8
gets $chan line

# call a function that checks if first line is <?...?>
# and if it is, returns the encoding we should use
set encoding [getHeaderEncoding $line]
if {$encoding == ""} {
    # if we found no <? ...?> line, let's read entire file
    seek $chan 0 start
} else {
    fconfigure $chan -encoding $encoding
}

set xml [read $chan]
close $chan

# Now, let's parse $xml somehow (see chapter 5)
```

Internationalization related issues are explained in more detail in *Chapter 5*. For more information about encoding handling in Tcl, please see the corresponding manual page at:
http://www.tcl.tk/man/tcl8.5/TclCmd/encoding.htm

For more details about all standard options, please see the fconfigure command manual page at:
http://www.tcl.tk/man/tcl8.5/TclCmd/fconfigure.htm

File management

Besides reading and writing to files, Tcl offers an additional command that aids in managing and working with files – the file command. This command has multiple subcommands, which allow copying, renaming, deleting, getting and modifying information about files. One of main features that file offers is ability to copy, rename, and delete files as well as directories.

The `file copy` command can be used to copy one or more files or directories. The last argument to this command is the target and all previous arguments are items to copy. If only one item to copy is specified and the target does not exist, then the file or directory is copied as the target. For example:

`file copy /etc/passwd /tmp/passwd`

If `/tmp/passwd` does not exist, then `/etc/passwd` will be copied as `/tmp/passwd`. If `/tmp/passwd` is an existing file, the command will fail, unless `-force` is specified as the first argument, as follows:

```
file copy -force /etc/passwd /tmp/passwd
```

If multiple source items to copy are specified or the target is an existing directory, then all items will be copied into the target directory. In the example above, if `/tmp/passwd` is a directory, then `/etc/passwd` will be copied as `/tmp/passwd/passwd`. Similar to previous case, unless `-force` was specified, `file copy` will fail in case of any existing files.

On systems that support symbolic links, `file copy` handles them correctly, which means that they will be copied as links instead of copying the targets that the links point to.

The renaming of files and moving them to different directories can be achieved using the `file rename` command. Similar to doing a file copy, the last argument is the target and all previous ones are source items that should be renamed or moved. If only one item is specified and the target does not exist, then the source item is renamed as the target. If multiple source items are specified or the target is an existing directory, all source items are moved to the target directory while preserving their name.

The `file delete` command is used to delete files and/or directories. It takes one or more arguments, each of them being either a file or directory name. For example:

`file delete /tmp/passwd`

Tcl will not delete non-empty directories and will raise an error in this case. Deleting directories recursively requires `-force` to be specified as the first argument. Using this option also causes Tcl to try and modify the permissions of items when permissions prevent them from being deleted. This, of course, is limited by the operating system, so Tcl won't be able to delete other users' files, unless it is run by an administrator. Tcl will ignore any attempt to delete a non-existent file, and it will not raise an error.

In order to create a directory, we need to invoke the `file mkdir` command. For example:

```
file mkdir /tmp/some/new/directory
```

This command creates a directory as well as all parent directories that do not exist. So, even if the directory /tmp was empty, Tcl will create /tmp/some, then /tmp/some/new, and finally /tmp/some/new/directory appropriately.

Filename related operations

The `file` command also offers multiple commands for platform-dependant management of file names. This can be used to effectively manage filenames, and handle joining paths so that different path types and different path separators are properly handled. The `file join` command joins all arguments into a full path. The `file split` command does the opposite — splits a path into a list of elements. For Unix systems the separator is /, while for Windows both / and \ are acceptable. Tcl uses / on both Windows and Unix when possible, though. On a Unix system, splitting and joining paths returns values similar to these:

```
% puts [file split /home/user/../tcluser/bin]
/ home user .. tcluser bin
% puts [file join / home user .. tcluser bin]
/home/user/../tcluser/bin
% puts [file join / home user /home tcluser bin]
/home/tcluser/bin
```

The last example shows that file join distinguishes paths that are absolute and if an element is an absolute path, the previous ones are discarded, similar to how all file accessing works. For Windows systems, the logic is a bit different to support multiple volumes — so C:/Tcl/bin/tclsh85.exe would be split into the elements C:/ Tcl bin and tclsh85.exe.

Using the `file` command we can also do typical path related activities in an easy way; `file tail` provides a convenient way to get the file name only, which is an equivalent of doing a `file split` and retrieving last element. We can also get the path to a parent directory by using the `file dirname`, which is equivalent to splitting, then removing the last element from the list, and finally running `file join` to get the path back. For example:

```
% puts [file tail /home/tcluser/bin]
bin
% puts [file dirname /home/tcluser/bin]
/home/tcluser
```

Similar to splitting and joining, these commands work regardless of whether the files and/or directories exist, and handle issues specific to the different operating systems.

Often, paths contain special entries such as . . that indicate that a parent directory should be used. The `file normalize` command can be used to normalize paths so that they are always full paths. In order to convert a path to use native file separator, we can use the `file nativename` command. For example:

```
% puts [file normalize [file join C:/WINDOWS .. Tcl bin tclsh85.exe]]
C:/Tcl/bin/tclsh85.exe
% puts [file nativename C:/Tcl/bin/tclsh85.exe]
C:\Tcl\bin\tclsh85.exe
```

Tcl also makes it possible to retrieve file extensions. The command `file extension` returns file's extension, along with last dot character preceding it. The command `file rootname` returns the opposite—returns filename up to but not including the dot and all characters after it. For example:

```
% puts [file extension mybinary-1.1.exe]
.exe
% puts [file rootname mybinary-1.1.exe]
mybinary-1.1
```

File information

The additional subcommands of the `file` command are available to gather information about files. In order to get all of the information about a specified file or directory, you need to use the `file stat` command appending a path to an item and an array name as arguments. Information about the specified file will be set in the specified array.

The following elements of the array are set:

Key	Description
type	Type of entry—`file` or `directory`
size	For files—size of file in bytes; for directories, value depends on operating system
atime	Last access time, as unix timestamp
ctime	File creation time, as unix timestamp
mtime	File modification time, as unix timestamp
gid	Unix group identifier owning the file
uid	Unix user identifier owning the file
mode	Unix file permissions

Values for the keys `gid`, `uid`, and `mode` are specific to Unix systems and are set to reasonable defaults on systems that do not support Unix file permissions. The owning user and group are specified as their integer identifiers.

For example, on Unix, this command would return information similar to following:

```
% file stat /etc/passwd myarray
% puts "Type=$myarray(type) Size=$myarray(size)"
Type=file Size=987
```

On Unix, performing `file stat` command on a symbolic link will return information about item that the symbolic link refers to. In order to access information about the actual symbolic link, the `file lstat` command should be used.

Symbolic links can also be read and created using the `file readlink` and `file link` commands accordingly. The first one returns information about the target a link points to for symbolic links and throws an error if either the file/directory does not exist or is not a symbolic link. The command `file link` creates a link, either symbolic or hard. It needs to be invoked with the new item to be created as the first argument and the source element as the second argument. In order to make a symbolic link the `-symbolic` flag needs to be provided before arguments. To create a hard link, the `-hard` flag needs to be provided. An attempt to create a link that is not supported on a particular operating system will raise an error. Currently, Unix platforms support symbolic links to files and directories and hard links to files. Modern Microsoft Windows systems allow symbolic links to directories and hard links to files on the NTFS filesystem. These are not done as Windows shortcuts (`*.lnk` files) and Tcl treats shortcut file as any other file.

For example, the following commands can create and read symbolic links on Unix:

```
% puts [file link -symbolic /tmp/passwd /etc/passwd]
/tmp/passwd
% puts [file readlink /tmp/passwd]
/etc/passwd
```

Getting and modifying the last accessed and last modification date can be done using the `file atime` and `file mtime` commands. When run with just a path as the first argument they return the appropriate time, as a Unix timestamp. When both a path and new value are specified, the appropriate time is set to a new value. Please note that not all operating systems and filesystems support setting this value and not all systems track it with the same granularity — in some cases, the new value will not be the same as the value that was set by the script.

Tcl also supports getting and setting operating system specific information about files and directories, using the `file attributes` command. When run with only the path to a file or directory, it returns a list of attribute name and value pairs, which can be used to retrieve all available attributes for an item. When run with a path and attribute name, it returns the current value for that attribute for the specified file or directory. When run with a path, attribute name and value, it sets a new value for that attribute for specified file or directory. For example, on Unix systems, we can work with ownership and permissions using this command:

```
% file attributes /tmp/passwd
-group tcluser -owner tcluser -permissions 00644
% file attributes /tmp/passwd -group admin -permissions 0660
% file attributes /tmp/passwd -permissions
00660
```

Tcl can also provide information about read/write access to particular items. The commands `file readable`, `file writable` return whether a particular file or directory can be read from or written to. For directories, this returns information about the ability to access files within that directory and the creation of new directories in that directory. In addition to this, the commands `file isfile` and `file isdirectory` can be used to check whether an item is a file or a directory.

Listing files

Listing items in a filesystem can be achieved by using the `glob` command. Each argument can be specified as a pattern of items to match or options that apply that to further patterns. The command returns a list containing all matched items in a filesystem or, by default, throws an error if no matches were found with any of the patterns.

Patterns can be specified as any character that the filename needs to match or a special character—? means any single character; * means zero or more characters. {ab,cd} matches any of the strings inside braces, split by a comma; in this case, it matches either a string containing ab or cd. [abcx-z] means any character inside the brackets, where x-z means any characters between x and z, inclusive; in this case, it matches a, b, c, x, y, or z. The form \x matches the character x and can be used to escape characters such as braces or brackets. Patterns can work with multiple levels of directories, for example by doing */*.tcl which will match all files with .tcl extension in all sub-directories of current directory.

The following will return similar information on many Unix systems:

```
% puts [glob /etc/pass*]
/etc/passwd /etc/passwd.bak
```

Specifying the base directory for matching patterns can be done using the
-directory flag. This causes all further patterns to be evaluated relative
to the specified directory. For example:

```
% puts [glob -directory /etc pass*]
/etc/passwd /etc/passwd.bak
```

Passing the flag -join causes all remaining arguments to be treated as one argument
and to be joined in the same way as file join does. For example:

```
% puts [glob -join /usr bin *grep]
/usr/bin/egrep /usr/bin/grep
```

When the -directory option was specified, adding the -tails option as well causes
the results list to contain only paths relative to one of the options. For -directory,
it causes only paths relative to this option's value to be returned, and for -path, it
causes the last element of the -path option to be appended as the first element in
all paths returned. For example:

```
% puts [glob -tails -directory /etc pass*]
passwd passwd.bak
```

We can also look for specific types of entries by using the -types option. It accepts a
list of one or more file types. When multiple types are passed, glob looks up entries
that are of any of the specified types. We can pass the d type to find directories, or
f to find files. In addition, on Unix systems, we can use l for a symbolic link, p for
a named pipe, and s for Unix sockets. In addition, b and c types can be used to find
block and character device entries, used to access devices on Unix systems.

We can also look for specific types of entries by using the -types option. It accepts a
list of one or more file types. When multiple types are passed, glob looks up entries
that are of any of the specified types. The following values can be used:

Type	Description
f	File
d	Directory
l	Symbolic link
p	Named pipe
s	Unix socket
b	Block device
c	Character device

The values l, p, s, b, and c are only used on Unix systems that provide support for
those kinds of file types.

In order to find symbolic links and directories in /tmp, we can do the following:

```
% puts [glob -type {d l} /tmp/*]
/tmp/hsperfdata_root /tmp/vmware-root /tmp/passwd
```

Besides file types, this option also accepts the permissions that a file needs to have. In case multiple access rights are specified, only entries having all of the access rights are returned. This can be r for readable, w for writable, x for executable, and hidden for hidden files on Microsoft Windows.

In order to find writable and executable files in /tmp, we can do the following:

```
% puts [glob -type {f w x} /tmp/*]
/tmp/sess1248
```

The package fileutil provides more high-level functionalities, such as recursive file lookups, searching for text within files, and so forth. It is available as part of the tcllib package, which is delivered with ActiveTcl installations. Please visit http://tcllib. sourceforge.net/doc/fileutil.html for more details on its available functionality.

Current working directory

All applications have the concept of the current working directory. This is the directory that is used as the base for any path that we specify — for example, if our working directory is /tmp, then opening the file tempfile will cause /tmp/tempfile to be opened. Specifying a full path — such as opening /etc/passwd will always the cause proper file to be opened. When starting the application, this is usually the place where the program running our application was. In many cases, our application will want to get current working directory or change it according to its needs.

Changing the current working directory in Tcl can be done using the cd command. It accepts one argument which specifies the new directory name. The command pwd can be used to return the full path to current working directory. For example:

```
% set oldwd [pwd]
% cd ~
% puts [pwd]
/home/tcluser
% cd $oldwd
```

This example stores the current directory, goes to the user's home directory, prints it, and returns to the original directory.

Packages in Tcl

Tcl offers a mechanism to look for and create packages—reusable pieces of code, either bundled with Tcl, created as additional projects or code you write and want to use in multiple applications. Packages are meant to provide an easy to use mechanism for using additional libraries—either your library or third-party libraries. Packages are identified using a package name and version.

Package name can be any string, but a good practice is to name the package using lowercase only and using the same name as the namespace used. For example, functionality to work with base64 encoded data is called base64 and all commands are in the base64 namespace.

Versions are one or more numbers separated by dots, where the first leftmost one indicates major versions, and remaining ones indicate additional versioning, with the leftmost being most significant, and the rightmost least significant. Tcl compares versions by separating the numbers using dots and comparing each part as numbers. version 3.2 is considered to be higher than 2.3 and version 10.1 is considered higher than 9.1. Tcl and Tk themselves are versioned in the same way.

Any code can be made into a package and this process is described in more detail later in this chapter.

Package loading

Operations related to the package system are accessible via the package command and its subcommands. In order to load a package, we need to invoke the package require command, specifying a package name and, optionally, the minimum version that is required.

If not specifying a version, the latest one is automatically loaded. If specifying a version to load, the package version that is larger or equal to the required version, with same major version as the required version is loaded. For example, if the package md5 is available in 1.3, 1.4.4, and 2.0.7 versions, then requiring any version would load the 2.0.7 version; and requiring 1.0 would load version 1.4.4.

If you are using ActiveTcl, then its documentation contains a full list of available packages along with documentation for each of the packages. This book only covers a small subset of all available Tcl packages.

Tcl package lookup works by having a variable that lists all directories Tcl should look for packages in. It then goes into each subdirectory of that directory and checks if the pkgIndex.tcl file exists and loads it. A list of these directories is stored in the global auto_path Tcl variable. In order to add a directory, it is enough to add it using lappend ::auto_path /path/to/new/directory.

Creating a package

Creating one or more Tcl packages is a trivial task and requires creating a directory, either in Tcl's lookup path, or in a place that we will later add to the list of directories. Our package can be stored in any directory. We need to have a file called pkgIndex.tcl, which is a script that should invoke the package ifneeded command, along with the name of the package, its version and the Tcl code to invoke to initialize a package. The scripts that provide a package need to invoke package provide command, providing package name and version as arguments.

While it is possible to create the pkgIndex.tcl file manually, Tcl provides a mechanism for building this file, which the authors recommend. Let's assume we want to build a package called mypackage, 1.0 version that will create a namespace called mypackage and an add command in it. What we need to start with is to set up a directory for our test packages and another for this particular package — for this example, we'll assume /tmp/packages and /tmp/packages/mypackage1.0 for the package. First create a file called /tmp/packages/mypackage1.0/mypackage.tcl containing the following code:

```
namespace eval mypackage {}

proc mypackage::add {a b} {
    return [expr {$a + $b}]
}

package provide mypackage 1.0
```

Next run the following command in any Tcl interpreter:

```
% pkg_mkIndex /tmp/packages/mypackage1.0
```

This will cause /tmp/packages/mypackage1.0/pkgIndex.tcl to be created. Every time you change your package names, package versions or filenames, the pkgIndex.tcl file will need to be rebuilt using the previous example.

Now in the same or new session of Tcl interpreter, type in the following commands:

```
% lappend ::auto_path /tmp/packages
/opt/ActiveTcl-8.5/lib /tmp/packages
% package require mypackage
1.0
```

More complex packages can include multiple files. If multiple files state that they provide the same package in the same version, then pkgIndex.tcl file will indicate that all those files need to be loaded. If multiple files provide different packages or different versions of the same package, then this will be reflected in the pkgIndex.tcl file as well.

For larger packages, the authors recommend building multiple smaller packages and having one larger package that only requires the remaining ones — for example, `mypackage::add` and `mypackage::sub` will provide actual commands and main `mypackage` command will just load the actual ones.

Tcl modules

Tcl 8.5 also introduces a new concept called **Tcl modules**. This is a simplification of packaging system we previously mentioned, which assumes that all packages reside in individual files. Tcl will load this file by loading this script, so it either needs to be a Tcl script or it can be a Starkit archive with a native library embedded in it. Starkit archives are introduced in *Chapter 3*.

The main reason for creating a modules system in Tcl is to be able to clearly map the directory structure to package names, similar to how it is done in languages such as Java or Python — by knowing the package name you can easily find directory and the files that define a particular package.

The path and filename reflect the actual package name and version. For example, the package `mypackage` with version `1.1` would reside in a file called `mypackage-1.1.tm`. If the package name contains one or more `::` strings, then those are used to map packages to directories. For example, `mypackage::common::misc` version `1.2` package would need to reside in `mypackage/common` directory with name `misc-1.2.tm`.

Loading a module does not differ in any way from loading a package — all we need to do is run the package `requiremypackage` and Tcl will find and load it in the same way regardless of whether it is a package or module.

Tcl looks for these modules in different set of directories so that the package lookup mechanism is separated from the modules lookup. In order to add a directory where modules should be looked for, we need to invoke the `tcl::tm::add` command with a directory where files should be looked for. For example, to create a package called `mypackage` with version `1.1`, we can create directory called `/tmp/tclmodules` and create a file called `mypackage-1.1.tm` in it with the following contents:

```
namespace eval mypackage {}

proc mypackage::add {a b} {
    return [expr {$a + $b}]
}

package provide mypackage 1.1
```

Then we can run the following code to test it:

```
% tcl::tm::add /tmp/tclmodules
% package require mypackage
1.1
```

Even though, internally, Tcl packages and modules differ slightly from each other in how they are handled, the authors have decided not to distinguish those two concepts where it is not necessary and always use the term package, whether Tcl uses modules or packages to load it.

Event-driven programming

Tcl is designed to use an event-driven model. This means that everything that should happen is either scheduled for a particular time or when an event occurs, such as data being read, a new connection is made, or an external application or database sends a notification. This means that your files, networking, and timers work in the same thread and use events to perform actions when something occurs. For example, in an application with user interface, an action can be bound to user clicking on a button, which causes specific code to be run whenever the user clicks on the button. Similarly, a network server will set up a listening connection and run specific code when a new connection is established. Similarly, whenever application can read or write to a network connection, the particular code can be run.

It is common to develop an application that is event driven. This means that in most cases the application will only do things when an event takes place or will perform scheduled tasks. For example, a server will take actions whenever a new connection comes in and will clean up its information once a day.

Tcl fits this way of creating applications very well. It comes with a built-in event loop that is used by all Tcl components. In addition to this, a large number of packages available for Tcl support working in an event-driven way — for example, many networking clients and servers allow defining what should be done when a process is finished or when a new request comes in. Commands that are invoked when an event takes place are often called **callbacks**.

Tcl event types

Different types of Tcl events are as follows:

- File/channel events — occur when a file or a channel (such as pipe, network connection, or serial port) can be read or written to
- Timer events — occur after specified time, used for periodic activity

- Idle events – these events are run as soon as there are no different types of events in the event queue

- GUI events – used in applications that use Tk for their user interface, these events are generated when the user generates an action – such as clicking on a button

In addition to events generated by Tcl itself, packages often provide higher level events. For example, network related packages handle channel related events to handle communication and invoke callbacks whenever it makes sense. A package to manage downloads over the network would invoke a callback whenever a download is completed or an error occurs.

Entering the event loop

In order for Tcl to process events, it needs to enter the event loop. When Tcl is started up, by default, it either sources the script file it was run with or it goes into interactive mode. In the majority of cases, this does not cause Tcl to enter the event loop. The best way to make sure that Tcl goes into the event loop once your application is initialized is to add the following command at the end of your script:

`vwait forever`

Normally, the command `vwait` enters the event loop and waits for the variable specified, because its argument is modified – in this case, it means that Tcl will be processing events until the variable `forever` is modified. However, `vwait forever` is an idiom that many programmers add to the end of their script when they actually don't want to wait for a variable, but just want to enter the event loop.

In some cases when your script exits, Tcl will enter the event loop anyway, so it might not be required. Usually, this means Tk applications and running your applications from within TkCon. We can add the following check to see if Tk is loaded, and only enter event loop if it is not available:

```
if {[info commands tk] == ""} {
    vwait forever
}
```

This checks if the `tk` command exists, and only invokes `vwait` if no Tk is available. If your application sources additional scripts or plugins, these should not enter the event loop themselves, because then actual loading of the script is blocked. It should only be invoked in the main script of your application.

Events and stack frames

All commands that are run as different types of events are always run at the global level — this is the same level that your application is loaded at. It also means that if an event initialization was done in a specific procedure or with various local variables, when the event is invoked, these variables will not be present. For example:

```
proc myFunction {} {
    set value 100
    puts "Current value: $value"
    after 1000 {puts "Value: $value"}
}
myFunction
vwait forever
```

This will schedule the `puts "Value: $value"` command to be executed one second after `myFunction` command is called. The `after` command causes a command to be evaluated after a specified time in milliseconds and is described in more detail in the coming sections of this chapter. The code will fail because the variable value is not accessible at this time and the `value` global variable was never defined. It is correct to use namespace variables and preferably a separate procedure for the actual event:

```
Namespace eval example {}

proc example::eventfunction {} {
    variable value
    puts "Value: $value"
}

proc example::function {} {
    variable value
    set value 100
    puts "Current value: $value"
    after 1000 example::eventfunction
}

example::function
vwait forever
```

This will cause the texts `Current value: 100` and `Value: 100` to be written to standard output as namespace variables are used in this case.

Channel events

Channel events are triggered whenever a channel can be read from or written to. Usually this is used for network connections, Unix sockets, and running processes using the open command. It is also used with non-blocking channel in majority of cases.

Channel events allow us to set up certain commands to be run whenever there is something to read or whenever we can write to a channel so that our code does not block other events from being processed — for example, so that while we are waiting for more data from a remote peer, scheduled events can still run.

Setting up events is done using the fileevent command. It accepts a channel as the first argument and an event type as the second argument — which can be either readable or writable, depending on which event we are interested in. If run with those two parameters, it returns the currently configured command to be run. We can also pass a new command that should be run whenever the specified event for this channel occurs. Usually this is combined with building commands as lists so that we can pass additional arguments such as the channel name to the command that will be run.

The following is an example of an echo server that sends each line back to the remote connection by using events:

```
proc echoHandler {chan} {
    if {[eof $chan]} {
        close $chan
    } else {
        gets $chan line
        puts $chan $line
        flush $chan
    }
}

proc echoAccept {chan remotehost remoteport} {
    # set buffering to line and non-blocking mode
    fconfigure $chan -buffering line -blocking 0

    # initialize readable event
    fileevent $chan readable [list echohandler $chan]
}

socket -server echoAccept 12345
```

This example also initializes a TCP server on TCP port 12345. Networking is discussed in more detail in *Chapter 6*. However, for the purpose of this example, we need to know two things — `socket -server` command sets up a listening connection and runs command, as yet another channel related event, to `echoAccept` command, adding new channel, remote host and remote port information as additional parameters. Next, this command sets up an event that runs `echoHandler` with the channel passed as an argument. It checks whether an end of file has been received, which happens when the remote peer closes the connection, and closes this channel if that happened. Otherwise, the command sends the same line that was read back to the remote peer.

Similarly the `writable` event can be used to send large chunks of data to a channel — if we wanted to send more data than our channel buffer can send, Tcl would need to wait until this data is sent — in which case all other events would not be processed until this operation was completed. Using the `writable` event, we can receive an event whenever we can write more data to a channel and send it in smaller chunks.

For both types of events, it is important to delete an event if we no longer want to handle this — for instance, if we won't read or write when an event occurs, Tcl will keep on invoking our event handler until we've read/written data. You can delete an event handler by invoking `fileevent` with the channel, event type, and an empty string as the third parameter.

For example, the command to send large data to a channel by temporarily setting an event can be done in this way:

```
proc sendMoreData {chan data} {
    # write first 4096 bytes of data to channel
    puts -nonewline $chan [string range $data 0 4095]
    flush $chan

    # trim data to contain remaining part of original data
    set data [string range $data 4096 end]
    if {[string length $data] > 0} {
        # if we have more data to write, set up next writable event
        fileevent $chan writable [list sendMoreData $chan $data]
    } else {
        # otherwise remove an event
        fileevent $chan writable ""
    }
}

proc sendData {chan data} {
    # set up initial event - we do not write now
    # since channel might not be accepting more data at the moment
    fileevent $chan writable [list sendMoreData $chan $data]
}
```

The previous example uses the writable event to write data whenever it is possible.

In many cases we will want to send data from one channel to another—for example, sending file contents over a socket. Tcl offers a command that allows synchronous (blocking) or asynchronous (using event system) copying of data from one channel to another. This can be done using the fcopy command. It accepts an input channel and an output channel as the first two arguments. If no other argument is specified, it copies data from the input channel to the output channel in blocking mode. Adding the -size option after those arguments we can specify the number of bytes that should be copied, in which case either all of the file is copied or only the specified number of bytes is copied, whichever comes first.

If we want fcopy to work in background, we need to specify a -command option along with a command as parameter. In this case fcopy will return immediately, set up sockets to work in non-blocking mode and start copying data. As soon as the copying is complete or an error occurs, the specified command is run, with one or two arguments appended. First argument specifies number of bytes copied. If no error occurred, only one argument is appended. If an error has occurred, the command is run with the error string added as the second argument.

Timer and idle events

Being able to perform certain tasks periodically is important, for example, periodically removing old entries from a database, sending daily reports. Tcl and its event loop offers a convenient way to run commands after specified time—it is possible to add a command to be run, remove it from the event queue, and query items currently in event queue. This functionality is accessible using after command.

In order to schedule a command to be run after some time, append the time (in milliseconds from now) and the command to be run, for example:

```
after 2000 {puts "Welcome back"}
puts "Hello"
vwait forever
```

What will happen is first a Hello text will be printed out, followed by a **Welcome back** message two seconds later.

Such invocation of `after` returns a unique identifier for this event. This can be used to cancel a timer event from running by invoking `after cancel` with the id. For example:

```
set id [after 2000 {puts "Welcome back"}]
puts "Hello"
after cancel $id
vwait forever
```

What will happen is the **Hello** message will be printed out, but **Welcome back** will not be printed as it has been cancelled. `after cancel` also accepts the command that was scheduled, and if it is found in the timer event queue, it is removed. For example:

```
proc myCommand {} {
    puts "My Command was invoked"
}
after 1000 myCommand
after cancel myCommand
```

In this example, `myCommand` will never be invoked — even though we did not store what the first after command returned, `after cancel` has removed the actual `myCommand` invocation from timer event queue.

If we want to add something to queue so that it is processed whenever the event loop is processing events, we can use the `after idle` command. It accepts a command to be run, similar to scheduling something to be run after specified period of time. For example:

after idle myCommand

The `after` command can also be used to wait for a specified amount of time without entering the event loop — it might be useful if our script needs to wait for something or a period of time, and we do not need to process other events during that time. In this case, the time in milliseconds needs to be added as the only argument to the command. For example, to wait for 5 seconds, we need to run this command:

after 5000

In many cases, what our application actually wants is to run a command at a specified time. In this case, we need to use the `clock scan` and `clock seconds` commands, and calculate after what time our command should be run. For example, to run a command at 8 p.m. we can do the following:

```
set seconds [clock scan "20:00"]
set seconds [expr {$seconds-[clock seconds]}]
if {$seconds < 0} {
    incr seconds 86400
}
after [expr {$seconds * 1000}] myTaskCommand
```

In order to periodically run a command the following code should be inside the scheduled command so it will reschedule the next event when done. In many cases, such as old data cleanup, it is okay to run the command when an application starts and schedule our command to after the entire application is started by adding `after 1000 ourCommand`. If the function should only be run at proper schedules, for example when doing daily reports, scheduling should be split from the actual task. For example:

```tcl
proc myTaskCommand {} {
    puts "Task is being performed..."
    scheduleMyTaskCommand
}

proc scheduleMyTaskCommand {} {
    set seconds [clock scan "03:00"]
    set seconds [expr {$seconds - [clock seconds]}]
    if {$seconds < 0} {
        incr seconds 86400
    }
    after [expr {$seconds * 1000}] myTaskCommand
}
```

Robust scheduling with tclcron

The Tcl community offers a package that provides robust scheduling capability called `tclcron`. It uses the `after` and `clock scan` commands internally. It allows us to register commands to be run in more intuitive ways.

The tclcron manual page can be found at `http://dqsoftware.sourceforge.net/tclcron_man.html`; download information can also be found on this page.

To add a command we want to run, we need to invoke the `tclcron::schedule` command, passing a command to be run as the first argument, the type of schedule as the second parameter, and arguments after that. The two most basic types of schedules are `once` and `every`. The first one schedules a task only once and second one invokes it repeatedly. For example:

```tcl
proc everyCommand {} {
    puts "Every 30 seconds"
}

proc onceCommand {} {
    puts "Once in 40 seconds"
}

tclcron::schedule everyCommand every 30 seconds
tclcron::schedule onceCommand once 40 seconds
```

This will cause **Every 30 seconds** to be printed out after half a minute has passed. **Once in 40 seconds** will be printed out 10 seconds after that and then first text will be repeated every 30 seconds.

Both schedule types accept all valid clock scan input which makes them very powerful while being intuitive to read. For example:

```
tclcron::schedule databaseCleanup every 03:00
tclcron::schedule weeklyReport every sunday 04:00
tclcron::schedule cacheCleanup every 15 minutes
```

This will cause `databaseCleanup` to be invoked every day at 3 A.M. and `weeklyReport` to be invoked each Sunday at 4 A.M. The command `cacheCleanup` will be invoked every 15 minutes.

Similar to `after`, `tclcron::schedule` returns a unique identifier that can be used to remove a command from being invoked by running `tclcron::unschedule`. This identifier can also be used to query the next planned invocations of a scheduled command by using the `tclcron::schedules` command, returning Unix timestamp of each time the command would be run. It needs an identifier as the first argument. We can also specify the maximum number of timestamps we want to receive as the second argument. In addition to this, we can specify a timestamp after which we will no longer be interested in the schedule as a third argument.

For example, to find out how a particular schedule would be run and then remove it from the schedule, we can do the following:

```
set id [tclcron::schedule {} every 2 days]

foreach time [tclcron::schedules $id 100 [clock scan "+3 months"]] {
    puts "Next planned run: [clock format $time]"
}

tclcron::unschedule $id
```

Multithreaded applications

Even though Tcl is designed to work efficiently in a single-threaded environment, it is possible to create separate threads in Tcl. While it can be used for performing any action, it is usually used for operations that take a lot of time to complete.

Threads in Tcl require that Tcl is built with threading enabled and has the package `Thread` installed, which is true for all ActiveTcl installations. Tcl builds from various operating system distributions may or may not be built with thread support enabled — in this case, the `Thread` package may not be present.

Managing threads

Tcl uses that approach that each thread is a separate entity and data is not normally shared across threads. It is possible to send commands to be evaluated in a thread, either waiting for them to finish or by having them performed asynchronously. In order to create a thread, we need to first load the `Thread` package and use the `thread::create` command:

```
package require Thread
set tid [thread::create]
```

This causes a new thread to be created and its ID stored in variable `tid`.

We can then use the `thread::send` command to tell a thread to evaluate Tcl code:

```
thread::send $tid {after 2000 ; puts "Printed after two seconds"}
thread::send -async $tid {after 2000 ; puts "Printed in the
background"}
```

The first command tells the thread to wait for two seconds, and print text to standard output. The `thread::send` command causes the main thread to wait for the command to finish, actually performed in the other thread. The second command asks the thread to run the command, but it does not wait for the command to complete. Instead, command is run in the background. Asynchronous commands are mainly used for jobs that do not need to pass results back to the application or they that use `thread::send` to send results back to the original thread.

All calls to `thread::send` add the commands to event loop queue, so there is no possibility that a command's execution will cause a race condition and it does not need to be synchronized in any way. Internally, thread communication adds idle events to the target thread's event loop so threads need to be in the event loop for this to work. When a thread is created using `thread::create`, it goes into the event loop so unless the thread blocks at some operation, this is not an issue.

Threads in Tcl do not share any data, unlike most languages, including Java, C/C++, and Python. It is common to use a two-way messaging approach, where we tell a thread to do something using the `thread::send -async` command and the thread sends results back also using `thread::send -async`. This approach prevents many of the most common mult-ithreaded programming issues such as deadlocks, and has the benefit that it is much easier to maintain.

A typical example is that the main thread initializes the thread and then sends it commands:

```tcl
namespace eval example {}

proc example::initializeThread {} {
    variable childtid
    set childtid [thread::create]
    thread::send $childtid {source childscript.tcl}
    thread::send $childtid [list \
        set example::mainthreadid [thread::id]]
}

proc example::parseDataDone {result} {
    # handling of parsed data
}

proc example::parseData {data} {
    variable childtid
    thread::send -async $childtid [list \
        example::childParseData $data]
}

example::initializeThread
example::parseData {data goes here}
```

And `childscript.tcl`, which is then loaded by child thread, should look like this:

```tcl
namespace eval example {}

proc example::parseDataActual {data} {
    # this actually does time-consuming calculations
    # and returns newly created data
}

proc example::childParseData {data} {
    variable mainthreadid
    set result [parseDataActual $data]
    thread::send -async $mainthreadid [list \
        example::parseDataDone $result]
}
```

The example will work in the following way—when somebody invokes `parseData` in main thread, it sends that data to the previously created thread in an asynchronous way and the main thread continues. The child thread receives it in `childParseData`. It then passes it to `parseDataActual` procedure, which performs the actual calculations and returns the results. When that happens, an asynchronous event is sent to the main thread with the result, and the child thread can then either parse the next events in its queue or will wait for new tasks to be sent. The main thread will then save the calculated data or pass it to the remaining parts of the application.

Shared variables

Even though variables are not shared in Tcl, the `Thread` package offers a mechanism for keeping data that is shared across threads, called **thread shared variables** (`tsv`). This works in a similar way to Tcl arrays—there are multiple tsvs and each of them can contain multiple keys. A tsv array does not need to be setup— the first operation that sets a key in an array automatically creates this array.

The command `tsv::set` can be used to set an item and needs to be invoked with the array name, key name, and a new value to set. Getting current value can be done using `tsv::get` command. The command `tsv::unset` is used to unset either an entire array or a specified key for this array—if only the array name is specified, the entire array is deleted; if both the array name and key name are specified, only a specific key is deleted. Increasing integer numbers can be done using `tsv::incr`, specifying array and key name. For example:

```
package require Thread
tsv::set myarray counter 1
tsv::incr myarray counter
puts "Counter: [tsv::get myarray counter]"
```

This will cause 2 to be printed out, as after incrementing, this will be the new counter value. As multiple threads can potentially be accessing your tsv variables at the same time, the `Thread` package uses a locking mechanism when performing operations. For this reason, `tsv::incr` is safer to use than a combination of `tsv::get`, incrementing using `expr` and `tsv::set`—it might happen that both threads get the current value, and if so, increase it by one and save it. In this case, both will get 1 as the input value, increment it to 2 and set this value—while after both increment it, the value of those operations should be 3.

In order to make sure that for your entire operation on a `tsv` array, no other thread will be able to access it, you can use `tsv::lock`. The first argument should be name of the array to lock and the second should be the command to execute. For example, a secure alternative to `tsv::incr` is:

```
tsv::lock {
    set value [tsv::get myarray counter]
    incr value
    tsv::set myarray counter $value
}
```

While basic operations for `tsv` arrays are provided by the `Thread` package, locking is useful in cases where your application performs non-basic operations and concurrent access to data should be prohibited while your operation takes place.

It is possible to operate on particular keys for `tsv` arrays as on regular Tcl lists using the same commands in the `tsv` namespace — `tsv::lappend`, `tsv::lindex`, `tsv::llength`, `tsv::lreplace`, `tsv::lsearch`, and `tsv::lset`. The only difference with their Tcl lists counterparts is that `tsv::lreplace` saves results back to the `tsv` array instead of returning a new list. In addition to these commands, `tsv::lpush` can be used to insert a new element to a list. It requires specifying an array and key name, followed by the item to insert and optionally the position to insert the element at. Here 0 means the first element in the list, 1 the second element, and so on. If a position is skipped, it is inserted as first element of the list. Command `tsv::lpop` can be used to retrieve and remove an element from a list. When invoked with only array and key name, it retrieves first element. If the element index is specified, the element at this position is retrieved — where 0 means the first element in the list, 1 the second element, and so on.

It is also possible to retrieve information about array names, key names within a specified array. Command `tsv::names` returns a list of all arrays and `tsv::array names` returns a list of all keys for a specified array. For example, to list all arrays and their keys, run:

```
foreach arrayname [tsv::names] {
    foreach keyname [tsv::array names $arrayname] {
        puts "Array $arrayname, key $keyname"
    }
}
```

Transferring channels

Tcl channels are associated with an interpreter, which means that a channel created in the main thread will not be accessible to other threads. It is possible to transfer a channel using `thread::transfer` command. It is invoked with the target thread id and channel name as arguments. For example, to create a thread each time a connection is accepted, the following code could be used:

```
proc acceptConnection {channel} {
    set threadid [thread::create]
    initializeThread $threadid
    thread::transfer $threadid $channel
    thread::send $threadid [list handleChannel $channel]
}
```

After a channel has been passed to a thread, the channel will no longer be accessible to the originating thread. In order to make it accessible again in the main thread, it needs to be transferred back from the thread that currently owns it to originating thread, also using the `thread::transfer` command in the exact same way, but using thread the id of originating thread.

Summary

In this chapter, we learned about some of Tcl features that are needed in order to progress to more advanced topics covered from next chapter on.

We've presented how Tcl handles dates and times, which is very similar to other programming languages. However, the ability to parse human readable date, time, and scheduling definitions is something specific to Tcl and is considered to be a very powerful feature.

We also talked about the internals of Tcl, and how variables and data types are managed, focusing on the fact that even though Tcl can store everything as a string, internally it optimizes objects based on the way we access them throughout our code.

We also discussed object oriented programming and how Tcl 8.5 standardizes the approach and provides mechanisms for compatibility with other implementations of object-oriented programming in the Tcl world.

This chapter also goes through file-related operations—from reading and writing files, through file operations such as up to getting information about specific files and querying the filesystem.

We've also described a packaging system in Tcl, which is a bit more complicated than what many languages offer. However, it also is very powerful, which you will be able to notice in detail in the next chapter which will focus on the topic of building standalone binaries that include packages.

Events and threads were also a major part of this chapter. While Tcl's approach of using events over threads is very different from many other languages, this approach allows us to build code that is more maintainable and has problems caused by threading and concurrency issues. For those tasks that need threads, we also showed how that can be achieved and gave some practical advice on building applications that use working threads for long running operations.

While some of our readers might be familiar with some of these topics, certain things had to be mentioned, because we're going to use them frequently throughout this book. Others needed to be covered to give you a better understanding of Tcl and its internals.

3
Tcl Standalone Binaries

How many times have you installed the application you need and found out that, as a side effect, it created a lot of files under different locations? The beginnings are usually promising—you download a single-file executable installer and start it, only to see that it extracts its contents to the location that the file was ran from. And have you ever tried to change the location of the already installed software? If you are looking for guaranteed troubles, go ahead. Then, you decide that you need to remove it, only to find out that even after following the recommended way of uninstalling it, some files and other data—such as application data, registry entries, file associations—remain on the system.

Why is there such a lack of flexibility? Why are there a lot of self-executable installers, but not ready-to-use applications? Is it really so hard to create a portable, one-file application? Have you ever wondered how such binaries are being developed and what their internal structure is? If you have, this chapter will bring you answers to these questions, explain how to do this using the Tcl language.

A few years ago, when Tcl was nothing more than just another scripting language for me, a friend showed me an application he had made. It was a normal `.exe` file, looking completely identical to any other software, and I was astonished to learn that it was developed entirely in Tcl in less than two hours! In fact, seeing that application inspired me to learn Tcl. Years have passed, but I still admire the charm and the elegant simplicity of this technology.

Our main objective, the Holy Grail of this chapter, is a self-contained, fully-functional single-file binary application. We will learn through step-by-step tutorials how to reach that goal using the most popular solution—the **Starpacks** technology which was developed by the Netherlands based company Equi4 Software (`http://www. equi4.com`). The choice of Starpacks is obvious when you realize that not only are the components freely available as open source software, they also provide a high degree of flexibility and support for a wide range of platforms.

First, the internal structure of such files will be presented with an explanation of how one file may contain many files in it. The underlying **Metakit** database will be introduced, but the real 'magic' is related to the Virtual File System (VFS), which allows us to treat the content of the database as a normal file system that contains a number of files.

We will also answer the question of how it is possible for a Tcl-based application to run on a system where no Tcl interpreter is installed. The trick is that the interpreter will now be a part of that application itself, and in our case, the solution is called **Tclkit**.

Following that, the Starkit, **Starkit Developer eXtensions (SDX)**, and Starpack mechanisms will be explained and discussed in detail in order to finally describe how create our standalone application.

Finally, having learned about all the technologies that we have in hand, we will review all the constraints and possible workarounds.

We will also mention alternative solutions to SDX.

This chapter will conclude with a real-life scenario example utilizing all the described techniques.

Understanding the executable file structure

In the context of normal files, two basic types exist—data and executable.

1. **Data**: These files contain raw data, which can be interpreted and used by software which understands the format of the data. Although the format of such files may be platform-specific, there is a pretty good chance that it is portable and can be used under other operating systems, either directly or after some conversion. Plain Tcl scripts (that is `*.tcl` files) are considered to be data files, because they need to be interpreted by the actual Tcl binaries in order to be run. On Unix systems, such scripts are correctly run by specifying the binary name, but the script itself cannot be run on its own.

2. **Executable**: An executable file contains a set of instructions that are executed by the system when you run the file. The instructions are usually formatted in machine code (assembler), which is directly related to the type of hardware platform and operating system you are using. Yes, there are also other kinds of files that appear to be executable, such as scripts, but in fact, these are just data files containing instructions for the scripting language's interpreter (for example Tcl), not for the CPU itself. The format of binary files is complex and depends on the operating system; describing it in detail is beyond the scope of this book.

In reality, an executable file contains not only binary instructions, but also various kinds of data (metadata) such as headers. At the end of this chapter, you will learn how to create an executable binary that will contain both the Tcl interpreter (executable) and your custom data (such as scripts, Tcl extensions, images, icons, and so on). To be more specific, these data are stored in a convenient structure referred to as the **virtual file system** (**VFS**). Just like a normal file system, the VFS allows us to have files and directories, but the difference is that they are not stored directly on the hard drive, but inside the file it contains, in a fashion similar to ZIP archives.

The overall structure of the executable file we are targeting will be similar to the following image:

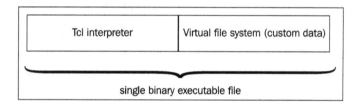

Looking at this, a basic question arises—how will the software that is intended to use this custom data be able to determine where it starts? At the end of entire file, the size of the custom data is written, so if you know the total size of the file and the size of the data part, it is easy to calculate the offset where the data starts.

The data could written in almost any format, but as you may have noticed already, Tcl-ers do not like to reinvent the wheel, and they also tend to reuse existing solutions and adapt them to their needs. In this case, the Metakit database was chosen.

Before you start creating your own standalone executable programs, we will explain the core technologies required to achieve this goal, starting with a description of Metakit as a database. Then we will talk about the Tcl's virtual file system, which allows us to use the Metakit database as a container for files.

Learning the Metakit database

Metakit is an embeddable database library which was created by the Netherlands based programmer Jean-Claude Wippler (Note that he is also one of the authors of TclKit, so it's no surprise that these two technologies are commonly used together.). In this section, we are going to explain how it works. This information is not crucial for building the standalone binaries, so you may skip it, but we do recommend that you take the time to get more familiar with it for at least one reason—whenever you use the TclKit, you will already have a Metakit within easy reach, so it is always useful to know about the possibilities it offers.

Metakit's main features are:

- Extreme portability—the entire database is stored in one file
- Platform independence—the file containing the database can be used directly on any other platform (such as Unix, Windows, Macintosh, and others) without any conversion
- High efficiency in typical operations, thanks to the specific internal format
- The ability to embed it in C++, Python, and Tcl based applications
- Support for transactions
- A small footprint—the library itself has a size of about 125 KB

The Metakit database format involves relational and hierarchical concepts. It introduces slightly different terminologywhen compared to typical relational databases.

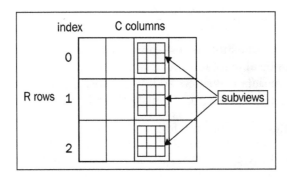

The most basic concept is a view, and it is nothing more than collection of *rows* (similar to a "table of records" in database terminology). A specific row is pointed out by an *index* (its values start from zero). Each row consists of a fixed number of cells, so basically a **view** is an RxC matrix, where 'R' is the number of rows and 'C' the number of columns (each cell belongs to some column). All cells belonging to the same column share the same data type (that is, they are homogenous):

- string
- numeric
- raw data (untyped)
- subview (nested view)

A **subview** is nothing more than a view nested inside another view. The availability of such nesting gives great flexibility to Metakit, and is also its biggest difference from traditional relational databases.

What is interesting is that data from a column is stored contiguously in the Metakit file. This is the opposite of a traditional database organization, where data is stored in a row-like perspective— where data from one specific row are adjacent to each other. The Metakit way means that the performance of adding / deleting rows is lower, but in return, loops iterating on data from a column are extremely fast.

The complete documentation of Metakit, along with downloads and support information is available at http://www.equi4.com/metakit/index.html.

Working with MetaKit from Tcl

Mk4tcl is an extension that allows operations on Metakit databases from Tcl scripts. The homepage, containing full documentation, is located at http://www.equi4.com/metakit/tcl.html. We do not intend to duplicate it, we will just review the most important Tcl commands introduced by this extension.

If you are using the prepared Tcl distribution, there is a good chance that the extension is already a part of it. Otherwise, you will have to download the extension from its homepage and install it. To start using the extension, you have to load it in your script using:

```
package require Mk4tcl
```

To operate on data files, use the mk::file command with the appropriate arguments. Mk4tcl introduces the concept of a tag—that is, an identifier for an opened data file.

To create or open an existing Metakit file, use `mk::file open`, for example:

```
mk::file open myTag myDatabase.mk
```

Here the tag is named `myTag` and the data file `myDatabase.mk`. Note that unless you use the option `-nocommit`, all pending changes will be saved to file when it is closed.

Other uses of `mk::file` include:

- `mk::file close myTag` — closes the data file identified by `myTag`
- `mk::file commit myTag` — commits all changes, this is useful when `-nocommit` is used. The other scenario when this may be useful is if you want to explicitly commit data — for example, before some time-consuming operations take place. Autocommit is done within the event loop, so it wouldn't occur in this situation, and if the user aborts the program, the data can be lost.
- `mk::file rollback myTag` — drops all pending changes
- `mk::file views myTag` — returns a list of views defined in the data file

To specify a view or a row with in a view, you can use a **path**. The way to construct a path can be easily described using the following examples:

- `myTag.myView` — specifies the top-level view called `myView` in database referred to by using `myTag`
- `myTag.myView!R` — specifies a row; R is a row number, starting from zero
- `myTag.myView!R.subview` — denotes an entire `subview` in the row R of `myView`
- `myTag.myView!R.subview!S` — denotes row S in a `subview` in row R of `myView`

To operate on a view, use the `mk::view` command. In the following commands, `myTag.myView` is an example of the path denoting the view, and it will sometimes be referred to by using `path` to make the syntax more readable:

- `mk::view size myTag.myView` returns the number of rows in the view named `myView` in the data file identified with `myTag`
- `mk::view layout myTag.myView` returns the current data structure of the view named `myView` in the data file identified with `myTag`

- The same `layout` command may be used to define a data structure:

  `mk::view layout myTag.people {name birthYear:I}`

  This command defines a `people` view with two columns—name and birth year. Note that the second one is of type integer (with suffix `:I`). The other suffixes are:

  - `:S`—string (default type)
  - `:L`—64-bit integer (long) value
  - `:F`—single-precision floating point value (32 bits)
  - `:D`—double-precision floating point value (64 bits)
  - `:B`—binary (un-typed) value

  If the suffix is not specified, it defaults to a string.

  To define a `people` view with the subview `addresses` (containing the columns `city`, `street`, and `number`), use the following command:

  mk::view layout myTag.people {name birthYear:I {addresses {city street number:I}}}

  What is more interesting is that this command may also be used to dynamically change the structure of the existing view — to add new or remove existing columns without losing other data.

  The command `mk::view delete myTag.myView` deletes the view.

Once you have opened the data file and defined the view, it is time to operate on the data. You can start operating on rows with the `mk::row` command:

- `mk::row append myTag.myView` appends new rows, for example:

  mk::row append myTag.people name "John Smith" birthYear 1945

  Note that you can also refer to a new, as yet undefined column, thereby effectively creating it. By default, the type of that column's data is `string`, unless an appropriate suffix is used.

- `mk::row delete path` deletes the row pointed to by the path.

- `mk::row create` creates a temporary row stored in memory and returns a unique path:

  set tempPath [mk::row create name "Will Bush" birthYear 1980]

- `mk::row insert path 1 tempPath` inserts a temporary row into the view in a position specified by `path`. `1` is the number of copies (the row may be inserted in multiple copies)

- `mk::row replace path tempPath` replaces the row with a new one
- `mk::row delete path` deletes the row

To get values from the row, use the `mk::get path` command. It returns a list of column names and values.

To set values in an already existing row, you can use the `mk::set path` command like this:

`mk::set path name "George S." birthYear 1978`

The path must denote the row number (in the `myTag.myView!R` format). If that row does not exist, it will be created. If you use a value higher than the index of the last row, the gap will be filled in with rows of empty values.

Knowing all this, lets consider the following example code:

```
package require Mk4tcl

proc printRows {path rows} {
    foreach i $rows {
        puts [mk::get $path!$i]
    }
}

mk::file open myTag myDatabase.mk

mk::view layout myTag.people {name birthYear:I}

mk::row append myTag.people name "George S." birthYear 1978
mk::row append myTag.people name "John Gray" birthYear 1973 sex male
mk::row append myTag.people name "Jeniffer Snake" birthYear 1982 sex
female
mk::row append myTag.people name "Judith Brow" birthYear 1987 sex
female
mk::set myTag.people!9 name "Johnny B." birthYear 1977 sex male
```

This set of instructions will create a database stored in the `myDatabase.mk` file and put inside it a total of 10 rows.

For easy selection of rows, use the `mk::select path ?options?` command. The command returns a list of row numbers that matched the selection criteria, which was specified in the `options` arguments. By default, the command will select all rows:

`set rows [mk::select myTag.people]`

`printRows myTag.people $rows`

The previous command will result in the following output:

name {George S.} birthYear 1978 sex {}

name {John Gray} birthYear 1973 sex male

name {Jeniffer Snake} birthYear 1982 sex female

name {Judith Brow} birthYear 1987 sex female

name {} birthYear 0 sex {}

name {} birthYear 0 sex {}

name {} birthYear 0 sex {}

name {} birthYear 0 sex {}

name {} birthYear 0 sex {}

name {Johnny B.} birthYear 1977 sex male

There is no point in doubling the documentation and describing all options of `mk::select`. Instead, we will show an example of the usage of some of them:

- Use –min and –max to specify a range of allowed values:

  ```
  set rows [mk::select myTag.people -min birthYear 1975 -max
  birthYear 1985]
  printRows myTag.people $rows
  ```

  This will result in selecting all the people born within 1975 and 1985:

  name {George S.} birthYear 1978 sex {}

  name {Jeniffer Snake} birthYear 1982 sex female

  name {Johnny B.} birthYear 1977 sex male

- Use –exact for an exact match:

  ```
  set rows [mk::select myTag.people -exact sex female]
  printRows myTag.people $rows
  ```

  The preceding command will find all women:

  name {Jeniffer Snake} birthYear 1982 sex female

  name {Judith Brow} birthYear 1987 sex female

- You can also use wildcard matching with `-glob`:

```
set rows [mk::select myTag.people -glob name J*]
printRows myTag.people $rows
```

The result of this command will be:

name {John Gray} birthYear 1973 sex male

name {Jeniffer Snake} birthYear 1982 sex female

name {Judith Brow} birthYear 1987 sex female

name {Johnny B.} birthYear 1977 sex male

- Also, in order to use regular expressions, we use the following command:

```
set rows [mk::select myTag.people -regexp name John.*]
printRows myTag.people $rows
```

The matching rows are:

name {John Gray} birthYear 1973 sex male

name {Johnny B.} birthYear 1977 sex male

Learning more about virtual file systems

Tcl, like almost every programming language, allows you to operate on files and directories existing in the underlying file system. In the 'good old days', the Tcl interpreter was able to operate only on native filesystems specific to the operating system it was compiled for. From version 8.4, Tcl incorporates the concept of virtual file systems (VFSs). The idea is to separate normal Tcl commands from the real file system calls. Such separation makes it easy to add support for additional filesystems, because all that is required is to create appropriate drivers. VFS allows us to redirect all FS related calls to the driver responsible for the proper handling of these calls.

Luckily for us, there is already a Tcl extension called `tclvfs` (`http://sourceforge.net/projects/tclvfs/`) that offers a number of drivers for various virtual file systems. The word 'virtual' means that the code operates in a unified manner on files / directories located inside something that seems to be a normal, native filesystem, but in reality, the filesystem could be anything - for example an FTP share or the contents of a `.zip` file. The real power of this solution is that you do not have to use any special commands to handle it once it is mounted.

Supported by `tclvfs`, VFSs are categorized as separate packages located in the `vfs` namespace. Before starting operations on any VFS, you have to mount it first. Two types of mount are available: a VFS can be mounted as a directory at the specified path, or more generally, the entire protocol is mounted. This second case is referred to as `urltype`, and it allows file paths starting with `ftp://`, `http://`, or `file://`. See the examples below in the FTP section.

The most important types of supported VFS are:

- **FTP**: Allows you to operate on files on FTP server as though these files were stored in a local directory. To start using it, use the `package require vfs::ftp` or `package require vfs::urltype` commands. Consider the following example:

  ```
  package require vfs::ftp

  vfs::ftp::Mount ftp ftp://ftp.kernel.org/pub/linux/kernel/v2.6 v2.6

  file copy v2.6/linux-2.6.31.4.tar.bz2 .
  ```

  In this case, we mount the FTP directory containing kernel sources as a virtual `v2.6` local directory (so this is the first type of mount), and then copy a file from it using the standard `file copy` command to the current directory.

  The second type of mount would be like this:

  ```
  package require vfs::urltype

  vfs::urltype::Mount ftp

  file copy ftp://ftp.kernel.org/pub/linux/kernel/v2.6/linux-2.6.31.4.tar.bz2 .
  ```

  Here you can assume that after the second line, a new kind of drive was created — `ftp://`, and any access to that drive causes the underlying `tclvfs` library to connect to the FTP server and make it available for usage. Effectively, it will also result in a call to `package require vfs::ftp`, so there is no significant difference between the two types of mounts.

- **HTTP** — this is similar to FTP and basically it is enough to replace `ftp` with `http` in previous examples.

- **ZIP** — allows access to files stored inside the compressed ZIP archive (note the `urltype` access does not apply here). Consider archive `test.zip`; to list its contents, the following could be used:

  ```
  package require vfs::zip

  set test_mnt [vfs::zip::Mount test.zip test.zip]

  puts [glob test.zip/*]

  vfs::zip::Unmount $test_mnt test.zip
  ```

The example code mounts the archive as virtual `test.zip` directory, lists its contents using the `glob` command, and unmounts the archive in the end. The output from that code is:

test.zip/README.txt

As you can see, the archive contains the `README.txt` file.

Note that the main drawback of support for ZIP files is that they offer only read-only access, so while reading their contents is easy, modifying it using only `vfs` is impossible.

- **MK4** — it is possible to use a Metakit database as a container for files and directories, thanks to the `mk4vfs` driver. In this way, such a database can be considered as an archive similar to a zip file. The driver offers full support for reading and writing files, so the Metakit database is a perfect candidate for keeping the files on our yet-to-be-created one file application.

  The following example shows the creation of empty archives, copying a file into it, and verifying if it's there:

```
package require vfs::mk4

vfs::mk4::Mount C:\\myKit.mk myKit

file copy C:\\README.txt myKit

puts [glob myKit/*]

vfs::unmount myKit
```

  The output from that code is:

  `myKit/README.txt`

  The first command, `package require vfs::mk4`, loads the appropriate VFS driver (`mk4vfs`). Next, we mount the Metakit database file located at `C:\myKit.mk` (note that the backslash character needs to be escaped with another backslash) to be available at the `myKit` mountpoint. If the file does not exist, it will be created. The `README.txt` file, containing the text "hello World!", is copied into the myKit mountpoint (and effectively into `.mk` file), and then we list its contents to check if the file is really there. The last line unmounts the database, causing all pending operations to commit. The `.mk` file created in this example will be the subject of investigation in the next section.

At the moment, Metakit has become a standard when it comes to storing and accessing files in an efficient and elegant way, but we are living in a fast-changing world and there is a possibility that soon some other, better solution will become popular and supplant the current one.

Getting into the details of VFS and Metakit

The good news is that it is not required for you to know or remember the internal structure of a Metakit database used with mk4vfs, because from the script level, you operate on its contents in a normal way, as you would on other file structures. If you feel that you do not need to know more about it, you can go directly to the next section.

Why was Metakit chosen as the practical implementation of the VFS container? It is the nested subviews feature that makes it a perfect candidate to reflect directories and files, as you will see in the next example.

So what really happens when you write a file into a directory that is mapped to a Metakit database? An appropriate VFS driver, in this case mk4vfs, captures the request to save files and stores them transparently in the database. Based on the knowledge that you already gained from this chapter, you can easily have a look into this database to get some idea of how the files are stored. The following simple code is one of the possibilities:

```
package require Mk4tcl
mk::file open myKit C:\\myKit.mk
puts -nonewline "layout of myKit: "
puts [mk::view layout myKit]
puts -nonewline "size of myKit.dirs: "
puts [mk::view size myKit.dirs]
puts "contents of first dirs entry:"
puts [mk::get myKit.dirs!0]
puts "contents of first files entry:"
puts [mk::get myKit.dirs!0.files!0]
mk::file close myKit
```

The code produces the following output:

```
layout of myKit: {dirs {name parent:I {files {name size:I date:I
contents:B}}}}

size of myKit.dirs: 1

contents of first dirs entry:

name <root> parent -1

contents of first files entry:

name README.txt size 12 date 1256126970 contents {hello World!}
```

What the code does may be described as a reverse-engineering of `mk4vfs` operations. Instead of going through the specification, we inspect the database directly to understand its layout. First we load the package `Mk4tcl` and open the `myKit.mk` database. Next we would like to learn what the layout of the database is, so `mk::view layout myKit` comes handy. Let's analyze its output carefully:

```
{dirs {name parent:I {files {name size:I date:I contents:B}}}}
```

We see that `myKit.mk` contains one view called `dirs`. This view (table) consists of the columns with `name` (by default, it is simply a string), `parent` (integer value), and the nested subview named `files`. The names are self explanatory. The `dirs` view represents the entire directory structure inside this virtual folder. `name` is the directory name and `parent` points to a directory at a higher level (the number in the `dirs` row represents that directory).

Each directory has a subview called `files` where all the files belonging to this directory are stored. Each row in this subview consists of:

- `name` — keeps the file name (string)
- `size` — size of the file (integer)
- `date` — creation date (stored as an integer)
- `contents` — contents of the file (binary raw data)

Next, the entire number of rows is printed out using `mk::view size myKit.dirs` command — in this case, there is only one entry corresponding to the top-level root directory. `mk::get myKit.dirs!0` is used for getting the first directory entry:

```
name <root> parent -1
```

`mk::get myKit.dirs!0.files!0` returns the entry for the only file in this directory:

```
name README.txt size 12 date 1256126970 contents {hello World!}
```

The filename is `README.txt`, its size is 12 bytes, and its content is the text 'hello World!'.

Learning Tclkit

Tclkit is another piece of technology without which our puzzle can't be completed. Basically, it is a single executable file that contains inside it a normal Tcl interpreter along with a set of extensions, such as:

- `Tk` — for graphic interfaces
- `IncrTcl` — for object-oriented programming — currently, it is an optional part of TclKit

- TclVFS — the virtual file system, explained earlier; Tclkit contains drivers only for ZIP and MetaKit

- Metakit — this was also explained earlier

The beauty and power of Tclkit comes from fact that it does not require installation, and that it is supported on a wide set of platforms, including:

- AIX

- FreeBSD

- various distribution of Linux on architectures including x86, PowerPC, S/390 and others

- HPUX

- IRIX

- MacOS Classic and MacOS X

- Solaris

- Windows

Tclkit may be obtained from the http://www.equi4.com/tclkit/index.html website.

At the time of writing this book, the latest version contains Tcl version 8.5.2. In the rest of this section, we will consider examples on the Windows platform. In this case, the Tclkit filename is strictly tclkit-win32.upx.exe (it is compressed internally with the UPX packer). Due to some differences between Windows and other platforms, an additional version with console support (but without Tk) is available as tclkitsh-win32.upx.exe. Running these examples on Unix platforms should require very little or no change, except for specifying different binary names.

Let's revisit the example from the *Chapter 1, Introducing Tcl*, which prints the "Hello World" message. Running it with Tclkit is as simple as running it with a normal tclsh interpreter:

```
C:\WINDOWS\system32\cmd.exe                                    _ □ ×
Microsoft Windows XP [Version 5.1.2600]
(C) Copyright 1985-2001 Microsoft Corp.

C:\workspace\TclHelloWorld>tclkitsh-win32.upx.exe main.tcl
Hello World one more time!

C:\workspace\TclHelloWorld>_
```

Starkit and SDX

As you could see in the previous example, Tclkit can be used as a replacement for `tclsh`, because it is able to run `.tcl` scripts. This feature, although useful, is nothing new. What is really innovative is that Tclkit is also capable of executing Starkits.

What is **Starkit**? It is a technology that allows you to pack (or wrap) the entire directory structure containing your scripts and other files crucial for your application into a single file with a virtual system inside of it. Having read the previous sections of this chapter, it won't be a surprise for you that Metakit, along with the appropriate VFS driver, is used to achieve this goal.

The structure and naming convention of directories and files to pack is precisely defined, so Tclkit will be able to locate appropriate scripts inside it and start your application.

The word 'Starkit' also refers to any file created with this technology. Such a file contains your application, is very portable, installation-free, and has no external dependencies. As a convention, these files are named using the `.kit` extension.

Creating a Starkit file

To create a Starkit file (we will also refer to it simply as 'starkit'), you may use the utility called SDX available at `http://www.equi4.com/starkit/sdx.html`. What is interesting is that SDX is nothing more than another application delivered in the form of Starkit, and the file is simply called `sdx.kit`.

SDX accepts a number of command-line options, where the most important ones are:

- `qwrap` — a convenient way for the quick creation of the `.kit` file, when your application comes in the form of a single-file Tcl script
- `lsk` — lists the content of a `.kit` file
- `unwrap` — unpacks a `.kit` file, so you can easily inspect its contents with the file manager of your choice
- `wrap` — allows the creation of `.kit` files based on a strictly defined directory structure that reflects VFS contents

Let's focus on the quick creation of the starkit first. Surely, you still remember our "Hello World" example, constituted from one single file named `main.tcl`. It is a perfect candidate to be wrapped into a `.kit` file. For better readability, we will rename `main.tcl` as `hello.tcl`, in order to more clearly reflect what the script does. To wrap up our example, put Tclkit and SDX in the same directory, and use the following command:

```
c:\workspace\TclHelloWorld>tclkitsh-win32.upx.exe sdx.kit qwrap hello.tcl
```

```
5 updates applied
```

Once finished, you will notice that a new file called `hello.kit` is created. Now you can verify if it is working according to your expectations:

```
c:\workspace\TclHelloWorld>tclkitsh-win32.upx.exe hello.kit
```

```
Hello World one more time!
```

At first glance, there is no logical reason to wrap this script, because you simply replace one file with another—but you will see what the differences are in a later section.

To unpack the file you have just created, use the `unwrap` command:

```
c:\workspace\TclHelloWorld>tclkitsh-win32.upx.exe sdx.kit unwrap hello.
kit
```

```
5 updates applied
```

As a result of this command, the `hello.vfs` directory is created. This directory reflects the contents of the virtual file system stored inside `hello.kit`. What you will obviously notice first is that this directory contains more files than just `hello.tcl`. As mentioned before, the structure of starkit's VFS is strictly defined, so SDX's `qwrap` command works like a wizard and adds all the necessary files and directories. The structure will be explained in more detail later.

Although the `qwrap` command is handy, it does not cover more complex variants. Imagine the opposite situation: instead of retrieving the full VFS structure from the `.kit` file, you would actually wrap your already prepared directory tree along with sources of your valuable application. This is where the `wrap` command becomes handy:

```
c:\workspace\TclHelloWorld>tclkitsh-win32.upx.exe sdx.kit wrap hello2.kit
hello.vfs
```

```
5 updates applied
```

The `wrap` command runs with two parameters—the name of the file to create and the name of the directory to wrap. Therefore, in this case, we simply wrapped the `hello.vfs` directory into the `hello2.kit` starkit file. Note that we describe the latest available version of SDX at the time of writing; the earlier releases had a slightly different syntax for this command.

The second parameter can be skipped. In this case, if first parameter is in the form of `<app-name>.kit`. The wrapper will search for the `<app-name>.vfs` directory to wrap, so the command line will be:

```
c:\workspace\TclHelloWorld>tclkitsh-win32.upx.exe sdx.kit wrap hello.kit

5 updates applied
```

It is important to notice that, by default, the starkits produced by SDX are read-only. If you would like your application to have the ability to modify or write files inside a wrapped VFS, you will have to specify the `-writable` flag:

```
c:\workspace\TclHelloWorld>tclkitsh-win32.upx.exe sdx.kit wrap hello.kit
-writable

5 updates applied
```

Internal structure of starkits

If you are thinking seriously about using Starkit technology, the structure of VFS inside it can not be any mystery to you. Let's first inspect the **hello.vfs** directory from the previous example, and then discuss how to improve it with additional files crucial for your application.

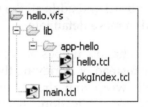

The top-level directory contains:

- The **main.tcl** file — this script is interpreted once the VFS has been mounted at start time.

- The **lib** directory — this holds additional packages required for your application. Every package is kept in a separate subdirectory. The most important thing is that, by default, your application is also automatically converted to a package. The naming convention for such a package is `app-your_application_name`, so in this case, the name is `app-hello`.

Let's focus on `main.tcl` first. In our case, this file was generated automatically by SDX's `qwrap` command, and its contents are:

```
package require starkit
starkit::startup
package require app-hello
```

The first line is obvious and causes the `starkit` package to be loaded. This package is an integral part of Tclkit, responsible for proper handling of the entire Starkit technology. Once this package is loaded, the `starkit::startup` command is available to be called. The command performs two important actions:

- It modifies the `auto_path` variable, so it includes the `lib` subdirectory, effectively causing all packages stored there to be available for your application.

- It sets `starkit::topdir` variable. The value of this variable is a (virtual) path that points to the directory where `main.tcl` is located.

After the `starkit::startup` command is run, we can assume that the packages from the `lib` subdirectory can easily be loaded—regardless of whether we run `main.tcl` from `hello.vfs`, a starkit, or a Starpack (which is described later). This feature provides great flexibility for code development—you don't have to generate a starkit after each change, because you will still be able to run the script in the normal way.

The `starkit::startup` command also returns a value that may be used to distinguish how the script was invoked. It returns the following values:

- `unwrapped`—the script was executed in a normal way, using the command `tclkit hello.vfs/main.tcl`

- `starkit`—the script is executed as a part of starkit, using the command `tclkit hello.kit`

- `starpack`—the script is executed as a part of Starpack (discussed in the next section), for example, `hello.exe`

- `sourced`—the script was sourced from the another script using the command `source hello.vfs/main.tcl`

This value can be used for altering the operations of the script depending on the way it was executed.

At this point, `package require app-hello` can be called successfully, causing your wrapped application code to be executed. What really happens is that the `pkgIndex.tcl` file is sourced. Its content is:

```
package ifneeded app-hello 1.0 [list source [file join $dir hello.
tcl]]
```

Therefore, effectively, it sources the `hello.tcl` file. If you look inside it, you will find that this is basically the original file you wrapped in, with a slight modification to the first line:

```
package provide app-hello 1.0
puts "Hello World one more time!"
```

The line with the package information was automatically added by qwrap.

It is important to mention at this point, that this structure is not obligatory. The mandatory items are only the main.tcl file and, in case you want to use some packages that are not built into Tclkit, the lib directory. You can put your entire application code into main.tcl, or some other files inside the VFS structure of your choice. You could even sacrifice the starkit::topdir variable (while handling the lib directory) and not use the starkit package at all. However, we do not recommend such a daring move—coding standards were not invented only to be, but also to facilitate understanding and development for other people. Just imagine what would happen if you wanted to maintain some weird code written by a bold programmer who believes standards are not his concern!

Using resource files in starkits

Often, your application will consist not only of script files, but also other items as well—for example, graphical images or sound files. There is no problem in putting additional files and directories inside the contents of the VFS, and the wrap command will put them all inside the starkit file. Assuming you placed a file, say image.jpg in a VFS subdirectory called images (images/image.jpg), you can refer to it in your scripts as follows:

```
$starkit::topdir/images/image.jpg
```

Putting additional packages into a starkit

As mentioned earlier, the starkit::startup command extends the $auto_path variable so it includes the lib directory. Therefore, adding additional packages is nothing more than putting them into this directory. Then the extension is available and you can use it in your code in the standard Tcl way:

```
package require <name_of_extension>
```

Format of the starkit file

If you display hello.kit (or any other .kit file) with any text viewer/editor, you will notice that it starts like a normal script file:

```
#!/bin/sh
# \
exec tclkit "$0" ${1+"$@"}
package require starkit
starkit::header mk4 -readonly
```

After this header comes the binary data (that forms the content of the Metakit database lying below the VFS). Such a header allows you to run .kit files directly on any Unix-like system by simply adding executable permissions and putting tclkit in your system path. On a Windows system, you will have to associate the .kit extension with a Tclkit program in order to achieve this functionality.

When the header is interpreted by Tcl, the starkit package is loaded. This package is included in all Tclkit versions. The last line causes the starkit package to mount the VFS and start processing the files stored inside it.

Interactions between different starkit files

Your application does not have to be limited to only one starkit file. It is possible to use the Tcl command source with .kit files, for example:

```
source hello.kit
```

It may seem a little magical at first, but as we already mentioned, a .kit file starts with normal Tcl script commands, and after interpreting the data, it effectively executes main.tcl inside that starkit. If that script includes a call to the starkit::startup command, it will expand the auto_path variable including libraries (extensions) from the new .kit file, and also replace the starkit::topdir variable's value (so it is important to store its value before sourcing):

```
set topdir $starkit::topdir
source hello.kit
set starkit::topdir $topdir
```

The main disadvantage is that the entire main.tcl file will be executed, and if you just want to make packages from another .kit file available, this is undesired behavior. In such a situation, instead of sourcing the .kit file, it is better to:

```
vfs::mk4::Mount /path/to/file.kit /path/to/file.kit -readonly
append ::auto_path /path/to/file.kit /path/to/file.kit/lib
```

The first line mounts the hypothetical file.kit file (located at /path/to) at the mountpoint named /path/to/file.kit (that's right, a good standard in case of VFS is to mount it under the same name as the original file containing it). On the other hand, the second line extends the auto_path variable.

Starkit files are perfect candidates for delivering ready-to-use pieces of code like extensions/packages. This idea is implemented in terms of sdarchive (found at the website http://tcl.tk/starkits), which is nothing more than a collection of ready-to-download and ready-to-use starkits. If your application uses a lot of packages, it is up to you to decide whether to put all of them into one main .kit file or use some starkits from sdarchive.

Knowing the Starpack technology

As mentioned in the previous section, the starkit file has a small header containing the initialization script that executes the externally available `tclkit`. What would happen if we replaced this header with a binary code of Tclkit? In such cases, we would get a **Starpack**, a self-contained starkit, and a Tcl interpreter — all in one single file. This is the solution we are searching for in this chapter — a standalone executable file without any dependencies that does not require installation or configuration!

A Starpack file can be created in the standard way using the `wrap` command, but with the additional flag `-runtime`, which specifies what Tclkit binary should be put together with the starkit that is being produced. A typical usage is:

```
c:\workspace\TclHelloWorld>tclkitsh-win32.upx.exe sdx.kit wrap hello.exe
-runtime tclkitsh-win32.upx.copy.exe
```

```
5 updates applied
```

Note that the Tclkit specified with `-runtime` must be different from the one actually executing this command, because a running Tclkit instance cannot copy itself. In this case we simply copied it, but here comes the beauty of this solution — you can use any Tclkit you want to, even for other platforms like Linux or Solaris. Therefore, you will be able to produce versions for different systems without even having access to them!

By default, when the output filename is of the form `<app-name>.exe`, or simply `<app-name>` in case of non-Windows platforms, SDX will search for the `<app-name>.vfs` directory holding the contents of your application.

After executing the `hello.exe` program, you will notice that it works in the same way as the `.kit` version:

```
c:\workspace\TclHelloWorld>hello.exe
```

```
Hello World one more time!
```

The benefits of using Starpacks are:

- The cleanest and the most elegant way of distribution and deployment — you deliver your entire application in the form of one file.
- The installation is as simple as downloading / copying the file
- Uninstalling the software is as simple as deleting the file
- No dependency problems — all the required libraries are stored inside Starpack's VFS

- Complete transparency and maturity—end users may not even be aware that the application is written in Tcl

- The time required to wrap your application is extremely less once you know the rules

The limitations of using Starpacks are:

- Starpack's size is larger than Starkit's, because the entire Tclkit interpreter is embedded inside it.

- A Starpack file will work only on the platform that the instance of Tclkit used to create that starpack was compiled for.

- Starpacks are incapable of modifying themselves, and the VFS structure is read only. If you really need to store some information, such as configuration information for your application, you will have to save it in some external file. We will address this issue in the next section called *Advanced topics – self updating*.

- Due to the VFS limitation, some Tcl commands, such as exec to run programs inside VFS will not work correctly.

- The practical Metakit database size limit is around 1 GB.

Practical example—the Hibernator application

Some time ago, I discovered that I needed a convenient way to hibernate my Windows-controlled PC after a specified amount of time. Of course, there were plenty of ways to achieve this, but what I really needed was an easy-to-use timer-like application, and that is why *Hibernator* was created.

Describing in detail how this application works is beyond the scope of this book, as we do not focus on GUI creation, but Hibernator is a perfect example of a portable standalone Tcl application that is successfully run almost every day. If you are interested in how the graphical interface is created, feel free to inspect the source of this application.

All the required files are stored in the **Hibernator** directory, displayed in the following structure:

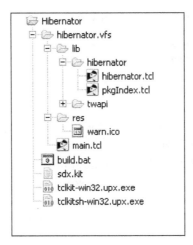

The `hibernator.vfs` directory holds the entire virtual file system of the application, and contains mandatory items such as the `lib` directory and the `main.tcl` initial script file.

The `lib` directory contains two packages. One of them, named `hibernator`, is my application. The other one is the Tcl Windows API extension called `twapi` (you can find more information on this at http://twapi.magicsplat.com/). This extension is needed to call appropriate actions—such as hibernate, suspend, or power off—directly on the Windows operating system. As mentioned earlier, all packages in `lib` are visible to the Tcl interpreter (thanks to the modification made to the `$auto_path` variable). Therefore, to use the functions offered by `twapi`, it is enough to do the following in any other file (for example, `hibernator.tcl`):

```
package require twapi
twapi::suspend_system -state hibernate
```

This command call causes the OS to hibernate.

The `res` directory holds additional files—in this case, it is a small icon `warn.ico`. This file may be referred to from anywhere in the application with the following path:

```
$starkit::topdir/res/warn.ico
```

The `build.bat` file contains nothing more than the appropriate invocation of the SDX extension, to build Hibernator standalone application:

```
tclkitsh-win32.upx.exe sdx.kit wrap hibernator.exe -runtime tclkit-win32.upx.exe
```

As the **Hibernator**! is a utility with a graphical interface and it requires `Tk`, `tclkit-win32.upx.exe` is used at runtime. After successful wrapping, the program is ready for use. Once you run it, you will be presented with the following window:

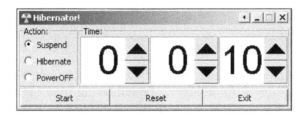

The GUI is simple, because the entire application is designed to be simple: on the left, you can choose the desired action (such as **Suspend**, **Hibernate**, or **PowerOFF**). On the right, you set the time left for completing this action, and at the bottom, you can control the countdown: start/pause it, reset the counter, or exit the application.

The entire `hibernator.exe` file has less than 2 MB of space. The main part of this size is the `Tclkit` (about 1.2 MB) and `twapi`—so, the entire package has 1.9 MB, but this contains documentation and tests that can easily be compressed (note that these can be removed, because they are not a crucial part of the extension). Nowadays, when typical storage is counted in terms of hundreds of gigabytes and the network link in Mbit/s, 2 MB may be considered as a small size.

Advanced topics—self updating

Imagine that you have just created your ideal, perfect application, wrapped into an easy-to-use self-executing file and made it available for public. People start using it, the count of downloads is getting higher every day, and suddenly you discover a terrible bug causing your software to be barely usable! Your product goes from 'wonderful' to 'pitiful' within moments.

And what if you manage a network with thousands of computers, each of them running your (defective) utility? Will you spend your entire weekend running from one computer to another and replacing the software manually?

Such scenarios have long been the worst nightmare of almost every software developer. The solution? Of course, the possibility of bugs can't be eliminated, but you can take care to minimize the impact of bugs on your users, and to be able to react as fast as possible by facilitating the process of replacing the bad software with a working version with the help of a blessed feature called autoupdate.

Of course, software defects are not the only reason to create a newer version of your application. You may new features to it, or make modifications, optimizations, and improvements. As part of easing deployment and management, you may want your application to automatically update itself. As the book deals with *network* programming, we assume that the update will be available to download over the network, and that every computer running the software is connected to that network.

Depending on how the application will work, there are different scenarios that we will consider. One option is that it will be a daemon running in the background – in this case, it is best to simply schedule periodic checking for updates, possibly with some smart algorithm to prevent all instances being updated at once, and therefore, generating network overload. The second option is an application that is started, used and eventually closed – in this scenario, the most obvious solution is to check for updates at start time.

Knowing the importance of automatic update, let's take a closer look at how to adopt this in terms of Starpack files. For the sake of simplicity, in the rest of this section, we assume that 'the update' that will be downloaded is a newer, full version of the application – in other words, we will not consider incremental updates.

Why do we focus on Starpacks and not Starkits? Starkits have the ability to modify their contents in terms of normal write operations to VFS, and that makes updating them as easy as downloading new VFS contents and replacing the old ones.

Starpacks, however, do not provide for such a possibility. On many operating systems (including all Microsoft Windows versions and many Unix variants), it is not possible to write to a file that is currently being run – that is, to replace our own binary file. Therefore, a typical approach is to use an additional binary for performing the upgrade.

Assuming our executable is in `<dirname>` and is called `<filename>`, after detecting and downloading an update, the steps to update our binary will be similar to the following:

1. First of all, part of the autoupdate code will write a new version of the binary as `<dirname>/autoupdate-<filename>`. Next, it will run `<dirname>/autoupdate-<filename>`, optionally passing to it all arguments that were passed to the original binary, and exit the main binary.

2. Now the `autoupdate` binary (which writes to our main application's executable file, because it is a separate file that is not being executed at the moment) will copy `<dirname>/autoupdate-<filename>` as `<dirname>/<filename>`. This can be implemented so that the initialization of the application checks the filename, and if it matches a specific pattern, performs the autoupdate actions. For example, we can check this by using:

```
set dirname [file dirname [info nameofexecutable]]

if {[regexp "^autoupdate-(.*)" \
    [file tail [info nameofexecutable]] - binaryname]} {
```

3. First, the name of the directory where the binary is located is stored in the `$dirname` variable, as it will be useful later. The check is performed by getting the name of the binary file (additionally, it is saved in the `$binaryname` variable) and checking if the filename begins with `autoupdate-`. If the filename matches with it, we'll perform autoupdate actions as follows:

```
after 5000
set targetname [file join $dirname $binaryname]
```

The code waits for 5 seconds for the parent process to exit — this is a relatively safe assumption, but some developers recommend using a wait of of 30 seconds.

4. Next, the main binary will be overwritten, make sure it can be run on Unix systems and eventually executed. Before that, we need to try and unmount our autoupdate the binary's VFS; this is required in order to copy our binary, otherwise Tcl would try to copy mounted VFS contents instead of the file itself, because the mountpoint name and filename are the same.

```
catch {vfs::mk4::Unmount exe [info nameofexecutable]}
file copy -force [info nameofexecutable] $targetname
catch {file attributes $targetname -permissions 0755}
exec $targetname {*}$argv &
exit 0
```

This will cause the autoupdate binary to exit and main binary to be run again, but this time it will be a newer, updated version of the binary that is run. `exe` is the name of a handle for the mounted VFS used internally by Tclkit.

5. As a cleanup step you should delete the autoupdate binary from the main binary if it exists at startup time. You can simply add the following code to check if the initial condition of a file with a name matching the autoupdate- prefix is met:

```
}  else  {
    set autoupdatename [file join $dirname \
        autoupdate-[file tail [info nameofexecutable]]
    if {[file exists $autoupdatename]} {
        after 5000
        catch {file delete -force $autoupdatename}
    }
}
```

There is a delay of 5 seconds before trying to delete the autoupdate binary. This is needed because of the delay between the beginning of the new process and the termination of the old one.

Other solutions

The Starpack/Starkit technology has gained huge popularity over the years, and is the "number one" solution when it comes to creating a single standalone executable file, and you will most likely be pleased with it, but it is worth mentioning, at least, some of the available alternatives.

One of them is a freeWrap program, available at `http://freewrap.sourceforge.net/`. Binary compilations are available for both Windows and Linux systems, but you can also attempt to compile the source code (also available on the website) on other platforms. Basically, the functionality of freeWrap is similar to Starpack technology: it can create executable files with Tcl/Tk and your wrapped application, and it has similar constraints such as the lack of the ability to modify its contents. Also, its licence allows you to use it free of charge. Personally, I found it hard to use and feel that there is no reason to leave Starpack in favor of freeWrap.

An other solution is TclApp, which comes as a part of ActiveState's TclDevKit package. You may consider it as a more advanced, commercial version of SDX. It also operates on starkit/starpack files. The GUI version of TclApp is also available, which make the entire process a bit easier for novice users. In general, it facilitates various tasks related to the creation of the output file. For example, the management of packages to include and even the selection of a program icon.

Summary

This chapter presented how to create a completely standalone single-file executable application entirely in Tcl, using Starpack technology. There are three core items that made this solution possible:

1. The Metakit database with its unique ability to nest subviews inside a view

2. The VFS feature that allows you to use the Metakit database as a normal file system

3. Tclkit—a complete Tcl interpreter compiled into one file

The beauty and power offered by this solution can't be underestimated. You can deliver virtually any application in terms of a single file that does not require installation/un-installation, doesn't mess up the user's operating system, and is extremely easy to deploy and use as it does not have any external dependencies. It is hardly possible to imagine or propose a better, easier-to-use solution.

What is also important, from a developer's point of view, is that the Starkit/Starpack technology does not have a significant impact on the way you create your code due to the low number of constraints it requires.

Throughout this chapter, you have been made familiar with Metakit database and VFS concepts. You also learned how to create Starkits/Starpacks, the benefits and constraints of this technology, and how to bypass them, if possible.

The next chapter will introduce you to concepts that are usually ignored at the beginning, only to be found as invaluable at the end—logging and debugging of an application. Experienced programmers already know these can save your life; and novices will soon learn the value of these concepts.

4
Troubleshooting Tcl applications

It is not uncommon for a developer to eagerly start to write a code, then to realize the brilliant idea that just came to your mind. You quickly implement the basics of the program and add functionalities one by one, each time running the code to check if it works as you wish. So far so good, but eventually you come to the point when adding additional functionality breaks existing functions for no obvious reason. Suddenly, your fast development stops because instead of coding you are reviewing sources and adding printouts, wherever possible, to get an idea what could have gone wrong.

Does that sound familiar? Well, you are not the only one who faces such problems. Luckily there are some well-known techniques to speed up investigation of the problem, and make it as less painful as possible. These techniques are **logging** and **debugging**.

The concept of logging is similar to adding printouts to your code, but in a more ordered and unified way. At runtime, the logging subsystem produces information, commonly referred to as logs or traces, which are basically a record of program flow. Such a record can be saved to a file, written directly to the console, emailed to a specified address, or used in some other way. It is up to you how many logging entries you put in your code. It may seem to be a waste of time in the beginning, but at the end you will either add them anyway, or abandon your project as it becomes too complex to maintain and develop further. In this chapter, we will describe logging with the usage of the `log` and `logger` packages, both coming from the `tcllib` collection. We will also mention an alternative `audit` package that serves the same purpose, but from a different perspective.

While logging allows you to analyze program flow after it finishes, debugging is a different concept. It allows you to take a look inside the working program, stop its execution at a specified point, and check the values of internal variables. The good news is that you do not have to put anything special in your code to debug it, but you have to use special tool that may seem to be awkward and complicated at the beginning. This chapter will describe the *Tcl Dev Kit Debugger*, and its older, freely available version — *TclPro Debugger*. We will also present the *Tcl Dev Kit Inspector*, which may be considered as an extended 'remote console', and discuss how it differs from a typical debugger.

Additionally, we will discuss proper handling of errors that may occur during the execution of your application, and how to prevent them from crashing it.

Logging

In the next few sections, we will describe a few logging packages that you may use in your code — `log`, `logger`, and `audit`. Of course these are not the only options available, but they give a good orientation in the topic. The first one — `log`, is the simplest one whereas the other two are more advanced.

In general, when it comes to adding log entries in the code, the question of performance impact arises, as too many calls to logging commands may significantly slow down the application. Tcl has the ability to completely ignore empty procedures (they are compiled to the `no operation` instruction at the bytecode level), and both `logger` and `audit` are able to take advantage of this feature, by aliasing unused commands to procedures with an empty body. Therefore, disabling the logging by setting the log level to minimum will result in almost same performance as for code without any logs.

Log package

One of the oldest libraries created for logging purposes is the `log` package, coming from the `tcllib` package collection. The manual page is available at `http://tcllib.sourceforge.net/doc/log.html`. The good news is that if you are using ActiveTcl, there is good chance that you do not need to install any additional items, because you already have the `log` package in your distribution. If you have any trouble, we recommend installing all Tcllib libraries with the following command:

```
teacup install tcllib
```

For more information about Teacup and how to use it, please refer to the appropriate section in *Chapter 2, Advanced Tcl features*.

Initialization

No special initialization is required. All you need to do to start using this package is to invoke the command `package require log`.

Available log levels

This simple library defines eight levels of logging, in the following order starting from the most important one:

Level name	Suppressed by default	Default output
emergency	No	stderr
alert	No	stderr
critical	No	stderr
error	No	stderr
warning	Yes	stdout
notice	Yes	stdout
info	Yes	stdout
debug	Yes	stdout

The four highest log levels are enabled by default, the other ones are disabled (suppressed) to avoid generating too much information.

Consider the following code:

```
package require log
set availableLevels [log::levels]

set availableLevels [lsort -command log::lvCompare -decreasing \
    $availableLevels]

foreach level $availableLevels {
    log::log $level "message logged on $level level"
}

foreach level $availableLevels {
    puts "---"
    puts "Level name: $level"
    puts "Is suppressed: [log::lvIsSuppressed $level]"
}
```

The first line loads the `log` package, to make it available for use. All commands provided by this package are located in the `log` namespace.

The command `log::levels` returns a list of all available log levels. Note that the list is NOT ordered according to the levels' importance. To get the list in the order presented in table, we sort it using `lsort` command. The `log` package provides a handy comparison command `log::lvCompare`, which is compatible with `lsort` (refer to *Chapter 1, Introducing Tcl*, for more details on `lsort` command).

Using this list, we first attempt to log a message on each level. To do this, we call `log::log` command that accepts two parameters: a level and a message:

`log::log` *levelName message*

Having done this, for each level the code displays information about its suppression state, using the command `log::lvIsSuppressed` *levelName*.

The code produces the following output (standard error output is in bold):

```
cs C:\WINDOWS\system32\cmd.exe                                    _ □ x
c:\tcl_book\chapter4\examples\tcllib_log>tclsh85 printLogLevels.tcl
emergency message logged on emergency level
alert     message logged on alert level
critical  message logged on critical level
error     message logged on error level
___
Level name: emergency
Is suppressed: 0
___
Level name: alert
Is suppressed: 0
___
Level name: critical
Is suppressed: 0
___
Level name: error
Is suppressed: 0
___
Level name: warning
Is suppressed: 1
___
Level name: notice
Is suppressed: 1
___
Level name: info
Is suppressed: 1
___
Level name: debug
Is suppressed: 1
```

As you can see, only the four messages on the highest levels get logged, because lower levels are suppressed.

Enabling or disabling log levels

To enable or disable particular logging levels, the following commands may be used:

- `log::lvSuppress` *levelName ?suppress?* – the first parameter is the name of level to alter. The second parameter is optional, and can take the values **0** or **1**. If a value is omitted, the default value is **0**. The command disables the specified level when `suppress` value is **1**, or enables it when value is **0**.

- `log::lvSuppressLE` *levelName ?suppress?* – similar to previous one, with the only difference being that the state of the specified level and all lower levels is altered. For example, the command: `log::lvlSuppressLE alert 1` will effectively disable all levels but **emergency**.

Each log level is capable of producing output to a specified channel. As mentioned earlier, by default these channels are `stdout` or `stderr`, but it is possible to specify a custom channel:

- `log::lvChannel` *levelName channel* – the first parameter is the name of level to alter. The second parameter is the channel where logs should be produced to.

- `log::lvChannelForall` *channel* – similar to previous one, but alters all log levels.

Replacing the default implementation of the logging command

When `log::log` is invoked, it first checks if the given level is enabled; if it is, then it calls `log::Puts` internal command, passing to it the level name and message text. This command automatically selects the appropriate channel, and writes a log entry to it.

By default, the log format produced by the `log::Puts` command is simple and each entry consists of a line as follows:

levelName message

Luckily, it is possible to replace `log::Puts` with a custom command, where some more sophisticated format and other message processing may be introduced:

- `log::lvCmd` *levelName commandName* – the first parameter is the name of level, for which you want to replace the log writing command. The second parameter is a command name. Note that this command should accept two parameters: the level of the message and the message text.

- `log::lvCmdForall` *commandName* – similar to previous one, but alters all log levels.

Knowing all this, we can implement modifications that would allow us to write well formatted logs to text file:

```
package require log
set availableLevels [log::levels]
set availableLevels [lsort -command log::lvCompare -decreasing \
    $availableLevels]

log::lvSuppressLE alert 0
set channel [open "messages.log" a]
log::lvChannelForall $channel
log::lvCmdForall myPuts

proc myPuts {lvl msg} {
    set now [clock seconds]
    set date [clock format $now]
    set channel [log::lv2channel $lvl]
    puts $channel [format "\[%s\] \[%-9s\] %s" \
        $date $lvl $msg]
    flush $channel
}

foreach level $availableLevels {
    log::log $level "some message"
}
```

The code starts in the same way as in the previous example. All log levels are enabled with log::lvSuppressLE alert 0. A channel related to the file messages.log is created and the reference stored in the channel variable. This channel is set for all levels with log::lvChannelForall $channel. Next, also for all levels, the writing command is replaced with myPuts.

The myPuts command accepts two variables—log level (lvl) and message text (msg). It retrieves the current date (and stores it in the date variable), channel for the specified log level (and stores it in channel), performs some formatting on the lvl string in order to achieve the fixed length of that variable, and finally writes a log entry with the puts command.

As a result, the `messages.log` file is created with the following
well-formatted content:

```
C:\WINDOWS\system32\cmd.exe                                    _ □ ×
c:\tcl_book\chapter4\examples\tcllib_log>type messages.log
[Wed Mar 17 17:14:43 CET 2010] [emergency] some message
[Wed Mar 17 17:14:45 CET 2010] [alert    ] some message
[Wed Mar 17 17:14:45 CET 2010] [critical ] some message
[Wed Mar 17 17:14:45 CET 2010] [error    ] some message
[Wed Mar 17 17:14:45 CET 2010] [warning  ] some message
[Wed Mar 17 17:14:45 CET 2010] [notice   ] some message
[Wed Mar 17 17:14:45 CET 2010] [info     ] some message
[Wed Mar 17 17:14:45 CET 2010] [debug    ] some message
```

Of course, it is also possible to send logs over the network using the socket channel.
To do this, we have to modify only one line in the code (now it can be called 'client
code'), the one defining `channel`:

```
set channel [socket localhost 1234]
```

We also need some kind of log server that will accept an incoming connection
and logs:

```
proc logServer {channel addr port} {
    puts "Receiving logs from $addr:$port"
    while {![eof $channel]} {
        puts [gets $channel]
    }
}
socket -server logServer 1234
vwait forever
```

This simple code will accept connections on port 1234 and just print logs to the
console for demonstration purposes. Once the server and the client code are
executed, the output on the console where the server was started will be similar to:

```
C:\WINDOWS\system32\cmd.exe - tclsh85 logServer.tcl              _ □ ×
c:\tcl_book\chapter4\examples\tcllib_log>tclsh85 logServer.tcl
Receiving logs from 127.0.0.1:2179
[Wed Mar 17 17:38:12 CET 2010] [emergency] some message
[Wed Mar 17 17:38:13 CET 2010] [alert    ] some message
[Wed Mar 17 17:38:13 CET 2010] [critical ] some message
[Wed Mar 17 17:38:13 CET 2010] [error    ] some message
[Wed Mar 17 17:38:13 CET 2010] [warning  ] some message
[Wed Mar 17 17:38:13 CET 2010] [notice   ] some message
[Wed Mar 17 17:38:13 CET 2010] [info     ] some message
[Wed Mar 17 17:38:13 CET 2010] [debug    ] some message
```

For more details on networking in Tcl, such as how to program a socket, refer to
Chapter 6, Networking in Tcl of this book.

Recap of the log package

In summary the log package offers a simple but still flexible mechanism for logging purposes. Its main disadvantage is that it is not able to read / write configuration, and lacks the ability to define more than one loggers, or at least targets (channels) for messages; for example, concurrent logging to multiple files and consoles with different formatting. These constraints can be bypassed to certain degree, with more sophisticated design of custom writing command and additional configuration code, but still it would be better to have it already included in package itself.

Logger package

The logger package is more advanced compared to the previous one. It also comes as a part of Tcllib bundle and you will already have it if you are using the *ActiveTcl* distribution. The documentation of the package is located at http://tcllib. sourceforge.net/doc/logger.html, but unfortunately it is not consistent and some information is incorrect or missing. The content of this paragraph is based not on the documentation, but on real life experience with the package in version 0.9.

The main difference in comparison to the log package, is that it introduces the ability to create many instances of the logger, each one with different configuration, which allows precise fine-tuning of the logger to reflect your needs. These instances are referred to as **services**, and we will use both terms interchangeably across this paragraph. Moreover, the instances can be organized hierarchically, which allows inheritance of configuration from the parent instance. Such a solution provides enough flexibility for even most demanding applications. Imagine that your complex application consists of various blocks (components). By creating separate loggers for each part, you gain an ability to easily inspect the behavior of only one component, instead of having to review logs from the entire program.

Another improvement is the ability to collect information, about entering and exiting to particular procedures along with data passed to it. Such behavior is called **tracing**, and collected logs are called **traces**. What's really important here is that this functionality leverages Tcl's native tracing mechanism. Therefore, changes in code are not required, and it does not generate any overhead unless enabled, either.

Initialization

To create a logger instance, use the logger::init *serviceName* command, as in the following example, where the instance is stored in the variable logger:

```
set logger [logger::init someService]
```

What is really stored in `logger` variable is the name of the namespace created by this command, for the particular service name. The command also imports some useful logging commands into this namespace, as we will see in the following section.

In case of version 0.9 of the `logger` package, the namespace created for `serviceName` is `::logger::tree::serviceName`. Actually, `serviceName` is nothing more than a part of a namespace and it may contain elements separated with `::`. This clever solution allows easy creation of hierarchical loggers:

```
logger::init parent
#... configuration of parent' logger goes here
logger::init parent::child
```

In this case, the second logger is simply referred to as a 'child' (although its full name is `parent::child`) which inherits all the configuration of `parent` logger. It is of course possible to fine-tune its configuration later.

Available log levels

Similar to `log`, there are eight log levels available. In contrast to the previous logging package, to log on a particular level you have to use appropriate command from the namespace described in the previous section. Luckily, the command names are identical to level names. The following table itemizes all levels in order of importance:

level name	logging command name
emergency	`${logger}::emergency` *message*
alert	`${logger}::alert` *message*
critical	`${logger}::critical` *message*
error	`${logger}::error` *message*
warning	`${logger}::warning` *message*
notice	`${logger}::notice` *message*
info	`${logger}::info` *message*
debug	`${logger}::debug` *message*

The level names are almost identical to those coming from `log`, with an exception of the `warn` level, which was called `warning`. In summary, logging any message is as simple as invoking:

```
${logger}::notice "this is test message"
```

By default, all levels are enabled but this behavior may be changed for newly created loggers with the usage of the `logger::setlevel` command which will be described later.

Once you start logging with these commands, you will quickly notice that using a variable name each time, in this example of `logger`, is not too convenient. The package authors also, noticed this and made it possible to import all logger service commands to the namespace of your choice, with the `logger::import` command. Typical usage of this command is:

`logger::import -all -namespace` *targetNamespace serviceName*

In this form, the command will import all logger commands related to the *serviceName* instance into the *targetNamespace* namespace. All parameters except for service name are optional. If the `-namespace` parameter is omitted, the commands would be imported into the current namespace. Skipping `-all` would cause logger to import only logging commands (`emergency`, `alert` , and so on.). When the option is specified, all commands (including some additional, described later) are imported.

Other possible parameters are:

- `-prefix` *prefixName* — the imported commands have a prefix prepended to their names specified as *prefixName*.
- `-force` — overwrites existing commands. If this option is not used and any of the commands imported already exist, the `logger::import` command will fail.

The `import` command is handy, but you will probably not use it. There is another, far better command — `initNamespace`:

`logger::initNamespace` *namespaceName ?level?*

The functions of the previously described commands are combined into this one, as follows:

- It creates a service with a name based on namespaceName
- It imports all logging commands into the namespace namespaceName
- It sets the logging level either to `warn` or to *level*, if specified

Enabling or disabling log levels

The `logger` package offers two possibilities for altering the log level: you can either change it for a particular logger instance, or globally (for all existing loggers):

global command	instance command	description
`logger::enable` *level*	`${logger}::enable` *level*	Enables logging at the specified level and all higher levels
`logger::disable` *level*	`${logger}::disable` *level*	Disables logging at the specified level and all lower levels
`logger::setlevel` *level*	`${logger}::setlevel` *level*	Enables logging at the specified level and all higher, and disables all lower levels

Additionally, the `logger::setlevel` command may be used to define the default log level for all newly created loggers.

Knowing everything that has been described up to this point, we can illustrate it with the following example:

```
package require logger
set logger [logger::init someService]
${logger}::debug "message logged on 'debug' level"

logger::import -all -namespace someService someService
someService::debug "another message logged on 'debug' level"
someService::emergency "message logged on 'emergency' level"

set child [logger::init someService::child]
logger::import -all -namespace someService::child \
someService::child

puts "Known log levels: [logger::levels]"
puts "Known services: [logger::services]"

proc listLevels {} {
    foreach service [logger::services] {
        puts "Current loglevel for $service is: \
            [${service}::currentloglevel]"
    }
}

listLevels
```

```
someService::setlevel notice
puts "after parent logger level change..."
listLevels

someService::child::enable debug
puts "after child logger level change..."
listLevels

someService::alert "this message will be logged"
someService::child::debug "and this one too"
someService::debug "but this one will be not"

someService::delete
```

The first lines demonstrate the creation of a logger instance for someService, for example logging on the debug level using this instance, then importing the relevant commands into the someService namespace, and again example logging to demonstrate the benefits of that import.

Next, a child logger named someService::child is created and similarly, its commands are imported into the someService::child namespace.

Subsequently, the code will print out all available log levels owing to logger::levels command, and all defined logger instances (services) up to this point, using the logger::services command. Both of these commands return results in the form of a Tcl list.

Then the procedure listLevels is defined. Its purpose is to print the enabled log level for every created logger. To get this information, ${service}::currentloglevel command is used, where the service variable is the service name (see the following section for more information).

The procedure is used next, each time the log level is altered for parent or child logger to see how it affected overall configuration.

At the end, the parent logger and its child are removed using delete command. This also cleans up all the resources used by that service.

The output of this example is as follows:

```
[Wed Dec 09 19:13:31 CET 2009] [someService] [debug] 'message logged
on 'debug' level'
[Wed Dec 09 19:13:31 CET 2009] [someService] [debug] 'another message
logged on 'debug' level'
[Wed Dec 09 19:13:31 CET 2009] [someService] [emergency] 'message
logged on 'emergency' level'
```

```
Known log levels: debug info notice warn error critical alert
emergency
Known services: someService someService::child
Current loglevel for someService is: debug
Current loglevel for someService::child is: debug
after parent logger level change...
Current loglevel for someService is: notice
Current loglevel for someService::child is: notice
after child logger level change...
Current loglevel for someService is: notice
Current loglevel for someService::child is: debug
[Wed Dec 09 19:13:31 CET 2009] [someService] [alert] 'this message
will be logged'
[Wed Dec 09 19:13:31 CET 2009] [someService::child] [debug] 'and this
one too'
```

Analyzing this output, we can clearly see that altering the parent logger has a direct impact on child instance — changing the logging level on the parent from debug to notice in both of them. However, changes in the child logger are not propagated to the parent, so after the someService::child::enable debug command, only the child logger changes its logging level to debug. We can also notice the rather obvious behavior that messages, logged on the level which is not currently enabled, are simply discarded.

The implementation of listLevels command should be improved, in order to make it more universal:

```
proc listLevels {} {
    foreach service [logger::services] {
        puts "Current loglevel for $service is: \
            [[logger::servicecmd $service]::currentloglevel]"
    }
}
```

The previous implementation worked only because of importing logger commands into namespaces, named identically to the corresponding services. To make it independent of the fact whether logger::import command was executed or not, additional command is used:

logger::servicecmd *serviceName*

This command returns the same value as logger::init — full namespace, where the logger package put all commands related to the particular instance for a specified service name.

Tracing

As mentioned earlier, this library allows the tracing of command execution. To achieve it, the ${logger}::trace command with appropriate parameters must be used:

- ${logger}::trace on : enables tracing. The mechanism is independent of logging, so enabling / disabling any log levels does not affect the ability to trace. Also, it uses some unique features of Tcl 8.4 and later, so the command will fail on earlier versions. ${logger}::trace off disables tracing.

- ${logger}::trace add *procName* : causes procedure(s) (the command accepts more than one procedure name) to be 'monitored'. If the procedure identified by *procName* is called, appropriate tracing information is generated. It is also possible to add all procedures from given namespace: ${logger}:: trace add -ns *namespaceName*

- ${logger}::trace remove *procName* : similar to add, removes one (or more) procedures from monitoring. Similarly, ${logger}::trace remove -ns *namespaceName* removes all procedures from the specified namespace.

- ${logger}::trace status : returns a list of monitored procedures. This command may be also called with an additional parameter, the name of the procedure, to verify if it is monitored or not.

The operation of the tracing mechanism is illustrated by the following example:

```
package require logger
set logger [logger::init someService]

proc second {} {}
proc first {} {second}
${logger}::trace on
${logger}::trace add first second
puts "monitored procedures are: [${logger}::trace status]"
first
${logger}::delete
```

Two dummy procedures, first and second are created and are registered for tracing. In the next step, we verify this by printing the status of tracer, and finally call the first command to observe the generated information (tracing.tcl is the script name that is being executed):

```
monitored procedures are: ::first ::second
[Wed Dec 09 19:20:56 CET 2009] [someService] [trace] 'enter {proc ::
first level 1 script tracing.tcl caller {} procargs {}}'
[Wed Dec 09 19:20:56 CET 2009] [someService] [trace] 'enter {proc ::
second level 2 script tracing.tcl caller ::first procargs {}}'
```

```
[Wed Dec 09 19:20:56 CET 2009] [someService] [trace] 'leave {proc ::
second level 2 script tracing.tcl caller ::first status ok result {}}'
[Wed Dec 09 19:20:56 CET 2009] [someService] [trace] 'leave {proc ::
first level 1 script tracing.tcl caller {} status ok result {}}'
```

Changing the implementation of the logging / tracing command

Every time you log a message, for example on debug level:

```
${logger}::debug "message"
```

what really happens is that debug (or other command) verifies if the log level is enabled, and if it is, then the appropriate underlying command is called.

For each log level of every instantiated logger, it is possible to replace the standard implementation of that underlying command with your custom one. Let's consider the following example first:

```
package require logger

proc myLogProc {txt} {
    puts ">>> $txt <<<"
}

proc listLogProcs {logger} {
    puts "== log procedures for $logger =="
    foreach level [logger::levels] {
        puts "$level --> [${logger}::logproc $level]"
    }
}

set logger [logger::init someService]
listLogProcs $logger
${logger}::debug "test message"
${logger}::logproc debug myLogProc
listLogProcs $logger
${logger}::debug "test message"


set anotherLogger [logger::init anotherService]
listLogProcs $anotherLogger
${anotherLogger}::delete
${logger}::delete
```

The output is as follows:

```
== log procedures for ::logger::tree::someService ==
debug --> ::logger::tree::someService::debugcmd
info --> ::logger::tree::someService::infocmd
notice --> ::logger::tree::someService::noticecmd
warn --> ::logger::tree::someService::warncmd
error --> ::logger::tree::someService::errorcmd
critical --> ::logger::tree::someService::criticalcmd
alert --> ::logger::tree::someService::alertcmd
emergency --> ::logger::tree::someService::emergencycmd
[Wed Dec 09 21:44:32 CET 2009] [someService] [debug] 'test message'
== log procedures for ::logger::tree::someService ==
debug --> myLogProc
info --> ::logger::tree::someService::infocmd
notice --> ::logger::tree::someService::noticecmd
warn --> ::logger::tree::someService::warncmd
error --> ::logger::tree::someService::errorcmd
critical --> ::logger::tree::someService::criticalcmd
alert --> ::logger::tree::someService::alertcmd
emergency --> ::logger::tree::someService::emergencycmd
>>> test message <<<
== log procedures for ::logger::tree::anotherService ==
debug --> ::logger::tree::anotherService::debugcmd
info --> ::logger::tree::anotherService::infocmd
notice --> ::logger::tree::anotherService::noticecmd
warn --> ::logger::tree::anotherService::warncmd
error --> ::logger::tree::anotherService::errorcmd
critical --> ::logger::tree::anotherService::criticalcmd
alert --> ::logger::tree::anotherService::alertcmd
emergency --> ::logger::tree::anotherService::emergencycmd
```

The first code defines two procedures: `myLogProc` which acts as simple implementation of logging command for *debug* level, and `listLogProcs` which prints implementing commands for all levels for the specified logger.

- To retrieve the current command that will be executed on specified level, we use
  `${logger}::logproc` *levelName*
  command. As we can see in the output, for example: for `debug` level the default command name is `debugcmd`.

- To change it, the additional parameter must be supplied:
  `${logger}::logproc` *levelName newCommandName*.
  In our example, we changed the procedure for `debug` from `debugCmd` to `myLogProc`, and this change can be verified by using `listLogProcs` again or by simply logging a message on this level.

At the end of the code, we verify that the procedure has been altered for only one logger, by instantiating the other one and listing implementations.

In a similar way, you can change the implementation of the trace logging command. To do this, run `logproc` with `trace` as the first parameter:

```
${logger}::logproc trace newCommandName
```

There is one significant difference—the new command (that will handle traces) will be called each time with a list variable as its argument, and not a text one. The list consists of two elements. The first one is `enter` or `leave` keyword that is rather self explanatory. The second item is a dictionary that contains the following name-value pairs:

Name (key)	Value
proc	The name of the procedure that was entered or left
level	The stack level for that procedure; stack frames are discussed in more detail in *Chapter 2, Advanced Tcl features*
script	The name of the file where the procedure is defined. May be empty in case of interactive mode
caller	The name of procedure which is calling the procedure being currently traced. May be empty in case the procedure is called from the global scope
procargs	A dictionary containing the names and values of arguments passed to the procedure
status	Only valid in the 'leave' case—the Tcl return code of the procedure, this is returned by the rarely used `return -code` *code* command. For example, values are: OK (or 0) or ERROR (1)
result	Only valid in the 'leave' case—the return value of the procedure

Appenders

In contrast to the previously described `log` package, you are not required to create your own logging procedure when you want to use the custom format of your log entries. The package `logger::utilities` makes it possible to easily create such procedures in predefined, template-based way, and names them **appenders**. In this paragraph, we will also refer to them as **formatters** as this is their main application.

Appenders are created per service (logger instance). Use `logger::utils::` `applyAppender` with following options to create one:

- `-appender` *type* : A mandatory option used to specify the type of the appender (described in the following section). Allowed values for *type* are: `console`, `fileAppend`.

- `-service` *serviceName* : A non-mandatory option used to specify the instance of the logger (identified by *serviceName*) to which the formatter should be appended.

- `-serviceCmd` *logger* : An alternative way to identify the logger instance. This non-mandatory option accepts the same values as returned by `logger::init` .

- `-levels` *levelsList* : if specified, applies the formatter only to messages logged on levels listed in the levels list. Otherwise all levels are included.

- `-appenderArgs` *args* : *args* is the list of arguments passed directly to the created appender.

One of the common arguments passed to the appender via the `-appenderArgs` option is the `-conversionPattern` *pattern*. This optional argument allows us to define a custom format (pattern) of the logged messages. Basically, this is a normal string that may contain special identifiers which will be expanded properly at runtime. The default pattern is: `[%d] [%c] [%M] [%p] %m`. The following table lists all items allowed to occur in pattern string:

Identifier	Expanded to
`%c`	Fully qualified name of logger instance (service)
`%C`	Short name of logger instance
`%d`	Current date (yyyy/MM/dd hh:mm:ss)
`%H`	Hostname
`%m`	Message
`%M`	Procedure name where the log event occurred ('global' in case of global scope)
`%p`	Level (priority) of the log event
`%P`	pid of the current process

Two types of appenders exist:

- `console`: this type of appender writes logs directly to the console—standard output and standard error.

- `fileAppend`: logged messages are sent to the channel (it may be a file channel, or the network one). The channel is passed as the appender option (`-appenderArgs`): `-outputChannel` *channel*.

To conclude the appenders description, let's have a look at working example:

```
package require logger
package require logger::utils

set fl [logger::init firstLog]
set sl [logger::init secondLog]

logger::utils::applyAppender -appender fileAppend \
    -appenderArgs "-outputChannel [open log.txt a]" \
    -serviceCmd $fl
logger::utils::applyAppender -appender console \
    -appenderArgs {-conversionPattern {\[%d\] %c:%p \"%m\"}} \
    -service secondLog

${fl}::notice "first logger message"
${sl}::notice "second logger message"
```

Two log services are created: `firstLog` and `secondLog`. The namespaces created for both of them are stored respectively in variables `fl` and `sl`.

Then the file appender (writing to `log.txt` file) is created and attached to the first logger, which is identified with `$fl` value.

After this, the console formatter is created with an example custom pattern `[%d]` `%c:%p "%m"`. This appender is applied to the second logger, thanks to the `secondLog` value for `service` option.

Consecutively, both loggers are used to log sample messages to verify if appenders work correctly. The `log.txt` file will then contain a line:

```
[2009/12/12 19:39:49] [firstLog] [global] [notice] first logger message
```

and the second log will be sent to the console as:

```
[2009/12/12 20:09:02] secondLog:notice "second logger message"
```

Recap of the logger package

The `logger` package is far more advanced than `log`. It allows us to create many logger instances (called services) with a different configuration. Appenders offer a convenient and flexible way to store log entries in the format of your choice.

However, it is still missing out the ability to read / write current configuration. Also, the available documentation is laconic and contains errors.

Audit

Another library worth mentioning is the one named `audit`. The documentation and all necessary files are located at `http://dqsoftware.sourceforge.net/audit_index.html`. `Audit` was created as a result of disappointment and a lack of some functionality in existing solutions. It is targeted for usage in long-running applications, working on servers, for example it allows logfile rotation. The library is very laconic and offers only essential information. It is closer to log than logger in terms of variety of features, yet offers a sufficient logging functionality. To start using it, you have to download and place it in your library directory, pointed by `$auto_path` variable.

The `audit` logger is able not only to save logs to text a file but also to create a special dump file, which may then be loaded in to a special graphical browser. What is more, the logger does not have to be initially configured to write to any files. As a part of its internal operations, it stores data in the memory and offers a possibility to write it later. For example, only in case some error occurs.

Let's analyze its usage starting with the following example:

```
package require audit::audit

audit::configure -level 9 -logfile log.txt
audit::audit main 5 "starting"
proc proc1 {} {
    audit::audit proc1 3 "message from proc1"
    proc2
}

proc proc2 {} {
    audit::audit proc2 3 "message from proc2"
}

proc1

audit::audit main 5 "ending"
```

The first line loads the package, after which some configuration must be done using the `audit::configure` command. The most important parameters for this command are (all are optional):

- `-limit` *integerValue* — defines the limit of log entries stored in the memory. Its default value is 20,000.

- `-level` *level* — defines logging level. By defaults logs are disabled — level set to 0. Audit accepts level values from 1(most important) to 9 (least important).

- -logfile *fileName* — the logs (in human readable format) will be written to a file named *filename*. An empty value "" disables writing to file.

- -logfilecount *integer* — the number of files with previous logs to keep during the log rotation process. By default the number is 10.

- -datafile *fileName* — the dump will be written to file named *filename*. An empty value "" disables writing to file. Such a dump may be later viewed in the Audit browser.

- -datafilecount *integer* — the number of files with previous dumps to keep during the log rotation process. By default the number is 10.

In this example, we enable all logging levels (by specifying value 9) and configure it to be written to the `log.txt` file.

To log anything, use the `audit::audit` command:

`audit::audit` *type level message ?varlist? ?parameter1? ?value1? ?parameter2? ?value2? ?..?*

The accepted arguments are:

Argument	Meaning
type	Any string identifier like method name
level	Level of log
message	Message to be logged
varlist	List of variables to dump
parameter value	Additional parameters and its values to store

The content of the `log.txt` file after running the previous example is as follows:

```
09-12-16 19:23:34.4203 | main  | 5 | 0 | starting
09-12-16 19:23:34.4221 | proc1 | 3 | 1 | message from proc1
09-12-16 19:23:34.4223 | proc2 | 3 | 2 | message from proc2
09-12-16 19:23:34.4225 | main  | 5 | 0 | ending
```

The first field contains the time of the log event, after which the value is specified as `type`, then level on which the message was logged, stack frame, and finally the message.

To force log rotation, as mentioned earlier, you can use the command `audit::logroll`. The best application is to call this method periodically; for example, from Tclcron (described in detail in *Chapter 2, Advanced Tcl features*).

The following example will demonstrate the usage of the Audit browser:

```
package require audit::audit

audit::configure -level 9
audit::audit main 5 "starting"
proc testProc {msg args} {
    audit::audit testProc 3 "message from testProc"
    anotherTestProc $msg $args
}

proc anotherTestProc {msg args} {
    audit::audit anotherTestProc 3 "message from anotherTestProc" \
{msg args} currentTime [clock format [clock seconds]]
}

testProc "Some test" name1 value1 name2 value2

audit::audit main 1 "some message"
audit::audit main 5 "ending"
audit::saveAudit audit.sav
```

This code is similar to the previous one, with the exception that no log file is defined at the beginning. Therefore, the information is stored in memory and at the end, the method `audit::saveAudit` is used to save a binary dump to the `audit.sav` file. Also, some additional information is passed to the `audit::audit` command to illustrate how they can be analyzed later.

To start the **Audit browser**, run `browser.tcl` file located among `audit` package files. The following screenshot shows the browser window with the `audit.sav` file loaded:

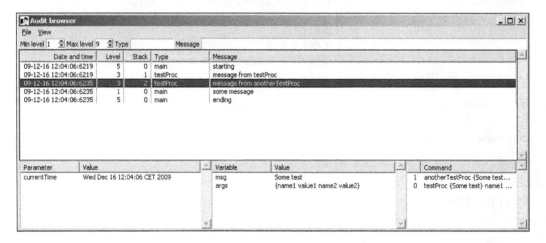

The main window shows a list of logged events in a similar format to the text file logs; each one can be clicked to obtain more information in lower windows. In this screenshot, event logged in `anotherTestProc` procedure is selected. It's also possible to search for entries by selecting the appropriate minimum and maximum levels, typing the text to `search for` in the type or message columns.

First, the lower window shows all parameters and its values logged with the `audit::audit` command. The next one contains the names and values of the variables, also put in with that command. The last one shows the stack trace, that the list of all procedures (along with their arguments) being currently executed when the log event occurred. Double clicking on any of items in lower part of the window will open an additional window, which will show detailed information about the selected item—such as being able to see the variables as a list or name-value pairs.

Recap of the audit package

The idea that stands behind `audit` is quite different compared to previous loggers. The package is designed to be suitable for long running server side applications (log rotation), and it also allows to dump logs only in some particular conditions for the end user software. You can easily imagine an on-error popup window that allows the user to send a dump to the application's authors with one mouse click.

Moreover, the graphical browser outperforms any other solution in the context of ease of usage and the level of details provided, allowing you to find out the source of the problem with as little effort and time as possible.

Debugging

While logging techniques save information about execution flow to allow you to analyze it later, debugging offers a different concept. It allows you to interact with a live, running application, review and modify its internal state, and halt execution at points of your choice using breakpoints.

The best graphical debugging tools, *Inspector* and *Debugger*, are offered by ActiveState as a part of the *Tcl Dev Kit* bundle, available at `http://www.activestate.com/tcl_dev_kit/`. There is a 21-day free trial period, so you do not need to buy it blindly. In this chapter, we will describe the tools offered by version 5.1.0. We will also describe its ancestor, the free *TclPro Debugger* (version 1.4), available at `http://www.tcl.tk/software/tclpro/`. Although it is based on old Tcl 8.3, it is still a free alternative worth considering.

Tcl Dev Kit Inspector

Before we focus on debuggers, we will first discuss the Tcl Dev Kit Inspector, which is not really a thorough-bred debugging application. It allows you to connect to a running program via a comm port and analyze its components. The comm package is described in *Chapter 7, Using Common Internet Services*, so we will not dive in to its details here. All you need to know is that the application itself must load a comm package, and configure it for listening on a specific port (across this book, we use value 1991 as the example port), or use the default value (returned by the comm::comm self command).

Across this and the next few paragraphs, we will base our description on the simple client that is the server code example. Here is the server code:

```
namespace eval ::server {}

proc ::server::initCounter {name} {
    variable counter
    set counter($name) 0
}

proc ::server::incrementCounter {name value} {
    variable counter
    if {[info exists counter($name)]} {
        incr counter($name) $value
    }
}

proc ::server::getAvg {} {
    variable counter
    set sum 0
    foreach name [array names counter] {
        incr sum $counter($name)
    }

    return [expr {$sum / [array size counter]}]
}

package require comm
comm::comm config -local 0 -port 1991
vwait forever
```

The concept is simple—the server application will allow the creation of variables named **counters** (with command `server::initCounter`), modification of its value (with `server::incrementCounter`), and retrieval of average value (`server::getAvg`). Each counter has a name and is stored in `counter` array. The server code defines appropriate procedures, initializes `comm` to listen on port 1991, and enters event loop.

The client code is also simple and boils down to remote execution of server commands:

```
package require comm

set id 1991

comm::comm send $id ::server::initCounter "testA"
comm::comm send $id ::server::initCounter "testB"
comm::comm send $id ::server::incrementCounter "testA" 8
comm::comm send $id ::server::incrementCounter "testB" 16
comm::comm send $id ::server::incrementCounter "testC" 10
puts [comm::comm send $id ::server::getAvg]
```

What we will do here is start a server process, and then execute some client code once to allow it to modify internal server application state. Once it is done, we can start the `Inspector`.

The first action to perform is to connect `Inspector` to our server application, by choosing **File | connect to comm port** and entering 1991 as the value (please note that it will use the same type of connection as the one between our example client-server, so effectively we are reusing `comm` port). Unfortunately, the `inspector` allows *only* local connections as there is no possibility of entering an IP address. Advanced users may bypass this limitation by using SSH tunnelling. If the target machine has a running SSH server (which is usually the case for applications running on Unix servers), it is enough to execute the following (we assume the target IP is 192.168.1.1):

- Windows: `plink -L 1991:127.0.0.1:1991 user@192.168.1.1` plink is a command-line interface for Windows SSH client PuTTY, available at: `http://www.chiark.greenend.org.uk/~sgtatham/putty/download.html`
- Unix: `ssh -L 1991:127.0.0.1:1991 user@192.168.1.1`

This command will tunnel the local port 1991 to the remote machine's port—also 1991, as a result allowing remote usage of `Inspector`.

`Inspector` allows you to take a look into the application. For example, you are able to review all defined procedures as follows:

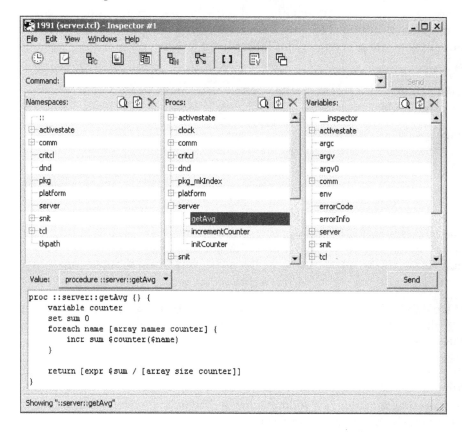

In the preceding screenshot, the `getAvg` procedure is selected (in **Procs** pane) and displayed (in **Value** pane). The bottom **Value** window is editable and you are given the possibility to redefine your procedure by editing its code, and clicking the **Send** button.

The following screenshot shows how to check value of the `counter` variable:

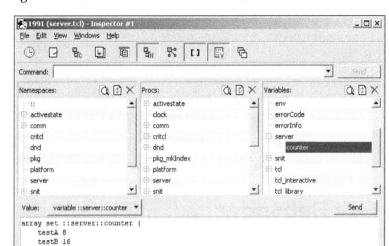

Note that the value is presented in the form of a ready-to-execute Tcl command that would set this value. Just as in the previous case, the **Value** window is editable, so you can easily modify the value of the variable. For example, change 8 to 12 and click the **Send** button.

You are also able to call any command of your choice, just as it would be called inside the application. All you need to do is to enter the command in the **Command** text field, and click **Send**. For example, the call to `server::getAvg` command will return the value 14 (the average of the values 12 and 16, as we already modified value of the `testA` counter):

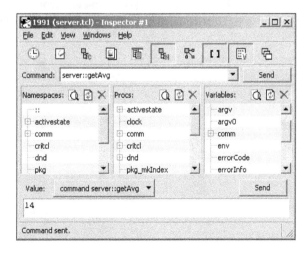

The preceding examples give you a taste of the possibilities offered by `Inspector`. Apart from the described components, there is also a possibility to inspect:

- The defined namespaces and items inside it
- Global items
- Classes and objects created with `incr Tcl`
- GUI elements such as windows, images, menus, and canvas
- Items declared with the `after` command

To sum up, `Inspector` offers you the ability to view the minute details of the application while it is running, to check, and to modify its internal state.

Tcl Dev Kit Debugger

Debugger is a full featured application that offers a complex set of features, aimed at finding and fixing bugs in your Tcl code. In this paragraph, we will describe how to debug our example server code. As usual, we do not intend to copy the documentation, but to present the potential offered by this tool. For more details, please refer to *Tcl Dev Kit User Guide*.

Debugger has the ability to work in two modes:

1. Local Debugging—the debugger and debugged code are executed on the same physical machine
2. Remote Debugging—the application that is a subject to debug connects remotely over TCP/IP network to the debugger

Local Debugging

Once you start *Debugger* and choose **File | New Project...** from menu, you are able to select the debugging mode. In this case, we select **Local Debugging** and load the server code:

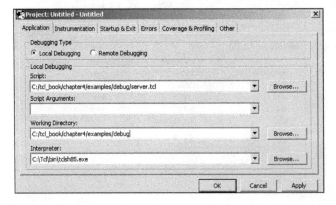

What this means is that the debugger will launch the server code (`server.tcl`) locally on the same computer, where it is run. The project may be saved, allowing us to keep your breakpoints and watch variables for later usage.

Once the code is loaded, you will be able to start interacting with it. Debugger offers typical scenario for this kind of application features:

- The ability to execute the code, line by line with stepping function
- Display of defined variables on all stack frames, along with stack information
- The ability to define line and variable breakpoints:
    - ° A line breakpoint will cause the application to stop, once the execution reaches the specified line
    - ° A variable breakpoint will cause the application to stop on any modification of specified variable
- The ability to modify internal state of the application by using Eval Console
- Measurements of coverage and profiling of the code

If there are more details, the code (`server.tcl`) will not simply be executed. The debugger will modify it transparently, enabling the debugging process to take place—this mechanism is called **instrumentation**. By default, all the code would be instrumented, but you have the possibility of explicitly excluding some of its parts. You may do this on the second tab of new project wizard (or later in **File | Project Settings...**):

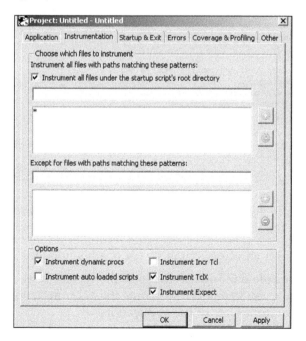

For example, you can precisely define which procedures should be left uninstrumented, or even ignore entire source files. The excluded code will still be executed of course, but you won't be able to use debugging features like setting breakpoints inside it. You may wonder why to bother yourself with such exclusions: for example, it would improve the performance of your code, or allow you to omit some parts like loading some libraries.

The following screenshot shows the Debugger with loaded and started `server.tcl` code:

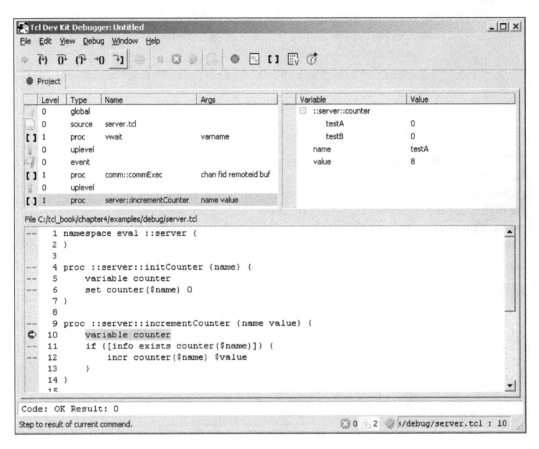

The upper toolbar contains buttons for stepping the application, stopping / and restarting it, and for displaying various additional windows, consecutively:

- **The Breakpoint** window contains a list of all defined breakpoints.
- **The Eval Console** window, is similar to the typical Tclsh console. This console allows you to enter and execute the Tcl commands, and effectively modify the runtime state of the application.

- **The Procedures** window contains a list of all procedures defined.
- **The Watch Variables** window offers the ability to watch values of the variables of your choice.
- **The Code Coverage** window.

The upper left pane holds the list of available stack frames. The right pane contains all variables and their values for the selected stack frame. It also offers you the possibility of creating a variable breakpoint (marked with the letter **V**), by clicking on the left margin of the variable:

	Variable	Value
V	⊟ ::server::counter	
	testA	0
	testB	0
	⊞ counter	
	name	testA
	value	8

Double clicking on any variable from this pane will open an additional **Data Display** window, where you can easily display the value of the variable in different formats (Hex, Octal, Unicode and so on).

It is worth noting that the version of the Debugger we used, at the time of writing, had problems when a breakpoint was defined for the array variable. Once the execution of that variable came to modification, the error `can't read "counter": variable is array` was shown.

The debugger may also fail when some core Tcl commands are renamed or redefined. For example, the `comm` package renames the `vwait` command that causes an appropriate warning once executed in Debugger.

The main pane displays the code for selected stack frame. By clicking on the left margin, you are able to define line breakpoints denoted by a dot (as shown in line **10** in the example screen). Once the server was launched and the breakpoint was defined, we executed the client code that caused the `server::incrementCounter` procedure to be executed. As a result, the execution was stopped at line **10**. The yellow arrow on the left points to the line where the execution is currently stopped. Once you decide to continue the execution with stepping functionality, you will notice the arrow moves to next line.

The client code (presented at the paragraph describing `Inspector`) attempts to increase the value for the counter named `testC`. However, once the average value is retrieved, it is calculated only from the first two counters. Quick debug action helps solve this issue:

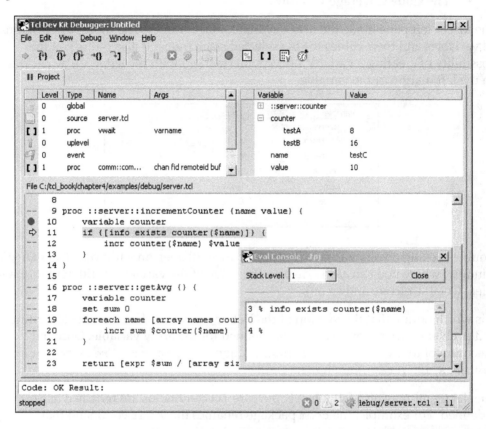

Having declared a breakpoint at line **10**, all we have to do is to wait until the `name` argument has the value `testC`. Once this happens, we can step to the next line, and using the Eval Console we can quickly check whether the *if* condition is fulfilled or not. As you can see, it is not fulfilled, and a quick look at the **counter** variable in the **Variables** pane proves that indeed the counter `testC` was never initialized. Once we return to client code, we check for the following:

```
comm::comm send $id ::server::initCounter "testB"
```

This line is missing indeed. This example 'bug' is trivial, as the client code is short and simple, but in the case of a complex application the odds of missing such a command may be pretty high.

Remote debugging

Remote debugging does not differ significantly from the local mode. The main difference is that the debugger and application are communicating via the TCP/IP network protocol.

The architecture of remote debugging is interesting: it is the debugged application's responsibility to connect to the debugger that is configured to listen on some specific port (let's use *1999* as an example value):

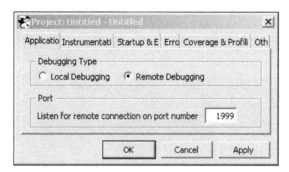

In order to connect (attach) to the listening debugger, the application must be modified. Tcl Dev Kit comes with the `tcldebugger_attach` package that offers all requisitive commands for the application to attach to the debugger. This package must be accessible for the debugged code, so you will probably have to copy it to the target machine.

You may either modify the application code itself or create some wrapper code that will do all that is necessary, and run the original script (see the User Guide for details). We choose second example as it is more elegant. Assuming that our original server code is stored in `server.tcl` file, we will create a new script with the following content:

```
package require tcldebugger_attach

debugger_init 127.0.0.1 1999

source server.tcl
```

As you can notice, basically only one command is required to enable remote debugging:

```
debugger_init host port
```

The *host* parameter is the address of the machine where Debugger listens on the specified port.

If you were to decide to modify the original `server.tcl` script, the start would be the same, but additionally you would have to encapsulate all the server code into the `debugger_eval` procedure call:

```
package require tcldebugger_attach
debugger_init 127.0.0.1 1999

debugger_eval {
namespace eval ::server {}

proc ::server::initCounter {name} {
        #body of the procedure
}

proc ::server::incrementCounter {name value} {
    #body of the procedure
}

proc ::server::getAvg {} {
    #body of the procedure
}

package require comm
comm::comm config -local 0 -port 1991
vwait forever
}
```

Once the application is attached to the debugger, you can interact with it in the normal way, identical to `local` mode, but in this case the interaction is transparently over the network.

The package also offers you the ability to programmatically define breakpoints with the `debugger_break` command, which behaves similar to a line breakpoint. For example, lets add it to the `::server::incrementCounter` command:

```
proc ::server::incrementCounter {name value} {
    variable counter
    if {[info exists counter($name)]} {
        debugger_break
        incr counter($name) $value
```

When the execution hits this line of code, the result is as follows:

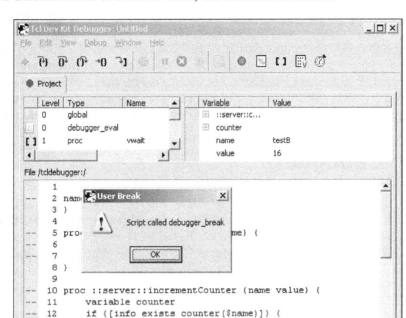

Note that you are still able to define breakpoints in the normal way, using the GUI. Usage of debugger_break may be particularly useful in the case of dynamically-generated code, where you wouldn't be able to set a breakpoint otherwise.

If the debugger is not started and is not listening then the application will continue its operations in the normal way, and debugging related commands will have no effect.

Recap of the Tcl Dev Kit Debugger

The Tcl Dev Kit Debugger is a simple but powerful tool that provides all the necessary functionality typical for this kind of application. Although it lacks some sophisticated options like conditional breakpoints (stop the execution only if some condition is met; for example, variable name has value testC), and in some circumstances it may fail (described in User Guide), there is no doubt it is the best Tcl debugger currently available.

The ability of remote debugging is especially important in the case of network programming, which is essence of this book. What's more, the debugger also offers the ability to perform code profiling, analyze the code coverage, and identify Hot Spots, that is the code fragments that have been executed multiple times. These features allow you to focus on the most critical parts of the application, and fine-tune and optimize the performance of them. For example, you may be dealing with the long running processes of a server application that are handling large volume of data, and reducing the CPU usage or response time may be a matter of life and death.

TclPro Debugger

TclPro Debugger is an older ancestor of its commercial successor, the Tcl Dev Kit Debugger. They both share almost identical user interface and functionality, but as the TclPro Debugger is no longer actively developed (at the time of writing the latest version is 1.4.1 which was released on 2000-11-21), it is based on an old Tcl version, 8.3, which is its main disadvantage. The upside is that it is freely available from the `http://www.tcl.tk/software/tclpro/` website. It also comes with a comprehensive user guide.

For example, the attempt to debug our example server code failed:

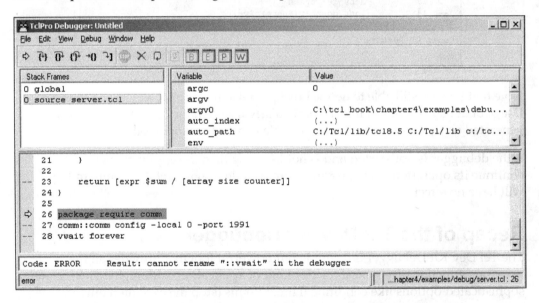

It may be considered as a proof that Tcl Dev Kit Debugger is more mature and advanced solution. However, there are still many situations where the free TclPro Debugger will work fine and satisfy your requirements. In general, this debugger will fail in cases when the subject of instrumentation is the code containing features specific to Tcl versions newer than 8.3, like 8.4 or 8.5. For example, `{$item in $itemlist}` or `{$string eq $otherstring}`. Consider the following code:

```
set animals [list cat cow aligator dog]

if {"dog" in $animals} {
    puts "dog is also an animal!"
}
```

This code is perfectly fine and will execute correctly with the Tcl 8.5 interpreter:

However, an attempt to run it in the debugger will finish with error:

You may try changing the interpreter used by the debugger in the **Project Settings** to the newer one, but the TclPro Debugger will complain about incorrect syntax:

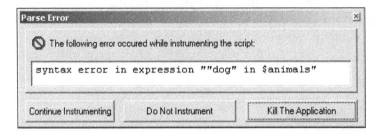

You can still disable the instrumentation of procedures / files that contain these commands. This way the debugger will skip syntax checking of commands that are potentially using features of Tcl 8.4 or newer, and will only inspect code you want to debug. Though this limits your functionality, which might be a reason to upgrade to the TclDevKit package that does not have such issues.

Summary

This chapter explored the concepts that would not be required in the "perfect world"—troubleshooting, which is basically finding out why your application does not work as expected.

First, we described the available solutions for logging and tracing your Tcl application. From the `log`, `logger`, or `audit` packages, you may chose the one that closest fulfils your expectations and requirements. We've shown how each of the packages work and what the key differences are between them.

Next, we described a variety of tools that allow you to take a good look at the internals, and analyse and interact with the running application. Starting from the TclDevKit Inspector, which is a tool that allows you to view the internal components of the application. It is a lightweight tool that can easily be used to connect to a running application, view or modify its parameters, and disconnect from it.

We then moved on to using a full-fledged TclDevKit Debugger with all its richness of features. We've shown how to use it to find and resolve a simple problem, and how to use it to debug remote applications.

In this chapter, we have learned:

- The available solutions for logging in Tcl
- How to configure and use it — how to create loggers, define log levels, write your logs to file or channel
- How to trace the execution of your code
- How to gain an insight into the running application by using the Inspector
- How to debug your application in both the local and remote way
- The key differences between the free TclPro Debugger and the paid ActiveState Tcl Dev Kit Debugger

After this chapter, troubleshooting and finding bugs in the code should be less painful, and allow you to spend more time on developing the functionality, not fixing it.

In the next chapter, we will focus on another fundamental concept: data storage, including topics such as accessing SQL databases, processing XML documents, and more.

5
Data Storage

It is not an overstatement to say that every software application processes some kind of data. Without data, an application's functionality would be rather modest, after all. Data can come from different sources—such as user input, network communication, and so on. It can also be stored locally on behalf of the application.

Knowing that data handling is an inevitable part of your code, this chapter will focus on it, and particularly on textual data. If you ask "why?", the answer is simple: binary data is rather simple and therefore simply boring—it is simply a sequence of bytes, and they can represent virtually anything. In case of text data, the situation differs—there are some common practices and libraries for processing it, and that's what we are going to discuss further. There is also a trend to prefer text data over binary in many cases—the success of text-based XML, for example, proves this.

The first topic will focus on the internationalization of your application. We will discuss the issues with proper encoding of your text data, and how to avoid common pitfalls. We will then briefly present how to create a multi-language program using the powerful package offered by Tcl—msgcat.

The next item will cover accessing relational databases using SQL. We will present how to access *MySQL* or *PostgreSQL* databases, and then we will focus on the Holy Grail of the Tcl database world, that is the *SQLite* database engine. Originally created by Tcl users for Tcl users, it was later widely recognized beyond that loop, and became a popular solution used in many programming languages and by many corporations, such as Adobe, Apple, Google, and Sun.

We will conclude by touching the topic strictly related to networking and data exchange—**XML**. The XML format is very relevant in case of transmitting text data over the network. With the focus on the tdom package, we will present how to parse XML data and access particular information stored inside it. You will also learn how to create an XML document.

Finally, we will discuss the possibility of storing raw, unformatted Tcl data structures such as lists or dictionaries inside the flat text files. The way Tcl treats such structures makes this task simple, and therefore a handy, yet primitive, solution.

Internationalizations

Almost every computer software application communicates somehow with the user or support person in terms of human-readable text messages. When you start developing an application, you may be tempted to use the easiest form, for example using `puts` (or some other command) command with the message in your native language. It may work pretty well in the case of small, one-evening applications, but when it comes to mature-level software that is going to be presented to the world, you will soon search for an easy way to make your application speak in different languages.

Encoding issues

Internally, Tcl uses Unicode to store any string data in memory. We assume the reader is familiar with Unicode and UTF-8 terms, and describing it is beyond the scope of this book. For more information, you can visit `http://www.unicode.org` or simply search the network for interesting articles, because the topic is widely covered.

As UTF-8 encoding solves most of the problems with internationalization (the term is often abbreviated to **i18n** for easier reading, as there are 18 characters in this word between 'i' and 'n'), Tcl may be considered a mature solution in this matter. You do not even have to remember about any encoding issues as long as you operate on Tcl string data.

Basically, Tcl reads all files using the system encoding (for example, for those using English in Windows, it is *Windows-1252*) and converts them to Unicode. The same is in case of writing—by default, data is converted to system encoding.

It may (and based on general experience, it will) happen that you want to read the contents of a file that is encoded in a different format than that of the system. Therefore, you will have to alter the default conversion by reconfiguration of data channel, and to do this, you can use the Tcl command:

```
fconfigure $channelId -encoding encodingName
```

channelId is nothing more than the identifier of the channel returned by the open command. When you select the encoding by specifying its name — encodingName — Tcl will treat incoming data as if it is encoded in the specified format and convert it to Unicode, and it converts outgoing data from Unicode to the target encoding. The encoding names command returns a list of all available encoding names. If you skip encodingName, the fconfigure command will return the current encoding for specified channel.

Let's illustrate what is written up to this moment with an example. Assume that we have two text files — utf8.txt and cp1250.txt, encoded in UTF-8 and Cp1250, respectively. The following code sample shows how Tcl will behave when reading them:

```
puts "system encoding is Cp1250, so the file will be read correctly:"
puts [read [open cp1250.txt r]]


puts "\nand this one will be malformed:"
puts [read [open utf8.txt r]]

puts "\nall known encodings are:"
puts [encoding names]

puts "\nafter proper configuration of encoding for the channel:"
set channelId [open utf8.txt r]
fconfigure $channelId -encoding utf-8
puts [read $channelId]
close $channelId
```

The output is:

```
system encoding is Cp1250, so the file will be read correctly:
This file is encoded with Cp1250 and contains some Polish characters:
zażółć gęślą jaźń

and this one will be malformed:
This file is encoded with UTF-8 and contains some Polish characters:
zaĹĽĂłĹ‚ĂŤ gĹ›lÄ… jaĹşĹ„
```

```
all known encodings are:
cp860 cp861 cp862 cp863 tis-620 cp864 cp865 cp866 gb12345 gb2312-
raw cp949 cp950 cp869 dingbats ksc5601 macCentEuro cp874 macUkraine
jis0201 gb2312 euc-cn euc-jp macThai iso8859-10 jis0208 iso2022-
jp macIceland iso2022 iso8859-13 jis0212 iso8859-14 iso8859-15
cp737 iso8859-16 big5 euc-kr macRomania macTurkish gb1988 iso2022-
kr macGreek ascii cp437 macRoman iso8859-1 iso8859-2 iso8859-3
macCroatian koi8-r iso8859-4 ebcdic iso8859-5 cp1250 macCyrillic
iso8859-6 cp1251 macDingbats koi8-u iso8859-7 cp1252 iso8859-8 cp1253
iso8859-9 cp1254 cp1255 cp850 cp1256 cp932 identity cp1257 cp852
macJapan cp1258 shiftjis utf-8 cp855 cp936 symbol cp775 unicode cp857

after proper configuration of encoding for the channel:
This file is encoded with UTF-8 and contains some Polish characters:
zażółć gęślą jaźń
```

The system encoding in this case is Cp1250, so the `cp1250.txt` file does not require any special action to be read properly. Ironically, when reading from a file in UTF-8, which is the core encoding for Tcl, the channel must be properly configured, otherwise the data is corrupted by incorrect conversion, as it is treated as encoded in Cp1250, not UTF-8. You can also see that the list of supported encodings is quite impressive.

Apart from altering configuration for the channel, Tcl also offers the possibility to convert a string to different encoding with the following commands:

encoding convertfrom *encodingName* **$string**

encoding convertto *encodingName* **$string**

The command syntax may strike you as confusing, but it is self explanatory; it always converts **from** *encodingName* to Unicode or from Unicode **to** *encodingName*. If the name of the encoding is omitted, the current default system encoding will be used. To clear up any confusion, let's illustrate it with one-liner example:

```
puts [encoding convertfrom cp1250 "za\xBF\xF3\xB3\xE6 g\xEA\x9C\xB9 ja\
x9F\xF1"]
```

In this code, \x and any following octal digits correspond to the appropriate character codes in Cp1250 standard, so the string is in Cp1250 encoding and after conversion it becomes UTF-8 encoded, which allows it to be printed correctly:

```
zażółć gęślą jaźń
```

In a similar way we can read the file `utf8.txt` mentioned earlier:

```
set channelId [open utf8.txt r]
fconfigure $channelId -encoding binary
set data [read $channelId]
puts [encoding convertfrom utf-8 $data]
```

Once the data is read in binary mode, it is treated as an array of bytes, so although the file content itself is encoded in UTF-8, `puts $data` would produce garbage, as each byte would be treated as separate character code, and in UTF-8 characters may be encoded in more than one byte. Usage of the `encoding convert from utf-8` command allows us to correctly decode the binary data into human readable content:

```
This file is encoded with UTF-8 and contains some Polish characters:
zażółć gęślą jaźń
```

In most cases Tcl does not have any problems with correct detection of system encoding. In the rare cases when it fails, it will fall back to ISO 8859-1. At any time you can retrieve the detected encoding with the command `encoding system`. There is also the possibility to force system encoding other than the detected one with `encoding system encodingName` command, but it is generally best not to alter this.

As mentioned earlier, by default Tcl reads files using system encoding. This is also true when it comes to loading additional scripts with `source` command, so generally it is advised that all script files should be encoded with the default system encoding.

When it comes to using some Unicode characters, you can always write them in the form *uxxxx*, where *xxxx* should be replaced with correct, four digit hexadecimal character Unicode code value.

If you have your Tcl script encoded in the format other than system one, you may use the following workaround (let's assume `script.tcl` file is encoded in UTF-8):

```
set channel [open script.tcl r]
fconfigure $channel -encoding utf-8
set script [read $channel]
close $channel
eval $script
```

What this does is read the content of file using correct encoding conversion into a variable, and next pass this variable to `eval` command.

Starting from Tcl 8.5, the `source` command may be instructed about the encoding of the file that is to be sourced. For example, to force our `script.tcl` file to be read as UTF-8 encoded, all we have to do is:

```
source -encoding utf-8 script.tcl
```

Translating your application into different languages

Tcl offers such a solution in the shape of the msgcat package (short for *message catalog*). The functionality it offers is so vital that the package is shipped with every Tcl interpreted since version 8.1. The manual may be found among the full documentation of Tcl—at the time of writing, the manual is located at http://www.tcl.tk/man/tcl8.5/TclCmd/msgcat.htm.

The basic concept is simple—you have to translate every string used in your application to the languages you are going to support. All translations should be stored in a directory (the name is your choice; in this chapter we assume it is *messages*). If a translation is missing, the untranslated source string will be used. For every language there should be one corresponding file with a .msg extension. The name of each file is directly related to the locale identifier for the language it contains. The following formats of locale identifier are supported:

- language_country_modifier—for example en_GB_Funky
- language_country—for example en_GB
- language—for example en

The language and country codes are defined in standards ISO-639 and ISO-3166, and the modifier may be a string of your choice. If there is more than one .msg file for given language, the best matching file is used. For example, if the system locale is "en_US", and we have both an en.msg and an en_US.msg files, the second one would be used. If only en.msg is present, then this file would be chosen as the best (and only) match.

Each of the translation files contains a set of calls to the command defining translations for every string used in your application. The command is:

```
::msgcat::mcset locale string translation
```

- locale parameter is in the same format as described earlier
- string is a source, untranslated string
- translation is a translated string; if the relevant translation has been is omitted, the source string will be used

In reality, each translation file will be evaluated as a normal Tcl script, so it should be encoded in UTF-8. For example, let's assume that we want to define translations for the Polish and Spanish languages. The `messages` directory will contain two files:

- `pl.msg`:

  `::msgcat::mcset pl "Hello World" "Witaj Świecie"`

- `es.msg`:

  `::msgcat::mcset es "Hello World" "Hola Mundo"`

Each of these contains a translation of "Hello World" string to the appropriate language.

To start using translations, all you have to do is load the translation with the command `::msgcat::mcload` *directory_name* (the parameter specifies directory where translations are located). Next, you use the `::msgcat::mc` *string* command, which will substitute *string* with appropriate translation.

The following example illustrates the usage of `msgcat` package:

```
package require msgcat

puts "system locale : [msgcat::mclocale]"
puts "system preferences: [msgcat::mcpreferences] \n"

foreach locale {pl_PL es en} {
    msgcat::mclocale $locale
    msgcat::mcload [file join [file dirname [info script]] messages]
    puts "current locale are: [msgcat::mclocale]"
    puts "current preferences are: [msgcat::mcpreferences]"
    puts "Translated message is: [::msgcat::mc "Hello World"]"
}
```

Basically the code sets each different locale: Polish, Spanish, and English, and allows verification that the string "Hello World" has been appropriately translated. The output of this example is:

```
system locale : pl
system preferences: pl {}

current locale are: pl_pl
current preferences are: pl_pl pl {}
Translated message is: Witaj Świecie
current locale are: es
current preferences are: es {}
Translated message is: Hola Mundo
current locale are: en
current preferences are: en {}
Translated message is: Hello World
```

The command `msgcat::mclocale` returns the current locale identifier (by default, system locale), but it can be also used to set a new locale, as depicted in the example. Note that after each change of the current locale, the command `::msgcat::mcload` must be called again, to find and load the matching translation file.

Another command, `msgcat::mcpreferences`, returns an ordered list (starting from the most specific) of locale identifiers that will be used to match the `.msg` file. As you can see, the preferences list for the locale `pl_PL` is: `pl_pl pl {}`, so the most preferred translation file would be `pl_pl.msg`, then `pl.msg` and finally no translation at all.

It is worth noting that the `msgcat` package is aware of namespaces. What this means is that translations from different namespaces are handled separately, which prevents possible side effects between different packages, which may arise if both packages were to try translating the same string to a different message. What is more, if the translation is not found in the current namespace, `msgcat` will search for it in the parent namespaces until the global namespace is reached. Here is an example of such a behavior — the content of translation file:

```
::msgcat::mcset pl "test message" "wiadomość testowa"
::msgcat::mcset pl "test message2" "wiadomość testowa2"
namespace eval ::test {
    ::msgcat::mcset pl "test message" "to jest wiadomość testowa"
}
```

Example code:

```
package require msgcat

msgcat::mclocale pl
msgcat::mcload [file join [file dirname [info script]] messages]

puts [::msgcat::mc "test message"]
puts [::msgcat::mc "test message2"]

namespace eval ::test {
    puts [::msgcat::mc "test message"]
    puts [::msgcat::mc "test message2"]
}
```

The output:

```
wiadomość testowa
wiadomość testowa2
to jest wiadomość testowa
wiadomość testowa2
```

As you can see, the *"test message"* translation will vary based on the namespace, and the translation of *"test message2"* is obtained from the global namespace, as the test namespace does not contain the definition for it.

It is worth noting that the `::msgcat:mc` command can accept additional parameters apart from the string to translate, and in such a case, the Tcl format command is used for parameter substitution. It also enables a different order of supplied values in the output string, as shown in the following example:

The translation:

```
::msgcat::mcset pl "January" "Styczeń"
::msgcat::mcset pl "date: the %d of %s" "Data: %2\$s, dnia %1\$d"
```

The code:

```
package require msgcat

foreach locale {pl en} {
    msgcat::mclocale $locale
    msgcat::mcload [file join [file dirname [info script]] messages]
    puts [::msgcat::mc "date: the %d of %s" 15 [::msgcat::mc January]]
}
```

The output clearly shows the different positions of the supplied arguments, depending on the locale:

```
Data: Styczeń, dnia 15
date: the 15 of January
```

Using SQL and databases in Tcl

It would be hard to talk about data storage and not mention relational databases. In this section, we will briefly review how Tcl interacts with different databases. We assume the reader is familiar with database concepts and SQL. If not, you can either skip this section, or learn about the topic from other sources first.

For demonstration purposes, in every database described, we will setup a database named *Bookstore* with the following tables and sample data:

```
CREATE DATABASE Bookstore

CREATE TABLE Books
(
title varchar(255),
```

```
isbn varchar(255),
PRIMARY KEY (isbn)
);

CREATE TABLE Persons
(
name varchar(255),
surname varchar(255),
CONSTRAINT pk PRIMARY KEY (name, surname)
);

CREATE TABLE Authors
(
book_id varchar(255),
name varchar(255),
surname varchar(255),
FOREIGN KEY (book_id) REFERENCES Books(isbn),
FOREIGN KEY (name, surname) REFERENCES Persons(name, surname)
);

INSERT INTO Persons VALUES ('Piotr','Beltowski');
INSERT INTO Persons VALUES ('Wojciech','Kocjan');

INSERT INTO Books VALUES ('Tcl Network Programming','978-1-849510-96-
7');
INSERT INTO Books VALUES ('Learning Nagios 3.0','978-1-847195-18-0');

INSERT INTO Authors VALUES ('978-1-847195-18-0', 'Wojciech','Kocjan');
INSERT INTO Authors VALUES ('978-1-849510-96-7', 'Wojciech','Kocjan');
INSERT INTO Authors VALUES ('978-1-849510-96-7', 'Piotr','Beltowski');
```

The structure of the tables and data are meant to reflect the current achievements of the authors of this book.

In the following sections we are going to discuss databases that can be divided into two general types:

- Client-server databases such as MySQL or PostgreSQL. In this case, the connection is done over network (in case of remote db) or local socket to the database server that is running as completely separate program. This solution is more flexible, but vulnerable to connectivity problems or low network performance that can really be a bottleneck. The main benefit is that the server where the database is running usually offers reasonable computing performance, so performing operations on large volume of data shouldn't be a problem. It also allows more efficient use of multiple applications using the same database.

- Embedded databases such as SQLite and mk4tcl. However, the latter does not support SQL and therefore is beyond the scope of this chapter. Such a database runs as a part of your application and is closed once you terminate the application. The data is usually stored in a local file or even in memory. This type of database is perfect for use when you are developing a standalone, single-user application.

Connecting to MySQL

MySQL is one of the most popular free databases. To work with it from Tcl, you can use the `mysqltcl` package that constitutes Tcl interface towards the database. The home page of this extension is located at http://www.xdobry.de/mysqltcl/index. html, and you can find the full manual here. Below we will briefly present how to use this package.

Assume that the database is installed on localhost, port 3306, the user name is *root* and the password is *toor*. To start working with it, we will first have to connect to it:

```
package require mysqltcl
```

```
set m [::mysql::connect -host localhost -port 3306 -user root -password toor]
```

The first line loads the package, the next one connects to the database using the `mysql::connect` command, and stores the connection handle in m variable for future usage. The options for the connecting command are rather self explanatory.

To select the database, use the `mysql::use` command with the handle and the DB name:

```
::mysql::use $m Bookstore
```

Assume we want to retrieve the details (title and ISBN number) of the books authored by Wojciech Kocjan. To facilitate this, first store the appropriate SQL query in the `query` variable:

```
set query "SELECT Books.title, Books.isbn FROM Books, Authors WHERE Authors.surname = 'Kocjan' AND Books.isbn = Authors.book_id"
```

To send the query to the server, we will use the `mysql::sel` function. This command is only for SELECT queries, and accepts the following parameters: the connection handle, the query string, and optionally:

- `-list` — this command will return the list of lists, where every list corresponds to one resulting row. For example:

```
puts [::mysql::sel $m $query -list]
```

  The preceding command will output:

```
{{Learning Nagios 3.0} 978-1-847195-18-0} {{Tcl Network
Programming} 978-1-849510-96-7}
```

- `-flatlist` — all rows will be concatenated into one single list:

```
puts [::mysql::sel $m $query -flatlist]
```

  And it returns:

```
{Learning Nagios 3.0} 978-1-847195-18-0 {Tcl Network Programming}
978-1-849510-96-7
```

  Such a list may be a perfectly suitable for use with a `foreach` statement, to iterate over the results.

If the third parameter is omitted, the resulting rows can be retrieved using the following commands:

- `mysql::fetch` — at every call to this command, retrieves one row of the result:

```
mysql::sel $m $query
while {[llength [set row [mysql::fetch $m]]]>0} {
    puts "[lindex $row 0] --> [lindex $row end]"
}
```

  And the output is:

```
Learning Nagios 3.0 --> 978-1-847195-18-0

Tcl Network Programming --> 978-1-849510-96-7
```

- `mysql::map` — this command maps every column from the resulting row to the variable and executes the provided script, from which these variables can be accessed. For example lets map the columns to variables named `title` and `isbn`, and then print them out:

```
mysql::sel $m $query
mysql::map $m [list title isbn] {
    puts "$title --> $isbn"
}
```

The result will be the same as in previous example:

```
Learning Nagios 3.0 --> 978-1-847195-18-0
Tcl Network Programming --> 978-1-849510-96-7
```

Both of these commands process one row at a time.

There is also another way to retrieve the result, with `mysql::receive`. The major difference is that this command does not buffer (cache) any data on the client side, but receives it directly from the server. This offers much better performance when a large number of results is received from the server.

When compared to `fetch` and `map`, it is not required to call `sel` first, as it accepts the query string directly:

```
mysql::receive $m $query [list title isbn] {
    puts "$title --> $isbn"
}
```

The output is identical to previous script. The command is very similar to `foreach` in the sense that it accepts a list of variables to assign values to.

If you would like to execute some SQL query other then SELECT, use `mysql::exec`:

```
::mysql::exec $m "INSERT INTO Persons VALUES ('John','Smith')"
::mysql::exec $m "INSERT INTO Authors VALUES ('978-1-849510-96-7',
'James T.','Kirk')"
```

This command returns the number of affected rows. The second call to the command will fail, as there is no record for *James T. Kirk* in the *Persons* table, so a foreign key constraint fails. To avoid execution interruption, you could use the appropriate `catch` clause.

Once you have finished working with the database, it is a good idea to disconnect and free the resources, by using the command:

```
mysql::close $m
```

Connecting to PostgreSQL

The support for *PostgreSQL* database is far better, than the support for *MySQL*, because we can choose from 2 available:

- The first one is `pgtcl` (http://pgtcl.projects.postgresql.org/), and its newer version `pgtcl-ng` (http://pgtclng.projects.postgresql.org/). This extension is built using native code, so you have to pick the correct version for your platform, or compile one from the source code. Once you do this, you will be rewarded with the high performance of this solution.

- The second extension is pgintcl (http://pgintcl.projects.postgresql.org/). This one is written in pure Tcl language, so it is portable and independent of the operating system and hardware you are using. Internally it uses TCP/IP protocol to connect to and carry on a dialogue with the database (so it is tightly related to the version of *PostgreSQL* protocol). The main disadvantage of this extension is its performance—it is slower than the previous extension, because native binary code will always perform better than Tcl-based code.

The good news is that both of these extensions share almost the same command set, so from the programmer's point of view there is almost no difference in usage. The first one, pgtcl, is loaded with:

```
package require Pgtcl
```

While to use pgintcl you have to call:

```
package require pgintcl
```

As usual, we are not going to duplicate the extension's manual it's already written by the extension's authors, and you can find it on appropriate homepages, but to make the reader aware of such a solution and get him familiar with it, we will be presenting the following example code:

```
package require pgintcl

set p [pg_connect -conninfo {dbname=bookstore host=127.0.0.1 port=5432
user=root password=toor}]

set query "SELECT Books.title, Books.isbn FROM Books, Authors WHERE
Authors.surname = 'Kocjan' AND Books.isbn = Authors.book_id"

pg_select $p $query result {
    puts "$result(title) --> $result(isbn)"
}

pg_execute -array result $p $query {
    puts "$result(title) --> $result(isbn)"
}

set handle [pg_exec $p "INSERT INTO Persons VALUES ('John','Smith')"]
puts [pg_result $handle -status]

set handle [pg_exec $p "INSERT INTO Authors VALUES ('978-1-849510-96-
7', 'James','T. Kirk')"]
puts [pg_result $handle -status]

pg_disconnect $p
```

In this case, we use `pgintcl`, but as mentioned before, you can easily switch to `pgtcl` by modifying the first line.

The example itself does the same operations as in case of the one presented in *MySQL* section.

First it connects to the database by calling `pg_connect`. The `-conninfo` argument specifies the list of connection options in form of *key=value* pairs. The full list of options may depend on version of the database, but the most common options are:

Key	Description
dbname	The name of the database to connect to
host	The host name or address where the server is running and listening for connections
port	The TCP port to connect to
user	The username used for the authorization
password	The user's password

If the values contain spaces, they should be entered in single quotes, following the typical escaping rules (\\ for \ and \' for ')

The next command, `pg_select`, is used to execute the query and work on the results. The command accepts the following attributes:

- The handle for the connection, returned by `pg_connect`
- The query string (this command accepts only SELECT queries)
- The name of the array, where the results of the query will be stored. Array keys are named after appropriate columns of returned rows.
- The script that will be executed for each row of the returned data. The script can be omitted, which makes sense in cases where only one row will be returned.

Next, another type of command — `pg_execute` — is used. The syntax is similar to the syntax of the previous command, but the order of arguments is different — first you have to specify the array name, which is done with `-array` argument. This command also accepts queries other than SELECT, and in such a case it simply returns the number of affected rows. In the case of a SELECT query, the (optional) script is executed for every row.

Once retrieving of the data is demonstrated, we attempt to execute some other types of query—in this case INSERT. To send a command to the database server, use the pg_exec command, with the handle and appropriate command string. The command returns another handle, this time to the result object, which can be further examined with the pg_result command. To use pg_result, you have specify the mentioned handle and which of the result attributes you would like to retrieve. For example, pg_result $handle -status will return the status (for other options, see the manual).

In our example the first INSERT query will succeed, and the next one will fail, which maps directly to the code's output:

```
Learning Nagios 3.0 --> 978-1-847195-18-0
Tcl Network Programming --> 978-1-849510-96-7
Learning Nagios 3.0 --> 978-1-847195-18-0
Tcl Network Programming --> 978-1-849510-96-7
PGRES_COMMAND_OK
PGRES_FATAL_ERROR
```

At the end, we close connection to the database server with pg_disconnect.

Using SQLite

SQLite is a free SQL database engine that has gained wide popularity among Tcl users. The reason for this is that it does not require installation or configuration, or dedicated server—you just start using it locally as an embedded database. It is fast, compact, efficient and very handy when it comes to rapid prototyping of the application, and this is the task which often happens in Tcl world. The details of SQLite can be found on its home webpage http://www.sqlite.org/.

What is particularly important from a Tcler's point of view is that *SQLite* was originally created as a Tcl extension, so it is supported in Tcl from the very beginning. It was meant to be very easy to use from Tcl code, and of course provides a comprehensive interface in terms of Tcl commands. As you will see, the usage is so simple that eventually even the most zealous antagonist will start using it as a default way to store application data.

To start using it, you have to load the appropriate package:

```
package require sqlite3
```

SQLite stores all data in database files. The file name can be anything, but by convention the extension for the file is .db. The following command connects to the file bookstore.db (or creates one if it does not exist) and defines the command named bs for handling the database from that file:

```
sqlite3 bs bookstore.db
```

Note that if you do not specify an absolute path to the file, it will be created in the current working directory of your Tcl interpreter. There is also the possibility to create and use a database that is stored in memory — in this case, instead of the filename, use `:memory:` as the name.

Once the database is opened, it is accessible via the command defined in the opening call; in our example the command is `bs`. Note that you have complete freedom in choosing the command name. What is more, you can open the same database more than once, each one with different command. You can consider a command name as the equivalent of a connection handle. Such a command provides a set of methods, where the most important is named `eval`. This method allows executing SQL queries on the database. The syntax is as follows:

`bs eval sqlQuery ?arrayName? ?script?`

- `sqlQuery` is a string containing an SQL query. Usually it is put in curly brackets {} to avoid Tcl substitution, because SQLite has the unique feature of understanding Tcl variables, so even though the variable will not be substituted by Tcl interpreter, the database engine will replace it properly with the correct value.

- `arrayName` is an optional name of the array where the columns from each result row will be stored (see the example below). Column names are used as array keys. Note that not every SQL query must return results.

- `script` is an optional Tcl script that will be executed for each result row.

Using the `eval` method is simple. For example to create a table called *Books*, all you need to do is:

```
bs eval {
    CREATE TABLE Books
    (
    title varchar(255),
    isbn varchar(255),
    PRIMARY KEY (isbn)
    );
}
```

Of course all SQL commands could be placed in a single `bs eval` call. In the rest of this paragraph we assume that `bookstore.db` database is populated with the example SQL structures presented at the beginning. Note that by default *SQLite* does not honor `FOREIGN KEY` constraints, and it must be enabled (the best option is to do it right after opening database) with the command:

`bs eval {PRAGMA foreign_keys = ON;}`

If the SQL query does return some results, the `eval` method will return a flat Tcl list containing all result records, suitable for using in a `foreach` loop:

```
set query "SELECT Books.title, Books.isbn FROM Books, Authors WHERE
Authors.surname = 'Kocjan' AND Books.isbn = Authors.book_id"
puts [bs eval $query]
```

The result from this query is as follows:

```
{Learning Nagios 3.0} 978-1-847195-18-0 {Tcl Network Programming} 978-
1-849510-96-7
```

The following illustrates how to use a script passed as additional argument for `eval`:

```
bs eval $query {
    puts "$title --> $isbn"
}
```

The script contained in {} is executed for every row. To access the returned data, use the variables named after appropriate column names. Note that instead of column names, identifiers specified with the SQL keyword *AS* can be used:

```
set query2 "SELECT Books.title AS TheTitle, Books.isbn AS ISBN_Number
FROM Books, Authors WHERE Authors.surname = 'Kocjan' AND Books.isbn =
Authors.book_id"
bs eval $query2 {
    puts "$TheTitle --> $ISBN_Number"
}
```

Using the array name is also trivial:

```
bs eval $query result {
    puts "$result(title) --> $result(isbn)"
}
```

In this case, the array name is `result`, and the keys for the array are named `title` and `isbn`. In all three examples, the output produced will be the same:

```
Learning Nagios 3.0 --> 978-1-847195-18-0
Tcl Network Programming --> 978-1-849510-96-7
```

As mentioned before, `eval` handles any SQL query, for example a query of type INSERT:

```
bs eval {INSERT INTO Persons VALUES ('John','Smith')}
```

In the case of such queries, `eval` does not return any value, but it can throw an error. For example, if the presented line were called second time, the PRIMARY KEY constraint would cause a failure, resulting in:

```
columns name, surname are not unique
    while executing
"bs eval {INSERT INTO Persons VALUES ('John','Smith')}"
```

As usual, such Tcl errors can be handled programmatically by using a `catch` command.

SQLite's origins in Tcl brings interesting feature — you are able to use Tcl variables directly in SQL queries:

```
set a 2
set b 3
set c "1+1"

puts [bs eval {SELECT $a + $b, $c}]
```

This will output: 5 1+1

When a query is put in curly braces, variables are not expanded by Tcl, but SQLite is able to map them to Tcl variables — its one of the reasons why SQLite3 is so popular in the Tcl world.

To close the database, use the `close` method:

```
bs close
```

As a result, the command controlling the database — in this case `bs` — is also deleted.

Managing databases from SQLiteStudio

SQLite database is so popular among Tcl users that a group of management tools aimed to facilitate the daily work were created. We would like to present one of them - *SQLiteStudio*, created by Pawel Salawa, available at `http://sqlitestudio.one.pl/`. Why do we mention this particular tool? It is a free, advanced, GUI based, cross-platform database manager, written in Tcl and offered in the form of a single standalone executable binary file (thanks to Starpack technology). What is more, you can easily download the source code and analyze it. *SQLiteStudio* offers you a number of features:

* Open an existing database file or create new one
* View and modify the structure of a database, for example to add new tables

- Display and modify (add, delete, edit) data values stored in the database
- Work with triggers, views and indexes

For illustration, in the below screenshot the `bookstore.db` database is loaded into *SQLiteStudio*, and data from table *Books* is displayed:

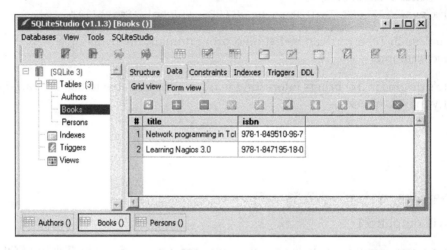

Other databases

There are of course a lot of other database engines, and the majority of them have some kind of Tcl bindings—for example `Oratcl` for Oracle or `db2tcl` for DB2. We should also keep in mind that Tcl world has another interesting database solution—Metakit, described in Chapter 3.

The last thing to mention is that you are also able to use ODBC data sources, by using `tclodbc` extension (`http://sourceforge.net/projects/tclodbc/`). It is supported for Unix and Windows, and allows you to connect to any database management system that provides ODBC interface.

Handling XML in Tcl

This section assumes that the reader is familiar with terms like XML, DOM, SAX, XPath and others related.

Just as with almost every modern programming language, Tcl offers comprehensive set of tools designed to facilitate the use of the XML standard. Basically Tcl is born to work with XML, thanks to native support for Unicode encoding. There are a lot of extensions for handling XML documents, but without a doubt one of the most important is tDOM (http://www.tdom.org). The power of this extension comes from the fact it is implemented in C language, therefore it is fast and efficient, with reasonable memory consumption; the extension supports XPath, XSLT and optional DTD validation. From a practical point of view it is also easy to get, as it is included in the *ActiveTcl* distribution.

The name of this extension clearly indicates that it works as an XML Document Object Model (DOM) parser. In other words, the document is treated as a tree-like structure. While we will focus on DOM, it is worth noting that tDOM is also able to act like an event-driven, SAX parser.

Across this section, we will use the following example XML document that pretends to define this book:

```
<?xml version="1.0" encoding="UTF-8"?>
<books>
    <book isbn="978-1-849510-96-7">
    <title>Tcl Network Programming</title>
    <authors>
            <author>Piotr Bełtowski</author>
            <author>Wojciech Kocjan</author>
    </authors>
    </book>
</books>
```

The document is saved in test.xml file. We do not intend to replicate the comprehensive tDOM manual available on the website, but rather to give a taste of using tDOM.

To start working with tDOM, we have to load the package first:

```
package require tdom
```

Next it is time to parse the XML document, which will affect the creation of complete DOM tree in the memory, using the dom parse command:

```
set channel [open test.xml]
fconfigure $channel -encoding utf-8
set doc [dom parse [read $channel]]
close $channel
```

As the `test.xml` file is encoded in UTF-8, the input channel must be correctly configured. The basic syntax of the `parse` command is `dom parse $xml`, where `xml` is the variable that holds the entire xml document. This command is also able to read directly from the channel (the encoding must still be configured correctly):

```
set doc [dom parse -channel $channel]
```

The command returns a Tcl command object (stored in `doc`) that provides a wide set of methods allowing interaction with the DOM document object that was created as a result of the parse action. The methods can be called according to pattern: `$doc` *methodName ?arg …?*

There is a convenient wrapper method `tDOM::xmlReadFile` that automatically handles encoding and some often annoying actions such as closing channels. The previous code sample can be expressed in one line:

```
set doc [dom parse [tDOM::xmlReadFile open.xml]]
```

As mentioned before, the DOM object is a tree-like structure, and the basic term is a *node*. Essentially, every XML tag in the document will be mapped to a corresponding node. By calling the appropriate commands on a DOM object (referred via `$doc`) you are able to get Node command object(s) that will allow direct interaction with nodes (again with the appropriate methods set). For example, let's inspect the authors of the book:

```
set authors [$doc getElementsByTagName authors]

puts "<authors> has child nodes: [$authors hasChildNodes]"
set author [$authors firstChild]
puts [[$author firstChild] nodeValue]
set author [$author nextSibling]
puts [[$author firstChild] nodeValue]
```

First, we retrieve all nodes having the name *authors*. In this case it is only one element, but more generally the command `$doc getElementsByTagName` *tagName* would return a Tcl list of elements. From this moment `$authors` refers to the `<authors>` node, and we are able to execute on it methods appropriate for nodes:

- `hasChildNodes` returns the boolean value 0 or 1 depending on the whether the node has child nodes
- `firstChild` returns the first child node of the node the method is executed on
- `nodeValue` returns the value of the node
- `nextSibling` returns the next sibling node to the node the method is executed on

It is important to note that the first `$author` value corresponds to *<author>Piotr Bełtowski</author>*, and [`$author firstChild`] returns a text node from its insides, which contains the text *"Piotr Bełtowski"*. Knowing all that, it is not a surprise that the output thus far is:

```
<authors> has child nodes: 1
Piotr Bełtowski
Wojciech Kocjan
```

The method `nodeValue` allows us not only to get the value, but also to set a new one:

```
[[$authors firstChild] firstChild] nodeValue "John Smith"
```

To verify that the value has been changed, let's print the authors again but in a different way:

```
foreach author [$authors childNodes] {
        puts [[$author firstChild] nodeValue]
}
```

As expected, the output is:

John Smith

Wojciech Kocjan

The method `childNodes` returns a list of child nodes, so it is made to iterate over it.

The node can be deleted:

```
[$authors lastChild] delete
```

So now the list of authors will be shorter:

```
set authors [$doc selectNodes /books/book/authors]
foreach author [$authors childNodes] {
        puts [[$author firstChild] nodeValue]
}
```

This time in the command: `$doc selectNodes xpathQuery` we used XPath expression /books/book/authors" to address all (in this case there is only one) `<authors>` elements.

Describing the XPath syntax is out of the scope of this book, but for quick introduction here are some examples:

Xpath expression	Result
/	Selects the root node
/tag	Selects the root node element(s) "tag"
/tag1/tag2	Selects all "tag2" elements that are direct children of the root node "tag1" element
//tag	Selects all "tag" element no matter of their real position in the document
/tag/text()	Selects the text content from all "tag" root node elements; in this case the value is returned instead of XML node

For more information visit `http://en.wikipedia.org/wiki/XPath` or read the tutorial at `http://www.w3schools.com/XPath/xpath_syntax.asp`.

The same result can be achieved more easily by directly addressing the appropriate text nodes:

```
set authorNames [$doc selectNodes \
/books/book/authors/author/text()]
foreach authorName $authorNames {
        puts [$authorName nodeValue]
}
```

In both cases, the output is the same:

`John Smith`

Talking about XPath, its syntax is completely normal, with one remark that square brackets [] have a special meaning in Tcl, so they have to be escaped correctly.

Thus far we have learned how to modify or remove nodes, so let's add some new authors:

```
set element [$doc createElement author]
$element appendChild [$doc createTextNode "Jean-Luc Picard"]
$authors appendChild $element
```

The method `$doc createElement` *elementName* creates an element of the given name — in this case the name is "author". Next, we create a text node with the content "Jean-Luc Picard" using `$doc createTextNode` *text* method. The text node is appended to the *author* element, and the element is finally added as a child of <*authors*>.

The tDOM package offers many ways to achieve the same result, and for example the author could be added using much shorter, but not so elegant way:

```
$authors appendXML "<author>James T. Kirk</author>"
```

appendXML takes a raw XML string as an input argument, parses it and creates an appropriate DOM sub-tree that is subsequently merged into the main document tree.

To verify that the authors were added we could again print the list of names, but this time let's convert entire DOM tree back to an XML document using asXML method:

```
puts [$doc asXML]
```

And the result is indeed:

```
<books>
    <book isbn="978-1-849510-96-7">
        <title>Tcl Network Programming</title>
        <authors>
            <author>John Smith</author>
            <author>Jean-Luc Picard</author>
            <author>James T. Kirk</author>
        </authors>
    </book>
</books>
```

XML elements do not only have a value, but it also may have attributes. The corresponding node command object offers the following methods to handle them:

- `$node attributes` — returns the list of all attributes existing for node `$node`
- `$node hasAttribute` *attributeName* — returns the Boolean value 0 or 1 depending on whether the attribute of name *attributeName* exists for the node `$node`
- `$node getAttribute` *attributeName ?defaultValue?* — returns the attribute value. The command will fail if the attribute does not exist, unless it is provided with a *defaultValue* that would be returned in this case.
- `$node setAttribute` *attributeName value* — sets the new value of the attribute. This command will create the attribute if it does not already exist.
- `$node removeAttribute` *attributeName* — removes the attribute.

Knowing this, we can play with book's attributes:

```
set book [$doc selectNodes /books/book]
if {[$book hasAttribute isbn]} {
    puts [$book getAttribute isbn]
}
puts [$book getAttribute notExisting "attribute not defined!"]
$book setAttribute year 2010
```

First the code will print out the value of the *isbn* attribute, and then it will attempt to get the value of the *notExisting* attribute, resulting in the output:

```
978-1-849510-96-7
```

```
attribute not defined!
```

Finally, it creates a new *year* attribute, so `puts [$doc asXML]` will now write:

```
<books>
    <book isbn="978-1-849510-96-7" year="2010">
        <title>Tcl Network Programming</title>
        <authors>
            <author>John Smith</author>
            <author>Jean-Luc Picard</author>
            <author>James T. Kirk</author>
        </authors>
    </book>
</books>
```

Memory conservation may be a goal, particularly in case of large XML documents, so once we finish working with the DOM document object, we should always delete it and free the memory it was using:

```
$doc delete
```

Until now we were working on an existing XML document, but we already know how to programmatically create nodes. The following example shows how to build the *text.xml* file from the scratch:

```
package require tdom

set doc [dom createDocument books]
set root [$doc documentElement]
set book [$doc createElement book]
$book setAttribute isbn "978-1-849510-96-7"

set title [$doc createElement title]
$title appendChild [$doc createTextNode "Tcl Network Programming"]
$book appendChild $title

set authors [$doc createElement authors]
$book appendChild $authors
set authorNames [list "Piotr Bełtowski" "Wojciech Kocjan"]

foreach authorName $authorNames {
    set author [$doc createElement author]
```

```
    $author appendChild [$doc createTextNode $authorName]
    $authors appendChild $author
}

$root appendChild $book
set channel [open test.xml w]
fconfigure $channel -encoding utf-8
$doc asXML -channel $channel
close $channel
```

The code is pretty self explanatory, similar to parse method, asXML can also produce output to the channel specified with -channel. While looking at this code sample, you have probably noticed that it is not too readable when it comes to being able to quickly determine what the produced XML will be. Luckily, there is far more legible alternative:

```
package require tdom

set doc [dom createDocument books]
set root [$doc documentElement]

dom createNodeCmd elementNode book
dom createNodeCmd elementNode title
dom createNodeCmd elementNode authors
dom createNodeCmd elementNode author
dom createNodeCmd textNode text

$root appendFromScript {
    book -isbn "978-1-849510-96-7" {
            title {text "Tcl Network Programming"}
            authors {
                    author {text "Piotr Bełtowski"}
                    author {text "Wojciech Kocjan"}
            }
}}
puts [$doc asXML]
```

What we do here is to use dom createNode *nodeType commandName* command. As a result, a special Tcl command named after *commandName* is defined. When used, such a command will generate a DOM node of type *nodeType*, named after *commandName*. The most common node types are:

- elementNode — will create normal DOM node

- textNode — will create text node

- commentNode — responsible for creating a comment

The created command cannot be used anywhere in the code, but only in a script supplied for the $node appendFromScript *script* method.

The invocation of every created command for element node is simple: it may take zero or more pairs of attribute names and values (the attribute name may be, but does not require, preceded by '-' character) and an optional Tcl script that may create the node's content and must be in the format accepted by appendFromScript method, as this will be recursively called. Commands generating text or comment nodes are simpler, as they accept only the text data to be inserted into it.

For example, a call to: author {text "Wojciech Kocjan"} will cause the creation of a text node, that will be appended as a child of *<author>* node, resulting in *<author>Wojciech Kocjan</author>*.

The result of both code samples described above is identical:

```
<books>
    <book isbn="978-1-849510-96-7">
        <title>Tcl Network Programming</title>
        <authors>
            <author>Piotr Bełtowski</author>
            <author>Wojciech Kocjan</author>
        </authors>
    </book>
</books>
```

But the readability of the second example is better, especially when correct indentation is preserved in appendFromScript script argument.

tDOM is capable of parsing HTML documents (that are often not compliant with XML specification). To achieve it, use -html option for parse command. For example, the HTML code for www.google.com in Poland is rather simple:

```
<HTML><HEAD><meta http-equiv="content-type" content="text/
html;charset=utf-8">
<TITLE>302 Moved</TITLE></HEAD><BODY>
<H1>302 Moved</H1>
The document has moved
<A HREF="http://www.google.pl/">here</A>.
</BODY></HTML>
```

And using the following code (the http package is described in Chapter 7):

```
package require tdom
package require http

set html [http::data [http::geturl "http://www.google.com"]]
set doc [dom parse -html $html]
puts [$doc asXML]
```

We are able to parse it, effectively obtaining the following XML document:

```
<html>
    <head>
        <meta http-equiv="content-type" content="text/
html;charset=utf-8"/>
        <title>302 Moved</title>
    </head>
    <body>
        <h1>302 Moved</h1>

The document has moved
<a href="http://www.google.pl/">here</a>
.

    </body>
</html>
```

The attempt to do the same without the -html option would cause an error:

```
error "mismatched tag" at line 2 character 26
">302 Moved</TITLE></H <--Error-- EAD><BODY>
<H1>302 Moved</H1>
The docum"
    while executing
"dom parse  $html"
    invoked from within
"set doc [dom parse  $html]"
```

The functionality of parsing HTML may be really helpful in terms of network programming—you can easily imagine a situation where you want to grab some information from a web page. A combination of tDOM and appropriate XPath queries may work some miracles, while the code will be less than brief. The following example will display links returned from a search for the 'tDOM' key word using the Bing search engine:

```
package require tdom
package require http

set token [http::geturl "http://www.bing.com/search?q=tDOM"]
set html [http::data $token]
http::cleanup $token
set doc [dom parse -html $html]

foreach node [$doc selectNodes //div/h3/a\[@href\]] {
    puts [$node getAttribute href]
}
```

And as we expect, the output is:

```
http://www.tdom.org/
http://tdom.com/
http://www.tdom.org/domDoc.html
http://www.phpclasses.org/browse/package/5690.html
http://packages.qa.debian.org/t/tdom.html
http://acronyms.thefreedictionary.com/TDOM
http://groups.yahoo.com/group/tdom/
http://www.ohloh.net/p/tdom
http://packages.debian.org/tdom
http://packages.debian.org/unstable/interpreters/tdom
```

As we only outlined the usage of the tDOM package, for more details please consult the manual (http://www.tdom.org) and freely available examples on the Web, especially on the Tcl wiki webpage (http://wiki.tcl.tk).

It is worth noting that there is another popular package for processing XML documents, named TclXML (http://tclxml.sourceforge.net). The functionality it offers is comparable to tDOM's, some elements of TclXML are written in pure Tcl, and that may be considered as a merit when it comes to supporting some platforms where C-based tDOM may not be available. On the other hand, tDOM has key features such as superior performance and lower memory consumption that can not be overestimated.

Storing raw Tcl values

In some cases, you may decide not to use any additional packages, yet you will need to save some data for future usage. In Tcl, it is easy to store data structures like lists or dictionaries in flat text file.

First, let's demonstrate how to write to and read from a list:

```
set book1 [list {Learning Nagios 3.0} 978-1-847195-18-0]
set book2 [list {Tcl Network Programming} 978-1-849510-96-7]
set books [list $book1 $book2]

puts [lindex [lindex $books end] 0]

set channel [open data.txt w]
puts $channel $books
close $channel
```

```
set channel [open data.txt r]
set books [read $channel]
close $channel

puts [lindex [lindex $books end] 0]
```

books variable is a list of two lists, each one containing the title and ISBN number, respectively. Before saving, we print out the name of the second book. Then, the $books is written to data.txt file, and in the next lines its contents are read and stored again into the books variable. It is the unique Tcl feature that allows treating lists as normal text strings and vice versa, therefore after reading the file we are able to access the variable in a list-like way and print the same title again, for verification:

```
Tcl Network Programming
Tcl Network Programming
```

Next, let's do the same thing, but with a dictionary object:

```
dict set books book1 title {Learning Nagios 3.0}
dict set books book1 isbn 978-1-847195-18-0
dict set books book2 title {Tcl Network Programming}
dict set books book2 isbn 978-1-849510-96-7

puts [dict get $books book2 title]
set channel [open data2.txt w]
puts $channel $books
close $channel

set channel [open data2.txt r]
set books [read $channel]
close $channel

puts [dict get $books book2 title]
```

Thanks to Tcl's way of internally treating of structures like lists or dictionaries, no additional conversion or serialization is required. As you can see, the procedure is identical, basically puts and read commands handle all the storage issues. In this case, the output is identical as in previous example:

Tcl Network Programming

Tcl Network Programming

Limitations

Note that such a way of storing and retrieving data works only with text information. If you have some other kind of data in your list, for example handles to objects, its meaning would be lost.

Encoding

We did not mention encoding in this section, it will not be necessary if you are using only one platform. If you are aiming for cross platform portability, we recommend the following configuration of the channel:

```
fconfigure $channel -translation lf -encoding binary
```

Another option is to set encoding to utf-8, which will preserve all Unicode data as well as binary data. For example:

```
fconfigure $channel -translation lf -encoding utf-8
```

Summary

After this chapter, topics related to text data storage and processing should not be a mystery for you any more. In particular, you have learned:

- How to handle different text encoding, dependent on the region you live in, and how to create a multi-language, internationalized application with msgcat package.

- How to work with SQL databases based on the example of *MySQL* and *PostgreSQL*. We learned how to access these databases, then we focused on *SQLite*, as it is a particularly interesting solution, thanks to its ease of use and the powerful features it offers.

- At the end, the last important topic was covered—how to work with XML data in terms of Tcl language. We presented how to parse and access information of your choice from an XML document, thanks to the tDOM package. Next, we also mentioned how to create such a document from the scratch, and additionally, how to use tdom to access HTML data.

All the chapters up to this moment constitute solid base for the main objective of the book—network programming in Tcl. The next and all remaining chapters are directly related to this topic, gradually introducing you to more advanced networking concepts.

6
Networking in Tcl

This chapter covers fundamental topics related to networking in the Tcl language, with a focus on the TCP and UDP protocols. It outlines the basic abilities offered by Tcl, and the following chapters will gradually approach more advanced topics. The entire subject is far too extensive to be described in one book. We assume the reader has basic knowledge of these protocols and IP networking in general, and is familiar with core concepts such as *client*, *server*, *peer*, *connection*, and other similar ones.

The importance of network programming cannot be underestimated nowadays. Even if your application does not interact with the network directly, there is a set of tasks or features such as checking the online availability of the updates that implies the 'network awareness' of your software. The programming language you are going to use to develop this software should allow the handling of network operations in an easy and convenient fashion, and yes, Tcl is such a language, as it fits in well with the Internet philosophy.

In general, reading or writing from/to a file and sending/receiving data over/from the network are similar concepts, because of the universal abstract concept of *channels*. When you open a file in Tcl, you operate on the channel leading to that file—you read data **from** that channel, and write **to** that channel. When you open a TCP connection to the server, you also get a channel that is essentially identical in usage; you can also read **from** and write **to** it. Moreover, for all types of channels, you use the same set of commands such as puts, gets or read. This is the beauty of the Tcl architecture that makes networking so simple.

Of course, some differences must occur, as the underlying devices are significantly different between a file on the disk and the connection over a network. This chapter is going to present how to deal with such network communication.

In this chapter, we will learn about:

- Tcl native support for TCP—starting from most basic usage, more advanced items like nonblocking sockets along with event programming are presented. A separate section is dedicated to issues related to correct error handling, because in case of network communication, such situations are not rare. Finally, networking using threads is discussed.

- Programming based on UDP protocol is presented on the basis of the TclUDP package. You will be able to get acquainted with both its similarities to and its differences from TCP programming, with the focus on avoiding possible pitfalls.

This chapter contains simple yet practical examples that not only illustrate the presented topics, but also form a good starting ground for further implementation of the network-related part of your application. As usual, we strongly encourage the reader not to settle for these examples, but to actively search for more examples over the Internet and write his/her own, as this is the best practical way to gain experience about the topic.

We will focus on the TCP and UDP protocols, but the Tcl architecture makes it extremely easy to operate on any protocol thanks to the ease with which it can be extended by additional packages. Support for UDP is a good example here, because it is provided by an external extension named TclUDP. By default, only TCP handling is built into the core of the Tcl interpreter.

Using TCP sockets

TCP communication forms the basis of modern networking, so it is no surprise that we will start with it. The basic Tcl command to use in this topic is socket, and it is built into the Tcl interpreter core. A **socket** is an abstract term representing the endpoint of a bidirectional connection across the network. In this chapter, we will often use the terms *socket* and *channel* interchangeably, although the channel term is more general (not every channel is a socket, but every socket is a channel). We do this because the execution of socket will result in using channels—the effect of executing this command is usually opening the connection over the TCP protocol (socket supports only TCP) and returning a channel identifier, which may be used for sending or receiving data through that newly created channel, in terms of commands like read or puts. The command may be used in two flavors in order to create client-side or server-side sockets.

Client sockets serve as the connection opened from a client application to a server of your choice. On the contrary, a server socket does not connect to anything by itself, its primary task is to listen for incoming connections. Such connections will be accepted automatically, and a new channel will be created for each of them, enabling communication to each of the connecting clients.

Let's explain the details of TCP networking based on simple, yet working example code consisting of two parts: a server and a client.

Creating server sockets

First look at the server code stored in the `server.tcl` file:

```
socket -server serverProc 9876
puts "server started and waiting for connections..."

proc serverProc {channelId clientAddress clientPort} {
    puts "connection accepted from $clientAddress:$clientPort"
    puts "server socket details: [fconfigure $channelId -sockname]"
    puts "peer socket details: [fconfigure $channelId -peername]"
    after 5000 set cont 1; vwait cont

    puts $channelId "thank you for connecting to our server!"
    close $channelId
}
vwait forever
```

To create the listening socket, you have to use the `socket` command in the following format:

`socket -server procedureName ?options? port`

The last argument is the value of the port on which the server will listen for connections. Throughout this chapter, the value 9876 will be used. Before this value, you can use optional parameters. To be more specific, only one option is available: `-myaddr address`, and it can be used if the computer where you run your server program has more than one IP interface, so you can specify on which IP address the server should accept connections.

The first parameter is the name of the command that will be called once a new connection is established. In our example, this procedure is called `serverProc`. The procedure has to accept *three* arguments: the **identifier of the channel** which can be used to send or receive data to/from the client program, the client IP **address**, and the **port**.

The procedure `serverProc` first prints out some details about the client — its IP address and port. Next, it prints information about the server and client sockets, illustrating the usage of `fconfigure` command (described later in this paragraph). After this, some time-consuming data processing is simulated, by forcing the execution to be suspended for 5 seconds. After that time, it writes a 'thank you' message to the channel, effectively sending it to the client and closing the channel (and thereby, a TCP network connection).

The server socket will listen for the connection only when the Tcl event loop is enabled (otherwise, the the program would end), so the last line enters the event loop with the `vwait forever` command.

The typical output produced by that code is:

```
c:\tcl_book\chapter6\TCPsockets\firstExample>tclsh85 server.tcl
server started and waiting for connections...
connection accepted from 127.0.0.1:1234
server socket details: 127.0.0.1 localhost 9876
peer socket details: 127.0.0.1 localhost 1234
```

As you can see, the server socket details returned by `fconfigure $channelId - sockname` reflect the actual configuration of that socket.

Note that the port from which client connection comes is generally random. In this case it was forced to 1234, however. You can also see that both the server and client were executed on the same machine, effectively using 127.0.0.1 as the IP address.

Connecting over TCP

The client code, saved in `client.tcl` file, is as follows:

```
set serverChannel [socket -myport 1234 localhost 9876]
set startTime [clock seconds]
puts "client socket details: [fconfigure $serverChannel -sockname]"
puts "peer socket details: [fconfigure $serverChannel -peername]"
puts [read $serverChannel]
puts "execution has been blocked for [expr [clock seconds] -
$startTime] seconds"
close $serverChannel
```

First let's present the output produced by this client code:

```
c:\tcl_book\chapter6\TCPsockets\firstExample >tclsh85 client.tcl
client socket details: 127.0.0.1 localhost 1234
peer socket details: 127.0.0.1 localhost 9876
thank you for connecting to our server!
execution has been blocked for 5 seconds
```

What happens in the client code is that in the first line we create a TCP connection towards the `localhost:9876` socket and save the channel reference in the `serverChannel` variable. We also store the current time (expressed in seconds) to calculate how long we had to wait for the answer from the server. The code prints out some details about the connection. In general, `fconfigure` allows us to get/set various options for a channel. As the types of channels may be very different (the `vs.network` file), at first glance, the task seems to be impossible. The beauty of this command is that although it operates on an abstract term of channels, depending on the underlying type, it supports a wide set of options. In the case of network channels, the command has new configuration options:

- `-sockname` — returns the details about the 'closer' end of the connection, that is about the socket used by the client: the IP address, the name of the host, and the number of the port. The data is returned as a three-element list. In this example, the client connects to the server from the port 1234, because this value was forced along with the `-myport` option for the `socket` command. In general, if this option is omitted, its value would be randomly chosen by the operating system.

- `-peername` — similar to previous option, but the data returned is related to second end of the connection. We can see that we are indeed connected to port 9876, the same one where the server is listening for connections. This option can not be used on the channel identifier returned directly by the `socket -server` command, as it is not connected to anything and cannot be used to send or receive any data — it will only listen for incoming connections.

- `-error` — returns the current error status for the connection. If there is no error, an empty string is returned.

Next, we read data from the network connection as we would do for any other type of channel — in this case, using the `read` command. This command reads all the data until the end-of-file marker (in this case, caused by `close $channelId` being executed on the server's side).

As we know, the server waits for 5 seconds before sending any answer. This effectively causes blocking of the entire client application, because execution hangs at the `read` command waiting for the data. In many cases such a behavior is unacceptable; therefore an alternative was introduced — nonblocking sockets.

Using nonblocking sockets

The concept of a nonblocking socket is rather simple—instead of executing the command that would wait for (and therefore block), and eventually read the data, you just register a procedure that should be called when there is some data to be read (in other words, when the channel becomes readable). It is the duty of the underlying nonblocking I/O subsystem to call this procedure. The advantages are obvious—your code does not block, is more responsive (which is crucial in the case of GUI-based applications) and may do some other work in the meantime. It can also handle multiple connections at the same time. As for the drawbacks, the code may become a bit more complicated, but this is not something you could not handle.

First, let's modify the server code a little:

```
socket -server serverProc 9876
puts "server started and waiting for connections..."

proc serverProc {channelId clientAddress clientPort} {
    after 5000 set cont 1; vwait cont

    puts -nonewline $channelId "12345"
    flush $channelId
    after 5000 set cont 1; vwait cont
    puts $channelId "6789"
    flush $channelId
    after 5000 set cont 1; vwait cont
    puts  $channelId "thank you for connecting to our server!"
    close $channelId
}
vwait forever
```

Now it returns 2 lines, wherein the first line is produced in two phases—first it sends *12345*, but without the end-of-line character (the -nonewline option for puts), and after 5 seconds, the rest of line *6789*. Following that it sends the line identical to the earlier one (also without the newline character), and closes the connection. Each time, the flush command is executed to make sure the data is sent—otherwise, the data could be buffered. Effectively, it takes 15 seconds to finish sending the data, and we would like to have client code that will not be blocked for that long.

The following is the client-side code that will not be blocked, due to usage of event programming:

```
set serverChannel [socket -async localhost 9876]
fconfigure $serverChannel -blocking 0
fileevent $serverChannel readable [list readData $serverChannel]
```

```
proc readData {serverChannel} {
    global end
    set startTime [clock seconds]
    set data [read $serverChannel]
    if {[eof $serverChannel]} {
        close $serverChannel
        set end 1
        break
    }
    puts "read: $data"
    puts "execution has been blocked for [expr [clock seconds] -
    $startTime] seconds"

}
vwait end
```

The first line is almost identical to that of the previous example, with the difference that the `-async` option is used. This option causes the `socket` command to not wait until the connection is established, and to exit immediately. This may matter in the case of slow, overloaded networks.

The next line causes the channel to be switched from the default *blocking* mode to *nonblocking*. In this mode, the command operating on this channel will not block—for example `read` will return only the data that is available at the moment in the input buffer, without waiting for the "end of the file" notification. The nonblocking mode will only make sense when Tcl enters the event loop, which is why the last line calls `vwait end`, effectively causing the interpreter to wait until the `end` variable is written.

Handling channel events

Once we know that reading commands will not wait for data, there must be another way to cause the client to react once the data is available. The `fileevent` command is useful for achieving this. By using this command, you can have your code executed only when some event related to the channel occurs. The command accepts the following as parameters:

- The channel identifier
- `writable` or `readable`, corresponding to the appropriate event
- The code to execute once that event has occurred:

  ```
  fileevent $serverChannel readable [list readData $serverChannel]
  ```

For example, the preceding code causes the `readData` command to be executed always when the channel becomes readable, that is, when there is some data to be read from it.

Handling the `writable` event is important when creating the socket with the `-async` option. As mentioned before, the `socket` command will end immediately, and the socket creation may be delayed (due to some network operations). Therefore, once it is ready to transmit your data, you will be notified with that event.

The `readData` command reads the data using the `read` command, calculates the time spent on this task, and if the channel was closed, also correctly closes this side of the channel and sets the `end` variable to `1`, which causes the client code to leave the event loop and end as a result.

The closure of the channel is detected using the `eof` command — `eof $serverChannel` returns `1` if the *end of file* event occurred during the most recently read operation on the channel.

The output from this client-side code is:

```
c:\tcl_book\chapter6\TCPsockets\firstExample>tclsh85 client_async1.tcl
read: 12345
execution has been blocked for 0 seconds
read: 6789

execution has been blocked for 0 seconds
read: thank you for connecting to our server!
execution has been blocked for 0 seconds
```

What we have achieved is that there is no single line in the code which would block waiting for any network connection related event. The output clearly illustrates that `read` does not block, but returns any data that came from the server.

More interesting is the behavior of the `gets` command. As we know, this command reads the entire line from the channel or the blocks. In nonblocking mode, when there is data available for reading, but it does not constitute the full line, `gets` will return an empty string without removing this data from the input buffer. Let's modify the `readData` procedure slightly:

```
proc readData {serverChannel} {
    global end
            puts "noOfChars: [gets $serverChannel data]"
            puts "fblocked: [fblocked $serverChannel]"
            puts "eof: [eof $serverChannel]"
```

```
if {![fblocked $serverChannel]} {
        if {[eof $serverChannel]} {
                close $serverChannel
                set end 1
                break
        }
        puts "read: $data"
}

}
```

We have removed the time calculations and replaced `read` with `gets`. The procedure also introduces us to the `fblocked` command. The command returns 1 in case there is some data to read from the channel, but it is not sufficient for the reading command. The typical example is just `gets`, which attempts to read the entire line, and when only the characters 12345 without newline character at the end are available, the `gets` command will read an empty string and return -1 as the read character count, leaving the data in the buffer, and causing `fblocked` to report properly.

```
c:\tcl_book\chapter6\TCPsockets\firstExample>tclsh85 client_async2.tcl
noOfChars: -1
fblocked: 1
eof: 0
noOfChars: 9
fblocked: 0
eof: 0
read: 123456789
noOfChars: 39
fblocked: 0
eof: 0
read: thank you for connecting to our server!
noOfChars: -1
fblocked: 0
eof: 1
```

Detecting the end of transmission may be a little tricky. In the current example, the server at the end sends the entire line (with the newline character at the end), so `gets` is able to read it properly. Following that, the channel is closed, resulting in another execution of the `readData` procedure on the client's side. This time `gets` also returns -1 as the number of characters read, but the channel is not blocked, and `eof` indicates that the connection is terminated.

So far so good, but what if the server sends the last line without the newline marker:

```
    puts -nonewline $channelId "thank you for connecting to our
server!"
    flush $channelId
    close $channelId
```

In this case, the client would get the following:

```
c:\tcl_book\chapter6\TCPsockets\firstExample>tclsh85 client_async2.tcl
noOfChars: -1
fblocked: 1
eof: 0
noOfChars: 9
fblocked: 0
eof: 0
read: 123456789
noOfChars: -1
fblocked: 1
eof: 0
noOfChars: 39
fblocked: 0
eof: 1
```

As you can see, the last call to gets resulted in 39 characters of data being read. However, in parallel, it caused eof to report 1, effectively causing the read data to be discarded. This allows a mistake in the logic of the readData function, which checks for the end of file first. A better design would include checking if gets returns a value other than -1:

```
proc readData {serverChannel} {
    global end
    set noOfChars [gets $serverChannel data]
    puts "noOfChars: $noOfChars"
    puts "fblocked: [fblocked $serverChannel]"
    puts "eof: [eof $serverChannel]"
    if {![fblocked $serverChannel]} {
        if {$noOfChars!=-1} {
            puts "read: $data"
        }
        if {[eof $serverChannel]} {
```

```
            close $serverChannel
            set end 1
            break
        }
    }
}
```

This makes the usage of `fblocked` redundant, because `gets` returns `-1` also when it was unable to read the entire line. Finally, the procedure would look like:

```
proc readData {serverChannel} {
    global end
    set noOfChars [gets $serverChannel data]
    if {$noOfChars!=-1} {
            puts "read: $data"
    }
    if {[eof $serverChannel]} {
            close $serverChannel
            set end 1
            break
    }
}
```

Transferring binary data

Up until this moment, we have been sending text data without paying attention to the formatting. When network communication occurs between potentially heterogenic systems, this subject must be considered more carefully. Let's illustrate these concepts using the example of uploading files to the server. For the sake of simplicity, the communication will be one way only, and for every file the following information will be sent:

- The file name encoded in UTF-8
- The size of the file
- The binary content of the file

The protocol we have just proposed allows you to send any number of files using a single TCP connection. On the server side, the uploaded files will be stored in the `uploaded` directory.

Firstly, let's look at the client-side code:

```tcl
set serverChannel [socket -async 127.0.0.1 9876]

fconfigure $serverChannel -blocking 0
fileevent $serverChannel writable [list socketWritable $serverChannel]

set end 0

set files [list tcl_logo.gif Tcl.png]

proc socketWritable {serverChannel} {
    variable files
    variable end
    if {[llength $files]!=0} {
        set fileName [lindex $files 0]
        set files [lreplace $files 0 0]
        uploadFile $fileName $serverChannel
    } else {
        close $serverChannel
        set end 1
    }

}

proc uploadFile {fileName serverChannel} {
    fconfigure $serverChannel -encoding utf-8
    fconfigure $serverChannel -translation auto
    fileevent $serverChannel writable ""
    set fileSize [file size $fileName]
    puts "uploading file $fileName of size $fileSize"
    puts $serverChannel $fileName
    puts $serverChannel $fileSize
    set fileInput [open $fileName r]
    fconfigure $fileInput -translation binary
    fconfigure $serverChannel -translation binary
    fcopy $fileInput $serverChannel -size $fileSize \
        -command [list fileUploaded $fileInput $serverChannel]
}
```

```
proc fileUploaded {fileInput serverChannel size} {
    puts "the file was successfully uploaded"
    close $fileInput
    fileevent $serverChannel writable \
            [list socketWritable $serverChannel]
}

vwait end
```

In this case, we are uploading two graphical files, both containing the Tcl logo (taken from http://www.demailly.com/tcl/about/logos.html and from Wikipedia respectively). The names of these files are stored in `files` list.

Every time the TCP channel opened to the server becomes writable, the `socketWritable` procedure is called. If there are any files on the list to be sent, the procedure pops the first element from the `files` list and calls the `uploadFile` procedure; otherwise, it closes the connection and writes the `end` variable, effectively causing the client code to exit the event loop and terminate.

The `uploadFile` procedure first configures the data encoding for the channel. As usual, `fconfigure` is used to set two new options: `-encoding` (described in detail in *Chapter 5, Data Storage*) and `-translation`. The second option is related to the fact that—for historical reasons—on various platforms newline characters are presented differently. Internally, Tcl always stores the newline indicator as a single LF (*line feed*, the ASCII code `0x0A`), just as on Unix systems. However, on other systems, the following combinations are used:

- CRLF on Windows and DOS
- CR on Mac OS

CR is the carriage return character, coded as `0x0D`.

For every read or written newline character, Tcl will convert it from/to the form specified by the channel configuration. The valid values for `–translation` are:

- `cr`, `crlf`, or `lf` — corresponds to the appropriate combinations of CR, CRLF, or LF characters respectively.
- `auto` — the format is chosen automatically depending on the underlying platform where the script is executed. This is the default value of the translation mode.
- `binary` — the translation of newline characters is disabled, and the channel encoding is set to `binary`, that is, any additional character conversions are disabled. This mode is extremely important when you are sending binary data, which could be easily damaged by the unnecessary conversion.

It is worth noting that fconfigure allows separate configuration of the input and output modes by specifying two values. The configuration of the channel encoding or translation can be modified dynamically at any time. We will use this later to set the socket channel to binary mode after the filename and size have been sent, but before the file data is sent.

In our example, we set the translation mode to lf, so effectively, no translation will occur, because this is the way Tcl stores newline characters. The encoding is set to UTF-8.

Following this, file events for the network channel are temporarily disabled, and the filename and size are sent to the server, both as the separate lines (no -nonewline option for puts).

Transferring data using the fcopy command

To copy the content of the file, a handy command called fcopy will be used, which copies data from an input channel to an output channel. The format of the command follows:

```
fcopy inputChannel outputChannel ?-size numberOfBytes? ?-command
commandName?
```

By default, the command will copy the data until *end of file* occurs, but this behavior can be altered by specifying the -size parameter—in this case, the command will copy only a numberOfBytes.

Normally, the command would block until the copying operation is completed, but in case the -command parameter is used, it will end immediately and the commandName command will be called once the data is copied.

In our example, we are using both options: we copy only the exact amount of bytes, that is, the size of the file, and on completion, the fileUploaded procedure will be called. The input channel allows us to read data from the file (returned by the open command). The output is the TCP channel to the server. Both channels are configured as binary at the moment.

During the fcopy operation, no other input/output operations are allowed on the involved channels, which is why we disabled the *writable* events earlier.

Once the file content is sent to the server using the TCP socket channel, the fileUploaded procedure closes the file channel and restores the handling of the writable events, allowing the repetition of the entire operation for the next filename in the list.

The server code that is able to understand the protocol described is:

```
socket -server serverProc 9876

proc serverProc {channelId clientAddress clientPort} {
    while {true} {
            fconfigure $channelId -encoding utf-8
            fconfigure $channelId -translation lf
            set fileName [gets $channelId]
            set fileSize [gets $channelId]
            if {[eof $channelId]} {
                    puts "end of transmission"
                    break
            }
            puts "incoming file $fileName of size $fileSize"
            set fileOutput [open "uploads/$fileName" w]
            fconfigure $fileOutput -translation binary
            fconfigure $channelId -translation binary
            fcopy $channelId $fileOutput -size $fileSize
            puts "file copied"
            close $fileOutput
    }
    close $channelId
}
vwait forever
```

All server logic is contained in the `serverProc` procedure. The server is designed to accept transmission of multiple files, so it enters an "infinitive" loop (`while {true}`). In each iteration, the channel is first configured to read text data from it. Then the name and size of file that is about to be uploaded are read. If any of these operations encounter the end of the file, the loop will be ended by calling the `break` command.

Following that, the file output channel is opened (all the incoming files will be stored in the `uploads` directory), and both this and the network channel are set to `binary` mode. Then the job of copying the data is done by the `fcopy` command, this time working in the blocking mode, because the `–command` parameter was not specified. Finally, the iteration ends with closure of the file.

If you exit the loop, the network channel will be closed and the `serverProc` procedure terminated.

The result of running the described example is illustrated in the following screenshot:

Handling errors

Network operations are especially vulnerable to various kinds of errors, so if you wish to create reliable application, proper handling of such a situation is indispensable. The basis of this is appropriate reaction to a *writable* event. The issue is that the channel is considered *writable* not only when it is possible to write to it, but also if some error occurred on the underlying device/file. Once an error occurs, your script will get a bunch of *writable* events to handle. Therefore, the proper implementation of the handler command must check the error condition, using the `fconfigure $socket -error` command.

Let's discuss error related issues using the following example:

```
if {[catch {
    set serverChannel [socket -async somehostname.com 9876]
} e]} {
    puts $e
    exit 1
}
fconfigure $serverChannel -blocking 0
fileevent $serverChannel writable [list socketWritable $serverChannel]
fileevent $serverChannel readable [list socketReadable $serverChannel]
```

```
set timer [after 5000 [list timeout $serverChannel]]

proc timeout {serverChannel} {
    fileevent $serverChannel writable ""
    catch {close $serverChannel}
    puts "custom timeout"
}

proc socketWritable {serverChannel} {
    variable timer
    set error [fconfigure $serverChannel -error]

    switch $error {
        "connection timed out" -
        "connection refused"
          {
                after cancel $timer
                catch {close $serverChannel}
          }
        ""
          {
                puts "all OK"
                after cancel $timer
          }
        default
          {
    puts $error
}
          }
}

proc socketReadable {serverChannel} {
    set error [fconfigure $serverChannel -error]
   if {$error == ""} {
        catch {gets $serverChannel}
        if {[eof $serverChannel]} {
            puts "the remote peer closed the connection"
            catch {close $serverChannel}
        }
    }
}

vwait forever
```

The socket command may throw an error—for example, if the specified target host domain name is invalid. In order to handle it properly, the catch command must be used.

Another important issue is timeouts. The network may be slow, or the target server may be unresponsive. If you do not want to rely on system defaults, there is no other way to specify your user-defined timeout value in Tcl. However, a little trick with after may be used. In our example, we decided that we would like to terminate it 5 seconds after the initial attempt to connect—the timeout procedure was executed to do so. First, we need to unregister ourselves from any new *writable* events and then close the channel. Note that the closing operation may also throw some errors (for example, the channel may already have been closed), so it is good practice to wrap it into catch. The same applies to commands such as gets or puts. So that we can cancel the timer in case the connection is successful, we store it in the $timer variable.

Once the writable event occurs, the socketWritable procedure is called. First, the current error status of the $serverChannel socket is retrieved by calling fconfigure $serverChannel -error, and then it's stored in the $error variable. If there is no error, an empty string is returned, and in the consecutive switch block, the "*all OK*" message is printed and the timeout timer is cancelled. If the returned string is not empty, it means that some error occurred, for example:

- Connection refused—the server refused the connection
- Connection timed out—the system-defined timeout has occurred

In case of these errors, the timer is cancelled and the channel closed manually. For any other non-empty error messages, the script (default section) will simply print out the error message, but of course, the appropriate clean-up actions can also be done here.

The other important situation is detecting that the remote peer has closed the connection. This case can **only** be handled in the procedure called for *readable* events—socketReadable in this example. This procedure first checks for errors, just as socketWritable does. Following that, some input operation must be called (in this case, gets), because without it, the eof command would not notify that the EOF state occurred, as mentioned earlier,. Once it is detected, the channel is closed. Note that any concurrent puts $serverChannel operations will throw an error if the channel was closed, so this should also be handled properly with a catch.

The following table sums up the most common issues along with the ways of detecting them:

Issue	Detection
Initial connecting issues	• `socket` may throw errors (for example, when the specified port is already being used by another application)
	• writable event along with appropriate error information from `fconfigure -error`
Peer disconnected	Detectable only in the readable event handler using `eof`
Transmission errors	Handled transparently by the TCP protocol

Buffering

When you are working with channels of various types, and especially the network type, all modern programming languages take advantage of buffering techniques that increase performance and make I/O operations more effective. As already mentioned in *Chapter 2, Advanced Tcl features*, Tcl is no exception. From the sender's point of view, the buffering is an automated process, where the data written with a `puts` command is not sent over the channel immediately, but rather gathered in internal memory (buffer) and transmitted in bulk, making the communication more effective. Each channel has its own buffer.

Basically, there are two commands allowing direct interaction with output buffers. The first is `fconfigure` with appropriate options—it allows either buffering configuration or reading of the existing parameters (assuming that $channel is a valid channel handle):

- `fconfigure $channel -buffering` *mode*—allows you to set the buffering for `$channel` in one of the following modes:
  - ° `full`—the data will be stored in the buffer until it is completely full (or until the `flush` command is executed) and then sent to the channel
  - ° `line`—the data is flushed (sent) any time the newline character occurs in input data
  - ° `none`—the data is flushed automatically after each output operation
  - ° If the `mode` is omitted, the command will return the actual value of the buffering mode.

- `fconfigure $channel -buffersize` *size*—allows you to define the size of the buffer, between ten bytes and one million bytes. Returns the current size if the last parameter is omitted.

In many cases of network programming, you would like the data to be sent right after you write it to the channel, so the none mode is useful here. All the more, it helps beginners to avoid some confusion—they may start writing networking code and may spend a considerable amount of time wondering why the data is not sent immediately or received in bulk different from those defined by the sender. Unless performance becomes an issue, setting buffering to none may be considered to be the best option.

The second command is flush $channel, and the result of calling it is a dump of the data stored in the buffer directly to the channel represented by the $channel handle. The command will block if the channel is in the blocking mode, until the data is transmitted.

Using threads for networking

Many languages focus on blocking the network model and using threads to handle each connection individually. Tcl also allows this model, using threads and transferring channels between threads. This concept was introduced in *Chapter 2*.

Using threads provides the benefit of being easier to write. However, it consumes more resources and makes it more difficult to provide scalability to a high number of simultaneous connections.

However, in some cases, it is a good idea to use this model for network connections in Tcl. One example can be when operations related to each connection can be blocked for a long period of time and/or a large amount of data processing needs to occur. Using threads allows one blocking operation not to block other ones from being completed and allows us to take advantage of newer CPUs that offer multiple cores, which can be more effective for data computations. As each thread or process can only use up one core of a processor, using multiple threads will allow us to perform calculations on multiple cores and/or processors.

Using threads and thread pools

For the purpose of this book, we'll create an example that uses threads and Tcl's thread pool. We'll use the thread pool to process requests from clients. Thread pools allow us to run commands within separated threads. It passes the specified job to the first available thread or spawns a new thread if it is needed. Jobs are specified as Tcl scripts to be run, so it is intuitive to use them. We also provide initialization and clean-up scripts for the thread.

The requests that the clients send will be read from the main thread and once read, the request itself along with the channel is passed to child thread, which handles the request and sends back the response. This optimizes how child threads are used — we do not need to make a thread wait until all data is readable, but instead use a single thread for reading all the incoming data.

The request is sent in such a way that a line indicating the number of bytes to read, as plaintext, is sent first and is followed by the specified number of bytes of the request itself.

Let's start with creating the server. We'll need to set up our namespace and load the Thread package first:

```
package require Thread

namespace eval tpserver {}
```

Next we'll set up a new thread pool. We use the command `tpool::create` for this purpose, which returns the new thread pool's identifier. We store it in `tpserver::tpool` variable for later use.

```
set tpserver::tpool [tpool::create \
        -initcmd [list source server-threads.tcl]]
```

Several options can be passed to the `tpool::create` command. The options `-initcmd` and `-exitcmd` specify commands that will be run in the new thread after it is created and before it is deleted accordingly. The options `-minworkers` and `-maxworkers` define how many threads should be running, and their values default to 0 and 4 accordingly. This means that, at most, four threads will be used and no thread will be created if not required. The `-idletime` option specifies a time (in seconds) after which a thread is terminated if it is not used. If not specified, threads are deleted as soon as they have no jobs to perform.

For this example, we specify a command to run to initialize the thread and use the default values for the remaining options. Child threads that will be used for operations will need to have their own code, which is responsible for handling requests. We have the thread source file called `server-threads.tcl`, which contains the code to run and respond to requests.

We now need to write the code for handling incoming connections. This code will be running in the main thread and will read the request using events. After reading the request, we'll add a job to the thread pool.

We start by setting the channel to the nonblocking mode and set up automatic translation of newline characters. We also set up a readable event so that whenever anything is sent, the command is run:

```
proc tpserver::accept {chan args} {
    fconfigure $chan -buffering none -blocking 0 \
        -translation auto

    fileevent $chan readable \
        [list tpserver::readInfo $chan]
}
```

We'll then execute the command for reading the first line that specifies number of bytes. We check if the end of file has been received first. If so, we will close the channel and exit.

```
proc tpserver::readInfo {chan} {
    if {[eof $chan]} {
        catch {close $chan}
        return
    }
```

Following that, we try to read the line. If a complete line is not available, the `gets` command will return `-1` and we'll wait for next readable event.

```
    if {[gets $chan line] < 0} {
        return
    }
```

In the next step we try to remove all the whitespace around the number of bytes and check if it is a valid integer. If not, we close the channel immediately and return.

```
    set bytes [string trim $line " \r\n"]
    if {![string is integer -strict $bytes]} {
        catch {close $chan}
        return
    }
```

After getting a valid number of bytes to read, we convert the channel into binary mode and set up a new readable event, which will read the specified amount of bytes.

```
    fconfigure $chan -translation binary

    fileevent $chan readable \
        [list tpserver::readData $chan $bytes ""]
}
```

The command for reading data accepts the number of bytes left to be read and the data read so far. For the initial event, we'll set up the specified number of bytes and empty the buffer. The subsequent events will be set up with data read so far until the specified number of bytes has been read.

The command to read data also begins by checking if the end of the file has been reached:

```
proc tpserver::readData {chan numBytes data} {
    if {[eof $chan]} {
        catch {close $chan}
        return
    }
```

Next we try to read data from the channel. If that fails, we close the channel immediately and return.

```
    if {[catch {
        set d [read $chan $numBytes]
    }]} {
        catch {close $chan}
        return
    }
```

Following that, we append the data that was read to the buffer and calculate the new number of bytes remaining—by taking the difference between the number of bytes read now and the previous value.

```
    append data $d
    set numBytes [expr {$numBytes - [string length $d]}]
```

If we have read the entire request, we remove the readable event and invoke the command to handle the request:

```
    if {$numBytes <= 0} {
        fileevent $chan readable [list]
        tpserver::handleRequest $chan $data
    } else {
```

Otherwise, we set up a new readable event with the current data buffer and the remaining number of bytes to read:

```
        fileevent $chan readable \
            [list tpserver::readData $chan $numBytes $data]
    }
}
```

When a complete request has been read, we will use the thread pool to deploy it. We first invoke the `tls::detach` command, which detaches a channel from the current thread. After this command, the current thread can no longer access the channel.

```
proc tpserver::handleRequest {chan data} {
    variable tpool

    thread::detach $chan
```

We then post a new job to be performed in the thread pool — the command to handle the response to a request along with request already read. We specify the channel to use and the request.

```
    tpool::post -nowait -detached $tpool \
        [list tpserver::respond $chan $data]
}
```

After that, this connection is handled by one of the threads in the thread pool.

Finally, we need to set up a listening connection to accept the requests:

`socket -server tpserver::accept 12345`

We now need to set up the `server-threads.tcl` file that handles responding to the requests.

We'll start by creating the `respond` command. It needs to attach to the channel using the `tls::attach` command. After running this command, the specified channel can be used like any other channel in this thread.

```
proc tpserver::respond {chan data} {
    thread::attach $chan
```

We will then run the command to handle the response and catch any potential errors. If the command does not fail, the `result` variable will store the value returned by the `respondHandle` command. If there are any errors, `result` will store the error information.

```
    set c [catch {
        respondHandle $data
    } result]
```

In the next step, we try to send the results as a list of two elements — the result from the `catch` command and the result or error, depending on value of the `c` variable.

```
    catch {
        puts -nonewline $chan [list $c $result]
        flush $chan
    }
```

We wrap writing output in a `catch` command because the write might fail, either because the client has already closed the channel or because of network issues.

Finally, we try to close the channel:

```
        catch {close $chan}
    }
```

We then need to write the command that handles the request itself.

```
proc tpserver::respondHandle {data} {
    return [eval $data]
}
```

While the `respondHandle` command can perform any action, for the purpose of this example, it simply evaluates the Tcl code sent by a remote peer.

Finally, we need to create a client that will allow us to send a command to any host and port, and will allow us to specify a callback to be run whenever results are available.

Connecting to our service

We'll start by creating a namespace for our client.

```
namespace eval tpclient {}
```

Following that, we'll create the command to send a request to the server. It accepts the host and the port, the request and callback data to invoke when results are retrieved, or if sending the request fails.

The callback will be run with two additional arguments specified — whether an error was encountered (`true` indicating an error and `false` indicating a successful request), followed by either error information or the result from the server.

We start by trying to open a TCP connection to a remote system and setup a channel for sending binary data:

```
proc tpclient::sendRequest {host port data callback} {
    if {[catch {
        set chan [socket $host $port]
        fconfigure $chan -blocking 0 -buffering none \
            -translation binary
```

Then we send the request by sending the length of the request followed by the request itself:

```
            puts -nonewline $chan \
                "[string length $data]\n$data"
```

Finally, we set up a readable event to read results as soon as they are available:

```
fileevent $chan readable [list \
    tpclient::readResponse $chan "" $callback]
```

If any of these operations fail, we close the channel if it was open and invoke the callback, specifying an error:

```
}]} {
    catch {close $chan}
    {*}$callback true "Unable to connect"
}
}
```

The command to read the response is written in a similar way to the command to read a request on the server — it reads the data and passes the current buffer to the next readable event. We also pass the `callback` command as the argument.

We start by trying to read data from the channel:

```
proc tpclient::readResponse {chan data callback} {
    if {[catch {
        set d [read $chan]
    }]} {
```

If the read fails, the callback is invoked with an error indication.

```
        catch {close $chan}
        {*}$callback true "Unable to read data"
        return
    }
```

Otherwise, we append the newly read data to the buffer and check if the end of file message has been received:

```
    append data $d

    if {[eof $chan]} {
```

If the end of file has been reached, we close the channel. We then take the first index of the resulting list as an indication of an error and the actual data as the second element of the list and invoke the callback with this data:

```
        catch {close $chan}
        set error [lindex $data 0]
        set data [lindex $data 1]
        {*}$callback $error $data
    } else {
```

Otherwise, we set up a new readable event with the current buffer:

```
        fileevent $chan readable [list \
            tpclient::readResponse $chan $data $callback]
    }
}
```

Further, we can invoke the command to send a request to the server, specifying the expr {1+1} command to be run and the requestCallback command to be run as the callback:

```
tpclient::sendRequest 127.0.0.1 12345 \
    {expr {1+1}} \
    requestCallback
```

We used 127.0.0.1, but if the server is located on any other machine, its IP address or hostname should be specified.

The callback itself simply prints either an error indication or a result from the command:

```
proc requestCallback {error data} {
    if {$error} {
        puts "Error: $data"
    } else {
        puts "Result: $data"
    }
    exit 0
}
```

Depending on whether the server (saved in server.tcl in the source code examples for this chapter) is running or not, the result should be either one of the following commands:

```
c:\tcl_book\chapter6\TCPsockets\threads>tclsh85 client.tcl
Error: Unable to connect
```

or:

```
c:\tcl_book\chapter6\TCPsockets\threads> tclsh85 client.tcl
Result: 2
```

Even though this example only does 1+1, using a thread pool to perform tasks can be useful if you need to offer functions that either use blocking functions (such as getting data from a database) or use CPU intensive operations (such as calculating an MD5 from a large file). Imposing limits on the number of threads itself prevents us from using up all available resources on one type of functionality.

Documentation for the `Thread` package as well as thread pools can be found on Tcl's wiki page - `http://wiki.tcl.tk/thread` in the Documentation section.

Using UDP sockets

TCP support is built in to the core of the Tcl interpreter. To be able to use the UDP protocol, you have to use an external package. The default choice is usually the `TclUDP` extension, which is available from `http://sourceforge.net/projects/tcludp/` (it also comes as a part of *ActiveTcl* bundle; if you don't have it, install it with `teacup install udp`).

In contrast to TCP, which is a connection-oriented protocol, UDP is connection-less. This means that every data package (datagram) travels from one peer to another on its own, without a return acknowledgement or retransmission in the case of lost packets. What is more, one of the peers may send packages that are never received (for example if the second peer is not listening at the moment), and there is no feedback information that something is going wrong. This implies a difference in the design for handling the transmission, which will be illustrated in the following example.

Creating a UDP-based client

Lets consider a simple 'time server', where the server sends the current time to any client application that subscribes for such notifications, of course using UDP connectivity. The format of each datagram will be rather simple: it will contain only the current time expressed in seconds.

First let's have a look on client code:

```
package require udp

set s [udp_open]
fconfigure $s -buffering none
fconfigure $s -remote [list 127.0.0.1 9876]
puts -nonewline $s "subscribe"

proc readTime {channel} {
```

```
    puts "Time from server: [read $channel]"
}
fileevent $s readable [list readTime $s]

vwait forever
close $s
```

As you have probably figured out, the first line loads the TclUDP extension. The next line creates a UDP socket, using the udp_open command, and stores its reference in the s variable. The UDP protocol uses ports in the same way as TCP. If we executed udp_open 1234, the port value *1234* would be specified, but if omitted, the operating system would assign a random port. Note that if you specify a port that is already being used by any other program, an error will be generated.

Next, we set the buffering mode to *none,* meaning that the output buffer will be automatically flushed after every output operation. We will discuss buffering issues more deeply later in this example.

The newly created UDP socket is not connected to anything, as the UDP is connection-less. Such a socket is able to receive packets as they arrive at any time from any source, without establishing a data connection of any type. To have datagrams be sent to a specific destination, you should use the fconfigure command with a new option (introduced by TclUDP) –remote, along with a two-item list containing the target address and port: fconfigure $s -remote [list 127.0.0.1 9876]. In this example the server will be executed on local host (so you are able to run it even if you are not part of a network). Note that you can call this command any time you wish, causing successive datagrams to be sent to different peers.

Now it is time to send a message to the server – in this case simply a string containing 'subscribe'. If –nonewline is omitted, puts would generate 2 datagrams (the second one containing the newline character) – it is likely that the puts implementation will write data twice to the buffer (the message, and then the new line character), and as the buffering is set to none, it is flushed immediately after each write. The other solution would be to set buffering to full and call flush $s after each socket write.

The handling of incoming data is implemented based on event programming. The line:

```
fileevent $s readable [list readTime $s]
```

defines that every time the socket has some data to read (is *readable*), the command readTime with $s as an argument is called. The command itself is simple – it prints to the screen every piece of data that comes from the socket, read with the read $s command.

Implementing service using UDP

The code for the server is a bit more complicated, due to a need to track subscribed clients:

```
package require udp

set clients [list]

proc registerClient {s} {
    global clients
    lappend clients [fconfigure $s -peer]
}

proc sendTime {s} {
    global clients
    foreach peer $clients {
            puts "sending to $peer"
            fconfigure $s -remote $peer
            puts -nonewline $s [clock seconds]
    }
    after 1000 [list sendTime $s]
}

set server [udp_open 9876]
fconfigure $server -buffering none
fileevent $server readable [list registerClient $server]

sendTime $server
vwait forever
```

The list named `clients` will hold an entry for each subscribed client; each entry is also a list containing IP address and port, so it suits perfectly for the `fconfigure $s -remote` command.

The server opens a UDP socket on port 9876. We would like to avoid the word 'listens' in this context, as this socket does not differ in any way from the one used by the client. By contrast, TCP requires a special server type socket, for listening purposes.

On every incoming data even, the `registerClient` procedure is executed. The command appends to the client's list information about the originator of the data (usually referred to as a peer) that has just arrived. This information is retrieved with `fconfigure $s -peer`. Although it may seem that this data is defined for the socket (represented by `$s`), in reality it refers to the most recent datagram received by this socket.

Every one second the procedure `sendTime` is called. The purpose of this command is to send the current time to all subscribed clients, so it iterates over the `clients` list, and for each one it first configures the socket with the target address and port (`fconfigure $s -remote $peer`), and then sends a datagram containing the time in the form of the output from the `clock seconds` command.

The server code is simple, it runs forever and there is no way to unsubscribe from receiving the data, but it demonstrates how to work with UDP in Tcl.

The following picture shows an example of the execution of the server (`timeServer.tcl`) and two clients (`timeClient.tcl`):

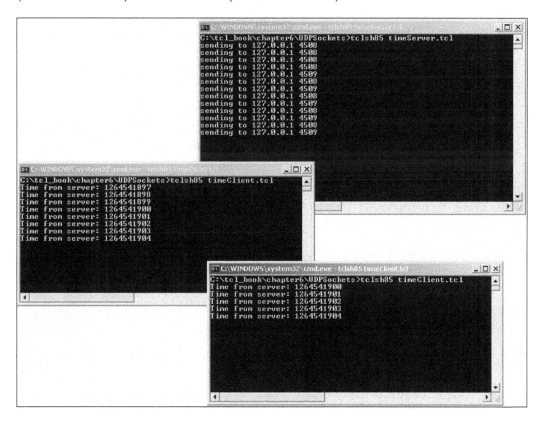

The first client connects from the port 4508, and the second one (started a few seconds later) from 4509.

The most important observation is that UDP sockets are handled identically on both the client and server, so the name 'server' is actually contractual.

It is worth mentioning that although we do not focus on this feature in this chapter, TclUDP supports multicasting and broadcasting of UDP packets. For details of how to perform this, please consult the package's manual.

Sending reliable messages

The UDP protocol lacks reliability, which is one of its main differences compared to TCP. Applications using UDP must either accept the fact that some of the datagrams may be lost, or implement equivalent functionality on their own. The same is true of topics like the order of incoming packets and data integrity.

The implementation of such logic could be as follows in the following example that follows — the sender calculates the MD5 checksum of the data, and sends both to the receiver. The receiver calculates the checksum again and compares it to the received one - and in the case of equality, sends acknowledgment (in this example, the checksum is sent back). The sender will repeatedly attempt to send the data until the confirmation is received, or the permitted number of attempts has been reached.

The sender code is as follows:

```tcl
package require udp
package require md5

set s [udp_open]
fconfigure $s -buffering none
fconfigure $s -remote [list 127.0.0.1 9876]

proc randomData {length} {
    set result ""
    for {set x 0} {$x<$length} {incr x} {
        set result "$result[expr { int(2 * rand()) }]"
    }
    return $result
}

proc sendPacket {chan contents {retryCount 3}} {
    variable ackArray

    if {$retryCount < 1} {
```

```
            puts "packet delivery failure"
            return
    }

    set md5 [md5::md5 -hex $contents]

    # if ack received, remove ack and do not send again
    if {[info exists ackArray($md5)]} {
            puts "packet successfully delivered"
            unset ackArray($md5)
            return
    }

    puts "sending packet, # of retries: $retryCount"
    puts "packet content: $md5$contents"
    puts -nonewline $chan "$md5$contents"
    flush $chan

    # handle retries
    incr retryCount -1
    after 1000 sendPacket [list $chan $contents $retryCount]
}

proc recvAckPacket {chan} {
    variable ackArray

    set md5 [read $chan]
    puts "received ack:    $md5"
    set ackArray($md5) 1
}

sendPacket $s [randomData 48]
after 5000 sendPacket $s [randomData 48]
after 10000 sendPacket $s [randomData 48]

fileevent $s readable [list recvAckPacket $s]

vwait forever
```

The main logic is located in the `sendPacket` procedure. The last parameter is the number of retries left to deliver the data. The procedure calculates the MD5 checksum of the data to be sent (stored in `contents` variable) and first checks if the appropriate acknowledgment has already been received – if the array `ackArray` contains the entry for the checksum (that is concurrently an acknowledgment), it is removed and the datagram is considered to have been delivered. If it is not, then the checksum along with the data is sent to the receiver, and a `sendPacket` is scheduled to be executed again after one second, every time with retries counter decreased. If the procedure is called when the counter is equal to zero, the delivery is considered to be negative.

The acknowledgments are received by the procedure `recvAckPacket`, which simply stores it into `ackArray`, allowing `sendPacket` to find it and react appropriately.

The helper procedure `randomData` allows the generation of a random string of zeroes and ones of a given length.

Note that this example does not cover the topic of received packets order.

The receiver code:

```
package require udp
package require md5

set server [udp_open 9876]
fconfigure $server -buffering none
fileevent $server readable [list recvPacket $server]

proc recvPacket {chan} {
    variable readPackets
    set data [read $chan]
    puts "received: $data"
    set md5 [string range $data 0 31]
    set contents [string range $data 32 end]

    if {$md5 != [md5::md5 -hex $contents]} {
            #the data are malformed
            puts "malformed data"
            return
    }

    # send an ack anyway, because original
    # might not have been received by other peer
    fconfigure $chan -remote [fconfigure $chan -peer]
    #simulate the ack package lost over network
```

```
        if {10*rand() > 7} {
                puts -nonewline $chan $md5
                flush $chan
        }

        # check if this packet is not a duplicate
        if {[info exists readPackets($md5)]} {
                return
        }

        set readPackets($md5) [clock seconds]

        # handle packet here...
}



proc periodicCleanup {} {
    variable readPackets

    set limit [clock scan "-300 seconds"]

    foreach {md5 clock} [array get readPackets] {
            if {$clock < $limit} {
                    unset readPackets($md5)
            }
    }

    after 60000 periodicCleanup
}
vwait forever
```

The receiver will send back the acknowledgement each time the correct datagram is received, that is when the checksums sent (first 32 chars) and calculated locally are equal. It also stores in the `readPackets` array the time of arrival of each packet, which allows us to detect duplicated data and processing it only once. To make the example more vivid, about 70% of data loss is simulated by randomly not sending confirmations.

The receiver also implements some simple logic for periodic clean up of the received datagrams log, to prevent it from becoming too huge and memory consumptive.

The result of running the example can be as depicted:

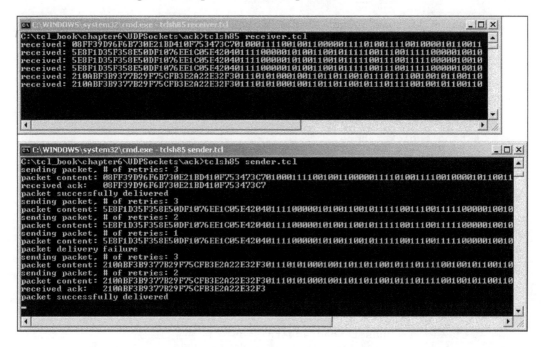

In this example, the first datagram was delivered successfully on the first attempt, the second one's delivery failed despite 3 attempts, and the last one was delivered on the second try.

Comparing TCP and UDP: streams vs. datagrams

Although from the Tcl point of view UDP sockets are identical in usage to normal sockets, you have to be aware of the differences. When you use file or TCP sockets, you operate on streams of data. Issues like buffering or the order of the data do not concern you. TCP features fit perfectly into the channel philosophy: the protocol offers reliable delivery of the stream of bytes in the correct order; transmission errors are detected and corrected automatically (with packet retransmission); flow and congestion control regulate the capacity of the channel.

In the case of UDP, the situation is different. You have to keep in mind that essentially everything you write to the UDP socket will end up in the datagram (UDP packet). In theory, a UDP datagram can carry **65507** bytes of data, but TclUDP has its own internal limit set to **4096** bytes. Therefore you should pay attention to the buffering settings:

- The buffer size (fconfigure -buffersize) must not be larger than 4096

- If the buffering mode is set to none, you should not write (puts) data larger than 4096 bytes to a UDP socket in one operation, otherwise the data will be lost

- In the case of buffering mode being set to full and the buffer size lower than 4096, you can write any amount of data you want, but note that the data will be split into pieces with the maximum size equal to the buffer size

The described behaviour can easily be illustrated with the following example: the sender code uses a buffer of the maximum possible size, 4096 bytes, and sends data of increasing size:

```
package require udp

set s [udp_open]
fconfigure $s -buffersize 4096
fconfigure $s -remote [list 127.0.0.1 9876]

proc randomData {length} {
    set result ""
    for {set x 0} {$x<$length} {incr x} {
        set result "$result[expr { int(2 * rand()) }]"
    }
    return $result
}

puts -nonewline $s [randomData 512]
flush $s
puts -nonewline $s [randomData 2048]
flush $s
puts -nonewline $s [randomData 8192]
flush $s
close $s
```

The function `randomData` produces strings of the specified length. First, 512 bytes is sent – the `flush` command makes sure that the buffer content is sent to the channel, and then packets of 2048 and 8192 bytes, similarly.

The receiver code prints on the screen the size of every received datagram:

```
package require udp

set server [udp_open 9876]
fconfigure $server -buffering none
fileevent $server readable [list recvPacket $server]

proc recvPacket {chan} {
    set data [read $chan]
    puts "received length: [string length $data]"
}
vwait forever
```

When both are executed, the output is as follows:

```
C:\tcl_book\chapter6\UDPSockets\largeData>tclsh85 receiver.tcl
received length: 512
received length: 2048
received length: 4096
received length: 4096
```

As you can see, the last bulk of data sent by the sender has arrived in form of two datagrams. If we modify the sender code — increase the output buffer size to 5000 bytes:

```
fconfigure $s -buffersize 5000
```

The receiver's output is:

```
C:\tcl_book\chapter6\UDPSockets\largeData>tclsh85 receiver.tcl
received length: 512
received length: 2048
received length: 3192
```

In this case, the 8192 bytes data bulk is split into two parts:

- The first one has a size of 5000 bytes (the buffer was completely filled upon writing, and then flushed) and is lost, as it exceeds the maximum datagram data size allowed by TclUDP

- The second one, of size 3192 bytes (that is the rest of the packet: *8192 – 5000 = 3192*) arrives successfully

The example clearly shows some of the pitfalls of using UDP, although from a Tcl perspective it looks like a 'normal' channel able to send data, you must be aware of the underlying mechanism and use it adequately.

In the case of a TCP socket, read would read data until the channel is closed (for example, when the client disconnects). In case of a UDP socket, read reads data from only one datagram at a time, as the datagrams are not connected to each other and must be treated separately (does not form a stream of data).

To summarize, treating UDP sockets as channels has the following pros and cons:

Pros	Cons
Consistent programming interface	Confusing; even though it seems to be a channel, you have to keep in mind that it is not
Common set of commands to operate on the channel: read/ write/configure	Creation of datagram is not too intuitive – for example to address it, you have to use `fconfigure` as if you were configuring the channel

Summary

After reading this chapter you are able to establish basic network communication using the TCP or UDP protocols, using Tcl code.

In this chapter, first, TCP connectivity was presented. Starting from the most basic blocking operation mode, we moved to nonblocking network handling based on event programming. Topics including binary data transfer, error handling or buffering issues were discussed along with appropriate examples. At the end, an alternative technique of programming based on threads was presented.

Next, the way how to handle UDP communication in Tcl was presented, with `TclUDP` extension as the implementation. The comparison of TCP and UDP philosophy was described, with the focus on the differences between streams and datagrams. We mentioned the limitations of both the UDP protocol and `TclUDP` package, and how to avoid some common pitfalls.

The contents of this chapter provided you with a knowledge of Tcl's philosophy when it comes to programming network operations, and constitute a solid basis for more advanced topics discussed in future chapters.

The next chapter will focus on using common internet services like FTP and HTTP from the Tcl scripting level.

7
Using Common Internet Services

By now we know that Tcl has the functionality to create networked applications. We also know how to build simple client-server communication. However, as with any programming language, being able to plug into existing protocols and communicate using standards that other systems are using as well is very important. This chapter talks about various standards, how Tcl fits into these technologies, and how to use Tcl for various types of protocols and data encoding.

First, we'll show how to manage files remotely over **File Transfer Protocol** (FTP). This can be used as the base for many operations, such as remote copies and filesystem synchronization. We'll also learn how to download a file from a website using **Hypertext Transfer Protocol (HTTP)**, which can then be used to get content from the Internet. This knowledge will also be valuable when we move on to embedding and using web servers in our application in the chapters that follow.

We will also talk about communicating with users using e-mail, starting with sending simple e-mails, followed by learning how to send attachments and multipart types. Using this we'll show how to send and receive e-mails in order to do tasks such as sending information to users and/or customers. You will also learn how to read e-mails in your Tcl code, parse them, and how simple mechanisms can be built to create an automated e-mail management system.

It's worth noting that whenever we're doing checks of any data retrieved from remote systems, we should check if all conditions are satisfied instead of checking for known problems; for example, we should check if the status is one of the acceptable status values instead of checking if it is one of the known error statuses. Troubleshooting Tcl applications and more recommendations for making applications less error prone are described in more detail in *Chapter 4, Troubleshooting Tcl Applications*.

Handling e-mail

Before working with e-mail, we need to understand a bit about how e-mail works, as well as what it provides and what our application needs to perform on its own. In general, e-mails are easy to understand—someone sends a message, the e-mailing system takes care of delivering it to the correct target machine(s), and the recipients are then able to retrieve that message. From the e-mail system's perspective, it does not care about what the e-mail contains, as long as it knows who it is from and who it should be delivered to.

From the user's perspective, he/she does not need to know how it is delivered—their mail application delivers the message to the server handling their e-mail, and all messages can be retrieved from that same server. When we interact with e-mails, it works the same way for us. In the majority of cases, our application only needs to interact with our e-mail server.

All e-mail messages are built using a common structure—each message consists of headers that describe the message and the body. Headers describe who the message is from, its recipients, and the subject of the message. They also provide the content type, which tells e-mail applications what type of data the message contains. Message headers can also contain a history of the servers it passed, additional information such as the e-mail application used to generate this message, and any other information that the e-mail application has added. The message body is the actual text and/or data that was sent. Information about what is in the message body is described in the headers, for example we can send plain text, HTML message, or simply an image.

Learning MIME

Multipurpose Internet Mail Extensions (MIME) is a standard that extends the e-mail format. It defines how messages can include character sets other than 7-bit ASCII in the message headers and body, and introduces the concept of multiple parts of an e-mail along with attachments. Over time, MIME became such an integral part of e-mail handling that all e-mails are now sent in accordance with MIME standards.

Content type

MIME introduced the concept of content type, which was originally meant for defining types of files in an e-mail. This was introduced so that e-mail applications could present the content of a message differently, depending on the actual file type. This grew to other protocols and can now be referred to as the **Internet media type** standard. The standard consists of two parts—MIME *type* and MIME *subtype* separated by a slash. The content type describes the type of a piece of media, for example, image. The subtype defines file format—for example, jpeg. In this example, the MIME type is image/jpeg.

A full list of standardized format types can be found on the following page:
`http://www.iana.org/assignments/media-types/`

Whenever an application needs to use its own content type, it is recommended that an `x-` prefix is appended to the subtype—for example, `application/x-tcl-dict` could be used to transmit a dictionary's contents.

The MIME standard defines several possibilities for embedding data that is outside a 7-bit ASCII character set, that is, data such as binary files, messages using different character sets, and so on. The **Base64** standard is commonly used for encoding binary files within an e-mail—this standard uses 64 characters only, and requires 4 bytes to encode 3 bytes of actual data. This means that a 1M file will use up over 1.3M when sent via e-mail. Base64 is described in more detail at:
`http://en.wikipedia.org/wiki/Base64`

The standard also defines the **quoted-printable** standard that is used for sending 8-bit data. Characters outside of 7-bit character set are encoded as multiple characters; this idea is described in more detail at:
`http://en.wikipedia.org/wiki/Quoted-printable`

For the purpose of this book, we do not need to go into details of how both Base64 and quoted-printable encodings work.

Multipart messages

MIME also introduces the concept of multipart content. An e-mail message can only consist of a single item. However, the MIME standard provides ways to send multipart content by enclosing multiple items in a single message. It can also be used recursively, one of the elements can also contain additional parts. We'll see this in the following example:

There are multiple types of multipart contents:

- `multipart/related` is used to send messages that should be treated as a whole. The first part is the content that the e-mail application should use and other parts are related to it, for example, images that are used in a HTML message. However, adding a part that should be inline requires that this element also has specific headers, which is discussed in more detail later in this chapter.

- `multipart/mixed` is used for sending mixed content types. It is up to the e-mail application to decide how to handle this, but parts that it can show inline will be shown within e-mail application, and parts that it cannot show directly will be shown only as attachments. A typical example is attaching images and documents—e-mail applications will show images inline, but require documents to be opened in an external application.

- `multipart/alternative` is used to define multiple parts, where each part is an alternate version of the same content. A typical example is sending plain text and HTML messages. E-mail applications choose the best format that they can handle. Representations should be sent in a way they are ordered by — preferable representation should be the last part.

Multipart content types allow each part to have its own individual headers — this is required in order to define which content type each part is, along with how it should be treated. Also, as each part can have its own type, each part can also be a multipart element on its own.

The following diagram illustrates how both `multipart/mixed`, `multipart/alternative`, and `multipart/related` can be used to send e-mail that contains plain text message and HTML message, *inlined* images as well as attachments. This is actually how the majority of e-mail applications will embed such a message. The structure of the entire message would look as follows:

1	E-mail message
1.1	E-mail headers
1.2	E-mail body; content type: **multipart/mixed**
1.2.1	Contents of the message; content type: **multipart/alternative**
1.2.1.1	Plain text version of the message; content type: **text/plain**
1.2.1.2	Container for HTML version of the message; content type: **multipart/related**
1.2.1.2.1	HTML message – actual HTML; content type: **text/html**
1.2.1.2.2	HTML message – inlined image; content type: **image/gif**
1.2.2	Attached image; content type: **image/jpeg**

Now that we know how our e-mail might appear, let's proceed to building such a structure from within Tcl.

MIME in Tcl

In order to send such an e-mail from within Tcl, we will need to use Tcl's `mime` package. It is a part of the `tcllib` package and is available in ActiveTcl distributions of Tcl.

This package allows the building and parsing of messages and handles all aspects of a message — headers, content, and support for multipart messages. It also handles conversion between various content encodings such as `base64` and `quoted-printable`. Thanks to this we'll only need to build the message parts and combine them into a final message.

Creating messages

The command `mime::initialize` is used to set up a part or the content of the entire message. This command accepts one or more options and returns a new token that identifies the new MIME part. Based on the options specified, there are two modes in which it can be used— the first is to parse content (such as parse a received e-mail message), and the second is to create content. We will focus on the second case and leave parsing for sections that talk about receiving e-mail.

Whenever we want to create a MIME part we need to specify the `-canonical` option and provide the content type for this part. Type is the MIME type described earlier. There are three possibilities for creating MIME objects—from a file or from a string, and when creating multipart content.

- To create it from a file or a string, we need to specify the `-file` or `-string` option and provide either the path to the file or the content of this part as string or binary data. We should also specify the `-encoding` option that states how content should be handled so that it can be passed over a 7-bit protocol such as SMTP. For binary files, we should usually use `base64` encoding and for text files, it is best to use `quoted-printable`.

- When creating a MIME part, we can also specify one or more headers that it should have by adding the `-header` option. This option can be specified multiple times and each parameter to this option should be a list containing a header name and corresponding value. These headers are then added to the actual MIME body. Their names and corresponding values are part of MIME's specifications. We'll cover a small subset that we need to know in order to send an e-mail with both *inlined* elements and attachments.

For example, in order to create a simple plaintext element, we can run the following command:

```
set token [mime::initialize -canonical "text/html" \
    string "Hello world!"]
```

If we want to send it, all we would need to do is use the `smtp` package:

```
smtp::sendmessage $token -recipients "someone@domain.com"
```

Sending e-mails is described in more detail later in this section—the preceding code simply shows that both packages can be combined very easily.

Multipart elements

In order to *multipart* content, we should provide the -parts option to the mime::
initialize command. The value for this option should contain a list of all parts that
should be included in this multipart content. Parts are included in the same order as
provided in the list.

Let's walk through an exercise of building up an e-mail that we described earlier.

This code uses several files, mainly message.html and message.txt for the
text of the e-mail, companylogo.gif for logo that is used in message.html, and
attachment.jpg as an attachment.

> The files as well as the complete source code for the example in this
> section are located in the 01mime directory in the source code examples
> for this chapter.

First we have to load the mime package and create an HTML part:

```
package require mime

# create actual HTML part
# (1.2.1.2.1 from diagram)
set part_html [mime::initialize -canonical "text/html" \
    -encoding quoted-printable -file message.html]

# create logo as inlined image
# (1.2.1.2.2 from diagram)
set part_logo [mime::initialize -canonical "image/gif" \
    -encoding base64 -file companylogo.gif \
    -header [list Content-Disposition "inline"] \
    -header [list Content-ID "companylogo.gif"] \
    ]
```

This code builds up two elements—a part containing HTML version of the message
and an image that we add, inline, in the message. Following that, we use these to
build up the multipart/related part (element 1.2.1.2 from preceding diagram)
that contains two elements created using the preceding code:

```
set part_htmlrelated [mime::initialize \
    -canonical multipart/related \
    -parts [list $part_html $part_logo]]
```

Next it's time to create a plain text version of the e-mail (element **1.2.1.1** from
diagram) and build the multipart/alternative element that binds the HTML
message and the plain text message into one piece, which is element **1.2.1**.

```
set part_txt [mime::initialize \
    -canonical "text/plain" \
    -encoding quoted-printable -file message.txt]
```

```
set part_alternative [mime::initialize \
    -canonical multipart/alternative \
    -parts [list $part_txt $part_htmlrelated]]
```

Finally, we create a part for the attachment (element **1.2.2** from diagram) and create an element that combines the previously created container for the plain text and HTML message along with the attachment—element **1.2** from diagram.

```
set part_attachment [mime::initialize \
    -canonical "image/jpeg" \
    -header [list Content-Disposition \
    "attachment; filename=attachment.jpg"] \
    -header [list Content-ID "attachment.jpg"] \
    -encoding base64 -file attachment.jpg]

set all [mime::::initialize -canonical multipart/mixed \
    -parts [list $part_alternative $part_attachment]]
```

This makes our code complete and a full version of the message is now ready.

There are three types of elements that we are building:

- HTML and plain text messages: Their context is defined by multipart elements they are included in, therefore, we only need to define content type.

- JPEG image: It is an attachment, therefore, we need to provide more information in the part headers—filename, Content-ID, and disposition.

- Multipart elements: These are used to combine other types of elements into a structure that we've described earlier.

Sending text messages also relates to character sets, encodings, and issues with internationalization. When sending messages that contain characters outside of 7-bit ASCII, we need to be aware of two things.

First of all, Tcl sends both strings and file contents in binary form. If we want to send text from a file, then that file needs to be encoded properly, using encodings such as UTF-8. If we want to send text from Tcl, we need to convert that text to proper encoding. Secondly, we need to specify the encoding of a part when specifying the canonical type—usually this means appending a semi-colon and `charset=<charsetName>`. For example:

```
set part_html [mime::initialize -canonical \
    "text/html; charset=UTF-8" \
    -encoding quoted-printable -string [encoding \
        convertto utf-8 "\u25ba Omega symbol: \u2126 \u25c4"]]
```

The previous example will cause our e-mail message to contain the text
▶ *Omega symbol*: Ω ◀ — in our example, \uxxxx means the Unicode characters
for ▶, Ω, and ◀ accordingly.

The command `encoding convertto` converts text to specified encoding and is
described in more detail in *Chapter 4*. For more information about standardized
character encodings, please refer to: `http://www.iana.org/assignments/`
`character-sets`.

Next we have an *inlined* image — in this case, we need to define additional headers.
The first header is `Content-Disposition`, which specifies how this part should be
handled. Specifying `inline` means that this is an element that will be referenced
from the main document and should not be shown as an attachment. The second
header is `Content-ID`, which identifies and names an element. This is how an
element can then be referenced from other parts. Any references should be made in
the format of `cid:<Content-ID>`, so in our case, it would be `cid:companylogo.gif`.
For example, our `message.html` file can contain the following HTML tag:

```
<img src="cid:companylogo.gif" width="400" height="40" />
```

Elements that are regular attachments should have `Content-Disposition` set to
`attachment`. Also, it is recommended to add `filename=<name>` to this parameter,
separated from the disposition type by a semi-colon. `Content-ID` in this case
specifies an attachment name and should be the same as the filename specified
in the `Content-Disposition` header. This is how the `attachment.jpg` file is sent.

There is also a difference between naming parts within an e-mail and actual
filenames. However, this example names files from MIME's perspective in the same
way as files are named on disk. It is common to add prefixes and/or suffixes to avoid
naming collisions, especially when a message contains parts from different sources.
For example, we add create inlined image in the following way:

```
set part_logo [mime::initialize -canonical "image/gif" \
    -encoding base64 -file "/path/to/template/logo.gif" \
    -header [list Content-Disposition "inline"] \
    -header [list Content-ID "template.logo.gif@$messageId"] \
    ]
```

We can then build the HTML to include such an image from Tcl by doing
something like:

```
set html "<img src=\"cid:template.logo.gif@$messageId\" />"
```

It is a good idea to generate unique identifiers for each message and append them to inlined parts' identifiers. This prevents poorly written e-mail applications from having issues with forwarding or replying to e-mails with such images. It can be done using the `uuid` package and the `uuid::uuid generate` command, but any mechanism for generating a unique ID, such as from a related database entry, will work.

Cleaning up a MIME item requires running the `mime::finalize` command and passing the token of a MIME part to it. In order to delete all elements that are used in that element recursively, we can add the `-subordinates` option with the value `all`. For example:

```
mime::finalize $all -subordinates all
```

The preceding code will delete the token created for the entire message along with all other elements we've created.

Information about all commands from `mime` package can be found in its documentation available at:
`http://tcllib.sourceforge.net/doc/mime.html`

Sending e-mails

Now that we're able to build MIME parts and the contents of messages, we can send our message. Messages are sent over the **Simple Mail Transfer Protocol (SMTP)**, which is the most popular standard for the delivery of e-mail messages. This is the protocol that almost all e-mail applications use to send e-mail and all service providers give you an SMTP server to send messages through.

From the Tcl perspective, we need to use the `smtp` package. This package uses the same tokens as MIME to send messages, which means that if you have created a message using the `mime` package, sending it requires only a few lines of code.

The package `smtp` offers a single command — `smtp::sendmessage`. This command requires passing a token to MIME part and accepts additional options. The first one is `-servers`, which is a list of SMTP servers to try. If this is not specified, then message is sent using the SMTP server on the local machine. If the machine our code is run on has an SMTP server, it is okay to not specify this option. If our SMTP server is using a non-standard port, the option `-ports` can be used to specify which ports we should try to connect to. For the majority of users, it is not necessary to use this flag.

We can also specify additional headers that should be added when building this e-mail by adding the -header option in one or multiple times. Similar to the mime package, it accepts a list where the first element is the header name and the second is the value. Usually when sending an e-mail, we want to set the From, To, and/or the Cc and Subject header fields. For fields such as To and From, we need to specify addresses in a specific way. If we want to specify both the full name and e-mail address, it should be in the form of "[Full Name]" <email@address>. If only the e-mail address is to be passed, it should be in the form of <email@address>. Multiple items should be separated by a comma succeeded by a space. For example:

```
smtp::sendmessage $token -header \
    [list To "<someone@domain.com>, <another-address@domain.com>"]
```

We should pass the -originator option in order to specify address from which an e-mail is sent. Specifying who the message should be delivered to can be done using the -recipients option. If -originator is not passed, the value is taken from the From or Resent-From header field. If -recipients was not specified, the value is taken from the To, cc, Bcc, or Resent-To header fields and is concatenated to one list. Please note that only headers specified to smtp::sendmessage are parsed, not headers set in the MIME token provided to the command.

Based on the previous example, we can use the message we have just created and add to it the code that will send it:

```
package require smtp

smtp::sendmessage $all \
    -recipients $recipient -originator $sender \
    -header [list Subject $mailsubject] \
    -header [list From "\"$senderName\" <$sender>"] \
    -header [list To "\"$recipientName\" <$recipient>"] \
    -servers $smtpservers
```

And a sample initialization of configuration variables needed for this code is as follows:

```
set sender sender@localhost
set senderName "My Tcl Application"
set recipient recipient@localhost
set recipientName "My Tcl Application User"
set mailsubject "Screenshot of Eclipse and DLTK"
set smtpservers 127.0.0.1
```

The complete example along with code from the previous example that creates all MIME elements is located in the `02smtp` directory in the source code examples for this chapter.

If our SMTP server requires authentication, we will need to pass this information to the `smtp::sendmessage` command. The options `-username` and `-password` can be used to specify credentials and if server requires authentication, the `smtp` package will use these. Usually authentication is needed if your e-mail server is being accessed remotely. In these cases, the username and password are provided by your ISP or network administrators.

Automated e-mail sending

Now that we know how to send an e-mail from start to end, we can move on to more advanced issues. Often our application will just send e-mails sporadically. However, there are many applications that mainly send e-mails. Many companies run their business by sending customized information to their customers and need a robust system that can send large volumes of e-mails, which handles failures of e-mail servers and needs to be customizable from both business logic and template perspectives.

If we plan on sending e-mail messages, we need to automate the process of building them and creating a system that will allow other people to customize both content and the appearance of our e-mails. We can either create a set of standalone tools or libraries that we can then use in our applications, depending on our needs.

One of the most important things that such an application will offer is an easy way to change contents of messages easily. In many cases, it is enough to have a separate directory for content of a message along with standardized file naming.

Creating template based e-mails

For example, let's assume our messages are stored in a separate directory. Files called `message.txt` and `message.html` will be used for body of the message. The subject of the message is in the `subject.txt` file. All files starting with the `inline_` prefix will be included and contained within `multipart/related` along with a HTML version of the message. We'll also assume our messages are in UTF-8 encoding, which allows support for various encodings around the world.

We'll reuse some of the ideas from the previous code sample and make it more generic. Let's start with creating a namespace, and create a procedure called readText for reading text files. This procedure will also use the subst command to allow substitution of commands and variables. We'll also load packages that we'll use throughout this example and initialize the proper namespace, which is needed before creating any procedures within that namespace:

```
namespace eval emailtemplate {}

package require mime
package require uuid
package require fileutil::magic::mimetype

proc emailtemplate::readText {filename messageId data} {
    set fh [open $filename r]
    fconfigure $fh -encoding utf-8 -translation auto
    set text [read $fh]
    close $fh

    set text [subst $text]

    return $text
}
```

This procedure also requires the messageId variable to be passed, which we'll later use to add inline images in the correct way. Our code reads a file as UTF-8, runs subst, and returns result of that command, which causes any occurrence of [command] or $variable to be evaluated as if it was part of Tcl code.

For example, we can add this to our HTML part of the message:

```
Welcome <b>[dict get $data firstname]</b>,
```

This causes value of firstname key from $data dictionary to be shown in bold.

Variable $data is passed to emailtemplate::readText command in the first place. We can use it for passing data to our templates as dictionaries. For example, if we were to send a notification that a payment is due, data would contain first name, last name, and other information about the recipient, and the amount and payment date. Our template would then include these values in the text by using dict get command as seen in this section.

We've loaded the uuid and fileutil::magic::mimetype packages. The first one is used to generate the message's unique identifier, whereas the second one is used to get the MIME content type from files, so that these don't have to be specified explicitly by e-mail template providers.

Next we'll create a `buildMessage` procedure that builds a MIME part containing each element based on directory where the template is placed and provided data. It also accepts an optional list of attachments, which allows us to add additional files, such as invoices as PDF files, if this is needed.

```
proc emailtemplate::buildMessage {directory data {files ""}} {
    set messageId [uuid::uuid generate]
```

The following steps are performed as part of `emailtemplate::buildMessage`:

The first step is to read the subject and both versions of messages. We'll also make sure that the subject does not include any newline characters as this will create errors when either building or parsing the message. We do this by splitting the subject into a list of lines and choose the first element from that list.

```
set subject [readText \
    [file join $directory subject.txt] $data]
set msgtext [readText \
    [file join $directory message.txt] $data]
set msghtml [readText \
    [file join $directory message.html] $data]

set subject [lindex [split $subject \n] 0]
```

After we've read the subject and both types of messages, we now build the MIME parts for these. Please note that, at this point, our messages are already formatted using the data that was provided. This step is very similar to how it was previously built for our first message.

```
set part_text [mime::initialize \
    -canonical "text/plain; encoding=UTF-8" \
    -string $msgtext -encoding quoted-printable]

set part_html [mime::initialize \
    -canonical "text/html; encoding=UTF-8" \
    -string $msghtml -encoding quoted-printable]
```

The third step is to build a list of parts for the `multipart/related` element that contains an HTML message along with sending images inline. We create a list of parts and add only one element to it for now — the actual HTML part.

```
set parts_related [list $part_html]
```

We then list all files in the template directory beginning — matching `inline_*` pattern. The variable `file` contains full path to the file and `filename` contains just the filename.

```
foreach file [glob -directory $directory \
    -nocomplain -type f inline_*] {
    set filename [file tail $file]
```

For each of these files, we'll find the proper MIME content type to use and add it to the list of items. We specify that this item should be added inline and that its identifier is `<filename>@<messageId>`.

```
set ftype [fileutil::magic::mimetype $file]
lappend parts_related [mime::initialize \
    -canonical $ftype -encoding base64 -file $file \
    -header [list Content-Disposition "inline"] \
    -header [list Content-ID "$filename@$messageId"] \
    ]
}
```

Finally, we'll build a `multipart/related` element by combining HTML along with the inline images and add this to a `multipart/alternative` element so that the e-mail application reading this message can choose between plain text or HTML.

```
set part_related [mime::initialize \
    -canonical "multipart/related" \
    -parts $parts_related]

set result [mime::initialize \
    -canonical "multipart/alternative" \
    -parts [list $part_text $part_related]]
```

The steps that follow take place only if this procedure has been passed any attachments. If this is the case, we create a new list of items for multipart/mixed. We initialize it to just one element — the result from previous step, the complete message containing plaintext, HTML, and images added inline.

Now we iterate through the list of attachments, taking two elements from the list at a time. The first one is the path to attachment file and the second one is the name that will be shown to the recipients.

```
if {[llength $files] > 0} {
    set elements [list $result]
    foreach {file name} $files {
```

For each of the attachments, we guess its MIME content type, and build its MIME element and add that to the list of elements.

```
set ftype [fileutil::magic::mimetype $file]
lappend elements [mime::initialize \
    -canonical $ftype \
    -encoding base64 -file $file \
    -header [list Content-Disposition \
        "attachment; filename=$name"] \
    -header [list Content-ID "$name"] \
]
}
```

Finally, we create a final `multipart/mixed` element that will contain the message and all attachments.

```
set result [mime::initialize \
    -canonical "multipart/mixed" \
    -parts $elements]
}
```

The last thing is to set the `Subject` header to indicate the subject that was provided by the template and return the element back to the caller of this procedure.

```
mime::setheader $result Subject $subject

return $result
}
```

This provides a complete mechanism for sending messages based on templates.

Setting the `Subject` header before sending the message is different from the previous example. Although the `From`, `To`, `Cc` and `Bcc` fields should be set during the `smtp::sendmessage` step, `Subject` and all other headers that are not related to message delivery can be set before sending the message.

Now that we have completed our code for preparing the messages, we can proceed with adding a small piece of code to send it:

```
set data [dict create firstname "John" lastname "Doe"]

set token [emailtemplate::buildMessage "template1" $data]

smtp::sendmessage $token \
    -recipients $recipient -originator $sender \
    -header [list From "\"$senderName\" <$sender>"] \
    -header [list To "\"$recipientName\" <$recipient>"] \
    -servers $smtpservers
```

This code is based on the same variables as the previous example. We're also passing two values to the message — `firstname` and `lastname`. If we want to send an attachment, all we need to do is add such a list to the `emailtemplate::buildMessage` invocation similar to the following example:

```
set token [emailtemplate::buildMessage "template1" $data \
    [list "attachment/attachment.jpg" "screenshot.jpg"]]
```

The directory `template1` is the location where the template of the e-mail is kept. It has to contain `subject.txt` and `message.txt`, and `message.html` which are the subject and content of the message in plain text and HTML respectively. The directory can also contain files that should be embedded as part of the message.

The list provided as the last argument is the list of attachments to include. While the actual file is called `attachment.jpg`, the user will actually see it named as `screenshot.jpg`. It is common to use this approach, for example, when file names are unique identifiers of the content, such as `customerinvoice_0013_0143.pdf` while we want the user to see a more readable filename such as `Invoice.pdf`.

 The example in this section is located in the `03emailtemplate` directory in the source code examples for this chapter. It also contains a sample template that uses data variables for passing information.

Documentation on `mime` and `smtp` packages can be found on the `tcllib` project website at SourceForge:
`http://tcllib.sourceforge.net/doc/mime.html` and
`http://tcllib.sourceforge.net/doc/smtp.html`

Receiving e-mails

In many cases, apart from sending e-mails, our application should also be able to **receive** messages sent via e-mail. One example is that if we send out mass e-mails to users, we might also want to be able to receive messages for unsubscribing from them and process them. Also, our application can also receive "delivery failed" notifications and process them — for example, starting with temporarily not sending messages and ending with removing failing e-mail addresses from our records permanently.

One of the most flexible options is to set up a dedicated SMTP server that will accept e-mails from other systems. This option, however, requires more setup and is discussed in the next chapter.

A simpler option that will allow us to receive e-mails is to use existing servers and read e-mails from them. This is similar to how e-mail applications work — the e-mail is stored on a remote server and you receive and/or delete it whenever your computer is online.

For this purpose, we'll use the **Post Office Protocol version 3 (POP3)**, which all e-mail servers offer. In order to read e-mail over POP3, we need to know the POP3 server name, and the username and password required to access our account. Usually, this is provided by our system administrators. For the majority of Unix servers, the hostname, username, and password are the same as for accessing it over SSH, Telnet, FTP, or any other protocol. POP3 works so that applications connect, list and read messages, delete the ones they have already read, and then disconnect. This is then repeated periodically.

POP3 uses positive integers to identify all messages. These messages range from 1 to the number of messages — therefore, if our inbox has 23 messages, they are 1, 2, 3, ..., 23 accordingly. Throughout the entire connection to a POP3 server, each number is guaranteed to point to the same message. Therefore, until we disconnect, message 19 will always point to the same message.

If we delete a message, we can no longer reference that particular message, but all other messages will still have the same index — for example, if we delete message 4, messages from 5 and up will still have the same identifiers. Also, when new messages arrive during our connection to the server, our connection will not be able to access them.

POP3 is designed so that the application logs in, reads messages, and disconnects. Our program might be doing this frequently, but it should always set up a new connection to the server.

Using POP3 protocol in Tcl

Tcl offers a pop3 package that allows you to retrieve e-mails from POP3 servers. Unlike SMTP, it is not integrated with the MIME package, but it can easily be used along with MIME to process messages.

In order to initialize a connection, we need to run the pop3::open command by providing it with the hostname, username, and password. Optionally, we can specify the TCP port to connect to as the next argument, otherwise the POP3 default port 110 is the used. This command returns a channel that is used by all other commands from this package.

For example, the following will connect to your Gmail account:

```
set h [pop3::open "pop.gmail.com" "user@gmail.com" "password"]
```

After that variable h will keep a handle, which we can use to issue commands later on. This token is used by all other commands from the pop3 package and is always passed to these commands as the first argument.

We can also provide this command with several options, which should be put before the host name. The first one is -socketcmd, which allows us to specify the command that should be used for creating the socket. Its main use is to support **Secure Socket Layer** (**SSL**) and for providing a command that connects using a proxy server if this is needed. While SSL is described in detail in *Chapter 12*, it is worth mentioning that if we are using SSL, we also need to specify the port to use, which is 995 for POP3 over SSL. For example:

```
set h [pop3::open -socketcmd tls::socket "pop.gmail.com" \
    "user@gmail.com" "password" 995]
```

Another flag is -msex, which takes a Boolean value and specifies whether the server we are communicating with is a Microsoft Exchange server. If this is the case, the POP3 package needs to work around some non-standard behavior that occurs when communicating with a Microsoft Exchange server.

Having the channel to a mail server open, we can now retrieve information. The command pop3::status can be used to find out about the total number of messages and bytes used, and requires passing only the POP3 channel. It returns two numbers — the first one being number of messages in your inbox and the second one specifies the total number of bytes used by all messages. For example:

```
lassign [pop3::status $h] numMessages bytesUsed
```

This will retrieve the status and assign it to numMessages and bytesUsed variables. The command lassign is described in more detail in *Chapter 1*. The number of messages specifies both how many messages are present in our inbox as well as the maximum value that we can use for specifying message identifier.

Listing all messages

We can also list all messages — by receiving either their sizes or their unique identifiers. The command pop3::list returns a list of messages that we can access as a list. The list consists of two elements for each message — its identifier (integer number) and size in bytes. For example, in order to list size of all messages, we can run the following:

```
foreach {id size} [pop3::list $h] {
    puts "Message $id has $size byte(s)"
}
```

The command pop3::uidl works similarly, but returns the unique identifier of a message instead of the size. For example:

```
foreach {id uidl} [pop3::uidl $h] {
    puts "Message $id is $uidl"
}
```

Both `pop3::list` and `pop3::uidl` can be run by specifying message number — in this case, data is returned for a single message only.

Please note that unique identifiers might not be supported by all e-mail servers and this command might return an error in this case. Otherwise, these identifiers allow for identifications of e-mails across POP3 sessions. The POP3 standard does not define the format of these identifiers, so our application should not assume anything about it and about the ways of comparing identifiers.

Unique identifiers combined with a persistent storage can be used to track which messages are new and should be processed, and which ones our application has already processed. This is especially useful if our application does not delete messages after receiving them.

Retrieving e-mails using POP3

Once we know which messages we want to retrieve, we can either retrieve just part of the message or the entire message. In order to retrieve headers and part of the message, we can use the `pop3::top` command. It accepts the POP3 channel, the number of the message, and the number of lines from the actual message to retrieve. For example, in order to retrieve the headers and 5 topmost lines from the first message, we can run the following:

```
puts [pop3::top $h 1 5]
```

Retrieving an entire message or a group of messages can be achieved by using the `pop3::retrieve` command, by specifying the channel name as the first argument and the index of message as the second argument. This command always returns a list of the messages, even if only one index was specified. For example, we can retrieve and print the entire first message by running:

```
puts [lindex [pop3::retrieve $h 1] 0]
```

We can also specify two indexes — the first being the start index and the second being the end index. In this case, the command will retrieve multiple messages and return a list containing them. For example, we can retrieve messages 1, 2, and 3 by running:

```
pop3::retrieve $h 1 3
```

We can also specify special values for the start and/or end indexes. The special index `start` means the first message and is the same as `1`. The special index `end` specifies the last message, based on how many messages are present on the server. For example:

```
set id 0
foreach msg [pop3::retrieve $h start end] {
    incr id
    puts "Message $id has [string length $msg] bytes"
}
```

This will print out the size of each message. The same values can be retrieved using the `pop3::list` command, because in both cases, the message is handled in a binary way — without encoding and/or newline translations.

Deleting one or more messages can be done using the `pop3::delete` command. It accepts the channel name, followed by one or two indexes. Similar to `pop3::retrieve`, if a single index is specified here, then only this message is deleted. If two indexes are specified, then multiple messages are deleted. The special keywords `start` and `end` can also be used. For example, deleting all messages can be done by invoking:

```
pop3::delete $h start end
```

As the POP3 protocol does not support retrieving or deleting multiple messages at a time, internally, both `pop3::retrieve` and `pop3::delete` iterate through the specified range.

When we have finished working with our remote e-mails, we should close the connection. The command `pop3::close` is used for this. The only argument it needs is the POP3 channel name. For example:

```
pop3::close $h
```

Parsing incoming e-mails

After retrieving our messages, we can parse them to properly handle their content. This can be done by using the `mime` package for this purpose, similar to how we built messages.

In order to have the `mime` package parse an already built message, we can use the `mime::initialize` command. It will parse the message, parse headers ,and split it into appropriate parts if we don't provide the `-canonical` flag. For example:

```
set message [lindex [pop3::retrieve $h $id] 0]
set token [mime::initialize -string $message]
```

It is a good idea to catch exceptions from `mime::initialize`, because if the message is not correctly formatted, the command will throw an error. As our messages can come from an unknown source, it is a good idea not to assume all messages can be properly handled.

We can use the token to access information in it and subsequent parts. In order to do this, we'll use three commands: `mime::getheader`, `mime::getproperty`, and `mime::getbody`.

The first command can be used to retrieve MIME headers such as `From`, `To`, `Subject` or `Content-ID`. The command `mime::getproperty` returns information about a particular token. The property `content` specifies content type, `encoding` specified content transfer encoding (base64 or quoted-printable), and `size` provides the size of the content before decoding it. The `parts` property provides a list of subordinates (children) of this node and it is only set if this node has children.

Both commands accept a MIME token as the first argument and, optionally, a property or header name as the second argument. If a name is not specified, the commands return a name-value pair list. Both commands also throw an error if a header or property is not set for this token.

The command `mime::getbody` decodes and returns the body of a message or a subordinate. It is used to extract the non-multipart elements of a message.

Let's use these methods in a more practical example. Assume we want to create an application that will check e-mails, look for messages that have an attachment with `jobdata.raw` filename and insert the contents of each of these attachments to a database. We'll also keep track of messages we've already parsed and will not delete them.

For the database, we'll use SQLite3, because it will not require the reader to set up any database server. SQLite3 is included in ActiveTcl, so we should have it installed already. More details about databases can be found in *Chapter 5*.

We'll start by initializing our code and database. We'll load the appropriate packages and initialize the database:

```
package require pop3
package require tls
package require sqlite3
package require mime

if {![file exists "database.db"]} {
    sqlite3 db "database.db"
```

```
        db eval {
            CREATE TABLE emails
                (uidl TEXT, status INTEGER)
        }

        db eval {
            CREATE TABLE jobs
                (uidl TEXT, id INTEGER, jobdata TEXT)
        }
    } else {
        sqlite3 db "database.db"
    }
```

If the database file does not exist, we'll create the appropriate tables. If the database exists, we'll assume it already has the proper tables set up. We're creating a table called emails that keeps unique identifiers of messages we've already parsed and a table called jobs which keeps track of jobs along with source messages.

As one of the first steps, we open the POP3 connection:

```
set h [pop3::open -socketcmd tls::socket \
    $hostname $username $password 995]
```

Now let's fetch the unique identifier information and iterate through it. We'll store a list of IDs and unique identifiers that we do not know in the idlist variable, which we'll initialize using an empty string:

```
set idlist [list]

# read all messages and find out which ones we should process
foreach {id uidl} [pop3::uidl $h] {
```

Following that, we fetch information for this UIDL from our local database and see if it is not empty:

```
        set status [lindex [db eval \
            {SELECT status FROM emails WHERE uidl=$uidl} \
            ] 0]
        if {$status == ""} {
```

If the status is empty, it means that the entry in the database does not exist— the database returned 0 items and first element from this list is empty. In this case, we'll add our message to the list of messages to process. Otherwise, we'll skip it. In both cases, we'll also print out the status to standard output.

```
            lappend idlist $id $uidl
            puts "We'll process message $id ($uidl)"
        } else {
```

```
        # this entry was already processed
        puts "Message $id ($uidl) was already processed\
            and has status $status"
    }
```

And that finishes our loop as well:

```
    }
```

Now the `idlist` variable contains a list of messages that we need to process kept as id-uidl pairs. We'll iterate through it and fetch the messages:

```
foreach {id uidl} $idlist {
    puts "Retrieving message $id"
    set message [lindex [pop3::retrieve $h $id] 0]
    if {[catch {
        set token [mime::initialize -string $message]
    } error]} {
        puts "Error while parsing message: $error"
        db eval {
            INSERT INTO emails (uidl, status)
                VALUES($uidl, "ERROR")
        }
    } else {
```

Our application retrieves a message and tries to parse it. If the parsing fails, we mark this fact in our database. If not, we proceed to handling the message:

```
        set attachments [findAttachments $token jobdata.raw]
        set aid 0
        foreach attachment $attachments {
            incr aid
            set jobdata [mime::getbody $attachment]
            db eval {
                INSERT INTO jobs (uidl, id, jobdata)
                    VALUES($uidl, $aid, $jobdata)
            }
        }

        set status "FETCHED; COUNT=[llength $attachments]"
        db eval {
            INSERT INTO emails (uidl, status)
                VALUES($uidl, $status)
        }
        mime::finalize $token -subordinates all
```

Once we have the token, we invoke `findAttachments` procedure. It's described in the following code, but returns a list of all MIME tokens that are an attachment and their filename is `jobdara.raw`. We'll go through this procedure in detail after finalizing our main part of the application.

Next we need to close our condition and loop, and close the POP3 connection:

```
        }
    }


    pop3::close $h
```

Our helper procedure to find attachments looks like:

```
proc findAttachments {token filename} {
    set result [list]

    # if it is a multipart node, iterate over children
    # otherwise process this part
    if {[catch {
        set children [mime::getproperty $token parts]
    }]} {
        # getting parts failed - it's a leaf
        # in this case, get Content-ID header
        # and compare it to requested filename
        if {![catch {
            set contentID [mime::getheader \
                $token "Content-ID"]
        }]} {
            # if filename matches Content-ID
            if {$contentID == $filename} {
                lappend result $token
            }
        }
    } else {
        # for multipart/*, we'll iterate over children
        # to see if any of them contains the attachment
        foreach token $children {
            set result [concat $result \
                [findAttachments $token $filename] \
                ]
        }
    }
    return $result
}
```

What we do here is try to get `parts` property for the token. If this fails, we proceed with finding `Content-ID` header. If this does not fail, and is what we expected to find, we add this token to results. If this part had children, we iterate through them and recursively call our procedure again. We also combine results from all of these calls so that it is possible to send multiple attachments, and/or they can be put in various parts of the e-mail.

 The example in this section is located in the `05pop3andmime` directory in the source code examples for this chapter.

Documentation on `pop3` package can be found on the `tcllib` project website on SourceForge: `http://tcllib.sourceforge.net/doc/pop3.html`

Transferring files and data

Transferring files over the Internet is one of the most common things that networked applications do. In this section, we'll focus on two very popular protocols—**HyperText Transfer Protocol (HTTP)** and **File Transfer Protocol (FTP)**. The first one is used to download websites, images, or other files from the Web and second one is used to download or upload files. There are subtle differences between the two and we'll need to go into a bit more detail to understand them.

HTTP is a for retrieving a single item over network. It allows us to retrieve a single element and is a lightweight protocol. It also allows us to handle large numbers of requests and is the protocol used for serving websites to web browsers. HTTP is used for both static files (such as HTML pages, images, downloads, and so on) and dynamic files (such as PHP or Tcl scripts building pages when users access them).

FTP protocol on the other hand is designed to transfer files over a network. It features authentication, and offers a lot of features that are specific to file management—creating directories, renaming and deleting items, listing contents of a directory, and the idea of a working directory. FTP is also a more heavyweight protocol and is less commonly used for offering downloads to wide audience.

Resources and uri package

Specifying locations of a resource on the Internet is done by specifying a **URL—Unique Resource Location**. It consists of a protocol, an optional username, a password, a hostname, and a port followed by the path to the resource. For example, a URL could look like `http://wiki.tcl.tk/tcllib`

Tcl offers the `uri` package, which is part of Tcllib, and can be used to split and join URLs from parts. These parts include `scheme`, `user`, `pwd`, `host`, `port`, `path`, `query`, and `fragment`. Not all of these are always present in all types of URLs. The first one is the only key only present and defines protocol that is used — for example, `http` and `ftp`. Credentials are optional and are specified as `user` and `pwd`. The parts `host` and `port` specify the hostname and port to connect to; `port` can be empty, which means it is the default port for specified protocol. The location of the resource is specified as `path`, and `query` is an optional part that defines a query sent via the URL (mainly for `http` requests); `fragment` points to a fragment of a page and is also used only for the HTTP protocol.

Currently, `ftp`, `http`, `https`, `file`, `mailto`, and news protocols are supported.

We can split a URL into elements using the `uri::split` command. It returns one or more name-value pairs which represent each part. For example, we can do the following:

```
set uridata [uri::split "http://wiki.tcl.tk/tcllib"]

foreach name {scheme user pwd host port path query fragment} {
    if {[dict exists $uridata $name]} {
        puts "$name = [dict get $uridata $name]"
    }
}
```

This will print the following result:

```
scheme = http
user =
pwd =
host = wiki.tcl.tk
port =
path = tcllib
query =
```

We can also create a URL by specifying various parts using the `uri::join` command. It takes all arguments and parses them as name-value pairs, specifying parts of the address it should generate. For example:

```
puts [uri::join \
    scheme http host www.packtpub.com port 80 path books \
    ]
```

The preceding code will print out the address `http://www.packtpub.com/books`. Please note that port part was skipped, because 80 is the default port for the HTTP protocol.

We can also use the result from splitting and join it back by running:

```
puts [uri::join {*}[uri::split "http://www.google.com"]]
```

This will split the address into parts and pass that to the `uri::join` command — `{*}` will cause all elements of the list to be appended as separate arguments, because the command expects it.

 The sample code shown in this section is located in the `06uri` directory in the source code examples for this chapter.

More information about the `uri` package can be found in its documentation available at:
`http://tcllib.sourceforge.net/doc/uri.html`

Using HTTP

HTTP is a stateless protocol that uses a simple request-response message exchange pattern. This means that whenever a client, such as our application, wants to access a particular resource, it sends a HTTP request. The server then processes it and sends back a response, usually being the requested response or information that it could not be found or an error occurred.

HTTP works by sending a request to the server. A request describes whether we are getting information or sending data to server, the path to the resource, and the version of the protocol we're using. A request also consists of several headers, which are name-value pairs and can either be standard or custom ones. Finally, a request can also provide data that we are uploading to server.

Retrieving data over HTTP

After receiving and parsing the request, the web server returns the response. The response consists of a status line, one or more headers, and the body of the response. After the response is sent, the current connection is either closed or reused for the next request. However, from the HTTP perspective, each of these requests is treated independently.

Tcl comes with a `http` package built-in. This package offers a basic, but complete HTTP client which can be used to perform both basic and more advanced operations. The command `http::geturl` is used to initiate or perform a request and is the starting point for performing HTTP operations. This command accepts a URL followed by one or more options.

A commonly used option is -binary, which specifies whether the transfer should be done in binary mode and defaults to false. By default, Tcl does newlines and encoding conversions for text documents — therefore, if a server sends out some HTML in UTF-8, Tcl converts that to proper string. If the -binary option is enabled, this is not performed and all types of documents are retrieved as bytes, not depending on whether it is a text document or not.

The http::geturl command always returns a token that can be used to get information and data related to this query. For example, in order to get the contents of Google's main page, we can simply run:

```
package require http
set token [http::geturl "http://www.google.com/"]
puts [http::data $token]
```

The second line receives the request and returns token that we can use later on. The command http::data returns body of server's response, which we then print to standard output.

The command http::cleanup should be used after we are done working with a request. It will clean up all resources used for this request. For example:

http::cleanup $token

We can also save contents of the response directly to any open channel. For example:

```
set fh [open "google-index.html" w]
set token [http::geturl "http://www.google.com/" -channel $fh]
http::cleanup $token
close $fh
```

This will cause a response to be written to the specified channel and not stored in memory. This can be used for downloading large files and/or if you plan to save the contents of the response to a file.

There are important things that our previous example is missing, for example, checking for errors. Although the http package will throw an error if the web server is unreachable, there are cases when a web server will send a response stating that a resource is unavailable or an error has occurred. In these cases, it is not translated into an error as this might be the desired response from our application's perspective.

We can check the status of handling the request by using the `http::status` command. It will return one of the following values:

Status	Description
ok	Indicates that the HTTP request was completed successfully
eof	Indicates that the server closed connection without replying
error	Indicates an error

If the status is `error`, we can also retrieve actual error message using the `http::error` command.

HTTP server sends status codes which specify the outcome of processing this request. We can retrieve the status code using the `http::ncode` command. Usually, it is sufficient to check if the code equals `200`, which means that the request has been processed correctly.

The most frequently used status codes are:

Code	Description
200	The request has been successfully executed
206	The request has been successfully executed and result is partial content, used to download parts of a file over HTTP
301	Moved permanently — indicates that resource has been permanently moved to a new location; response header `Location` gives new location to resource
302	Moved temporarily — indicates that resource has been temporarily moved to a new location; response header `Location` gives new location to resource
401	Unauthorized — indicates that a server has requested the client to authenticate
403	Forbidden — this indicates that access to this resource is forbidden
404	Not found — indicates that a specified resource cannot be found
500	Internal error — indicates that there was a problem serving this request; for example, because HTTP server configuration is broken or module/script failed

For example, we can print out the status of our request by running:

```
switch -- [http::status $token] {
    error {
        puts "ERROR: [http::error $token]"
    }
    eof {
        puts "EOF reading response"
    }
    ok {
```

```
            puts "OK; code: [http::ncode $token]"
            puts "Data:"
            puts [http::data $token]
        }
    }
```

We can also get all headers from an HTTP response by using the `http::meta` command. It returns a list of name-value pairs that can be used as dictionaries or arrays. For example, to get contents of the `Location` header, we can do the following:

```
set code [http::ncode $token]
if {($code == 301) || ($code == 302)} {
    set newURL [dict get [http::meta $token] Location]
    # go to new location
}
```

The complete example is located in the `07httprequest` directory in the source code examples for this chapter.

Submitting information using GET and POST

We can also use the `http` package to submit information to a web server – for automating things such as filling in forms. Data from a form can be formatted using the `http::formatQuery` command. It can now be sent in two ways – either as part of the path in the URL or sending data as separate data. The first case is done using a GET request and an example is searching using Google, like `http://www.google.com/search?q=tcl` – the query is passed after `?` character. The other approach is sending a POST request and the data is sent after the actual request.

POST is used for sending a larger amount of data and usually takes place when the request is modifying/sending data. GET is usually used for reading information as it can send smaller amount of data. POST requests are used for sending data, they can send much larger amount of data and POST requests are not cached by proxy servers.

For both GET and POST, data is sent as name-value pairs – `q=tcl` means value for field `q` is `tcl`. Multiple values are separated using `&` character. Tcl offers a command for generating such data, that is `http::formatQuery`. It accepts zero or more name-value pairs as arguments and formats proper query as an output.

Sending data using GET requires that we append the query to actual URL, for example:

```
set query [http::formatQuery q "Tcl Programming"]
set url "http://www.google.com/search?$query"
```

Sending POST data requires passing the data as a `-query` option to `http::geturl`. For example, we can do the following:

```
set query [http::formatQuery search "tcl programming"]
set url "http://www.packtpub.com/search"
set token [http::geturl $url -query $query]
```

This will cause a query to be sent as POST and data from `-query` will be sent.

By default, data is sent as encoded form data, it is also possible to send different query data. Usually, this is accompanied by sending the appropriate query type to the server. We can do this by adding the `-type` flag when sending the query. If a type is not specified, it defaults to `application/x-www-form-urlencoded`, which is the default MIME type for encoded form data. Many applications expecting XML or **JavaScript Object** Notaktion (**JSON**) data require that data sent in XML/JSON is sent with the appropriate MIME type in the headers of the request.

For example, we can send XML with accompanying data by doing:

```
http::geturl $url -command onCompleteXMLPost \
    -type "text/xml" \
    -query [$dom asXML]
```

This will cause the appropriate value for the `Content-Type` header to be sent in the query. Details on XML and its handling can be found in *Chapter 5* and show how to read and write documents.

 Examples related to basic HTTP functionality are placed in `basic.tcl` file in the `07httprequest` directory in the source code examples for this chapter.

By default, `http` queries are done in a synchronous way, meaning that the `http::geturl` command returns after the command has been executed. In many cases, it is better to use an asynchronous approach, where the command exits instantly, uses events to process requests, and issues our callback, which is a Tcl command that will be run when the operation is completed.

The `http` package also offers advanced features such as passing additional headers to requests. This can be done by providing both the `-timeout` and `-command` options to the `http::geturl` command. In this case, the command returns immediately and returns a token that will be used. Accessing the data should be done from the command passed to the `-command` option. In asynchronous requests, `http::geturl` might still throw an error, for cases such as "no existing hostname". It is still recommended to catch such exceptions and handle them appropriately.

For example, in order to download the Google page asynchronously, we can do the following:

```
if {[catch {
    set token [http::geturl "http://www.google.com/" \
        -timeout 300000 -command doneGet]
} error]} {
    puts stderr "Error while getting URL: $error"
}
```

Next we can create the command that will be invoked as the callback. It will be run with an additional parameter—the token of the request. For example, our command, based on previous examples, can be run as follows:

```
proc doneGet {token} {
    switch -- [http::status $token] {
        error {
            puts "ERROR: [http::error $token]"
        }
        eof {
            puts "EOF reading response"
        }
        ok {
            puts "OK; code: [http::ncode $token]"
            puts "  Size: [http::size $token]"
            puts "  Data:"
            puts [http::data $token]
        }
    }
    http::cleanup $token
}
```

The token can be used in the same way as we used it with synchronous requests. We are also responsible for cleaning up the token, which is done in the last line of the example.

 Examples related to basic HTTP functionality are located in the `async.tcl` file in the `07httprequest` directory in the source code examples for this chapter.

Advanced topics

The package `http` can also be used for more advanced features such as partial content downloading, sending cookies, and HTTP-level authorization.

The majority of these functions can be carried out using the `-headers` option passed to the `http::geturl` command. This option accepts a list of one or more name-value pairs. These can be any headers and values, but these should be headers that the server can understand. For example, we can use it to send cookie values to a site or authorize over HTTP for sites that use it.

There are two common ways that users are authorized within the Web — at the HTTP level and using HTML forms and cookies. The first one provides the username and password information as a HTTP header. The latter uses sending form data and cookies to track users, and is mainly related to handling cookies properly at the HTTP level.

For now, we'll focus on HTTP level authorization. A lot of web-based applications and data are protected using this mechanism. Let's assume we want to retrieve data from a specified URL. We need to connect to it without providing any credentials, and at this point, the server should include HTTP status `401`. The following code would be a good start for checking if authorization is needed:

```
set token [http::geturl $url]
if {[http::status $token] != "ok"} {
    puts stderr "Error while retrieving URL"
    http::cleanup $token
    exit 1
}


if {[http::ncode $token] == 401} {
```

If this condition is `true`, we should resend our request. The server will provide the `WWW-Authenticate` header in the response that will indicate the type of authentication and realm, which specifies the descriptive name of the resource we are currently trying to authenticate to. We can print it out by running:

```
set realm [dict get [http::meta $token] \
    "WWW-Authenticate"]
puts "Authenticate information: $realm"
```

Next we need to clean up the previous request and send a new one with proper authentication information. Except for a few cases, the authentication type of `Basic` is used by HTTP servers. It requires sending a `<username>:<password>` string encoded as `base64`, preceded by the word `Basic`. We'll use the package `base64` for this along with the `base64::encode` command:

```
package require base64
set authinfo [base64::encode ${username}:${password}]
set headers [list Authorization "Basic $authinfo"]
```

The second line contains the `Authorization` header to be sent to the server, along with the credentials as `base64`. Next we're sending a new request by doing:

```
set token [http::geturl $url -headers $headers]
if {[http::status $token] != "ok"} {
    http::cleanup $token
    puts stderr "Error while retrieving URL"
    exit 1
}
```

We can then check if our current username and password were correct. If not, then the status for a new request will also be `401`:

```
if {[http::ncode $token] == 401} {
    puts stderr "Invalid username and/or password"
    http::cleanup $token
    exit 1
}
```

An example related to basic authorization is located in the `auth.tcl` file in the `07httprequest` directory in the source code examples for this chapter.

Cookies in Tcl

An additional feature that headers are useful for is supporting **cookies.** While the `http` package itself does not provide this functionality, it is easy to support this in the majority of cases. Standards for setting and getting cookies define expiration dates, and paths and domains that cookies should be valid for. However, in the majority of code that we write, it is enough to assume that the cookie you're getting is needed for all subsequent requests.

Cookies work in such a way that HTTP responses from servers may include one or more `Set-Cookie` headers. These headers need to be parsed and all cookies should be passed in the `Cookie` header. The server might send a response similar to this one:

```
Set-Cookie: mycookie=TEST0123; path=/
Set-Cookie: i=1; expires=Thu, 27-Oct-2011 11:07:24 GMT; path=/
```

This causes the cookie `mycookie` to be set to `TEST0123` and `i` to be set to `1`. Each subsequent request to this server should include the following header:

```
Cookie: mycookie=TEST0123; i=1
```

All changes to existing cookies overwrite them and new cookies cause a new value to be set, which is similar to behavior of arrays and dictionaries in Tcl. Writing code that handles cookies without taking parameters into account is relatively easy.

Let's start by writing a command that processes the HTTP response for cookies. We define the namespace for our code, the reference variable specified by user, and iterate over HTTP headers from the provided token:

```
namespace eval cookies {}

proc cookies::processCookies {varname token} {
    upvar 1 $varname d
    foreach {name value} [http::meta $token] {
        if {[string equal -nocase $name "Set-Cookie"]} {
```

If the header is Set-Cookie, we process its value by taking part only until the first occurrence of a semi-colon and separating it into name and value using regular expressions:

```
            set value [lindex [split $value ";"] 0]
            if {[regexp "^(.*?)=(.*)\$" $value \
                - cname cvalue]} {
                dict set d $cname $cvalue
            }
        }
    }
}
```

This will cause the dictionary that is stored in the varname variable to be updated. Next, in all requests ,we need to pass all cookies. A small function to generate the appropriate value for the Cookies header would look like:

```
proc cookies::prepareCookies {var} {
    set rc [list]
    dict for {name value} $var {
        lappend rc "$name=$value"
    }
    return [join $rc "; "]
}
```

Here we only take each cookie, append it, and join all cookies using a semi-colon followed by a space. In order to use this to query Tcler's wiki we can do the following:

```
set c [dict create]
set h [http::geturl http://wiki.tcl.tk/]
cookies::processCookies c $h
http::cleanup $h

set query [http::formatQuery _charset_ utf-8 S cookie]
set h [http::geturl http://wiki.tcl.tk/_/search?$query \
    -headers [list Cookie [cookies::prepareCookies $c]] \
    ]
```

The first request gets the main page of the Wiki, which causes a cookie to be set. We need to pass this cookie to the second request in order to be able to perform a search. In this case, we're searching for the cookie string. Without passing the cookie from previous request, this site will not allow us to perform the search.

 An example related to basic authorization is located in the cookies.tcl file in the 07httprequest directory in the source code examples for this chapter.

HTTP and encryption

HTTP can handle both encrypted and unencrypted communication. The default is not to encrypt the connection, which is in fact http protocol when specifying URLs. It is also possible to use HTTP over SSL encrypted connection, which is usually called https.

The Tcl package http allows registering additional protocols to run HTTP on with the command http::register. It requires that we specify the name of the protocol, default port, and command that should be invoked to create a socket. This is mainly used for SSL connections. In order to enable the use of the https protocol, we need to add the following code to our application:

```
package require tls
http::register https 443 tls::socket
```

The tls package provides SSL-enabled sockets to the Tcl language and it provides the command tls::socket, which is an equivalent of the socket command, except for enabling SSL for connection. SSL and security is described in more detail in *Chapter 12*.

More information about the http package as well as remaining configuration options can be found in its documentation at:
http://www.tcl.tk/man/tcl8.5/TclCmd/http.htm

Retrieving RSS information

Really Simple Sindication (RSS) is a format for publishing frequently updated information, such as blog entries, news headlines, audio, and video in a standard format. An RSS document (often also called a **feed** or **channel**) provides a list of items recently published along with metadata about these items. RSS is provided by an majority of content providers, such as portals, blog engines, and so on. Even Packt Publishing has its own RSS feed that we'll use later on in an example.

RSS itself is an XML document published over HTTP. This means that using the `http` and `tdom` packages, we can easily retrieve and parse an RSS feed and find out about recent documents. The RSS standard describes the structure of the XML document, which we'll learn later. All we need to know is the URL to RSS feed to start with. Information about the address to the RSS feed is usually stored in the website's metadata. This as well is standardized and usually looks like this:

```
<link rel="alternate" type="application/rss+xml" href="/rss.xml"
title="Packt Publishing News" >
```

The previous example is from Packt Publishing's website. Your browser also probably supports this and a small icon on the bottom or near address of the page indicates that an RSS feed is present—clicking on it will go to the RSS feed and allow you to subscribe to it from your browser and get the address of the actual RSS feed.

Packt Publishing website's RSS feed address is `http://www.packtpub.com/rss.xml`. Tcler's Wiki is available at `http://wiki.tcl.tk/`, and it also has its feed available at: `http://wiki.tcl.tk/rss.xml`

We'll start with Tcler's Wiki and its feeds. The feed looks as follows:

```
<?xml version='1.0'?>
<rss version='0.91'>
  <channel>
    <title>The Tcler's Wiki - Recent Changes</title>
    <link>http://wiki.tcl.tk/</link>
    <description>Recent changes to The Tcler's Wiki</description>
    <item>
        <title>tDOM</title>
        <link>http://wiki.tcl.tk/1948</link>
        <pubDate>Wed, 14 Apr 2010 01:05:27 GMT</pubDate>
        <description>Modified by CMcC (898 characters)
(actual description of the Wiki change goes here)
        </description>
    </item>
    <item>
        <title>WISH User Help</title>
        <link>http://wiki.tcl.tk/20914</link>
        <pubDate>Wed, 14 Apr 2010 00:59:10 GMT</pubDate>
        <description>Modified by pa_mcclamrock (194 characters)
(actual description of the Wiki change goes here)
 </description>
    </item>
  </channel>
</rss>
```

In order to read RSS, we need to find the `<rss>` tag and iterate over all `<channel>` tags. The first one includes information about the RSS feed and each `<channel>` instance can describe a different channel. It is possible that one RSS feed describes multiple channels, although usually an RSS feed covers only one channel. Each channel has a title, link, and list of items.

In order to get all items in a channel, we need to iterate over the `<item>` tags inside the channel. Each item describes a single element in a feed, such as one entry on a blog, in this case, one change in the wiki. Each item has a title, link, publication date, and description. Many RSS feeds provide additional information, which can be checked and handled properly if needed.

We can retrieve the RSS by simply doing:

```
set token [http::geturl "http://wiki.tcl.tk/rss.xml"]
if {[http::status $token] != "ok"} {
    puts "Error retrieving RSS file"
    exit 1
}
set data [http::data $token]
http::cleanup $token
```

We now have the RSS document in the `data` variable, and we can parse it using `tdom`:

```
set dom [dom parse $data]
```

The `tdom` package is described in more detail in *Chapter 5*.

Now we can iterate over each channel by doing:

```
foreach channel [$dom selectNodes "rss/channel"] {
```

This will use the `selectNodes` method to find all channel tags. We can then find the `<title>` tag in our channel and use `asText` method for that node to get title of current channel and print it:

```
set nodes [$channel selectNodes "title"]
set title [[lindex $nodes 0] asText]

puts "Channel \"$title\":"
```

We can now iterate over all items for a channel in similar way:

```
foreach item [$channel selectNodes "item"] {
    set nodes [$item selectNodes "link"]
    set link [[lindex $nodes 0] asText]

    set nodes [$item selectNodes "title"]
```

```
set title [[lindex $nodes 0] asText]

puts "- \[$link\] $title"
}
```

We first use the `selectNodes` method to find `<item>` tags, iterate over them, get the link and title by finding proper nodes and using the `asText` method. We then print information on each element.

Finally we need to close the loop iterating over channels:

```
}
```

 The source code in this section is located in the `rss-basic.tcl` file in the `08rss` directory in the source code examples for this chapter.

In many cases our applications will need to check and retrieve RSS periodically. In such cases, it is a good idea to cache the RSS on disk or in memory. If our application offers a web interface to consolidate multiple RSS channels or filter them to only include specified items, this would be the best approach.

In order to do this, all we need to do is change how our DOM tree is created. We'll start by setting URL of the feed and name of the file to store it:

```
set url "http://www.packtpub.com/rss.xml"
set filename "packtpub-rss.xml"
```

Next we can check if the local copy exists and if it was created in the last 30 minutes by doing:

```
if {(![file exists $filename]) ||
    ([file mtime $filename] < [clock scan "-30 minutes"])} {
```

This checks whether the file does not exist or if it has been created earlier than 30 minutes ago. If any of these conditions are met, then we download the RSS by doing:

```
set token [http::geturl $url -binary true]

if {[http::status $token] != "ok"} {
    puts "Error retrieving RSS file"
    exit 1
}

set fh [open $filename w]
fconfigure $fh -translation binary
puts $fh [http::data $token]
close $fh
http::cleanup $token
}
```

This is similar to previous example and to the HTTP examples shown earlier. The main difference is that we're downloading the file in binary mode. This prevents the `http` package from converting the file's encoding.

We will use the `tDOM::xmlReadFile` command to read the RSS. This command is part of the `tdom` package and handles encoding issues when reading files such as detecting encoding. It also handles the **Byte Order Mark (BOM)** markers that many RSS feeds have. This is a set of bytes at beginning of XML file that specifies encoding of the file and is described in more detail at: `http://en.wikipedia.org/wiki/Byte_order_mark`

In order to read and parse the file, all we need to do is:

```
set dom [dom parse [tDOM::xmlReadFile $filename]]
```

After that, we can use the same set of iterations as previously to list all entries in the RSS feed:

```
foreach channel [$dom selectNodes "rss/channel"] {
    set nodes [$channel selectNodes "title"]
    set title [[lindex $nodes 0] asText]

    puts "Channel \"$title\":"
    foreach item [$channel selectNodes "item"] {
        set nodes [$item selectNodes "link"]
        set link [[lindex $nodes 0] asText]

        set nodes [$item selectNodes "title"]
        set title [[lindex $nodes 0] asText]

        puts "- \[$link\] $title"
    }
}
```

 The source code in this section is located in the `rss-file.tcl` file in the `08rss` directory in the source code examples for this chapter.

Using FTP

The **File Transfer Protocol (FTP)** is a stateful protocol for transferring files. It requires logging in, keeps the connection alive across transfers, and is not a lightweight protocol. It is mainly used for retrieving or transferring multiple files.

Tcl has a package called `ftp`, which is a part of Tcllib, and can be used to download and upload files over FTP. It offers functionality for connecting, getting file information, and uploading and downloading files.

Establishing connections

The command `ftp::Open` can be used to set up a connection to an FTP server. It accepts the server name, username, and password followed by any additional options we might want to provide. It returns a token that we can later use for all other operations.

 The package `ftp` differs from the majority of Tcl packages in that its commands start with uppercase, such as `Open` instead of `open`. This is not common in the Tcl world, but is the case for the FTP package for historical reasons.

Anonymous FTP connections require specifying `anonymous` as the username and the e-mail as the password. For example, in order to open an anonymous connection to `ftp.tcl.tk`, we can do:

```
set token [ftp::Open ftp.tcl.tk anonymous my@email.com]
```

An FTP session has a dedicated connection to the server. For each additional FTP transfer such as listing files, downloading and uploading, additional connections are made with the server for the purpose of each transfer. The FTP protocol uses two modes for communication—active and passive. Active connections work in such a way that FTP server connects to its client for sending data, passive connections work the opposite way, the client connects to FTP server.

While the default for `ftp` package is to use active mode, it might be necessary to use passive mode if our computer does not have a public IP address. Passive mode is also the default for majority of clients as it works regardless of having a public IP address, so it is a good idea to use passive mode whenever possible. Specifying the mode can be done using the `-mode` flag appended to the `ftp::Open` command. Acceptable values are `active` and `passive`. For example:

```
set token [ftp::Open ftp.tcl.tk \
    anonymous my@email.com -mode passive]
```

Retrieving files

Another important aspect of FTP we should be aware of is transfer type. Due to how different operating systems store information, FTP differentiates between text (ASCII) and binary files. We can do this using the `ftp::Type` command. It accepts a token as the first argument and the transfer type as additional argument. It can be either `ascii` or `binary`. To set our transfer type to binary, we can do:

```
ftp::Type $token binary
```

We can now retrieve files over FTP. We can use the command `ftp::Get` for this purpose. It works in different modes depending on the arguments supplied. It first accepts the token of the connection, followed by the path to the remote file. We run this command without any arguments — in this case, the file will be downloaded with the same name as the remote path. If we specify a local filename as the next argument, it will be downloaded as that name. Instead, we can also specify `-variable` or `-channel` options, followed by a value. This will cause file data to be downloaded to a variable or saved in a specified channel. In case of a channel, it will not be closed after file is retrieved.

For example, we can retrieve remote file `tcl8.5.7-src.tar.gz` from `pub/tcl/tcl8_5` remote directory as same file in local filesystem by doing:

```
ftp::Get "pub/tcl/tcl8_5/tcl8.5.7-src.tar.gz" \
    "tcl8.5.7-src.tar.gz"
```

Similarly, we can download a file to variable by doing:

```
ftp::Get "pub/tcl/tcl8_5/tcl8.5.7-src.tar.gz" \
    -variable fileContents
```

Please note that due to how this is implemented, the variable name is global and not local to the code invoking `ftp::Get` command. It is best to use namespace-based variables or object variables for this.

We can also resume an interrupted transfer by using the `ftp::Reget` command. It requires that we specify a token, a remote filename and, optionally, a local filename. If a local name is not specified, it is assumed to be the same as remote name. We can also specify offsets at which to begin and end download at, but by default, Tcl will download remaining part of the file.

For example, in order to complete transfer of `tcl8.5.7-src.tar.gz` file, we can simply invoke:

```
ftp::Reget $token tcl8.5.7-src.tar.gz
```

Uploading files

Similarly, there are commands for putting and appending to remote files. The command `ftp::Put` can be used to upload a file, while `ftp::Append` will append data to an already existing file, which can be used to continue an interrupted transfer. In both cases, the syntax is the same — the first argument is the token of the FTP session to use, followed by either the local filename, `-data` or `-channel` options. In the first case only a filename is needed, in the second option actual data or channel to use needs to be specified. The last argument is the remote filename to use. If the remote filename is missing, it is assumed to be the same as the local one.

For example, to upload a file, we can do:

```
ftp::Put my-logs.tar.gz
```

In order to append data to a file, we can do:

```
ftp::Append -data "Some text\n" remote-logs.txt
```

When downloading or uploading data, it will be treated as binary data — that is, if we are downloading text, we can use the encoding command to convert it from/to proper encoding.

Listing files and directories

FTP also introduces the concept of the current directory for a specified FTP session. We can change the directory by invoking the ftp::Cd command and retrieve the current directory by invoking ftp::Pwd. The first command expects the FTP session token and the path to the directory, which can be relative or absolute. The second command always returns an absolute path, which can be used when comparing and/or analyzing current location.

For example:

```
puts "Changing directory"
ftp::Cd $token "pub/tcl/tcl8_5"
puts "Changed to [ftp::Pwd $token]"
```

We can also retrieve information about remote files. The command ftp::FileSize returns size of a file in bytes. The command ftp::ModTime returns the time when a file was last modified, as Unix time. Both commands require a token to the FTP session and a filename. For example:

```
set size [ftp::FileSize $token tcl8.5.7-src.tar.gz]
puts "tcl8.5.7-src.tar.gz is $size bytes"
set mtime [ftp::ModTime $token tcl8.5.7-src.tar.gz]
set mtext [clock format $mtime]
puts "tcl8.5.7-src.tar.gz last modified on $mtext"
```

We can also list the contents of a directory. The command ftp::NList can be used to list all files and directories in the current or specified directory. It accepts a token to the session and we can also provide directory to list. If this is not specified, listing of current directory is performed. This command returns a list of all items found in a directory, each element of a list being the name of the file or directory.

For example:

```
foreach file [ftp::NList $token] {
    puts $file
}
```

The command `ftp::List` returns a long listing of a directory. This returns a list of items, where each item is represented by a line, similar to output of `ls -l` command in Unix. For example:

```
foreach line [ftp::List $token] {
    puts $line
}
```

The preceding code would print out the following line, among others:

```
-rw-r--r--  1 ftp ftp 4421720 Apr 15 2009 tcl8.5.7-src.tar.gz
```

While this provides much more information, we need additional code to parse such lines. Let's start with creating a command for this:

```
proc parseListLine {line} {
```

First we try to search for filenames with spaces and remove symbolic link definitions (which are in the form of `filename -> actual_file` it points to).

```
if {[regexp {(([^ ]|[^0-9] )+$} $line name]} {
    # Check for links
    if {[set idx [string first " -> " $name]] != -1} {
        incr idx -1
        set name [string range $name 0 $idx]
    }
}
```

Following that we remove any multiple spaces and create a list of items by splitting the resulting string by spaces:

```
regsub -all "\[ \t\]+" $line " " line
set items [split $line " "]
```

If we did not match the name with previous attempt, we assume that filename is the last element:

```
if {![info exists name]} {set name [lindex $items end]}
```

We then try to get the permissions and file size information, if possible:

```
set perm [lindex $items 0]
if {[string is integer [lindex $items 4]]} {
    set size [lindex $items 4]
} else {
    lappend result ""
}
```

Based on the permissions we've extracted, we take the first character and gather the actual file type based on it:

```
switch -- [string index $perm 0] {
    d {
        set type "directory"
    }
    c - b {
        set type "device"
    }
    l {
        set type "symlink"
    }
    default {
        set type "file"
    }
}
```

We then return a list that consists of the filename, type, size, and permissions:

```
    return [list $name $type $size $perm]
}
```

This code is based on `ftp.tcl` from the `tclvfs` package, which is licensed under the BSD license. The package is available at:
`http://sourceforge.net/projects/tclvfs/`

We can then test it in the following way:

```
foreach line [ftp::List $token] {
    puts "\nOriginal line: $line"
    lassign [parseListLine $line] \
        name type size perm
    puts "Filename '$name' ($type), size $size,  $perm"
}
```

In addition to this, we can also modify remote filesystem contents. The command `ftp::MkDir` can be used to create a directory. It expects a token to the session as the first argument and the name of the directory to create as the second argument.

The command `ftp::Rename` can be used to rename a file or directory. It requires a token of the FTP session, and the old and new names.

The commands `ftp::RmDir` and `ftp::Delete` can be used to delete a directory or file, respectively. Both accept token of the FTP session and name of the directory or file to delete.

Closing a connection to an FTP server can be done using the `ftp::Close` command, specifying token of the FTP session. For example:

```
ftp::Close $token
```

 The source code in this section is located in the `09ftp` directory in the source code examples for this chapter.

More information about the `ftp` package as well as the remaining configuration options can be found in its documentation in SourceForge project at:
`http://tcllib.sourceforge.net/doc/ftp.html`

Summary

Tcl can communicate with applications and devices using a variety of protocols and talk to different types of hardware—embedded devices, routers, desktops, and servers.

We can use e-mail to communicate with users and/or applications. Tcl allows us to send and retrieve e-mails. It also offers mechanisms for parsing and building MIME messages that include support for attachments, *inlined* images, multiple document types, and different encoding systems.

We can use Tcl to transfer files over FTP and HTTP. We can use this to retrieve information, communicate with server part of our application, download updates, upload results as well as many other operations. We can also automate web-based operations using HTTP client.

In this chapter, we have learned how to:

- Send e-mails from Tcl
- Build e-mails containing HTML and plain text message, attachments, and *inlined* images
- Retrieve, parse, and process e-mail messages
- Get data over HTTP
- Read RSS feeds
- Upload and download files over FTP

The next chapter talks about some of additional network protocols and how they can be used from Tcl. It describes how to query for DNS information, and retrieve the current date and time from remote servers.

8
Using Additional Internet Services

By now we know that Tcl has the functionality to create *networked* applications. We also know how to build simple client-server communication functionality. However, as with any programming language, being able to plug into existing protocols and communicating using standards that other systems are using is very important. This chapter talks about various standards, how Tcl fits into these (technologies), and how to use Tcl for various types of protocols and data encodings.

We will also talk about communication with users using e-mail. We'll start with sending simple e-mails, followed by learning how to send attachments and multipart types. Using this we'll show how to send and receive e-mails in order to do tasks such as informing users and/or customers. We'll also show how to read e-mails, how to parse them and how simple mechanisms can be built to create an automated e-mail management system.

This chapter also talks about many other protocols that we can use Tcl with. We'll talk about using **Lightweight Directory Access Protocol (LDAP)** to look up information and/or authenticate users, manually querying host names and time servers.

We'll also show Tcl's comm protocol, which is an RPC mechanism that can be used to invoke remote procedures on same or different machines. We'll show how this can be used both for running commands remotely and locally. We'll also show how we can introduce basic security features and how Tcl can be made to offer limited access to commands.

When writing our applications, it is essential to remember that there are many cases where all network-related functions may throw errors — a network can be down, the server we are communicating with might not be responding or may prevent us from gaining access due to invalid credentials, misconfiguration, or some other reason.

At all stages of writing an application, you should remember to make sure that you handle such errors properly. This is especially important for networked applications. Packages for handling network communication take care of catching such errors. Our application also needs to handle this properly and clean up all resources, inform the user or create a log of such errors—and when it makes sense, the application should retry communication periodically.

Also, when performing checks of any data retrieved from remote systems, we should check if all the conditions are satisfied instead of checking for known problems. For example, we should check if the status is one of the acceptable ones instead of checking if the status is a known error status. Troubleshooting Tcl applications and more recommendations for making applications error prone are described in more details in *Chapter 4, Troubleshooting Tcl Applications* .

Checking DNS

Tcl can be used to query Domain Name Servers using the dns package. This package allows us to query for various domain-related information. The package is an implementation of the DNS protocol client and it uses the DNS servers configured on the system by default. Although, it can also be configured to use different name servers.

The main command for querying DNS is dns::resolve, which returns a token that can then be used to get results. This command should be invoked with the query as the first argument and all options appended after it. The query can have multiple formats—the first one being the hostname. It can also be specified as dns:<hostname> or dns://<servername>/<hostname> where servername is the name of DNS server sent to the query.

The result from a query can be multiple servers. For example, in order to check the IP addresses of www.google.com, we can do the following:

```
package require dns

set token [dns::resolve "www.google.com"]
```

As DNS queries are always asynchronous, we should now wait for the query to finish. The dns::wait command can be run to achieve this and accepts one argument, which is the token that was returned by dns::resolve:

```
dns::wait $token
```

It is best to check whether the query has worked or not. Similar to the `http` package, the `dns::status` command is used for this. The status can be `ok`, `error`, `timeout`, or `eof`. For errors, the actual error message can be retrieved using the `dns::error` command. . For example, we can check if DNS query succeeded by doing:

```
if {[dns::status $token] != "ok"} {
    puts "Problem querying DNS"
    exit 1
}
```

Now we can retrieve IP addresses from the query. We can do this using the `dns::address` command:

```
set iplist [dns::address $token]
puts "Google.com IP addresses: [join $iplist ", "]."
```

Finally, we need to clean all the information related to this query by running:

```
dns::cleanup $token
```

Depending on query types, the results can be retrieved using different commands:

- `dns::name` — for queries that return hostnames.
- `dns::address` — for queries that return addresses.
- `dns::cname` — for queries that return canonical names.

  All these commands return a list of results with zero or more entries. The command `dns::result` can be used to retrieve raw results as Tcl list. In this case each element is a sublist with one or more name-value pairs that can then used for `dict` command and/or `array set`.

For example, we can also query DNS servers that serve the `google.com` domain by doing:

```
set token [dns::resolve "google.com" -type NS]
dns::wait $token
if {[dns::status $token] == "ok"} {
    puts "DNS servers: [join [dns::name $token] ", "]."
}
```

There are multiple types of queries that can be performed and they map to DNS query types.

Below is a table of commonly used query types:

Type	Result type	Comment
A	dns::address	IP addresses for specified hostname
PTR	dns::name	Reverse DNS (host name from IP address)
NS	dns::name	Name servers that should be asked about specific domains
MX	dns::name	Mail servers that should be used when delivering an e-mail to specified domain; each server specified as `<priority> <servername>` where lower priority indicates higher precedence

For example, in order to list the mail servers for the gmail.com domain, we can do the following:

```
set token [dns::resolve "gmail.com" -type MX]
dns::wait $token
if {[dns::status $token] == "ok"} {
    set mxlist [dns::name $token]
    set mxlist [lsort -index 0 -integer $mxlist]
    puts "MX servers:\n[join $mxlist \n]"
    puts "--"
}
```

After retrieving the results we can sort them. We are using the fact that the format of MX definitions can be treated as Tcl sublist. We tell `lsort` to sort the list, treating each element as a sublist and compare using the first element of this sublist, comparing items as integers. Finally, we join the list with each entry being a separate line and print it out.

Using callbacks

By default, DNS queries are asynchronous and we used dns::wait to wait for the results. In order to perform queries using callbacks, we can use the -command option from dns::resolve command. Command is specified as a value for this parameter, Callbacks described will be run with a DNS token appended as additional argument after the query has been performed as specified.

For example, from our previous example we know the IP addresses of all hosts that were resolved for www.google.com. We can now query what names those IP addresses resolve to by running:

```
set counter [llength $googleiplist]

foreach ip $iplist {
    dns::resolve "dns:$ip" \
    -type PTR \
    -command [list onResolveDone $ip]
}

vwait done
```

This will cause the onResolveDone command to be run after each IP address is resolved. We've also set counter variable to track how many queries are left—initially being number of IP addresses. The final line enters an event loop in order to avoid exiting the application before our queries are completed.

The command we're invoking will print out the result, decrease the counter, and if it was the last query, exit:

```
proc onResolveDone {ip token} {
    global counter
    set name [dns::name $token]
    if {[dns::status $token] == "ok"} {
        puts "$ip resolves do $name"
    } else {
        puts "Failed to resolve $ip"
    }
    dns::cleanup $name
    incr counter -1
    if {$counter == 0} {exit 0}
}
```

 Examples of querying DNS in Tcl are located in the 01dns directory in the source code examples for this chapter.

More information about the dns package, as well as the remaining configuration options can be found in its documentation at the package's SourceForge project at: http://tcllib.sourceforge.net/doc/dns.html

Getting the current date and time

Tcl offers time package that can be used to query current time using either official servers for providing it or local servers within our network.

One of the reasons is that applications that operate over the network need to know and use the current time. For example, if multiple machines register events and/ or data updates based on the time they occurred, if their system clocks are not synchronized, events might be reported out of order.

In majority of cases the system clock is synchronized so all applications use the correct time, but in some cases it might only be possible for the application to synchronize its time and handle it properly whenever sending a time.

The time package offers similar commands to dns and http ones. The query can be run using the time::gettime and time::getsntp commands. The first command queries the time using the **Network Time Protocol (NTP)** and second one uses the **Simple Network Time Protocol (SNTP)**, which is a simplified version of NTP. The majority of servers on the Internet use SNTP.

Both commands take the time server as the first argument. Additional options can be specified before the time server. Both commands also return a token that can be used for invoking other commands to get information and/or finalize the query. By default it works in synchronous mode, which means that the commands will exit after the time is retrieved or a timeout occurs. For example:

```
package require time

set token [time::getsntp pool.ntp.org]
```

This will query the time from pool.ntp.org. This hostname is a pool of all publicly available time servers and is updated dynamically, it should always point to a valid time server on the Internet. These servers serve the SNTP protocol, which is why we're using time::getsntp command. Details about publicly available time servers and the project can be found on its home page at: http://www.pool.ntp.org/.

Next we should verify if an error has occurred. We can use the time::status command which returns status of the query. The status can be one of ok, error, timeout, or eof. For errors the actual error message can be retrieved using the time::error command. For example:

```
if {[time::status $token] != "ok"} {
    puts "Error while retrieving time"
    exit 1
}
```

The final step is to clean up our request. This can be done by invoking `time::cleanup` command, which takes token as its only argument. We can then show both the local and the remote time and print out both along with the difference between them. Getting the time from the request can be done with `time::unixtime` command, which accepts a token as an argument and returns a Unix timestamp, which is the same as the `clock` command it operates with. For example:

```
time::cleanup $token

set remoteclock [time::unixtime $token]
set localclock [clock seconds]
set diff [expr {$remoteclock-$localclock}]

puts "Local time: [clock format $localclock]"
puts "Remote time: [clock format $remoteclock]"
puts "Difference: $diff secons(s)"
```

It is also possible to use the `time` package in an asynchronous way. We can provide `-command` option and this command will be run whenever a query finishes and will have token appended as argument, similar to `dns` and `http` commands. For example:

```
time::getsntp -command onGetDone pool.ntp.org
```

This will cause the command to exit instantly and call the `onGetDone` command as soon as the query is completed. Our command can then use the token to parse the time, for example:

```
proc onGetDone {token} {
    if {[time::status $token] != "ok"} {
        puts "Error while retrieving time"
    }
    set time [clock format [time::unixtime $token]]
    time::cleanup $token
    puts "Remote time retrieved: $time"
}
```

This command will work similarly to the previous example—it will check the status of the query. If there was a problem, we print out an error message. If everything went okay, we will print out the current time and exit.

An example of synchronizing the clock periodically is located in the `main.tcl` file in the `02time` directory in the source code examples for this chapter.

As mentioned earlier, just retrieving the time might not be very useful for our application. Usually we want to make sure that all the time and date information we're using is based on the same time, retrieved periodically. We can create a procedure that periodically queries the time and stores the difference between the local clock and the remote server. Let's start with defining the namespace and creating the procedure:

```
package require time

namespace eval centraltime {}

proc centraltime::periodicUpdate {} {
    variable centraltimediff
    if {[catch {
```

We'll store the difference in the `centraltimediff` variable, which is referenced in the first line of the command. We'll then run the entire retrieval process in a `catch` to handle any errors. We can now proceed with retrieving information:

```
        set token [time::getsntp pool.ntp.org]
        if {[time::status $token] != "ok"} {
            puts stderr "Error synchronizing time"
        } else {
            set remote [time::unixtime $token]
            set localclock [clock seconds]
            set centraltimediff [expr {$remote-$localclock}]
        }
```

We're retrieving the current time over SNTP and if it succeeds, we store difference between the remote and local clock in our variable. We can then finalize our catch statement, clean up our request, and reschedule the next check for 10 minutes later:

```
    } error]} {
        puts stderr "Error while synchronizing time: $error"
    }
    catch {time::cleanup $token}
    after 600000 centraltime::periodicUpdate
}
```

We now have a function that will try to query the time server, store the time difference if it succeeded, and reschedule the next check. We can also write a function that will return expected current time:

```
proc centraltime::getCorrectTime {} {
    variable centraltimediff
    set result [clock seconds]
```

```
    if {[info exists centraltimediff]} {
        incr result $centraltimediff
    }
    return $result
}
```

This command takes the current clock time, and if we know the last offset when comparing the local and remote time, it applies the difference. We can use this as replacement for the `clock seconds` command and get the time that we expect other systems we communicate with to have.

> An example of synchronizing the clock periodically is located in the `periodicsync.tcl` file in the `02time` directory in the source code examples for this chapter.

More information about the `time` package as well as the remaining configuration options can be found in its documentation at the package's SourceForge project page: `http://tcllib.sourceforge.net/doc/ntp_time.html`.

Using LDAP from Tcl

Lightweight Directory Access Protocol (LDAP) can be used to retrieve and/or modify a directory, in this case a directory is understood as a set of objects that are organized in hierarchical way and have attributes, such as directory of users. LDAP allows us to access this directory, query it, and modify certain attributes, based on the level of privileges we have.

Often, LDAP is deployed in larger companies to provide centralized information about users, along with their authentication details. This allows applications that can work using LDAP to authenticate users and/or get additional information about users.

LDAP operates on standardized attribute names and same names are used for the same values in different LDAP implementations. For example:

- o stands for organization
- ou means organization unit
- cn is canonical name
- c is country

For contact information, these are `mail`, `telephoneNumber`, `mobile` among others. Usually the best way to learn about the available fields is to retrieve a list of all available fields for particular entry/entries and print them.

The Tcl package `ldap` offers the functionality to query information over LDAP. Similar to other protocol related packages, we start off by connecting to a service. We can use the commands `ldap::connect` or `ldap::secure_connect` for this. The first command connects over an unencrypted connection and the second connects using SSL. Both commands require a hostname as the first argument. Specifying a port as the second argument is optional and usually not needed.

For example:

```
set s [ldap::connect ldap.itd.umich.edu]
```

In order to query information we can use `ldap::search` command which returns a list of all matching items. It accepts the following arguments:

- The first argument is the handle to the LDAP session
- The second is base object to query on
- The third argument specified filter string
- The fourth argument specifies list of attributes to retrieve – or an empty list to retrieve all arguments.

Both the base object and filter string are specified in the form of `name=value` separated by a comma, such as `o=University of Michigan,c=US`. This means the organization name is `University of Michigan` and the country `US`.

For example we can perform a simple query similar to:

```
set base "o=University of Michigan,c=US"
set query "cn=*test*"

foreach item [ldap::search $s $base $query {}] {
    foreach {name value} [lindex $item 1] {
        puts "$name: [join $value ", "]"
    }
    puts ""
}
```

Each search result is a list that contains two elements: first one is a distinguished name, which can be used to uniquely identify an object. It can be in the form of:

```
uid=username,c=US,o=University of Michigan
```

Second item is a list of name-value pairs, where name is the attribute name and value is a list of values for this attribute. For example, if a user has 2 telephone numbers which can be used to reach him/her, the value for the `telephoneNumber` attribute would be a list of 2 items. For a single e-mail address, the value for the `mail` attribute would be a one-element list.

Closing the connection can be done using `ldap::disconnect` command, regardless of whether it was set up over SSL or not. For example:

```
ldap::disconnect $s
```

LDAP allows users to authenticate themselves in order to perform various operations. We can do this by invoking `ldap::bind` command. It requires that we specify a handle to the connection, distinguish the name of the user to authenticate and password to authenticate against. It authentication fails, an error is thrown. For example we can log in by doing:

```
set dn " uid=username,c=US,o=University of Michigan"
set password "secret"
ldap::bind $s $dn $password
```

This might be needed before modifying, adding, or deleting objects.

Authenticating users over LDAP

Often, `ldap::bind` is used to authenticate users. However, since users are often asked to type in other fields, such as e-mail, this needs a bit more complex. A typical example is that authentication is based on user e-mail, since it uniquely identifies a user.

Let's write a generic command that does an `ldap::search` first, makes sure that it gets a distinguished name for this user, and then authenticates him/her. We start by running a query:

```
proc authenticateLDAP {s base query password} {
    set results [ldap::search $s $base $query {cn}]
```

We only retrieve `cn` field to reduce network and server resource usage.

We then need to make sure that exactly one item was found. If this was not the case, the result is same as if the authentication failed:

```
    if {[llength $results] != 1} {
        # Multiple or no results found
        catch {ldap::disconnect $s}
        return false
    }

    set dn [lindex $results 0 0]
```

If we got a single result, we get the distinguished name, which is the first element of the first result. Next we try to authenticate and if the authentication fails, report a failure:

```
if {[catch {ldap::bind $s $dn $password}]} {
    catch {ldap::disconnect $s}
    return false
} else {
    catch {ldap::disconnect $s}
    return true
}
}
```

In all cases we've also disconnected the LDAP connection. Usually base is a constant defining pool of objects (usually users) that we will be authenticating against. The value for query is usually a combination of user input and a constant value, for example, mail=<what the user specified>.

As users can specify any string, we need to make sure that it gets properly escaped. LDAP standard specifies that backslash (\) character is used for escaping various characters. Therefore, we can write a small command that escapes text for LDAP:

```
proc escapeLDAP {str} {
    return [string map [list \
        "=" "\\=" " " "\\ " \
        "," "\\," "+" "\\+" \
        "+" "\\*" "\"" "\\\"" \
    ] $str]
}
```

This way if a user specifies *, we'll escape it to * which LDAP will treat, literally, as an asterisk, not as wildcard matching. Next we can use such functionality to authenticate users by asking for an e-mail and a password, and performing authentication:

```
puts "Enter your e-mail address:"
gets stdin mail

puts "Enter your password:"
gets stdin password

set s [ldap::connect ldap.itd.umich.edu]

set base "o=University of Michigan,c=US"
set query "mail=[escapeLDAP $mail]"

puts [authenticateLDAP $s $base $query $password]
```

For the simplicity of the example we ask users to provide their username and password using the `gets` command, which reads a line from standard input. Usually this is done over a Tk or web based form.

Modifying information in LDAP

We can add items into LDAP by using the `ldap::add` and `ldap::addMulti` commands. Both accept a handle as the first argument, followed by a distinguished name of the new item and followed by a list of name-value pairs for attributes this object should have.

The command `ldap::addMulti` treats each value as a list of actual values to add, similar to what `ldap::search` returns whereas `ldap::add` treats the name-value pair as specifying the actual value to add. The command `ldap::addMulti` is the preferred way to add items to LDAP and using it makes LDAP related data management in Tcl more consistent.

For example, the following command will cause the same entry to be added:

```
set dn "uid=newuser,ou=People,o=University of Michigan,c=US"
ldap::add $handle $dn {
    objectClass      OpenLDAPperson
    cn               {New User}
    uid              newuser
    telephoneNumber  12345678
    telephoneNumber  12345679
}

ldap::addMulti $handle $dn {
    objectClass      {OpenLDAPperson}
    cn               {{New User}}
    uid              {newuser}
    telephoneNumber  {12345678 12345679}
}
```

The difference is that with `ldap::addMulti` all items need to be created as one element list. Also, items that have multiple values are specified as multiple items for `ldap::add` and as single list with multiple elements for `ldap::addMulti`.

Modifying existing objects can be done using `ldap::modify` and `ldap::modifyMulti` commands. The difference is the same as between `ldap::add` and `ldap::addMulti` in how attributes are passed, except that for `ldap::modify` it is not possible to change the attribute to contain multiple values – it is always replaced with a single value.

Both commands accept a handle as the first argument, followed by a distinguished name of an element. The third argument is a list of name-value pairs with attributes to replace. Specifying the attribute that was not previously set for this object will set it to a new value, specifying an empty list of values will cause an attribute to be removed if it was previously set. For example, in order to change phone number and add mobile phone we can do:

```
ldap::modifyMulti $handle $dn \
    [list telephoneNumber {87654321} mobile {74201234}]
```

We can also specify a name-value pairs list of items to delete as fourth argument and name-value pairs list of items to add as fifth argument. For example, to delete both phone numbers we can do:

```
ldap::modifyMulti $handle $dn {} \
    [list mobile {} telephoneNumber {}]
```

Please note that `ldap` package needs name-value pairs for list of attributes to delete. We can also add a new mobile phone number by doing:

```
ldap::modifyMulti $handle $dn {} \
    {} [list mobile {74201235}]
```

If we'll need to change a distinguished name of an object, we can do this using `ldap::modifyDN` command. It accepts a handle to the LDAP connection, the current distinguished name, and a description of changes to perform. For example:

```
ldap::modifyDN $handle $dn "uid=testuser"
```

This will cause `uid` part of the distinguished name to be changed to `testuser` while preserving other attributes' values.

The command `ldap::modifyDN` can also take two more arguments. The first one is whether to delete an old entry, if this is set to `true`, which is the default, this operation is a move operation. If it is set to `false`, it will cause a copy of the current object to be created. The second argument specifies a new base object. This can be used to relocate objects to different branches of the object hierarchy.

For example, to create a copy of our user assigned to the UK we can do:

```
ldap::modifyDN $handle $dn "uid=newuser" false \
    "ou=People,o=University of Michigan,c=UK"
```

Similarly we can also delete objects using the `ldap::delete` command. This command takes a handle to the session and distinguished name as its arguments and deletes an item. It throws an error if a specified object does not exist. For example, in order to delete an object we can do:

```
ldap::delete $handle $dn
```

 Examples of querying DNS in Tcl is located in the `031dap` directory in the source code examples for this chapter.

More information about the `ldap` package as well as the remaining configuration options can be found in its documentation on SourceForge project: `http://tcllib.sourceforge.net/doc/ldap.html`.

Communicating with Tcl applications

Often, our application needs to be able to accept commands from a local and/or remote application or troubleshooting utility. In many cases it is enough to set up a service that will accept connections and evaluate commands sent over them.

We can do this by using the `comm` package that offers both client and server functionality. This package allows many use cases – from a simple server that evaluates all commands to a system that allows only certain tasks to be performed. This package uses TCP connections so it is possible to handle both local and remote connections. However, it is configurable whether connections from other computers are allowed.

Using a `comm` package we can also connect to our application from applications such as *TclDevKit* inspector from *ActiveState*, which can help in troubleshooting daemon-like applications. This is described in more detail in chapter 4.

Comm client and server

Using the `comm` protocol requires the use of the `comm::comm` command by providing an actual command to perform as its first argument.

One of the subcommands is `config`, which allows us to get and set the configuration. It accepts either no arguments, in which case it returns list of name-value pairs specifying all options and their values, or one or more arguments. Specifying only the name of an option returns its current value. Specifying one or more name-value pairs causes those to be set to specific values.

The most important options are `-port` and `-local`. The first one allows us to specify the TCP port to listen on, or to retrieve the port currently used – by default the system assigns an available port. The second option allows us to specify whether only local connections should be accepted or if both local and remote connections are allowed – by default only local connections are accepted.

In most cases it is best to assign a port – either hardcoded or read from a configuration file. However, in some cases it makes sense to have it assigned by the operating system– in this case we can simply load comm package and get port that was assigned by default. We can then read it using the `self` subcommand, which returns the currently used port.

For example:

```
package require comm

puts "Comm port: [comm::comm self]"
```

If we want to define which port to use, we can simply set the `-port` option. For example:

```
package require comm

comm::comm config -port 1991
```

For the purpose of this section we'll use port `1991` throughout all further examples.

Assuming that our application is in an event loop – for example by invoking `vwait forever`, we can now send commands to it. We can do this by invoking the send subcommand, specifying identifier of the application and command to run. In the case of processes on the same system identifier is simply the port number – `1991` in our case. In case of remote systems, identifier is a list containing port and hostname – for example `{1991 192.168.2.12}`.

For example, in order to calculate 1+1 using remote interpreter we can do:

```
package require comm

set result [comm::comm send 1991 expr {1+1}]
puts "1 + 1 = $result"
```

Similarly calculating the same value using a remote computer can be done by changing our client's code to:

```
set result [comm::comm send {1991 192.168.1.12} expr {1+1}]
```

The remaining parts of the example are the same. In addition, the server needs to be configured to accept remote connections:

```
comm::comm config -port 1991 -remote 1
```

We can also perform asynchronous operations that will not block the client until the server completes the operation. One case is when our application only needs to send a command without needing its result. In this case, we simply need to provide the -async flag before the identifier of the remote system. For example:

```
comm::comm send -async 1991 {after 3000}
```

This will cause the remote system to wait for 3 seconds, but the send command returns instantly.

Asynchronous commands can also be used to perform long running operations, or for actions that will require user input. In this case we need to specify the -command option followed by the command to be run when the results have been received.

This command will be run with name-value pairs containing information about both the channel and the result appended to it. The item -result contains the result from the command or the error description for errors. The item -code will specify result of the command as 0 indicating successful evaluation of the command and 1 indicating an error. In case of an error -errorinfo and -errorcode are set respectively to indicate error information. More details on error information can be found in Chapter 4. These items can be retrieved using dict command.

For example, in order to calculate the MD5 checksum of a large remote file we can run:

```
comm::comm send -command oncallback 1991 \
    {md5::md5 -hex [string repeat "Tcl Book" 16777216] }
```

And in order to define the command that handles the result we can do:

```
proc oncallback {args} {
    if {[dict get $args -code] != 0} {
        puts "Error while evaluating command"
    } else {
        puts "Result: [dict get $args -result]"
    }
}
```

This callback checks whether the command returned an error and if not, prints out the result from the command.

 Source code for both synchronous and asynchronous communication is located in the 04comm-basics directory in the source code examples for this chapter.

Performing commands asynchronously

In many cases, we want our remote procedure to send a result that needs operations which might not happen immediately, such as passing a request to another machine or application.

A typical example can be sending a request to an other Tcl application over comm or sending a request over HTTP. In such cases we can receive the result after long period of time and we might want to return information to our caller when our event handler returns.

In such cases we can use the return_async subcommand from the comm::comm command in the Tcl interpreter that is the server for a particular connection. This command returns a new command, usually called future that we can invoke later on in order to pass the result.

In order to return a value we can invoke the return subcommand of the future object. It accepts a value to return, optionally preceded by the return code, which can be supplied by providing the -code option before the actual result.

For example, we can return the result after several seconds by doing:

```
proc returnAfter {after code value} {
    set future [comm::comm return_async]
    after $after [list $future return -code $code $value]
}
```

In this case, whatever we return from within the procedure will be ignored. Invoking the return subcommand also cleans up the future object.

We can invoke the command from the client in the same way regardless if it uses asynchronous return or if it returns instantly. For example we can run:

```
set v [comm::comm send 1991 returnAfter 3000 0 1]
```

Asynchronous returns are usually used when we need to invoke asynchronous operations, such as sending an HTTP request. A good example might be how to implement a comm proxy service:

```
proc proxy {id args} {
    set future [comm::comm return_async]
    comm::comm send -command [list proxyReturn $future] \
        $id {*}$args
}
```

This command takes the id of the next hop as an argument and the remaining arguments are treated as commands to pass on to the next hop. It also sets up asynchronous return command which is used in `proxyReturn` procedure. It can look like this:

```
proc proxyReturn {future args} {
    $future return -code [dict get $args -code] \
        [dict get $args -result]
}
```

This simply passes the result back to the client calling the `proxy` command. For example assuming our proxy `comm` server is listening on port 1992, we can pass the query to actual server on port 1991 by doing:

```
set v [comm::comm send 1992 proxy 1991 \
    returnAfter 3000 0 1]
```

We can also use multiple hops and over network – assuming we need to send all requests first via comm on host `192.168.2.12` and further via host `10.0.0.1`, we can do:

```
set v [comm::comm send \
    {1991 192.168.2.12} proxy \
    {1991 10.0.0.1} proxy \
    returnAfter 3000 0 1]
```

All of the proxy `comm` servers will perform this operation without waiting so it is possible to proxy multiple requests at a time this way, regardless of how much it takes to complete the operation.

 Source code for proxy based communication is located in the `05comm-proxy` directory in the source code examples for this chapter.

Security aspects

An obvious concern is that this allows everyone to send commands to be run – either only from local machine or from the entire network. While for some operations this is perfectly acceptable, there are cases where such a model might not work. An example could be that if our system is shared among users – in this case anyone knowing the port might send commands to our application. Another case is when our application accepts commands from remote machines, unless access to the network is strictly limited.

The comm package allows the specification of hooks that are evaluated whenever an event occurs. These can be used for both comm clients and servers.

We can set up a script that will be evaluated when an event occurs by invoking the hook subcommand of the comm::comm command. It accepts event type and script as its arguments. These can be used to authenticate and optionally reject incoming connections, validating commands to evaluate as well as their responses.

Hook scripts can read various information using variables that are accessible while it is running. These variables are:

Variable	Description
chan	Comm command that is associated with the event, by default it is comm::comm; additional channels are described further in the section
id	Id of the remote interpreter
fid	Tcl channel associated with connection
addr	IP address of the remote peer; used for authenticating remote connection
remport	Port used by the remote peer; used for authenticating remote connection
cmd	Command type for evaluating a script – sync or async
buffer	Tcl command to evaluate
host	Host to connect to; used by client hooks
port	Port to connect to; used by client hooks

Not all variables are accessible for all hooks and availability is described along with each of the events.

The event type incoming is run for listening connections whenever a remote interpreter is connecting. It can be used to log incoming connections and/or reject connections based on remote address. This hook can reject a connection by throwing an error. This hook allows access to chan, fid, addr and remport variables.

For example, in order to accept connections only from hosts matching 127.* or 192.168.* pattern, we can add the following hook:

```
comm::comm hook incoming {
    puts "comm—Connection from $addr"
    if {(![string match "127.*" $addr])
        && (![string match "192.168.*" $addr])} {
        error "Connection from unknown host $addr"
    }
}
```

This hook prints information about incoming connections to standard output. Then if the `addr` variable (provided by `comm` package) does not match any of defined patterns, an error is thrown. This error causes comm to close the connection and pass this error to client.

Event type `eval` is run whenever a command is to be evaluated. It provides information in `chan`, `id`, `cmd` and `buffer` variables. In this case it is possible to modify command to evaluate, return any result from within the hook or throw an error in case a specified command should not be run.

If the `eval` hook returns with an error, this error is passed back to the original client. For example, in order to refuse all commands except for the known ones we can do:

```
comm::comm hook eval {
    if {[lsearch $::validcommands [lindex $buffer 0]] < 0} {
        error "Command not authorized"
    }
}
```

In this case, we search for first element of the command in global `validcommands` variable – if it contains the command we allow execution of the command.

Usually it is a better idea to either pass the command to a procedure that will handle it, which can do additional checks or make sure that only a subset of functionality is exposed. For example we can rewrite the `buffer` variable to pass actual command as argument by doing:

```
comm::comm hook eval {
    set buffer [list [list myhandler $buffer]]
}
```

This way we pass the original buffer as first argument to `myhandler` command. As the `comm` package tries to concatenate all elements into a single list, we need to build a list of lists so that our `myhandler` is invoked with just one argument. We can then write a simple function that writes the actual command and result by doing:

```
proc myhandler {command} {
    puts "Evaluating '$buffer'"
    set rc [eval $command]
    puts "Result: '$rc'"
    return $rc
}
```

This command prints out the command to execute, evaluates it and prints out results.

Another option is to evaluate the command on our own instead of having it done by the comm package. We can use the return command inside the hook to force the comm package to pass our result back to the client. For example, we can invoke myhandler in the same way by doing:

```
comm::comm hook eval {
    return [myhandler $buffer]
}
```

It is also possible to use an asynchronous handler for commands that are evaluated by our hook. For example, we can do the following:

```
proc myhandler {command} {
    if {$command == "asynctest"} {
        set future [comm::comm return_async]
        after 5000 [list $future return "After 5 seconds"]
        return
    }
    set rc [eval $command]
    return $rc
}
```

This command has a special case where if the command invoked is asynctest, we return the result after 5 seconds. Otherwise we just evaluate whatever command user provided and return it.

 Source code for server side hooks is located in the 06comm-hooks directory in the source code examples for this chapter.

Limiting available commands

In many cases it is good practice to limit the operations remote applications can perform – provide only a set of commands that user can access and allow only access to a subset that user has access to. We can even introduce an idea of a session identifier – which is given when authenticating a user and can expire after some time.

For example we can work in the following way – first operation a user should perform is authorizing using username and password. Next the server provides a session identifier that can be used to invoke other commands. We can do this by sending a session identifier as the first argument and assume that if session is not set, remaining arguments are username and password. If the session is valid, we can assume that the second argument is a command name and the remaining arguments are passed to the command.

We can create a command that handles buffer in this way by doing:

```
proc so::handle {buffer} {
    set session [lindex $buffer 0]
    if {$session == ""} {
        lassign $buffer session user pass
        set sid [authorize $user $pass]
        return $sid
    } elseif {[check $session [lindex $buffer 1]]} {
        return [so::service::[lindex $buffer 1] \
            {*}[lrange $buffer 2 end]]
    } else {
        error "Authorization failed"

    }

}
```

What the procedure does is check first element of a list – if it is empty, we assign the second and third argument as the username and password and invoke the `authorize` command, which returns a new session identifier or an empty string. If the session is set, and if the user is authorized to run specified command, we run it assuming it is in the `so::service` namespace – to avoid running commands outside of the specified namespace. If the session is not valid or the user is not authorized to run a specified command, we throw an error.

We also need to set up a hook for `eval` event:

```
comm::comm hook eval {
    return [so::handle [lrange $buffer 0 end]]
}
```

We're using the `lrange` command to make sure the user input is a valid list, just as a precaution.

Our sample authorization command should authorize the user, generate a session ID (for example using `uuid` package) and return it. A simple one, with a hardcoded username and password could be as follows:

```
proc so::authorize {user password} {
    variable sessions
    if {($user == "admin") && ($password == "pass")} {
        set sid [uuid::uuid generate]
        set sessions($sid) $sid
    }
    return $sid
}
```

This checks if the username is admin and the password is pass – if so, it sets up a session and stores it in namespace variable sessions. We can also implement a trivial checking by doing:

```
proc so::check {sid command} {
    variable sessions
    if {[info exists sessions($sid)]} {
        return true
    }
    return false
}
```

And now we have a safe comm based service that can be used to offer services. We can also add a simple command on top of this infrastructure, for example:

```
proc so::service::add {a b} {
    return [expr {$a + $b}]
}
```

In order to use it we can now use the following code on the client:

```
set sid [comm::comm send 1991 {} admin pass]

if {$sid == ""} {
    error "Unable to authorize"
}

set v [comm::comm send 1991 $sid \
    add 1 2]
```

The main issue we need to implement is support for sessions to expire, for example if no operation is performed for some time, session is removed from sessions variable.

 Source code for examples related to providing services on top of the comm package is located in the 07comm-service directory in the source code examples for this chapter.

Summary

In this chapter, we've learned to use Tcl with different protocols that our application can benefit from — synchronizing time with other servers, querying user information and authenticating users over LDAP and perform DNS queries.

Tcl has its own protocol for remote procedure calls locally and remotely. This can be used for both accessing our application from different processes and troubleshooting. We can also use this for distributed computing of information. In addition to this, the comm package can also be used to offer service-based approach, including authentication.

In this chapter we have learned to:

- Get DNS information
- Get current date and time
- Query and modify information over LDAP
- Authorize users using LDAP
- Creating and using networked applications using comm package

The next chapter shows how to embed a web server in our application, and how this can be used to both create a simple web server as well as use HTTP protocol for communication between our applications.

9
Learning SNMP

In this chapter, we'll learn about the **Simple Network Management Protocol** (**SNMP**), which is often used for monitoring and gathering information from various devices; such as routers, gateways, printers, and many other types of equipment. We'll start by introducing SNMP and the various concepts surrounding it, which will be useful for readers who do not have much experience with SNMP.

We'll talk about the Tcl package Scotty, which handles SNMP, and how it can be used to query information from within our application. It also provides a Tk-based GUI application that can be used for inspecting devices, discovering systems within our network, and browsing data that can be retrieved over SNMP.

We'll show how Scotty can be used for retrieving SNMP values, and mapping between raw values and readable representations. You will also learn how to set any values that a particular device allows us to set.

This chapter also talks about SNMP traps and how they can be both sent and received using Scotty. We'll find out how to send additional information along with a trap and how to retrieve this information when handling an incoming trap.

We'll also implement our own SNMP agent, which will allow any SNMP-aware application to query data from our application.

Finally, we'll show additional features package Scotty offers, such as **ICMP** functionality. **ICMP** stands for **Internet Control Message Protocol** and is used for diagnostics, routing, and troubleshooting of networks. It can be used to check how much time it takes for a packet to get to a host and back, detect the route to an IP address and other features needed for monitoring and troubleshooting networks. We'll create a simple ping-and-traceroute application, which can be used in applications which monitor network status.

Introduction to SNMP

The Simple Network Management Protocol is designed to be easy to implement and provide a uniform way to access information on various machines. Before we can use it from within Tcl, we need to understand how it works so that we know what is happening when we are running commands and examples.

The SNMP protocol is designed so that the footprint of its services is minimal. This allows devices with limited size of storage and operating memory to use the protocol. SNMP uses the UDP protocol which requires much less resources to handle than TCP. It also uses only one packet for sending a single request or response operation so the protocol itself is stateless.

Each machine that is managed by SNMP has a running application that responds to requests from it, and also other computers. Such application is called an **agent**. For UNIX systems, it is usually a daemon working in the background. Many devices with embedded systems have SNMP support included in the system core. In all cases, a device needs to listen to SNMP requests and respond accordingly.

All agents are managed by one or more machines called the SNMP **manager**. This is a computer that queries agents for data and might also set their attributes. Usually this is an application running in the background that communicates over SNMP and stores the information in some data storage.

Usually SNMP uses UDP port 161 to communicate with the agent and 162 for sending information from the agent to manager. In order to use SNMP, these ports need to be correctly passed by all network routers and should not be filtered at the firewall.

Two types of communication are carried out in SNMP:

- The first type is when a manager sends requests to an agent. In such cases, these can be **get** requests, in which case the manager wants to retrieve information from an agent. If the information needs to be modified, a set request is sent out.

- Another type of communication is **traps**. These are sent when an agent wants to notify a manager about a problem. An agent needs to know the IP address of the manager to send the information out to it. A manager needs to be listening for SNMP traps and should react to them.

The following is an illustration of possible SNMP communication types:

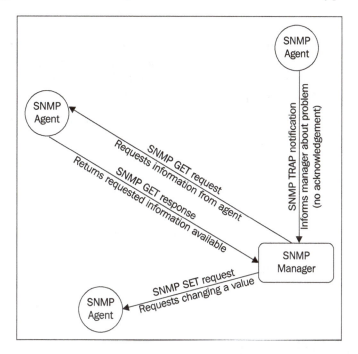

Learning SNMP protocol versions

SNMP has several versions that an agent can communicate over. SNMPv1 was the first version of the protocol. It featured get, set, and trap operations. The standard defined scalar data objects as well as tabular objects. It also featured the `getnext` operation that can be used to iterate over tables of data objects.

The security model related with SNMPv1 is relatively unsophisticated. A `get`, `set`, or `getnext` request is authenticated based on the IP address of the manager and the community string that it uses. All SNMP devices communicating over SNMPv1 use a community string for verifying the request—whether none, only get, or both get and set operations can be performed. By default, the `private` community string allows both reading and writing of information, and the `public` community string allows reading only.

SNMP version 2 introduced improvements in terms of performance and security. Instead of using get and getnext, it had a getbulk operation. This allows the retrieval of all entries in a table in a single operation. It also introduces an **inform** packet— this is a trap that must be acknowledged by the manager. This avoids a problem where a trap is not received by a manager because a single UDP packet failed to reach its destination. This version also introduced the party-based security model, which did not gain wide acceptance as it was very complex.

The most common version 2 implementation is **SNMPv2c—Community-Based Simple Network Management protocol 2**. It uses features of version 2 without implementing the new security model, instead using the community string mechanism that was introduced in SNMPv1.

The **User-Based Network Management Protocol version 2**, or **SNMPv2u**, is another variant of SNMP version 2. It includes changes in security, but also does not include all of the security features originally developed for SNMPv2. SNMP version 3 features an improved security model with authentication, privacy, and access control. This version introduced much better security than that available in SNMPv2, and one of its security frameworks uses the functionality from SNMPv2u. This standard is now gaining more attention than SNMPv2; mostly because it offers better security without the high level of complexity that SNMPv2 introduced.

Most SNMP server implementations that come with operating systems support SNMPv1, SNMPv2c, and SNMPv3. Some devices support only SNMPv1 and others also offer SNMPv2. Packets from different SNMP versions are incompatible, so a device only using SNMPv1 will not recognize SNMPv2c packet. However, an application that knows both SNMPv1 and SNMPv2 will understand an SNMPv1 packet.

In many cases, devices that are used across your network will offer a different subset of versions that they support. There are two strategies that can be used to work in such an environment:

- The first approach is to use a proxy agent. Some SNMP management software uses SNMPv3 and devices that do not support this version will need to have the packets translated. In such cases, all requests from the manager are received by the proxy agent, which translates and passes them to the actual agent, and sends the results to the manager. The proxy agent receives traps from the actual agent. It then passes them to the manager as a trap or inform packet using a newer SNMP version. The proxy agent is usually an application on a computer, however, it can also be a physical device that works as a proxy agent.

- Another approach is for the SNMP manager to use multiple versions of SNMP, based on the device it is trying to get information from. Which version should be used can either be defined in some form of database, but SNMP also supports verifying which version can be used with a particular device.

Often SNMP managers allow configuring which version of the protocol should be used for specific devices.

Data objects

SNMP uses **Object Identifiers (OIDs)** to identify data objects that it refers to. They define an object uniquely for a specified SNMP agent. They are identified by using a hierarchical definition, in a fashion similar to how Internet domains work.

Object identifiers are a series of numbers separated by a period. Each number represents a part of the tree. Often, the first number in the series is also preceded by a period to indicate that this is an OID; this is not necessary, though. An example OID can be `.1.3.6.1.2.1.1.5.0`, which maps to the system name of a machine.

As it is very hard to memorize, read, and compare OIDs written as series of numbers, there is also a standard of naming and describing the object tree.

The standard is called **Management Information Base (MIB)** and it defines how various parameters are defined — both how they are named and what types of values these objects might return. Each MIB definition is a text file written in a subset of ASN.1 (Abstract Syntax Notation One) notation. A file can describe a small or large subset of the MIB trees.

As of now, the latest standard is MIB SMIv2 and it defines all commonly used attributes along with additional information that can be used for visualization applications.

MIB files describe fields that are used in SNMP. They define parent nodes in a hierarchy, numeric identifier, and the type of data that this field is associated with. SNMP uses the following basic data types:

- String — a string, written as bytes, that can have 0 to 65535 bytes
- Integer and Integer32 — a signed 32-bit integer value
- Counters32, Counter64 — non-negative integers that increase, and after they reach maximum value, they are reset to 0
- Gauges — non-negative integers that can increase and decrease in a defined minimum-maximum range

- Time tick — defines a time span, where a value of 100 represents one second
- IP address — represents an address from a protocol family; SNMPv1 only supports IPv4

In many cases, a field is returned as an enumeration type integer — this means that some predefined numbers represent several predefined values. A good example might be the ifType field when defining network interfaces, as it specifies type of a network interface. Some examples can be 23 for PPP4 connection or 6 for Ethernet interfaces.

An example OID is .1.3.6.1.2.1.1.5.0. The following table describes each element, both as a string and as the corresponding numbers:

Identifier	Description
1	iso: ISO standard tree
3	org: Organizations; this node is a placeholder for all national and international organizations
6	dod: Department of Defense; this is the node for U.S. department of defense
1	internet: sub node for Internet; since originally Internet was a project for U.S. military defense, its placeholder is under the dod sub-tree
2	mgmt: systems management node
1	mib-2: Management Information Base, version 2 root node
1	system: Operating system information
5	sysName: Name of this machine; usually a fully qualified domain name
0	Index of the elements; in this case it is always 0

The string representation of this OID is iso.org.dod.internet.mgmt.mib-2.system.sysName.0. Often, it is also referred to as SNMPv2-MIB::sysName.0.

The .1.3.6.1.2.1 part of the OID defines root elements for all MIB-2 standardized parameters. This means that all standard SNMP parameters that various devices use are under this OID node or its descendants. This node is also called SNMPv2-MIB namespace, therefore, the SNMPv2-MIB::sysName.0 OID also maps to the same object.

The MIB tree has a few major nodes that are the base for many other sub-trees that might be significant to you under various circumstances:

- .1.3.6.1.2.1 which stands for iso.org.dod.internet.mgmt.mib-2

  This is the base for all attributes that are available on the majority of SNMP-aware devices.

- `.1.3.6.1.4.1` which stands for `iso.org.dod.internet.private.`
  `enterprise.`

  This is a root node for all corporations and companies that use their private objects; this is used by companies such as Microsoft, Motorola, and many other hardware and software vendors.

- `.2.16.840.1.113883` which stands for `joint-iso-itu-t.country.`
  `us.organization.hl7.`

  This is a root node for Health Level 7 and is used mainly in health care and public health informatics.

The most important node is `.1.3.6.1.2.1`, which is used by all SNMP-aware devices to report information. This part of the MIB tree is the root node for majority of standard objects. It is also mandatory for all SNMP-enabled devices to provide at least basic part of information in this sub-tree. For example, information such as contact information, location, system name, and type should be provided by all SNMP-aware devices.

SNMP can be used to retrieve different kinds of information. They are usually grouped into various categories. All categories also have corresponding aliases that they are usually referenced with, in order to avoid putting entire structure along every OID definition or MIB name. All applications that offer communication over SNMP allow specifying attributes using both OID and MIB names. Let's go over a few of the most important sections of the MIB tree.

Information in `IF-MIB`, `IP-MIB`, `IPv6-MIB`, `RFC1213-MIB`, `IP-FORWARD-MIB`, `TCP-MIB`, and `UDP-MIB` describes network connectivity: interfaces, IP configuration, routing, forwarding, and TCP and UDP protocols. They support querying of the current configuration as well as the currently active and listening sockets.

Data contained in `SNMPv2-MIB` and `HOST-RESOURCES-MIB` describes system information and current parameters. It can contain information on disk storage, current processes, installed applications, and the hardware that the computer is running on.

Working with SNMP and MIB

Various operating systems come with different SNMP applications. Many hardware vendors also offer additional software that manages multiple machines using SNMP; for example, HP OpenView or Sun Management Center. For this and the following sections, the Net-SNMP package, available from `http://net-snmp.sourceforge.net/` will be used.

Binaries for Microsoft Windows can be downloaded from the project's file repository at: `http://sourceforge.net/projects/net-snmp/files/net-snmp%20binaries/`

Installers for 32-bit and 64-bit processors can be downloaded and Net-SNMP is installed in `C:\Usr` by default, having binaries such as `snmpget.exe` in `C:\Usr\bin`.

This package is included in all Linux distributions and works with almost all Unix operating systems.

In order to install this package on Ubuntu Linux, we need to run the following command:

```
apt-get install snmp
```

For `yum`-based Linux distributions, the package is called `net-snmp` and the command to install it is:

```
yum install net-snmp
```

Despite being named differently, both are actually packages for SNMP handling based on the Net-SNMP package.

The Net-SNMP project homepage also offers binaries for several platforms, including HP-UX and Fedora Linux. Fedora packages should also work on Red Hat Enterprise Linux systems.

It is also possible to build everything from source for Unix operating systems such as AIX, HP-UX, and Solaris. Exact instructions are provided on the project page.

After a successful installation, we should be able to run any SNMP-related command like `snmpget` and check the Net-SNMP version by doing the following:

```
root@ubuntu:~# snmpget -V
NET-SNMP version: 5.3.1
```

Assuming we have a host with an SNMP agent set up and it accepts SNMP protocol version 1, we can now try to communicate with it and query a few parameters:

```
root@ubuntu:~# snmpget -v 1 -c public 192.168.2.2 \
    iso.org.dod.internet.mgmt.mib-2.system.sysName.0
SNMPv2-MIB::sysName.0 = STRING: WAG354G
```

As you can see, the device returned that the system name is WAG354G. This is actually a Linksys/Cisco router and the only way to access its information is over the web interface or SNMP.

The Net-SNMP package comes with a couple of useful commands that can be used to check current values as well as perform a dump of part of whole MIB tree. These vary from simple tools used to query a single attribute to very complex ones that print out a df-like report of partitions on a remote system. There are also commands for displaying tables and for setting parameters remotely.

Throughout this section and the next one, we'll mainly use SNMP version 1, because it is supported by almost all SNMP-enabled devices. When using SNMP in production, it's better to check which devices accept SNMP versions and use the latest one that a device handles correctly.

The first command that is worth getting familiar with is snmpget. This allows you to query a single attribute or multiple attributes, over SNMP.

The syntax of the command is as follows:

```
snmpget [options] IP-address OID [OID] ...
```

All Net-SNMP commands accept a huge amount of parameters. The following are the ones we will be using throughout this chapter, or those worth knowing:

Option	Description
-h	Provides help
-V	Prints Net-SNMP version
-c	Specifies community name to use
-v	Specifies SNMP version to use; should be one of 1, 2c, or 3
-r	Specifies number of retries
-t	Timeout in seconds
-O	Output options; should be one or more of the following:

- n – print OIDs as numerical values without expanding them from MIB
- e – print enum and OID fields as numbers instead of string values
- v – print values only instead of name = value format
- f – print full OID names; does not permit shortcuts like SNMPv2-MIB

The -O option allows us to retrieve values without MIB shortcuts being applied. Therefore, we can see the entire branch. It also allows us to change the output so that only values along with data types are printed out, instead of the object names themselves.

```
# snmpget -O ef -v 1 -c public rtr SNMPv2-MIB::sysObjectID.0
.iso.org.dod.internet.mgmt.mib-2.system.sysObjectID.0 =
OID: .iso.org.dod.internet.private.enterprises.ucdavis.ucdSnmpAgent.linux
```

All of these options can also be used with other Net-SNMP commands.

Net-SNMP also offers a command to iterate through entire or part of MIB tree. The snmpwalk command accepts the same options as shown earlier. Most versions of Net-SNMP's snmpwalk command do not need to be passed any OID to work. For older versions in order to list the entire tree .1 can be specified as OID.

The following command will list entire MIB tree of a SNMPv1 agent:

```
root@ubuntu:~# snmpwalk -v 1 -c public 192.168.2.2
```

Depending on the underlying operating system and the SNMP agent itself, the actual data will be different. Please note that if the device is not on a local network, then this operation might take a long time to complete.

In order to retrieve only a part of the MIB tree, simply pass the prefix of the tree you are interested in. For example:

```
root@ubuntu:~# snmpwalk -v 1 -c public 192.168.2.2 1.3.6.1.2.1.1
```

The previous command will limit the query to iso.org.dod.internet.mgmt.mib-2.system node along with all its children. It will also be completed much faster than querying the entire tree.

Walking over a part of a tree is mainly useful when trying to check which objects are available on a remote device that does not respond quickly to SNMP requests — either because of network lag or the computations required for some objects. It is also commonly used to find out what values are available in a specific part of the MIB tree.

Another useful utility is the snmptable command. This allows you to list various SNMP tables and shows them in a human readable form. The syntax is as follows:

```
snmptable [options] IP-address OIDprefix
```

For example, to list all TCP/IP connections, the following command can be used:

```
root@:~# snmptable -v 1 -c public 192.168.2.2 tcpConnTable
SNMP table: TCP-MIB::tcpConnTable
```

connState	connLocalAddress	connLPort	connRemAddress	connRPort
listen	0.0.0.0	23	0.0.0.0	0
listen	0.0.0.0	80	0.0.0.0	0
listen	0.0.0.0	199	0.0.0.0	0

Net-SNMP also allows you to set new object values which can be used to reconfigure various devices. The `snmpset` command can be used to perform this. The syntax is as follows:

```
snmpset [options] IP-address OID type value [OID type value] ...
```

The command accepts all the standard options, just like the `snmpget` command. A single command invocation can be used to set more than one parameter by specifying more than one set of OIDs to set. Each set operation needs to specify the new value along with the data type it should be set to.

The value type can be one of the following:

Type	Description
i	Integer
u	Unsigned integer
s	String
x	Hex string—each letter is specified as 2 hexadecimal digits
d	Decimal string—each letter is specified as a 1-2 digit
n	NULL object
o	OID—for objects that accept object
t	Timeticks
a	IP address
B	Series of bits

Most common types are String, Integer, and OID. The first two require you to pass the number of a text that the object's value should be set to. Setting the OID type of the object requires that you either provide the full OID identifier or a string that can be matched by the MIB definitions.

An example of the code which can be used to set a system's contact name and hostname is as follows:

```
root@ubuntu:~# snmpset -v 2c -c private 192.168.2.2 \
    SNMPv2-MIB::sysContact.0 s admin@net.home \
    SNMPv2-MIB::sysName.0 s RTR

SNMPv2-MIB::sysContact.0 = STRING: admin@net.home

SNMPv2-MIB::sysName.0 = STRING: RTR
```

Some attributes cannot be set via SNMP. It is not possible to modify objects that are used for monitoring the system. These usually include IP address configuration, counters, or diagnostic information—for example TCP/UDP connection tables, process lists, installed applications, and performance counters. Many devices tend to support command-line administration over SNMP and, in this case, the parameters might be read-only.

MIB definitions specify which attributes are explicitly read-only. Using a graphical tool to find out which attributes can be modified will ease the experience of automatic device configuration over the SNMP protocol.

Setting up SNMP agent

The previous section talked about how to communicate with SNMP agents. If you have a network device such as a router or WiFi, WiMax, or DSL gateway, it will most likely already come with a built-in SNMP agent.

The next step is to set up SNMP agent on one or more computers so that we can use SNMP to monitor servers or workstations. This way, the majority of the networked equipment will allow querying data and/or monitoring from a single machine using SNMP protocol.

Let's start with various Unix boxes. The SNMP agent is a part of Net-SNMP and several distributions come with the command-line tools, libraries, and an SNMP agent—usually as optional packages.

In our case, we will install the SNMP agent on Ubuntu Linux. To do this we will run the following command:

```
apt-get install snmpd
```

This will cause the SNMP daemon from Net-SNMP to be installed. By default, the Ubuntu Linux SNMP agent which comes from the Net-SNMP package accepts connections on 127.0.0.1 only, which is the IP address that always reflects the same machine we are on. This is due to security reasons, in many cases, an SNMP agent is mainly used by tools like MRTG to gather usage statistics.

To change this we will need to either enter the IP address the SNMP agent should listen on or remove it completely from the /etc/default/snmpd file, using the SNMPDOPTS variable.

If the SNMP agent should listen on all available IP addresses, then the line should look similar to the following example:

```
SNMPDOPTS='-Lsd -Lf /dev/null -u snmp -I -smux -p /var/run/snmpd.pid'
```

Changing this option requires restarting the SNMP agent by invoking the following command:

```
/etc/init.d/snmpd restart
```

After a successful installation, the SNMP agent should be up and running and doing a walk over the entire tree should produce some output.

To test the SNMP agent simply launch the following command on the same machine, assuming Net-SNMP command line tools are installed:

```
snmpwalk -v 1 -c public 127.0.0.1
```

The agent that we have just installed supports SNMPv1, SNMPv2c, and SNMPv3 protocol versions. It also features an extensive security model that you can configure in order to provide a more secure setup.

Net-SNMP agent allows you to define one or more OIDs along with all subnodes that can be retrieved by specific security groups. These groups can be mapped to specific communities that originate from all IPs, or specific IP addresses. Security groups are also mapped using SNMP versions used by the remote machine.

A sample configuration that only allows read-only access from all hosts is:

```
com2sec readonly default public
group readonlyGroup v1   readonly
group readonlyGroup v2c readonly
group readonlyGroup usm readonly
view all     included  .1                              80
access readonlyGroup "" any noauth    exact  all    none   none
syslocation Home

syscontact Administrator <admin@yourcompany.com>
```

The first line defines a mapping between community and `readonly` security group. The lines that follow assign `readonlyGroup` access rights to it. Then it is assigned access to read all objects from `.1` OID node and its children. The last two lines indicate system administrator and location where the machines are stored.

For SNMPv3, it is also possible to specify one or more users by calling the `snmpusm` command. It allows real-time configuration of the user list for local or remote SNMPv3 agents.

SNMP can also be set up on all modern Microsoft Windows operating systems. As with Unix systems, the SNMP agent must be installed. In order to do this on Windows XP and 2003 Server, we need to go to the **Control Panel** first. Then we need to select the **Add or Remove Programs** applet and select **Add/Remove Windows Components** option. The following window will appear:

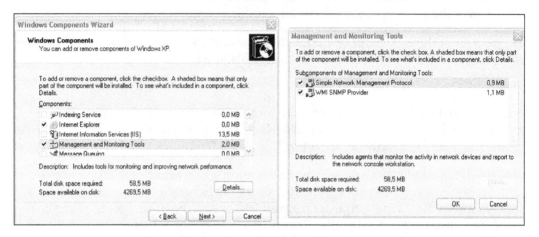

Next, we need to select **Management and Monitoring Tools** as shown in the preceding screenshot. We can also click the **Details** button and choose only the **Simple Network Management Protocol**. The **WMI SNMP Provider** makes it possible to retrieve SNMP parameters over WMI and can be left unchecked if you do not need it.

The Windows SNMP agent exports information about the system similar to other platforms. You can use it to query the underlying hardware, operating system version, and network configuration along with currently active connections. It is also possible to list active processes and monitor system load. The Windows SNMP agent also exports all installed applications along with security patches from Microsoft. This mechanism can be used to monitor whether all critical system patches are installed, or it may be used to monitor compliance with software licenses.

After a successful installation, we can go to the **Administrative Tools** folder and run the **Services** applet. When selecting the **SNMP Service** and choosing **Properties**, the service properties window along with SNMP configuration will appear:

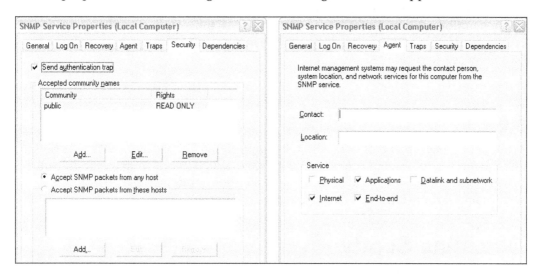

The window has three additional tabs: **Agent**, **Traps**, and **Security**. The **Agent** tab allows us to configure which parts are exported over SNMP and lets us set up contact and location information.

The **Security** tab allows us to configure how SNMP information from this host can be accessed. The Windows SNMP agent offers support for SNMPv1 and SNMPv2c, so the security model is based on a community string and IP addresses for authentication.

The agent can either accept SNMP queries from all hosts or only specific hosts listed in the bottom part of the tab. It is also possibile to specify one or more readable and writable communities. By default, only queries on the `public` community string are accepted and these allow read-only access.

The **Traps** tab allows configuring Windows to send or forward traps to specific IP addresses and which SNMP community to use for communication.

Tcl and Scotty package

Tcl features a powerful engine for managing SNMP, MIB, and many additional features called **Scotty**. It is an extension for Tcl that provides mechanisms for querying information over SNMP, receiving SNMP traps, and even allows us to create our own SNMP agents so that our application can be queried from other SNMP-aware applications.

It also features an extensive GUI application called **TkInEd** (Tcl/Tk-based Interactive Network Editor), which can be used to interactively discover, monitor, and graph data using SNMP.

While Scotty is the name of the project, the underlying Tcl package that offers SNMP and other network-related functionality is called **Tcl Network Management (Tnm)**. When talking about project in general, we'll mention Scotty. On the other hand, when using it from Tcl, we'll use the package name Tnm.

Obtaining Scotty

Scotty can be downloaded as source code, is part of several Linux distributions, and has pre-built binaries for Microsoft Windows systems and a port to Mac OS X is also created. More information about Scotty can be found on its website at:
http://www.ibr.cs.tu-bs.de/projects/scotty/

The source code as well as project information and the project's bug tracker can be found on its website at: https://trac.eecs.iu-bremen.de/projects/scotty/

Installing a pre-built version on Microsoft Windows requires copying Scotty to a location where Tcl looks for packages, such as C:\Tcl. Information on installation for the Mac OS X platform can be found at http://scotty.darwinports.com/.

Installing Scotty from source is a bit more complex and is usually needed for Linux and other Unix-based systems. For the purpose of building it, we'll assume ActiveTcl 8.5 is installed in /opt/ActiveTcl-8.5 and Scotty the source code is already unpacked in /usr/src/scotty. While some basic Unix administration skills might be required, Scotty's compilation from source code resembles building any other package and requires no additional Tcl skills.

As a prerequisite, we'll need development files for X11 and the gcc compiler. For example, in order to install these on Ubuntu, you should run:

```
sudo aptitude install libx11-dev gcc make libc-dev
```

The first thing we need to do is go to the `/usr/src/scotty/unix` directory, where the configuration script is located, and run it. We'll need to pass location of Tcl and Tk libraries to `--with-tcl` and `--with-tk` options. We will also use the `--prefix` option to specify where the package should be installed.

The following is a sample invocation:

```
# cd /usr/src/scotty
# sh ./configure --prefix=/opt/ActiveTcl-8.5 \
    --with-tcl=/opt/ActiveTcl-8.5/lib \
    --with-tk=/opt/ActiveTcl-8.5/lib
```

After running the configuration script, we will need to build Scotty:

```
# make
```

This process should cause the build to be complete in around a minute on modern hardware. Then we'll need to install it:

```
# make install
```

This will also cause MIB files to be generated and parsed, which will take several minutes.

SNMP uses privileged UDP ports and the ICMP protocol. This means that any application communicating over SNMP must be run by an administrative user. Scotty provides an alternative that allows non-root users to communicate over SNMP. It comes with binaries that are installed using `suid-root` — meaning that whoever runs them will have administrator access on your system. These binaries are only used if we use the Tnm package, and will be used by a non-root user.

These binaries are only used from within the Tnm package and do not cause a large security issue. If you want to use Tnm as a non-root user, you should proceed with the next step, which is installing these binaries:

```
# make sinstall
```

If they are not installed everything will still work for the root user. However, all other users will not be able to perform any communication using the Scotty package.

Scotty also comes with large number of examples on how to use its functions. They can be found in the `examples` subdirectory and also come with a documentation of what each of the examples do.

As Scotty is a large package and depends on specific Tcl features, it is not possible to embed it in a Starkit or Starpack. While the majority of packages can easily be embedded in a VFS, Scotty is one of the not so many packages that do not work in this way.

The best choice is to set up ActiveTcl on systems where we want to use SNMP and set up Scotty on these systems. Your Starkit can then be run using the `tclsh` binary from ActiveTcl and by taking advantage of all packages set up for this ActiveTcl instance, including Tnm package from Scotty.

An alternative is to use the MIBSmithySDK, which is a commercial Tcl implementation of the SNMP protocol from Muonics. It is available at: `http://www.muonics.com/Products/MIBSmithySDK/`. It can be wrapped in single-file binaries and offers a compatibility wrapper that mimics `Tnm` package's API.

The TkIned application

TkIned comes as part of Scotty package. After building and installing Scotty, it should be available in the same directory as other Tcl/Tk binaries — for our example, the path would be `/opt/ActiveTcl-8.5/bin` and the file is called `tkined<version>`; for example, `tkined1.5.0`. While the application offers an extensive set of features, we'll focus on a small subset of features that can be used to interactively play with your network and its SNMP features before actually interacting with it from scripts.

After running it, we should see an empty diagram, a menu, and a toolbar similar to the following screenshot:

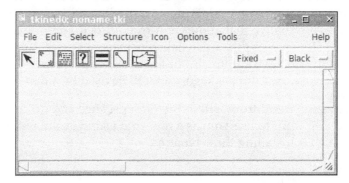

If you want to test how SNMP and Tnm work with your network, it is a good idea to start by discovering machines within your network. Open the **Tools** menu and choose **IP Discover**. This will cause a new menu **IP-Discover** to be shown — choose **Discover IP Network**, provide your network address (such as 192.168.2.0), and proceed. After some time, the application will show a separate window with results similar to the following one:

```
Discover 192.168.2 from kubuntu [192.168.2.12]

9 nodes found on network 192.168.2 in 82 seconds.

9 routes traced in 3 seconds.

9 netmasks queried in 3 seconds.

5 snmp agents queried in 6 seconds.

9 ip addresses queried in 3 seconds.

1 networks discovered in 0 seconds.

0 gateways discovered in 0 seconds.

9 links discovered in 0 seconds.

19 tkined objects created in 0 seconds.

Discover finished in 97 seconds
```

The UI will also show what hosts were discovered within your network, and display a screenshot similar to the following:

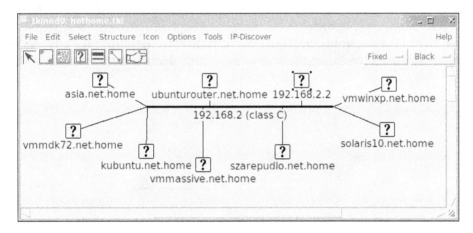

In order to check what was discovered, you can right-click on an item, and then choose **Attribute** and **Edit…**. This will show information about a node, such as its IP address, SNMP information (if SNMP was detected), and any information returned over SNMP. For example:

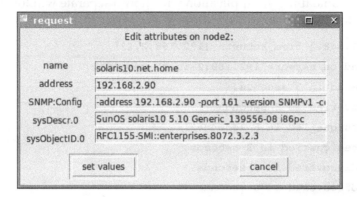

Fields such as **SNMP:Config** won't be visible for devices that are not SNMP aware or that did not respond to the defaults that TkIned tries, such as using SNMPv1 and `public`/`private` communities. Also, **SNMP:Config** is a direct mapping to SNMP session configurations from `Tnm` package, which is described in this section, and can be used when configuring how to talk to particular systems.

We can also set up graphing of specific values, for example, monitoring system usage and/or network traffic. In order to do that we can either use the **SNMP Monitor** package or **IP Monitor**, found in **Tools**. We can then set up graphs for any variable, for specific interfaces and monitor round-trip time, which is the time it takes for a message to get to a server and back. For example:

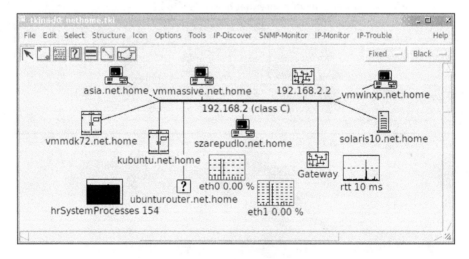

We recommend that you get familiar with TkIned and explore its functionality. However, as far as SNMP is concerned, the authors of this book have focused only on the features that will aid you in using Tnm package and writing scripts that communicate over SNMP.

Using Tcl for SNMP communication

Now that we have performed SNMP queries using TkIned, we can move on to using Scotty from Tcl directly to communicate over SNMP.

Querying SNMP in Tcl

The Tnm package offers a large number of features. Main part of its functionality is related to SNMP and MIB.

A quick example to query SNMPv2-MIB::sysContact value over SNMP can be as follows:

```
set session [Tnm::snmp generator]
$session configure -address "192.168.2.2" \
    -version "SNMPv1" -community "private"
puts [$session get SNMPv2-MIB::sysContact.0]
```

This will create a connection handle, configure it to query the IP 192.168.2.2 over SNMPv1 protocol and get sysContact value. This will print out something like the following:

{1.3.6.1.2.1.1.4.0 {OCTET STRING} root@router}

This is a list of a single element, which is a sub-list with three elements—OID of the item, data type, and actual value. In order to print out just the value we can get get the third element from the first item by doing:

```
puts [lindex \
    [$session get SNMPv2-MIB::sysContact.0] 0 2]
```

All commands used in the previous example are shown and explained in more detail later in this section.

All values related to SNMP are defined as **varbind** lists in Tnm. These are Tcl lists that define one or more SNMP attributes. Each attribute is a single element in the list and consists of three elements—OID, datatype, and value. An example answer from querying for sysContact ({1.3.6.1.2.1.1.4.0 {OCTET STRING} root@router}) is a varbind list.

Another example of a varbind list that describes the speed of an interface along with its type is:

```
{
  {1.3.6.1.2.1.2.2.1.5.1 Unsigned32 10000000}
  {1.3.6.1.2.1.2.2.1.3.1 Integer32 softwareLoopback}
  {1.3.6.1.2.1.2.2.1.2.1 {OCTET STRING} lo}
}
```

Regardless of whether a varbind list contains single or multiple elements, it always assumes that one item in the list represents one OID — it is a common mistake to specify a varbind list with a single item as a flat three-element list while it should be a one-element list where that element is a sublist with three elements. When getting an element, it is okay to provide only the first element as varbind list, which can either be the OID or its name — for example:

```
{IF-MIB::ifSpeed.1 IF-MIB::ifType.1 IF-MIB::ifDescr.1}
```

When specifying or parsing a data type, it can be one of the following:

Tnm types	Description
OCTET STRING	An octet-based string, in Tcl, it is mapped to an 8-bit string; when setting a value, characters outside of 8 bit are not handled properly.
OBJECT IDENTIFIER	It specifies another OID; when retrieving Tnm extension, tries to convert it from its numeric form to MIB representation; when setting a value, both MIB and numeric representation can be supplied; for example `IF-MIB::ifMIB`.
IpAddress	IPv4 address; represented in typical IP notation, for example `192.168.2.2`.
TimeTicks	The time interval; specified in the form of `nd hh:mm:ss.cc`; the first element is number of days, followed by number of hours, minutes, seconds, and hundredths of a second; for example `12d 11:38:12.40`; when setting a value, Tnm allows you to skip number of days and/or number of hundredths of second as well as accepts including number of days when specifying hours; for example `132:20:00`, which is an equivalent of `5d 12:20:00.00`.
INTEGER, Integer32, Counter, Counter32, Gauge, Gauge32, Unsigned32	Integer values of different characteristics; types and gauges are read-only, and cannot be set to any value. Integer values can be set; they can also be mapped to named values if the MIB definition specifies what each value maps to. For example, `softwareLoopback` maps to specific integer value for network interface type field Counter, Counter32, Gauge, Gauge32, and Unsigned32 can only store positive values. INTEGER or Integer32 values can be negative.
Counter64	64 bit counter that can only be read.

Usually, we will be able to handle values and their meaning accordingly by knowing the OIDs we are working with. However, in some cases, this might require the use of the `Tnm::mib` command, which can be used to query MIB-related information.

We can convert an OID to its name by invoking `name` subcommand of `Tnm::mib` command. For example:

```
% puts [Tnm::mib name 1.3.6.1.2.1.1.5.0]
SNMPv2-MIB::sysName.0
```

Subcommand `oid` does the opposite — it converts a label to an OID. Both subcommands accept OIDs and names, so it is perfectly safe to invoke them if we want to make sure an OID is specified.

A similar operation can be carried out for integer values that are mapped to string representations. By using the `scan` and `format` subcommands, we can convert such named integer values to and from integer representation. The OID/name of the object whose value we want to convert, and the value, must be specified. This is required because different values are mapped to different string representations for various MIB objects. For example:

```
% puts [Tnm::mib scan IF-MIB::ifType softwareLoopback]
24
% puts [Tnm::mib format IF-MIB::ifType 24]
softwareLoopback
```

In this case, we need to make sure that what we are passing is either a string or an integer representation — in some cases, especially with string or IP address-based values passing an already scanned value to the `scan` subcommand will throw an error.

We can now proceed to communicating over SNMP with our devices and/or computers. Let's assume we want to create a SNMP session. We'll start by running:

```
    set session [Tnm::snmp generator]
```

This will create a new SNMP session command. The first argument sent to `Tnm::snmp` command is the type of session. The `generator` session type is a session that generates requests and/or gets responses — usually used for getting or setting values.

We now need to configure the IP address, protocol to use, and community string. We can do that by running:

```
$session configure -address "192.168.2.2" \
    -version "SNMPv1" -community "private"
```

This configures our session to use SNMP version 1 and private community, which can be used for my wireless router, for example, in order to both get and set variables, such as the administrative e-mail contact.

Getting a value can be achieved by invoking the get subcommand of the session object. This command accepts a varbind list. However, this is because when *getting* we only need to specify the OID or name, querying a single element can be done by just specifying its name or OID. This is an equivalent of specifying a list that contains a sublist with just this element. For example, in order to retrieve the administrative contact for a device we can do:

$session get SNMPv2-MIB::sysContact.0

This will return a list with single element that is a sub-list with three elements. In order to extract an e-mail we can run the following command:

```
set addr [lindex \
    [$session get SNMPv2-MIB::sysContact.0] 0 2]
```

We can also retrieve multiple values by specifying multiple items in the varbind list. For example, in order to retrieve multiple values and iterate them, we can run:

```
foreach item [$session get \
    {IF-MIB::ifSpeed.1 IF-MIB::ifType.1 IF-MIB::ifDescr.1}] {
    lassign $item oid type value
    set oidname [Tnm::mib name $oid]
    if {$type == "Integer32"} {
      set value "$value ([Tnm::mib scan $oid $value])"
    }
    puts "$oidname ($oid) = $value"
}
```

Our example iterates over each varbind list. The values retrieved are configuration items of network interfaces — specifically, its speed (in bytes per second), type, and descriptive name.

We can map OIDs to names using Tnm::mib name. Also, if the type of an item is Integer32 then we map the value to integer value using Tnm::mib scan. The output from this script would be similar to:

```
IF-MIB::ifSpeed.1 (1.3.6.1.2.1.2.2.1.5.1) = 10000000
IF-MIB::ifType.1 (1.3.6.1.2.1.2.2.1.3.1) = softwareLoopback (24)
IF-MIB::ifDescr.1 (1.3.6.1.2.1.2.2.1.2.1) = lo
```

Performing asynchronous queries

It is also possible to use get in an asynchronous way by adding the script you want to execute as an additional parameter. In this case, the command will return instantly and whenever data is retrieved or an error occurred, our command will be invoked. This command is modified. %V is replaced by resulting varbind list, %E is replaced with error status, and %% is replaced by a single percent sign. In addition to this, %A will be replaced by IP address of remote peer. Error status of noError indicates that operation succeeded. All other values indicate an error.

In the case of callback scripts, the varbind list is not passed as list of lists, so it is best to pass it as the last argument to a procedure and use the args parameter name in the procedure to catch all remaining arguments to it.

For example, let's write a procedure to write the address and location in an asynchronous way:

```
proc onComplete {error args} {
    if {$error == "noError"} {
        puts "Address:  [lindex $args 0 2]"
        puts "Location: [lindex $args 1 2]"
        exit 0
    } else {
        puts "Error: $error"
        exit 1
    }
}
```

And in order to query this data using an SNMP session object, we need to do the following:

```
$session get \
    {SNMPv2-MIB::sysContact.0 SNMPv2-MIB::sysLocation.0} \
    [list onComplete %E %V]
```

This causes SNMP to query in the background, so we might need to add the following command after this to make sure our test script does not exit before data is retrieved:

```
vwait forever
```

We can also set the values of elements using the set subcommand. It can set multiple values:

```
$session set [list \
  [list SNMPv2-MIB::sysContact.0 {OCTET STRING} $address] \
  [list SNMPv2-MIB::sysLocation.0 {OCTET STRING} $location] \
  ]
```

This will cause the contact address and location values of a device to be set to a different value.

> The previous example is located in the `snmpget_set.tcl` and `snmpget_async.tcl` files in `01smtp-basics` directory in the source code examples for this chapter.

Walking over MIB trees

`Tnm` also supports walking over MIB trees. This is useful if you want to list multiple entries such as network interfaces, configured IP addresses, routes or existing connections. The subcommand `walk` can be used for this in a way similar to `foreach` command from Tcl.

The first argument is the variable name which `Tnm` will set to varbind list of current item and the second argument is the script to execute. We can also query multiple elements and, in this case, they will be iterated over simultaneously.

For example, in order to enumerate network interfaces, we can run:

```
$session walk items {
    IF-MIB::ifIndex IF-MIB::ifDescr
    IF-MIB::ifType IF-MIB::ifOperStatus
} {
    set index [lindex $items 0 2]
    set descr [lindex $items 1 2]
    set type [lindex $items 2 2]
    set status [lindex $items 3 2]
    puts "Interface $index \"$descr\" ($type) is $status"
}
```

This code tells us to walk over the iteration over four items — for the interface index, name, type, and its current status. The output of this script would be similar to the following:

```
Interface 1 "lo" (softwareLoopback) is up
Interface 2 "eth0" (ethernetCsmacd) is up
Interface 3 "tunl0" (tunnel) is down
Interface 4 "gre0" (tunnel) is down
Interface 5 "ipsec0" (tunnel) is down
```

> The following example is located in the `snmpwalk.tcl` file in `01smtp-basics` directory in the source code examples for this chapter.

Receiving traps

Aside from generator types of sessions which are used for querying data, the Tnm package also provides different types of session. The `listener` type can be used to listen for SNMP traps. They are used by SNMP agents to notify SNMP monitoring software about critical conditions, errors, or other things that might require actions to be taken.

Listener sessions are created in a way similar to generator sessions. For example, creating an SNMPv1 session to receive traps can be done this way:

```
set session [Tnm::snmp listener]
$session configure -version SNMPv1
```

Please note that it is common to have an snmptrapd daemon running on your system, which forwards traps depending on their type – in this case, Tnm will not be able to listen for notifications and will throw an error. If this is the case, please make sure you disable this service, for example, by invoking:

/etc/init.d/snmptrapd stop

Next we need to bind an event to this session so that our script is invoked whenever a trap is received. This is done using the `bind` subcommand of the session. It requires you to specify an empty argument as the first parameter. The reason for this is explained later in this chapter. Following that, we specify event type, `trap`, in this example. Finally, we need to supply our script. This script will be substituted in the same way as callbacks just as with the `get` command. Therefore, we can use %V to retrieve varbind list and %A to retrieve IP address of originator.

For example:

```
$session bind trap \
    [list ontrap SNMPv1 [list %A] %V]
```

This will cause the ontrap procedure to be invoked whenever a trap is received. Our command will receive the SNMP version as the first argument, and IP address as the second argument. In some cases, IP address can be empty; therefore, it is wrapped in a list command. This is caused by Tnm, which passes arguments to scripts and it is recommended that you implement bindings in this way.

In addition to this, SNMPv2 introduced inform packages, which are similar to traps, but require a confirmation response. We can create another session for the SNMPv2c (which is SNMPv2, community-based security) version by running:

```
set session2 [Tnm::snmp listener]
    $session2 configure -version SNMPv2c
```

We need to bind to the `inform` event as `Tnm` treats both types of packages separately:

```
$session2 bind inform \
    [list ontrap SNMPv2c [list %A] %V]
```

Now we can proceed by writing the `ontrap` procedure that handles `trap` / `inform` packages:

```
proc ontrap {version ip args} {
    puts [clock format [clock seconds] -format %H:%M:%S]
    puts "Trap using $version from $ip:"
    foreach item $args {
        lassign $item oid type value
        set name [Tnm::mib name $oid]
        puts "$name = $value ($type)"
    }
    puts ""
}
```

This will cause text similar to the following to be printed out whenever an SNMP trap is sent to our application.

```
20:45:35
Trap using SNMPv1 from 127.0.0.1:
SNMPv2-MIB::sysUpTime.0 = 284 (TimeTicks)
SNMPv2-MIB::snmpTrapOID.0 = IF-MIB::linkUp (OBJECT IDENTIFIER)
IF-MIB::ifIndex = 10 (Integer32)3
```

Sending traps

In order to test this, we can use the `Tnm` package to send trap and inform packages. In order to do that, we need to create a `notifier` type of SNMP session by running:

```
set session [Tnm::snmp notifier]
$session configure -address "192.168.2.12" -community public
$session configure -version SNMPv1
```

This will create a SNMPv1 session that can send traps. All we need to do now is to invoke the `trap` subcommand of this session. It accepts the OID of the trap to send as its first argument. The third argument is a varbind list of all additional information we want to provide.

In order to send a `linkUp` trap that sets `ifIndex` to 10, we can run the following:

```
$session trap IF-MIB::linkUp {
    {IF-MIB::ifIndex Integer32 10}
}
```

Similarly, in order to send an SNMPv2c inform package, we need to set up a session using the SNMPv2c protocol:

```
set session [Tnm::snmp notifier]
$session configure -address "192.168.2.12" -community public
$session configure -version SNMPv2c
```

Sending an inform package looks exactly the same, but uses the inform subcommand:

```
$session inform IF-MIB::linkUp {
    {IF-MIB::ifIndex Integer32 10}
}
```

While it is more common to listen for traps than to send them, there are instances in which our application might forward events to other computers in the network.

The preceding example is located in the snmptrap_receive.tcl and snmptrap_send.tcl files in 02snmp-traps directory in the source code examples for this chapter.

SNMP agent

It is also possible to create your own SNMP agent using Tnm. This can be used to have an application respond over SNMP. It can then be used with standard software and hardware network-monitoring solutions. We can also create a proxy agent that will send requests to other hosts and optionally perform calculations on some of the fields. We can also use it to test other SNMP-aware software.

The first thing we need to do is to create a responder session by invoking the Tnm::snmp responder command. For example:

```
set session [Tnm::snmp responder -port 5161 -community public]
```

In many cases, our system already has an SNMP daemon listening, so it is wise to run our agent on a separate port. This way we won't collide with the system's SNMP agent and can safely test everything as a non-root user on Unix systems.

Just this line is enough and our SNMP agent is now listening. You can check it by running the following shell command:

```
snmpwalk -v1 -c public 127.0.0.1:5161
```

We should see basic subset of SNMP values returned. Here is a subset of the result:

```
SNMPv2-MIB::sysDescr.0 = STRING: Tnm SNMP agent version 3.0.0 (i686-
Linux-2.6.28-16-generic)
SNMPv2-MIB::sysObjectID.0 = OID: SNMPv2-SMI::enterprises.1575.1.1
DISMAN-EVENT-MIB::sysUpTimeInstance = Timeticks: (477) 0:00:04.77
SNMPv2-MIB::sysContact.0 = STRING:
SNMPv2-MIB::sysName.0 = STRING:
SNMPv2-MIB::sysLocation.0 = STRING:
SNMPv2-MIB::sysServices.0 = INTEGER: 72
```

These values are bound to Tcl variables. Contact, name, location, and description are bound to the Tcl array tnm_system. We can modify these by invoking:

```
set tnm_system(sysDescr) "My Tnm SNMP agent"
set tnm_system(sysContact) "root@net.home"
set tnm_system(sysName) "My test machine"
set tnm_system(sysLocation) "Rack 1"
```

We can also bind additional fields to be mapped to Tcl variables using the instance subcommand of the session command. These will always be read whenever a request comes in, so simply updating values is enough for them to be reflected when querying over SNMP. For example:

```
$session instance \
    HOST-RESOURCES-MIB::hrSystemInitialLoadDevice.0 \
    hrLoad(device)

set hrLoad(device) 1234
```

This will cause OID HOST-RESOURCES-MIB::hrSystemInitialLoadDevice.0 to be mapped to the Tcl variable hrLoad(device). This variable is always read as global variable, so when setting it from a procedure, we either need to use command global or reference it as ::hrLoad(device).

We can also bind strings to an OID in the same way:

```
$session instance \
    HOST-RESOURCES-MIB::hrSystemInitialLoadParameters.0 \
    hrLoad(params)

set hrLoad(params) "Unknown"
```

As all these values are read, we can use the `trace` command to set a value before it is actually returned by SNMP session. For example, we can set `hrLoad`(device) to a random value each time it is read:

```
proc traceLoadDevice {args} {
    set ::hrLoad(device) [expr {int(rand() * 1000)}]
}

trace add variable hrLoad(device) {read} traceLoadDevice
```

The `traceLoadDevice` procedure its sets value to a random value within a range of 0 to 1000. Following that, we add a trace before `hrLoad(device)` is read to invoke `traceLoadDevice`. More information about the `trace` command can be found in its documentation which is available at `http://www.tcl.tk/man/tcl8.5/TclCmd/trace.htm`.

 The previous example is located in the `snmpagent.tcl` file in `03snmp-agent` directory in the source code examples for this chapter.

Additional features

The `Tnm` package also offers access to ICMP functionality, available via `Tnm::icmp` command. We can use it for including functionality such as monitoring, network diagnostics, and troubleshooting.

Similar to SNMP, all commands are implemented as subcommands of this command. The main difference is that, for ICMP, there is no concept of a session. All operations are atomic and there is no need to keep a state.

One of the features of ICMP is the ability to ping one or more systems. This can be used to check whether a machine is responding to ping requests, which usually is equivalent to whether this machine is up and running. It can also be used to check time needed for a packet to be sent to the machine and received back.

This command accepts a list of all hosts as its arguments. For example, in order to pass all arguments to your script as list of hosts, we can do the following:

```
set result [Tnm::icmp echo $argv]
```

The result is a list of name-value pairs. For each host, we get a value. If it is empty, it means that a host has not responded. Otherwise, the value is the number of milliseconds after which a response was received. For example, in order to ping `192.168.2.2` and `192.168.2.20`, we can run:

```
Tnm::icmp echo {192.168.2.2 192.168.2.20}
```

If the first IP is up and the second is down, the result would be similar to:

```
192.168.2.2 8 192.168.2.20 {}
```

In this case, the result means that it took 8 milliseconds to ping 192.168.2.2, and that 192.168.2.20 has not responded.

We can easily iterate over results by doing the following:

```
foreach {ip value} $result {
    if {$value != ""} {
        puts "$ip is up"
    } else {
        puts "$ip is down"
    }
}
```

It is also possible to trace route to a particular computer or a set of computers.

 Thr preceding example is located in the icmp_multiping.tcl file in 04icmp directory in the source code examples for this chapter.

It is also possible to trace the route to one or more IP addresses by using the ttl and trace subcommands. These commands hop number to find and list hosts to check against. The **hop number** is the distance in terms of machines that the IP packages pass, from your computer. The index starts with 1, where 1 will probably indicate your local router or modem.

The subcommand ttl returns the IP addresses of machines that have responded to requests while trace returns the IP addresses of machines that packages have been sent to. Usually both will return the same IP addresses; combining both can be used to detect multi-homed systems.

Both commands return a list with two elements for each host— the IP address of specified hop and the number of milliseconds it took between sending and receiving packet from that machine. For example, we can write a simple route tracing application by doing:

```
set i 0
set ip ""
while {$i < 256} {
    set old $ip
    lassign [Tnm::icmp trace $i $argv] ip ttl
    puts [format "%-20s%4s" $ip $ttl]
    if {$ip == $old} {
```

```
        break
    }
    incr i
}
```

This example increases the i variable and gets the next hop for the specified IP address or hostname. When the IP address returned is the same as the previous one, this means that this is the last hop and we can now stop iterating. This example also stops if the number of hops exceeds 256.

 This example is located in the `icmp_traceroute.tcl` and `icmp_multitraceroute.tcl` files in `12smtp` directory in the source code examples for this chapter.

Summary

Tcl has a powerful extension for communicating over SNMP. The Scotty package covers all aspects of SNMP — all commonly used versions of the protocol and offers all aspects of SNMP communication.

In this chapter, we learned:

- TkIned application — this can be used as both a simple network monitoring tool and base for learning SNMP.

- Using Scotty for getting and setting SNMP values, for iterating over SNMP tables and finding attributes that a particular device offers. This can be used to, periodically or on demand, query data from devices or automatically configure devices.

- How to send and receive traps — this is especially useful if we need to support devices that communicate only over SNMP, such as routers, printers, and embedded devices. We can also send traps from our application, which can be used to notify our monitoring system if something is wrong.

- To set up SNMP agent so that our application can be monitored and/or queried using SNMP. This can be an integration point with monitoring systems that communicate over SNMP, such as Cacti or Nagios.

Readers are encouraged to play with the application more, and learn SNMP using it. It can also be used to discover devices and computers within our network that we can test it on.

The next chapter introduces the embedded Tcl web server that can be used for communicating with users and across applications using HTTP. It also shows how it can be used to build a website and serve content similar to other web servers.

10

Web Programming in Tcl

In this chapter, we will introduce you to concepts related to web programming in Tcl. To be more specific, server-side web programming — processing the requests coming from clients via the HTTP protocol and responding to these requests.

The invention of HTTP and HTML revolutionized the perception of Internet and had a significant impact on the way we are using it today. These technologies became so common that it is almost impossible to imagine our day-to-day life without them. It is no wonder that every modern language is web-enabled, that is it offers a rich variety of libraries and extensions facilitating the web programming. Tcl, of course, is one of these languages, but it offers more than that — a high grade, stable and efficient web server written entirely in Tcl, able not only to serve the content, but also easily extendable, so it may be boldly considered as a kind of application server. The existence of such a solution proves the maturity of Tcl as the tool that can be used to develop complex solutions.

We assume the reader is familiar with the basic concepts of web programming, and abbreviations such as HTTP, HTML, CGI, or MIME are not a mystery. Otherwise, although we attempt to use simple language and easy-to-understand examples, we recommend reading about them before proceeding with this chapter, as it will significantly help you to get more familiar with topics covered in this chapter. The amount of available sources of such knowledge is so high that there would be no point to repeating this information once again.

In this chapter, the following topics will be covered:

- First, we will discuss how Tcl code can be used as CGI scripts — the solution was once very popular, and even now is important for historical reasons. CGI is a strict interface that defines how a web server can cooperate with an application (written in the language of your choice) to generate an answer. The interface is so simple that any language could be used, but Tcl offers some extensions to facilitate CGI scripting development, particularly the package ncgi, which we will present.

- Next we will take a closer look at `html` package that is designed to make the generation of HTML output easier. It is only one of many extensions offered by Tcl world, so you may consider it an incentive to learn about others and choose the solution that will suit you the best.

- Finally, we will focus on `TclHttpd` — a mature web server written entirely in Tcl. Make no mistake here — it is not just a 'toy' or proof of concept. For example, the entire Tcl wiki (`http://wiki.tcl.tk`) is running on top of it. As a matter of fact, the Tcl language, thanks to its well-designed and efficient I/O system and event programming, suits the purpose of concurrent handling of multiple HTTP requests quite well. For example, take *AOLserver* (`http://www.aolserver.com`) — a Tcl-enabled web server that is used in mature business-grade implementations around the world. It is not a coincidence that from a variety of languages Tcl was chosen to shape this product.

  Talking about `TclHttpd`, we will present how to obtain, install, configure, and run it. After having a look at its basic capabilities, we dive into extending the server with your custom code. You will learn how to use CGI here, and map a URL to a Tcl procedure, so its invocation is as simple as one mouse click in web browser. We will show you how to create a document handler; a piece of code that processes and generates the content served to the client, effectively allowing you to extend the server in any way you would like to. Next, we will discuss domain handlers, which are pieces of code responsible for handling the website sub-domains of your choice. Then, you will become familiar with rapid development of websites based on a template system, which allows you to mix HTML and Tcl code together.

- Once you learn how to program the `TclHttpd` server, we will show you how to debug it, and finally how to embed it into your application, effectively making it web-enabled. You will be presented with a real-life example of when the server is successfully incorporated into standalone executable distribution created with the *Starpack* technology — that's right, you can have your program in one binary file, and it can be accessed via the web browser! Here is where the flexibility and richness of techniques, available in Tcl, allow you to create impressive solutions.

We do not in tend to mirror the official documentation of described libraries/ packages, but to show the possibilities and applications they offer through simple yet interesting examples of usage. For every example, the complete source code and other resource files are available in the source code examples for this chapter.

Tcl scripts as CGI application

The **Common Gateway Interface** (**CGI**) is the standardized way the CGI-compliant web server can use external application to do some tasks, and essentially to generate the HTML output to the client. We do not intend to describe CGI itself—as it is beyond the scope of this book, but to focus how Tcl can be arranged here. The full specification of CGI, is described in detail in RFC 3875 (`http://www.ietf.org/rfc/rfc3875.txt`).

The CGI standard defines that the application may be written in any language. The communication between the server and the application is as follows:

* The input for the application is provided in terms of environmental variables (see CGI manual for detailed list of these variables). In the case of HTTP POST request, the content of that request is available as standard input.

* The application writes the resulting document to standard output. This output must contain at least the HTTP header defining the MIME type of the document, and the content.

To sum up, all operations boil down to reading standard input and/or environmental variables, and writing to standard output.

The following is simple example of a Tcl script that may serve as application CGI:

```
#!C:/tcl/bin/tclsh85.exe
puts "Content-type: text/html"
puts ""

puts "<pre>"
parray ::env
puts "\nStandard input:"
puts [read stdin]
puts "</pre>"
```

All this code does is write to the standard output all environmental variables available (in form of Tcl $env variable) and the contents of standard input. For the sake of clarity, we do not even care about the correct HTML formatting of the output—fortunately, the web browser will still display it correctly.

You can run this code with any web server that is able to handle CGI applications correctly. Consult your server's manual for details on how to enable and configure CGI.

For demonstration purposes, we decided to use Apache, coming in the form of a portable XAMPP distribution (http://www.apachefriends.org/en/xampp.html). In this case, no special configuration was required. Assuming the distribution is installed in C:\xampp directory, all you have to do is save the code in the c:\xampp\cgi-bin\. We decided to name it cgi_example.tcl. Once you start the web server, you can access the application using http://127.0.0.1/cgi-bin/cgi_example.tcl:

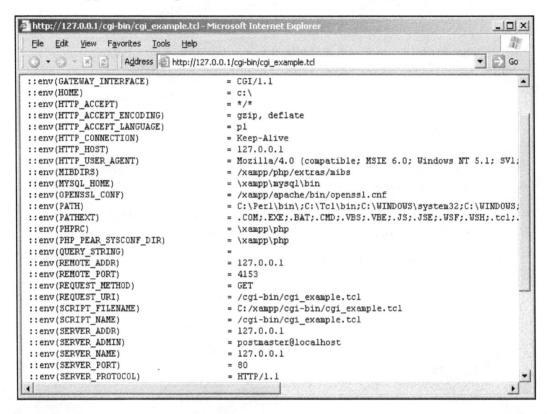

In a typical use-case scenario, the web browser sends some user entered data to the application. Two options are possible:

- The data is sent using an HTTP GET query. For example, if you decide to send a variable named "key" of value "value", you could simply type in the browser: http://127.0.0.1/cgi-bin/cgi_example.tcl?key=value. In the code, you can access this data by reading the QUERY_STRING environmental variable, which will contain all the characters from the URL after the question mark ('?'); each new key=value is separated by an ampersand character ('&')

- The data is sent using HTTP POST query, for example, by this simple HTML form:

```
<form action="/cgi-bin/cgi_example.tcl" method="POST">
  <input type="hidden" name="key" value="value" />
  <input type="submit" />
</form>
```

In this case the QUERY_STRING is empty, and the data is available on standard input. The encoding of the data depends on the encoding type used by the browser that is sending the query. The default type is application/x-www-form-urlencoded, but if you are uploading some files, the type multipart/form-data must be used. In the HTML page code, the encoding type is specified using the enctype attribute of the form tag.

To work with this data, you would have to detect which HTTP request method has been used (by reading env(REQUEST_METHOD) variable) and read the data from the appropriate source (standard input or env variable). Note that they are encoded, so you have first to check what type of encoding was used (by checking the env(CONTENT_TYPE) variable) and decode them adequately.

Of course, you are not limited to outputting only text/html type of data; you can produce the response of any allowed MIME data. For example, you could create a script that adds a watermark to an image and returns it—in this case, the content type would be like image/* (for example image/png or image/jpeg), and then the binary data would be written.

 The source code of the examples presented in this section is located in the in the 01cgi directory in the source code examples for this chapter.

Using ncgi package

All these tasks, although simple, are really annoying and error prone when it comes to doing them on your own; fortunately, there is a package named ncgi. What the package does is to provide an abstract overlay over the CGI interface, boiling down the entire operation to the invocation of a few commands from the :ncgi namespace in your Tcl script. The package is part of the tcllib library, and you can find its documentation at http://tcllib.sourceforge.net/doc/ncgi.html. To illustrate its usage, let's revisit and modify the previous example. We will use simple a HTML form to upload both text (name, surname, age) and binary (file) data:

```
<form action="/cgi-bin/ncgi_example.tcl" method="POST"
enctype="multipart/form-data">
Name:<br /><input name="name" value="John" /><br />
```

```
Surname:<br /><input name="surname" value="Smith" /><br />
Age:<br /><input name="age" value="54" /><br />
Image:<br /><input type="file" name="file"><br />
<input type="submit" />
</form>
```

The following screenshot shows the form:

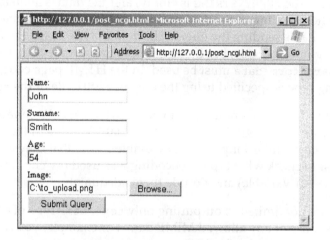

Upon upload, the ncgi_example.tcl CGI script will be executed. The file contains the following code:

```
#!C:/tcl/bin/tclsh85.exe
package require ncgi

::ncgi::parse

::ncgi::header
set keys [::ncgi::names]
puts "<pre>"
puts "query data names: $keys \n"
foreach key $keys {
    if {$key eq "file"} {
        puts "uploaded file details:"
        puts "client sent: [::ncgi::importFile -client $key]"
        puts "type: [::ncgi::importFile -type $key]"
        puts "saved as: [::ncgi::importFile -server $key uploaded.png]"
    } else {
        puts "$key: [::ncgi::value $key]"
    }
}
puts "</pre>"
```

What the file does first is load `ncgi` package. All commands from that package are accessible in the `::ncgi` namespace. The `::ncgi::parse` command, once executed, performs all the behind-the-scene magic—it automatically reads data from the CGI environment and decodes it appropriately, so you don't have to bother about it anymore. You may have no idea how HTTP/CGI works, and you'll still be able to successfully code the CGI script! You have to call this command first, before you start accessing the uploaded data. The command takes care of all aspects like detecting the encoding type and using it to decode the data correctly—in our example, it transparently handles the support of multipart/form-data, which would be quite awkward to perform manually.

After the incoming request was parsed with `::ncgi::parse`, we get the list of uploaded data names using `::ncgi::names` and store it into the `keys` variable. Next, for each data we print its name and value, except the image—we print image file details and save them as the `uploaded.png` file. The details of uploaded file are retrieved using the following commands:

- `::ncgi::importFile -client key`—returns the full path and name of the file as it is on the client's side. The last `parameter—key`—it is the appropriate name of input field used in uploading HTML form. In our example, the client uploaded the file `C:\to_upload.jpg` from the local drive.

- `::ncgi::importFile -type key`—returns the MIME type of the file, allowing to process it appropriately.

- `::ncgi::importFile -server key uploadedFileName`—saves the uploaded file as `uploadedFileName` (in our case, as `uploaded.png`) and returns that name. Note that it is your responsibility to remove the created file when it becomes dispensable.

In fact, before we start printing anything to the standard output, the HTTP response header must be written to it. In the earlier example, it was done manually:

```
puts "Content-type: text/html"
puts ""
```

But `ncgi` package offers handy command `::ncgi::header` that automates it. By default, it outputs only `Content-type` header with `text/html` value, but you are able to alter this behavior by specifying additional (optional) parameters:

`::ncgi::header` *contentType additionalHeaders*

- `contentType` is a new value of type to send to the browser
- `additionalHeaders` is a list of additional headers to send, in the form of name-value pairs

The response produced by the script to standard output is sent by the server to the web browser, as shown in the next screenshot:

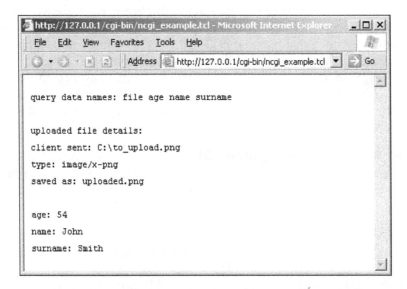

We do not intend to describe all of `ncgi` commands—interested readers will find them in the package's manual. Some of the most useful are:

- `::ncgi::cookie cookieName`—returns the value of the cookie named `cookieName`.

- `::ncgi::setCookie options`—writes the HTTP cookie header to `stdout`. This command must be called before other commands that write headers (for example `::ncgi:header`). The argument options are a list of option names and values:
    - `-name` *name*—specifies the cookie name.
    - `-value` *value*—the value of the cookie.
    - `-expires` *date*—the expiration date.
    - `-path` *path*—the cookie's path attribute.
    - `-domain` *domain*—the domain attribute.

- `::ncgi::import name ?tclName?`—imports the data identified by *name* from the HTTP query as the `tclName` variable (or as `name`, if `tclName` is omitted), for easy access to the script. There is also a command that allows importing a set of variables: `::ncgi::import ?names?`, where `names` is a list of variable names to import. If that parameter is omitted, all variables are imported.

As the cookies are commonly used, let's have a closer look at them. The following example will either ask the user for his name, or print a welcome message if the cookie `name` is set:

```
#!C:/tcl/bin/tclsh85.exe
package require ncgi

::ncgi::parse
set name ""
if {[::ncgi::exists name]} {
    set name [::ncgi::value name]
     ::ncgi::setCookie -name name -value $name
} else {
    set name [::ncgi::cookie name]
}
::ncgi::header

if {$name != ""} {
    puts "Hello, $name"
} else {
    puts "<form action=\"/cgi-bin/ncgi_example2.tcl\" method=\
"POST\">"
    puts "Enter your name:<br /><input name=\"name\" /><br />"
    puts "<input type=\"submit\" />"
    puts "</form>"
}
```

The code is rather simple. If the `name` parameter is sent to the script, its value is used to set a cookie of the same name.

Next, depending on whether the cookie is set or not, one of the following screens may be presented:

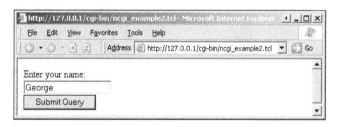

If you refresh the page multiple times, you will still get the greeting message, as your name is already stored as a cookie.

 The source code of the examples presented in this section is located in the in the 02ncgi directory in the source code examples for this chapter.

Using html package

The package ncgi significantly eases server-side programming in Tcl, but there is still a need to manually generate the output—and by manually we mean that you have to take care of every output character on your own. Tcl programmers tend to make life as simple as it can be so it is easy to guess that there are some solutions for creating HTML code. One of them is the html package, also a part of tcllib (http://tcllib.sourceforge.net/doc/html.html).

As usual, instead of duplicating the manual, we will present the abilities of the package in some simple yet working example code:

```
#!C:/tcl/bin/tclsh85.exe
package require ncgi
package require html

::ncgi::parse
::ncgi::header

::html::author "Piotr Bełtowski"
::html::keywords "html tcl package learning"
::html::description "example web page that illustrates \
the usage of html (and ncgi) package"
puts [::html::head "package html example"]
puts [::html::bodyTag]
if {[::ncgi::exists name]} {
    puts [::html::h3 "thank you for posting the data:"]
    puts [::html::tableFromList [::ncgi::nvlist] border="1"]
} else {
    puts [::html::openTag form \
        action="/cgi-bin/html_example.tcl"]
    puts [::html::h3 "please fill in the form:"]
    puts [::html::nl2br "Name:\n \
        [::html::textInput name John]"]
    puts [::html::nl2br "Surame:\n \
        [::html::textInput surname Smith]"]
```

```
    puts [::html::nl2br "Age:\n \
        [::html::textInput age 54]"]
    puts [::html::submit "Submit"]
  }
  puts [::html::end]
```

We assume this code is saved as `html_example.tcl` in CGI directory (`cgi-bin` in the case of Apache).

The code starts in similar way as previous examples, by parsing the HTTP request and writing the HTTP response header to the standard output, respectively with `::ncgi::parse` and `::ncgi::header` commands.

In general, the commands from the `html` package do not produce any standard output on their own, but return an HTML fragment string. That is why in the example these commands are usually surrounded by a `puts` invocation. This allows us to create HTML text, storing it in a variable, and performing more advanced processing such as caching HTML text. The second thing about them, as you have already noticed, they are all available in `::html` namespace.

The problem of generating the HTML content is that every tag has to be eventually closed, which may be cumbersome in the case of deeply nested tags. The package solves this problem in an interesting way: the information of every opened tag (for example `<html>`) is stored (pushed) on some kind of stack. At the end, all you have to do is call the appropriate command that pops the tag back from the stack and generates an appropriate closing sequence (like `</html>`).

The command `::html::head pageTitle` generates the `<head>` section with the title set to `pageTitle`. It also creates the `<html>` *tag*, pushing the information about it on the stack mentioned before. In a real web page, the `<head>` tag usually contains additional information. To put them there, all you have to do is to call some commands earlier, before generating the `<head>` section. In our example, we use the following:

- `::html::author string` — this command will result in a `string` (that, as the command name suggests, may contain details about the author of the web page), which will be put as the comment into the `<head>` element

- `::html::keywords` and `::html::description` — calling these commands will place their arguments into the appropriate `<meta>` tags (`keywords` and `description`) that will be a part of `<head>`

There is also a more general command `::html::meta` that allows you to create virtually any `<meta>` tag.

Once we have dealt with the `<head>` section, we create opening `<body>` tag with the `::html::bodyTag`. Again, this command will store information about any unclosed tags in the stack.

Now it is time for some logic. The same CGI script will either generate a simple form to be filled-in, or will present the results from the form. Using `::ncgi::exists name` we check if the HTTP request contains a variable named `name`. If yes, we assume that the form was submitted, and generate some kind of summary page:

- The `<h3>` tag is created using the `::html::h3` *tagContent* command. All such tags from `<h1>` to `<h6>` have corresponding commands, named adequately.

- Next, a two-column HTML table is created using the `::html::tableFromList` command. Its first argument must be a list of name-value pairs — in our case, we get this using `::ncgi::nvlist`, which produces a list of all query variables in complaint format. The second (optional) argument is a string that will be put inside the `<table>` tag, so it should contain the appropriate tag's attributes.

In case no data was sent to our script, it will respond with an HTML form. First the `<form>` tag is created using `::html::openTag`. This command allows you to create any tag — its first parameter is a tag name, and the second — the tag's attributes. As you probably guessed, it also pushes the tag on the stack, allowing it to be closed later. We want the form to invoke the same current script on submission, so the action target `/cgi-bin/html_example.tcl` is used. In case you would like to use a web server other than Apache, or in different configuration, please consult the server's manual on how to access your CGI script.

Our form will ask the user for three input data values: `name`, `surname`, and `age`, proposing as default values *John Smith, 54*. To achieve this, some `<input>` elements are created using `::html::textInput`, with the variable's name and the default value as parameters. Note that this command will set the `<input>` size attribute to the value `45` by default. It is a bug that should be fixed in future releases of the library.

In order to avoid manual encoding of new lines using `<br/>` tags, we use `::html::nl2br` that converts all new line characters (\n) occurrences to that tag. In this example, it is a bit over the top, but may be really useful in the case of generating more complex web pages.

Finally, an `<input>` element of type `submit` is created with "Submit" as the label on the button, by using `::html::submit "Submit"` command.

Now it is time to close all opened tags — we can do it almost magically with `::html::end`; this command will pop all unclosed tags from the stack and produce the appropriate HTML content to close them. There is also another command — `::html::closeTag` — that pops from the stack and closes only one tag.

Having said all that, let's see the generated HTML code along with its appearance in the web browser. First, the page with the form to send:

```html
<html><head>
    <title>package html example</title>
    <!-- Piotr Bełtowski -->
    <meta name="keywords" content="html tcl package learning">
    <meta name="description" content="example web page that
illustrates the usage of html (and ncgi) package">
</head>

<body bgcolor="white" text="black">

<form action="/cgi-bin/html_example.tcl">
<h3>please fill in the form:</h3>

Name:<br>   <input type="text" name="name" value="John" size="45"><br>
Surname:<br>   <input type="text" name="surname" value="Smith"
size="45"><br>
Age:<br>   <input type="text" name="age" value="54" size="45"><br>
<input type="submit" name="submit" value="Submit">

</form>
</body>
</html>
```

The preceding code should produce a screenshot like the following one:

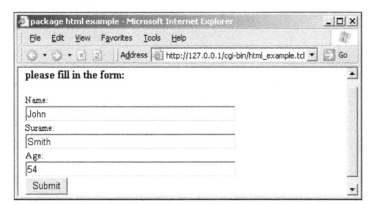

The page presenting the uploaded data is as follows:

```
<html><head>
    <title>package html example</title>
    <!-- Piotr Bełtowski -->
    <meta name="keywords" content="html tcl package learning">
    <meta name="description" content="example web page that
illustrates the usage of html (and ncgi) package">
</head>

<body bgcolor="white" text="black">

<h3>thank you for posting the data:</h3>

<table border="1"><tr>
    <td>name</td>
    <td>John</td>
</tr>
<tr>
    <td>surname</td>
    <td>Smith</td>
</tr>
<tr>
    <td>age</td>
    <td>54</td>
</tr>
<tr>
    <td>submit</td>
    <td>Submit</td>
</tr>
</table>
</body>
</html>
```

The screenshot produced with the preceding code is:

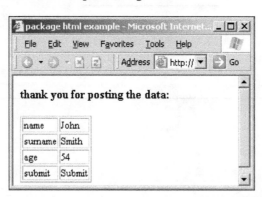

As you can see, the produced HTML code, although simple, is clean and correct. Using the `html` package you may probably not be able to produce perfect, 100% valid HTML code in all cases, but in most applications, the results should be satisfying. The package offers many more commands than described here, and we encourage the reader to study the manual to get acquainted with its full possibilities.

 The source code of the examples presented in this section is located in the in the `03html` directory in the source code examples for this chapter.

Introduction to TclHttpd

The possibilities offered by Tcl go far beyond plain CGI scripting—the entire web server can be written using this language. But before you eagerly start writing your own, know that this task was already done by *Brent Welch*, the author of `TclHttpd`—the powerful web server completely implemented using the Tcl language. The author claims that at the beginning the entire code had about 175 lines. Tcl's input/output subsystem is well crafted, and it offers maximum usability with minimum coding.

The homepage of `TclHttpd` is located at `http://www.tcl.tk/software/tclhttpd/`. The latest available officially released version 3.5.1 was released on May 27th, 2004. This is both bad and good information: the code is pretty old and not actively supported, but it reached the maturity level long time ago. The code has its years, but you can't question its usability.

 The source code of the examples presented in this section is located in the in the `04tclhttpd` directory in the source code examples for this chapter.

Installation

You can download the server from `http://sourceforge.net/projects/tclhttpd/` in two ways:

- `tclhttpd3.5.1.tar.gz` (or `tclhttpd351.zip`)—contains the server code
- `tclhttpd3.5.1-dist.tar.gz` (or `tclhttpd351dist.zip`)—contains the server code, a full Tcl/Tk distribution of version 8.4.5, `TclLib` version 1.6, and the `Thread` extension (2.5.2)

In most cases, you will already have a Tcl interpreter installed and configured on your system, and for the rest of the chapter, we will focus on this option. The version of server we describe requires Tcl version 8.3 or higher, with the Tcl Standard Library (`TclLib`) installed (as the server makes use of some of its packages). If you have set up ActiveTcl 8.4 or 8.5, it also contains all the packages that TclHttpd needs; all that you need to do is use it now!

The entire installation process is simply to download and unpack the compressed archive. After unpacking, the server's files will be found in the `tclhttpd3.5.1` directory—you may rename it and put it anywhere you like, and in our examples we assume it is moved to `C:\ tclhttpd` location. We will also refer to this as the "home directory".

It is also worth mentioning that TclHttpd server is available in form of a Starkit one-file distribution—*tclhttpd3.5.1.kit*.

Retrieving source code from the CVS repository

The source code of the server is stored in the SourceForge cvs. It contains a newer, never released version 3.5.2 that fixes some known bugs. If you wish to use this version, the following are the command-line instructions to run. When prompted for a password, hit the *Enter* key.

```
cvs -d:pserver:anonymous@tclhttpd.cvs.sourceforge.net:/cvsroot/tclhttpd
login
```

```
cvs -z3 -d:pserver:anonymous@tclhttpd.cvs.sourceforge.net:/cvsroot/
tclhttpd co -P tclhttpd
```

The code will be downloaded to the `tclhttpd` subdirectory of current folder.

Documentation

The server comes with documentation, moreover, with a complete chapter from Brent Welch book, dedicated to TclHttpd—you can find it in the directory: `htdocs/book/TCLHTTPD.html`

First run

The start of the server is done by running the `httpd.tcl` script located in the `bin` directory of the `TclHttpd` home directory (in our example it is `C:\tclhttpd\bin\ httpd.tcl`).

Once launched, the server is available by default on the 8015 port. You can also see a randomly generated password (in this execution, it was `rf4lohm7.np`), allowing you to access debug information. See `http://127.0.0.1:8015/hacks.html` for more details.

When accessed via the web browser, the server presents its default homepage:

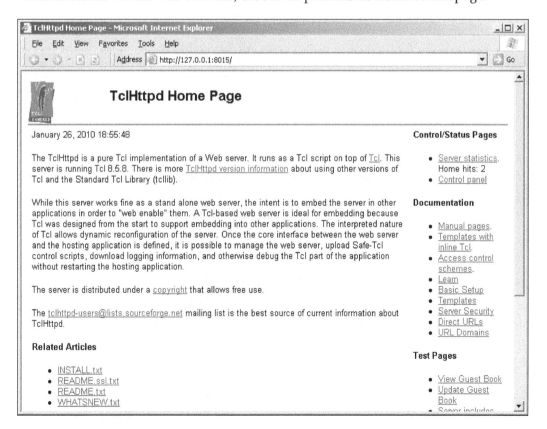

When you first run `TclHttpd`, there is a pretty good chance you may witness some trivial yet annoying problems, especially on MS Windows.

First, the default configuration assumes that the server will store its log and runtime files in the `/tmp` directory. It is quite a good default value in a Unix environment where that directory usually exists, but on Windows you will get an error like:

```
Error processing main startup script "C:\downloads\tcl\
tclhttpd3.5.1.kit\bin\httpdthread.tcl".
couldn't open "/tmp/tclhttpd.default": no such file or directory
```

The solution is either to create the `C:\tmp` directory (because the Tcl 'understands' the philosophy of Windows paths; `/tmp` will eventually be translated to `C:\tmp`), or to use the 3.5.2 version, where the bug seems to be fixed (although it is still attempting to write to `/var/run/tclhttpd/tclhttpd.pid`). As previously mentioned, version 3.5.2 can be retrieved from the CVS repository.

The second issue may be related to running the server from the `.kit` distribution, and occurs on Windows. `TclHttpd` offers some debugging mechanisms, and as mentioned earlier, at each start, it generates a random password that allows access to this functionality. This password is written to standard output at startup. The problem is that if you are using MS Windows and Tclkit as the runtime, you will not be able to see that output, and in particular the password. The solution is to instead use the command-line version of Tclkit — Tclkitsh, which is able to handle this situation correctly. However, you will lose the ability to see the GUI (not a real loss anyway). Version 3.5.2 offers a circumvention of the problem — the password is printed in the GUI window.

Talking about the GUI, if run with `wish` instead of `tclsh`, the `TclHttpd` will display a simple graphical window with some basic information and counters (**computername** is the name of the computer on which it is executed):

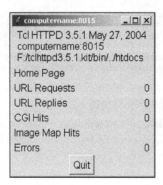

Note that the screenshot was taken from the version 3.5.1, so the password is not displayed.

Startup parameters

The `httpd.tcl` script can be run with additional parameters that override the default configuration of the server. The most important ones are:

Parameter	Description
`-port portNnumber`	Overrides the default port value.
`-docRoot directoryPath`	Defines the root directory for the top level URL (like `http://127.0.0.1:8015/`). By default, it is `htdocs` in the server home directory.
`-config configFileName`	Specifies the configuration file to use. The default `config` is `tclhttpd.rc`.
`-library directoryPath`	Defines the directory where the custom code should be stored — all files from this location are sourced by the server at startup. By default, it is `custom` in the server home directory.

Such a form of invocation is useful for the quick change/customization of configuration. If you need the changes to be permanent, you should rather modify (or create new) configuration file (described as follows).

Default directory structure

When you unpack downloaded server distribution, you will observe a lot of files and directories inside it. Fortunately, only some of them are crucial and worth knowing. The most important subdirectories of the server home directory are:

Subdirectory	Description
`bin`	Contains the file `httpd.tcl` that starts up the server, *tclhttpd.rc* that holds the default configuration. Also, the mini subdirectory has a minimalistic version of server that may be a base for your modifications and development
`custom`	Your custom Tcl code should go here—on startup, the server will source every file from this directory
`htdocs`	Constitutes the base for / URL hierarchy. All documents that should be accessible via HTTP should be located here, for example, the file htdocs/test/test.txt will be accessible with `http://127.0.0.1:8015/test/test.txt`.
`htdocs/cgi-bin`	All CGI scripts go here
`lib`	TclHttpd Tcl source files are stored here

Configuration

When started, the server first reads the configuration. The `config` file—by default, it is `tclhttpd.rc`. This file is looked for in the same directory where `httpd.tcl` resides. As mentioned earlier, you can force `TclHttpd` to use an other file using the `-config` command-line attribute. Of course, it should have the same format, so you will probably make a copy of the default one and enter your modifications, rather than writing from the scratch.

The `tclhttpd.rc` is well commented. Its syntax will appear similar to you—basically, it is a Tcl script that runs the internal `Config` command to set configuration properties. For example, the following line configures the HTTP port value to 8015:

```
Config port 8015
```

Some other important configuration items include:

config file entry	Description
Config gui 1	Enables simple GUI. Change to 0 to disable it.
Config LogFile path	Defines location where to save log files.

Internally, the configuration is stored in the `::Config` array.

The second way of configuration is to use some commands in scripts loaded by the server. For example, you can register another document root directory (`C:\tclhttpd\htdocs2`) to be available at the specified URL prefix (`/backup`):

```
Doc_AddRoot /backup C:\\tclhttpd\\htdocs2
```

Therefore, all the content of that directory is available as a subtree of `http://127.0.0.1:8015/backup/`.

Performance

As for the performance of `TclHttpd`, not too much data is available. According to information from Brent Welch (`http://www.tcl.tk/software/tclhttpd/tclhttpd-tcl2k.pdf`), the author of the server, it runs about 2-3 times slower when compared to other servers like Apache or IIS. This is a good result, when you take into consideration that those servers are not created in scripting languages, and have many performance improvements. Keep in mind that the data was gathered some time ago and is probably not too accurate. Nevertheless, the performance of `TclHttpd` should be enough for most applications.

Programming TclHttpd server

Providing the static content to the client, although crucial, is not the most passionate feature of modern web servers. The entire magic and source of extreme success of WWW in today's world comes from server-side programming and the ability to deliver dynamically generated responses — it may include a web page, image, or any other type of media.

In this section, we are going to present how `TclHttpd`, being the fully-featured web server, is able to fulfill these challenges.

Providing static content

There is not much to write about it. The basic feature of the type of content referred to as **static** is that it does not depend on the request's parameters — the client is always served with exactly the same content they had requested, and usually, it is taken directly from the server's file system. Needless to say, `TclHttpd` is able to do this. For example, the graphical file located at `htdocs/images/lake.gif` will always be served as the answer to a request for `http://127.0.0.1/images/lake.gif`. A feature as important, as boring!

Using CGI in TclHttpd

Note that running external Tcl scripts from a Tcl-based web server is a really bad idea and we present it only to prove that the CGI interface works here. In the next section, you will get to know how to embed your Tcl code in a far more elegant and efficient way.

TclHttpd is able to handle CGI applications correctly. You have to place your application in the `htdocs/cgi-bin` directory to make it work. The way this application is created has no meaning here—it must be executable in the underlying operating system, so it may even be a Tcl script. You can verify it quickly with the example at the beginning of this chapter, `cgi_example.tcl`:

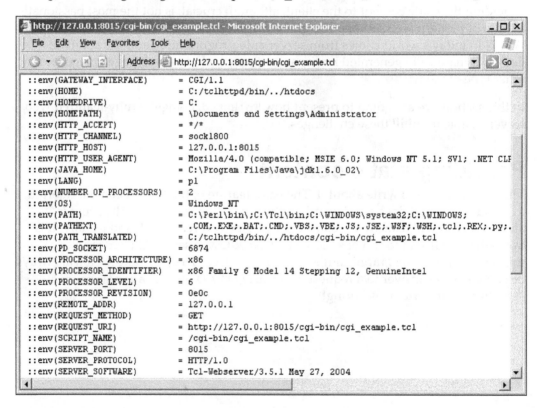

Mapping URL to application

Here is where the interesting part begins. `TclHttpd` offers you the ability to create Application Direct URLs. In other words, you are able to map an URL to a particular Tcl procedure.

Does this sound a bit similar to CGI? It may, but this solution brings you much more flexibility and ease of implementation. Running the code inside the same process has a lot of benefits, for example, caching the data as a Tcl variable for usage on the next invocation. Also, the performance is far better, as the procedure will execute in the already running Tcl interpreter, rather than spawning a new one. When you run an external application using a CGI interface, it works outside the TclHttpd server environment, so you are not able to alter its internal state or perform any other action that is beyond the CGI specification.

The idea is that once the HTTP request for a particular resource occurs, a Tcl procedure of your choice will be called. The arguments of the procedure will be automatically obtained from the query data, along with the following rules:

- The name of the argument must match the name of the request parameter.
- If the corresponding parameter is missing, the argument will be assigned with an empty string or the default value (if defined).
- If the last argument of the procedure is named args, all superfluous query parameters will be assigned to it in the form of a list containing name-value pairs.

After a call, the procedure should return HTML or any other value that should be delivered to the HTTP client. TclHttpd offers a set of commands that may be used, for instance, to set the content type of the output, so no manual coding of HTTP headers is required.

Let's consider this functionality in the following example:

```
Direct_Url /app_example Test

proc Test {{name John} {surname Smith} {sex male} address args } {
    set result "<h1>Welcome !</h1><pre>"
    foreach {key} {name surname sex address args} {
        append result "$key: [set $key]\n";
    }
    foreach key [::ncgi::names] {
        append result "\n(ncgi) $key: [::ncgi::value $key]"
    }
    append result "</pre>"
    return $result
}
proc Test/printenv {} {
    set result "<pre>"
    foreach {key value} [array get ::env] {
        append result "$key -> $value\n";
    }
    append result "</pre>"
    return $result
}
```

To make it do anything, you have to save it in the `custom` subdirectory (in our environment, it is `C:\tclhttpd\custom`) as the Tcl script of any name (for example, `app_example.tcl`) and restart the server.

`Direct_Url` is one of the commands offered by `TclHttpd`. It allows defining that any access to `/app_example` URL (`http://127.0.0.1/app_example`) will result in a call to `Test` procedure. You should be careful in case the URL overlaps with static resources reachable at the same location, and rather avoid such a situation.

The procedure takes a set of arguments. Some of them, `name`, `surname`, and `sex` have default values, and others — `address` — do not. The last argument named `args` will hold all additional parameters from the query. Once called, the procedure will print a welcome message and a list of arguments along with their values:

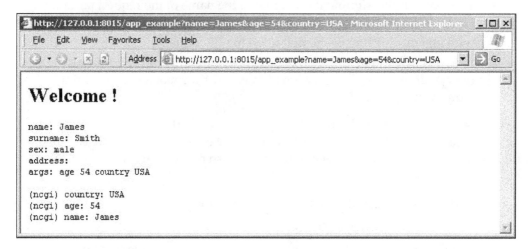

Note that:

- As expected, variables not present in a HTTP query (in this example, we use GET query for better readability) have a default value assigned
- The value from the query for the `name` argument is used instead of default one
- It is perfectly legal to also use the `ncgi` package here

Apart from the `Test` procedure, we have defined a second procedure named `Test/printenv`. Why such a cumbersome name? The specification of `TclHttpd` states that when `Test` handles the `/app_example` domain, the `Test/printenv` will handle `/app_example/printenv`. Of course, you can use any path of your choice (it may contain multiple '/' characters) — there is only one rule, the name must be appropriately reflected in the procedure name that you want should be executed upon accessing the URL.

This second procedure does a similar job to our previous CGI scripts—it prints out the ::env array. The environmental variables are initialized in a manner compliant with the CGI specification, allowing you to retrieve information about both the server and the request that is being processed. Besides CGI-related variables, there are also other, system-specific variables available.

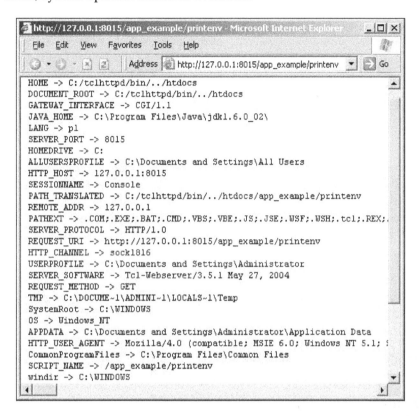

```
HOME -> C:/tclhttpd/bin/../htdocs
DOCUMENT_ROOT -> C:/tclhttpd/bin/../htdocs
GATEWAY_INTERFACE -> CGI/1.1
JAVA_HOME -> C:\Program Files\Java\jdk1.6.0_02\
LANG -> pl
SERVER_PORT -> 8015
HOMEDRIVE -> C:
ALLUSERSPROFILE -> C:\Documents and Settings\All Users
HTTP_HOST -> 127.0.0.1:8015
SESSIONNAME -> Console
PATH_TRANSLATED -> C:/tclhttpd/bin/../htdocs/app_example/printenv
REMOTE_ADDR -> 127.0.0.1
PATHEXT -> .COM;.EXE;.BAT;.CMD;.VBS;.VBE;.JS;.JSE;.WSF;.WSH;.tcl;.REX;.
SERVER_PROTOCOL -> HTTP/1.0
REQUEST_URI -> http://127.0.0.1:8015/app_example/printenv
HTTP_CHANNEL -> sock1816
USERPROFILE -> C:\Documents and Settings\Administrator
SERVER_SOFTWARE -> Tcl-Webserver/3.5.1 May 27, 2004
REQUEST_METHOD -> GET
TMP -> C:\DOCUME~1\ADMINI~1\LOCALS~1\Temp
SystemRoot -> C:\WINDOWS
OS -> Windows_NT
APPDATA -> C:\Documents and Settings\Administrator\Application Data
HTTP_USER_AGENT -> Mozilla/4.0 (compatible; MSIE 6.0; Windows NT 5.1; S
CommonProgramFiles -> C:\Program Files\Common Files
SCRIPT_NAME -> /app_example/printenv
windir -> C:\WINDOWS
```

The procedure assigned to handle a specific URL is not limited to return only HTML string. In fact, you have the full capability to return data of content type of your choice, which we will show in the next example. This time we want to have the code that will return a graphical image file tagged with watermark.

Let's present the source code first:

```
package require Img

Direct_Url /image getImg

proc getImg {name} {
```

```
        set watermark [image create photo -file [file join \
            $::Config(library) "watermark.png"] -data png]
        set image [image create photo -file [file join \
            $::Config(docRoot) $name]]
        set iw [image width $image]
        set ih [image height $image]
        $image copy $watermark -to 0 0 160 30
        $image copy $watermark -to [expr {$iw - 160}] [expr {$ih - 30}] \
            $iw $ih

        global getImg
        set getImg "image/jpeg"
        return [::base64::decode [$image data -format jpeg]]
    }
```

The code makes some use of Img package that was not discussed earlier, but it is enough to know that as a result, the binary data of image with watermark are eventually returned by the getImg procedure. As that package is dependent on Tk, it's usage has some drawbacks — it will not work in text-only environment (in real-life cases, you can consider using dummy X server or TclMagick package that does not require Tk).

We refer to the watermark file by using $::Config(library) (by default, its value is *custom* so the file path would be <TclHttpHomeDir>/custom/watermark.png), and search for target file in the $::Config(docRoot) (typically htdocs) directory.

The picture to be tagged is specified via the name parameter. Note that you have to be extremely cautious when it comes to accepting any type of file path from the request — a malicious user could use it as a security hole.

Before the image data is returned, one more task must be completed. To set the type of content returned by the procedure, all you have to do is set the global variable after the procedure, getImg, to the desired content type MIME value:

```
    global getImg
    set getImg "image/jpeg"
```

In this case, we have decided that regardless of the source image format, we will always generate a JPEG picture.

The overall result is that we have a possibility of returning to web browser, a picture with watermark:

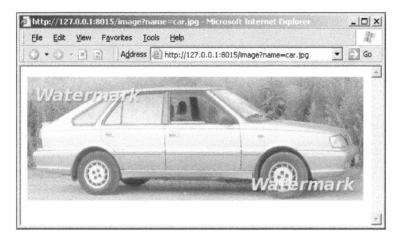

Creating document type handlers

The presented way of tagging files works, but is far from perfect. In particular, the URL is complex, and the user still has the ability to access the untagged file by simply requesting `http://127.0.0.1/car.jpg` file. It will be good to flip over this situation—by default all graphic files should be tagged, but there should be the possibility to return the untagged image (for example, for premium users). We can achieve this by defining the special `handler` procedure for all files of the MIME type *image/jpeg*.

In general, almost any resource served by the web server can be categorized to be one of the media content types, commonly referred to as MIME types. For a full list of defined types you can visit `http://www.iana.org/assignments/media-types/`. The web servers are usually aware of the most common MIME types. For a list of the types known to `TclHttpd`, have a look at the `lib/mime.types` file.

Using the watermark example

A Document type handler is a piece of code that is invoked only when a resource of a given type is being requested. Consider the following code, which will be responsible for applying a watermark to every picture requested from the server:

```
package require Img
proc Doc_image/jpeg {path suffix sock} {
    set watermark [image create photo -file [file join \
        $::Config(library) "watermark.png"]]
    set image [image create photo -file "$path"]
```

```
        set iw [image width $image]
        set ih [image height $image]
        $image copy $watermark -to 0 0 160 30
        $image copy $watermark -to [expr {$iw - 160}] [expr {$ih - 30}] \
            $iw $ih

        set mtype [Mtype $suffix]
        set format [string replace $mtype 0 [string last / $mtype]]
        if {$format eq "gif"} {
            set mtype [Mtype .[set format png]]
        }

         Httpd_ReturnData $sock $mtype [::base64::decode \
            [$image data -format $format]]
    }
}
Mtype_Add .png image/png

#PNG handler
proc Doc_image/png {path suffix socket} {
    Doc_image/jpeg $path $suffix $socket
}

# GIF handler
proc Doc_image/gif {path suffix socket} {
    Doc_image/jpeg $path $suffix $socket
}

Direct_Url /untaggedimage getUntaggedImg
proc getUntaggedImg {name} {
    global getUntaggedImg
    set getUntaggedImg [Mtype $name]
    set f [open "htdocs/$name"]
    fconfigure $f -translation binary
    return [read $f]
}
```

Just save it as customs/doctype_examle.tcl and restart TclHttpd to make it work.

To define a document handler for a *MIMEType* of your choice, all you have to do is define the Doc_*MIMEType* procedure—for example, Doc_image/jpeg will handle all requests for files of type image/jpeg. Once a resource of that type is requested, the server finds the matching procedure and executes it with three arguments: the full path to the requested resource (path), the name of the resource (suffix), and the network socket that can be used to return the answer (`socket`). Luckily, there is no need to use the socket directly—once your code has calculated the return data, you may use a function offered by `TclHttpd`:

`Httpd_ReturnData` *socket type data*

that as a response will send the *data* of a given *type* using the *socket*. There are more useful functions offered by the server, so we recommend studying the manual—for example, it is possible to return the HTTP error code or redirect.

The procedure `Doc_image/jpeg` is designed to be flexible—in particular it does not make any assumptions about the type of file, but checks it using another useful `TclHttpd` function—`Mtype filename`. This command attempts to return the correct MIME type by matching the filename extension to the ones defined in `lib/mime.types` (or added with command `Mtype_Add`); if the specified extension is not known, it returns *text / plain* as the default value. Due to the constraints of GIF support, in case of this format we convert and send back a JPEG instead.

The flexibility of `Doc_image/jpeg` allows us to use it for other types like image/gif or image/png, by creating some simple wrapper procedures `Doc_image/gif` and `Doc_image/png` which calls that procedure. `TclHttpd` is not familiar with the type image/png, so we have to define it first. In this example, we use the `Mtype_add extension MIMEType` procedure that defines that all files with the specified `extension` are of `MIMEType` type. Alternatively you could simply add the appropriate entry to the `lib/mime.types` file.

Let's verify if the code is working with, for example, GIF files by using the *lake.gif* that is already included in the `TclHttpd` distribution:

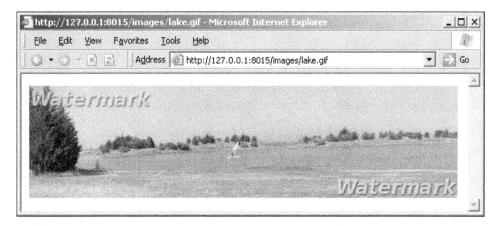

As mentioned earlier, we decided to have a backdoor that will allow us to retrieve the original image, without the watermark. It is done by the procedure getUntaggedImg bound to /untaggedimage URL:

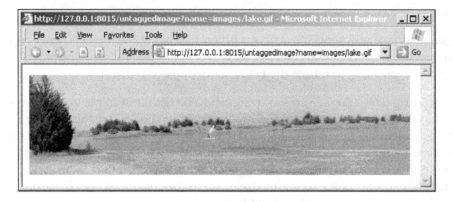

Creating custom templates

Another example of using handlers for specific MIME types is to handle dynamically created pages, similar to template files with the .tml extension (described later in this chapter).

As an example we can use the substify package to parse files. This package allows for parsing text which contains code in specified delimiters and converts it, so that it can then be directly passed to the Tcl subst command. This way the file can be parsed once and evaluated multiple times, by passing the result from invoking substify::substify to the subst command. The command substify::substify accepts three parameters — the text to convert, the delimiter that specifies the beginning of code, and the end of your code. The package is an open source project and source code is available at: http://sourceforge.net/projects/dqsoftware/files/substify/0.1/

The package allows us to specify commands to be run without appending their results by enclosing them in delimiters — for example, <% set now [clock seconds] %>.

Prefixing the command with an = causes the result of the command to be appended in the current location — for example, <%=[clock seconds]%> will be replaced by number of seconds since January 1st 1970. We can also put variables to get their value — such as <%=$now%>, which will be replaced with contents of now variable at this time.

This is a convenient alternative to .tml files, which require all [and $ characters to be escaped. It is also useful for placing Tcl code in existing HTML pages, where escaping all characters that Tcl would interpret might be an issue.

For example, in order to convert a sample code using `<%` and `%>` as delimiters we can do:

```
% set code [substify::substify {
   <% set now [clock seconds] %>
   Now = <%=[clock format $now -format "%H:%M:%S"]%>
} "<%" "%>"]
```

We tell the command that `<%` is the delimiter for starting the code section and `%>` ends a code section. We can then get the resulting string multiple times by doing:

```
% subst $code
```

This will return a string similar to *Now = 20:31:20.*

We can now proceed with writing a MIME type handler for this file. Let's start by loading `substify` package so we can call the `substify::substify` command:

package require substify

We can also add the association that `.thtml` files should be associated with `application/x-html-tcl-template` mime type.

```
Mtype_Add .thtml application/x-html-tcl-template
```

The mime type chosen was based on the name that `Tclhttpd` uses for `.tml` files — `application/x-tcl-template`.

The following information can also be added to the `mime.types` file instead of invoking a command, to add a MIME type manually. In such a case, we would need to add the following line to `mime.types`:

```
application/x-html-tcl-template thtml
```

We can now write the `Doc_application/x-html-tcl-template` command for handling `.thtml` files.

The command will treat all files as being UTF-8 encoded to ease support for international websites, so we'll read all templates using this encoding. Internally `Tclhttpd` treats all files and data as binary by default, therefore, we'll convert all output passed to the web browsers to `utf-8` as last step of handling the request.

1. We'll start by mapping a global array called `templateCache`, which is used for storing parsed representation of files. The array will keep mapping between file names (as specified in `path` argument), and will keep the file's last modification time, size, and the parsed content of the file. We'll use the last modification time and size to check whether file needs to be re-read. The value for each file will be a list of three elements — the first one being the file modification time, the second being the size of the file, and the third being parsed content of the file in UTF-8.

```
proc Doc_application/x-html-tcl-template {path suffix sock} {
    global templateCache
```

2. We'll now set the MIME type of returned content. It defaults to text / html with the implicit specification that the character set for this page is UTF-8. This value is interpreted by the web browser. While the character set can also be specified in the body of the HTML page, it is better to provide this at the HTTP level so that all browsers can use this value immediately.

    ```
    set ctype "text/html; charset=UTF-8"
    ```

3. Next we try to get information on the file specified by the `path` argument. If the `file stat` command fails, we return `error 404`, which means that a file was not found and return from the procedure.

    ```
    if {[catch {file stat $path stat}]} {
        Httpd_Error $sock 404
        return
    }
    ```

4. The next step is to check whether we already have read the file and if the parsed version of the file is up to date:

    ```
    if {![info exists templateCache($path)] ||
        ([lindex $templateCache($path) 0] != $stat(mtime)) ||
        ([lindex $templateCache($path) 1] != $stat(size))} {
    ```

    The condition checks if the `templateCache` array does not contain information for the specified file, if the file modification time does not match or if the file size is different. If any of these conditions fail, we read or re-read the file from disk and parse it.

    We try to open the file for reading. If this step fails, we return `error 404` to the client and return from the procedure.

    ```
    if {[catch {set fh [open $path r]}]} {
        Httpd_Error $sock 404
        return
    }
    ```

    If opening the file succeeded, we then configure the encoding to `utf-8` and read the file.

    ```
    fconfigure $fh -encoding utf-8 -translation auto
    set content [read $fh]
    close $fh
    ```

    Next we convert contents of the file using the `substify::substify` command, specifying `<%` and `%>` as the delimiters.

We then store the file modification time, the size, and the parsed contents of the file in the `templateCache` array:

```
set content [substify::substify $content "<%" "%>"]
set templateCache($path) \
    [list $stat(mtime) $stat(size) $content]
}
```

Finally, we end the condition that was met only if `templateArray` did not contain any information about the file or if it was out of date.

5. We can now pass the cached representation of the file to the `subst` command, convert the results to `utf-8` and send them back to the client:

```
set html [subst [lindex $templateCache($path) 2]]
set html [encoding convertto utf-8 $html]

Httpd_ReturnData $sock $ctype $html
}
```

To verify if it runs correctly, you have to put our handler along with the `substify` package in the `custom` directory to make it available for `TclHttpd` server, and create the sample `htdocs/index.thtml`:

```
<html>
    <body>
        <h2>Hello world - it is now <%=[clock format [clock seconds]
-format "%H:%M:%S"]%></h2>
    </body>
</html>
```

The result of accessing this file via the web browser will be as follows:

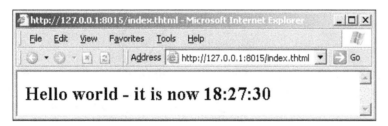

Learning domain handlers

Another interesting feature of TclHttpd is a possibility to use command Url_ PrefixInstall for sub-domain handling. This command can be used to register a handler for all requests with a specified prefix. For example, if we register a command to be run for prefix /myprefix, requests for /myprefix, /myprefix/info, as well as /myprefix/long/suffix/with/multiple/elements will be handled by that command. We will show the power and flexibility offered by this command in a few examples.

Setting up request handlers

The command Url_PrefixInstall requires specifying two arguments – the prefix to register and the command to be run upon each request for the URL starting with this prefix. The command also accepts three options, which can be appended after the two mandatory parameters.

The option -thread specifies whether a request should be handled in a separate thread and whether or not it accepts a boolean value. This option applies only to multi-threaded the Tclhttpd. If the server is configured not to use threads or the version of Tcl it is using does not offer threading support, the request will always be served in the main thread. If it is not specified, this option defaults to 0 which means that the request will be handled in the main thread. The main use for this is when the request needs to perform a long running action – such as performing calculations or querying a database.

The option -callback can be used to specify the command to be run upon each request completion. The command will be invoked with two attributes appended – the socket identifier and error message, in the case of an error or an empty string in the case of success. If not specified, no command will be run upon each completion of a request.

The option -readpost can be used to tell Tclhttpd whether it should read POST data, and is enabled by default. Usually this option should not be used – in this case the server reads the POST data then the data sent by the browser or application can be instantly read. This option is mainly meant for advanced users who might want to send files directly over HTTP(S) requests. In this case, we can disable reading information sent by the HTTP(S) client and read the data directly from the file.

As an example of using Url_PrefixInstall, we'll create a sample handler that will print out information about the request. Tclhttpd keeps track of information related to each connection in global arrays. The name of each array is in the form of Httpd<socket> – for example, if the connection identifier is sock3, then the variable would be called Httpdsock3. It contains information about the request – the HTTP headers, request content type, HTTP version, remote IP address, and much more.

The following are a few of keys in the array along with the information they store:

Key	Information
headerlist	A list of name-value pairs that specify all HTTP headers received by this request
ipaddr	The IP address of remote peer for this connection; for example, `127.0.0.1`
pathlist	A list of elements in the suffix part of the request; for example, `{}` `long suffix with multiple elements`
prefix	The prefix of the connection – same as registered in Url_PrefixInstall
proto	The HTTP method used – it can be either `HEAD`, `GET`, or `POST`
query	The query passed in either GET or POST response as raw data; for example, `q=some+query&lang=en`
self	A list consisting of three elements – the protocol (http or https), name of the host specified and listening port of the server – for example, `http localhost 8015`
suffix	The suffix of the request; for example, `/long/suffix/with/multiple/elements`
url	The full path in the request; for example, `/myprefix/long/suffix/with/multiple/elements`
version	The HTTP version – this should be either `1.0` or `1.1`

The array also contains all HTTP headers in the form of `mime,<header>` where `<header>` is the HTTP header in lowercase. For example, in order to get the User-Agent HTTP header, which identifies the browser that invoked the request, we can read it using the `mime,user-agent` key.

In order to create our sample handler, we'll need to register a handler for the specific prefix first. In our example, the prefix will be `/helloworld/prefix/httpstate`:

```
Url_PrefixInstall /helloworld/prefix/httpstate \
    urlHandleHttpstate
```

Whenever a new request is received the command is run with two parameters appended — the socket that corresponds to the request and the suffix. Our command has to accept these parameters:

```
proc urlHandleHttpstate {sock suffix} {
```

1. The first thing we'll do is map the `Tclhttpd` state array as local variable. We're using the `upvar #0` command. It will map a variable with name the `Httpd$sock`, where `$sock` will be expanded to the actual socket passed as an argument and map the array as the local `data` array. This will allow us to access any HTTP state array data as `$data(<keyname)` — such as `$data(headerlist)` for list of all headers.

   ```
   upvar #0 Httpd$sock data
   ```

2. Our handler will create output in HTML, so we need to start creating the actual HTML. We start by adding the `<html>` and `<body>` tags:

   ```
   set html "<html>\n"
   append html "<body>\n"
   ```

   First we'll print out the `data` array. We'll create a HTML table for the array prefixed with title of the table using the `<h1>` tag. The table will have 2 columns — parameter name and value:

   ```
   append html "<h1>HTTP state array</h1>\n"
   append html "<table border=\"1\">\n"
   append html "<tr>\n"
   append html "<th>Parameter</th>\n"
   append html "<th>Value</th>\n"
   append html "</tr>\n"
   ```

   Next we'll iterate over all elements in the array and print them. We invoke `array names` to get list of all keys in the array and then sort them for easier reading:

   ```
   foreach name [lsort [array names data]] {
   ```

   Next we print each item to a separate row in the HTML table:

   ```
   append html "<tr>\n"
   append html "<td>$name</td>\n"
   append html "<td>$data($name)</td>\n"
   append html "</tr>\n"
   }
   ```

   Finally we need to close the HTML table.

   ```
   append html "</table>\n"
   ```

3. Similarly we can print all HTTP headers as list by accessing `$data(headerlist)` to get the name-value pairs and iterate over them:

```
append html "<h1>HTTP headers</h1>\n"
append html "<table border=\"1\">\n"
append html "<tr>\n"
append html "<th>Name</th>\n"
append html "<th>Value</th>\n"
append html "</tr>\n"

foreach {name value} $data(headerlist) {
    append html "<tr>\n"
    append html "<td>$name</td>\n"
    append html "<td>$value</td>\n"
    append html "</tr>\n"
}
```

Finally we can close the table and finalize our HTML.

```
append html "</table>\n"
append html "</body>\n"
append html "</html>\n"
```

4. The last thing we need to do is to send the response to the client:

```
    Httpd_ReturnData $sock "text/html" $html
}
```

Once you put the code in `custom` directory, the result of accessing the `http://127.0.0.1:8015/helloworld/prefix/httpstate` URL may be as follows:

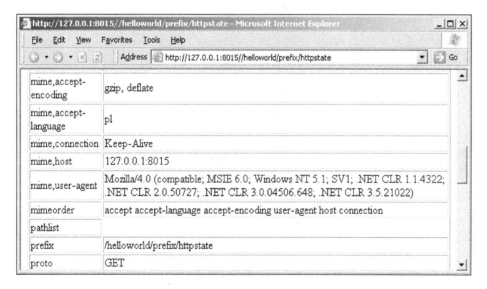

We can also access query information to get parameters using query key in the http state array. We'll use `Url_DecodeQuery` command, which takes the query as argument.

Similar to `substify` based templating, we'll also convert information from and to UTF-8. This allows the handling of non-latin characters and is good practice for all `Tclhttpd` based applications.

1. Let's start by registering a new prefix for query printing:

```
Url_PrefixInstall /helloworld/prefix/printquery \
    urlHandlePrintquery
```

2. Next, we'll create the procedure that handles the request. The first thing it does is map the state array as data local variable and decoding query:

```
proc urlHandlePrintquery {sock suffix} {
    # map HTTP state array as local array data
    upvar #0 Httpd$sock data
    set querydata [encoding convertfrom utf-8 \
        [Url_DecodeQuery $data(query)]]
```

3. We can then generate our HTML, similar to how we did in the previous example:

```
set html "<html>\n"
append html "<body>\n"
```

4. For testing of submitting values, we'll also create a small HTML form. It contains two fields — `value1` and `value2`. It will also contain a submit button to allow the form data to be sent:

```
append html "<form method=\"GET\">\n"
append html "Value1=<input name=\"value1\"><br />\n"
append html "Value2=<input name=\"value2\"><br />\n"
append html "<input name=\"go\" type=\"submit\""
append html "  value=\"Submit\"><br />\n"
append html "</form>\n"
```

5. Next, we'll create a HTML table that prints out the results:

```
append html "<table border=\"1\">\n"
append html "<tr>\n"
append html "<th>Parameter</th>\n"
append html "<th>Value</th>\n"
append html "<th>Value in uppercase</th>\n"
append html "</tr>\n"
```

6. Next, we'll iterate over the query information and print it. For this example, we'll also print the value of each parameter in upper case. This will show that UTF-8 is handled properly, and non-latin characters are also correctly converted to their upper case equivalents.

```
foreach {name value} $querydata {
    append html "<tr>\n"
    append html "<td>$name</td>\n"
    append html "<td>$value</td>\n"
    append html "<td>[string toupper $value]</td>\n"
    append html "</tr>\n"
}
```

7. Finally, we can finalize our HTML by closing all open tags:

```
append html "</table>\n"
append html "</body>\n"
append html "</html>\n"
```

8. One final step is to convert the HTML to UTF-8 encoding and return it to the client:

```
set html [encoding convertto utf-8 $html]
Httpd_ReturnData $sock "text/html; charset=UTF-8" $html
}
```

We're also specifying `charset` as the MIME type in the HTTP response.

Once you run this example and enter some test values, you will get a result similar to the following:

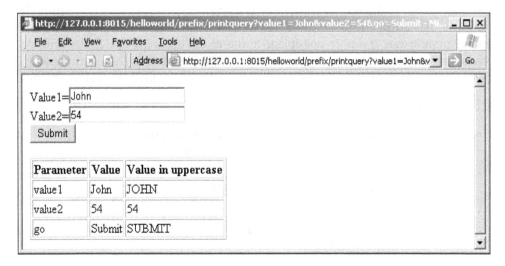

Comparing domain handlers to application direct URLs

While working through the past few sections, you have probably started to analyse what are the real differences between the domain handlers and Application direct URLs described earlier. The following table describes some of those differences:

	Domain handler	Application direct URL
Command	`Url_PrefixInstall`	`Direct_Url`
Access to query parameters	using `ncgi` package or `Url_DecodeQuery`	parameters are matched to corresponding arguments of the procedure; also using `ncgi` package
Access to other data	has access to various HTTP Request related parameters via state array `Httpd$sock`	CGI defined parameters via `env` array
Response	procedure must call one of relevant commands (like `Httpd_ReturnData`)	procedure returns a string with HTTP response
Scope	handles entire domain and subdomains	handles only specific URL (the one bind to the procedure)
features	powerful	easy to use, similar in usage to CGI

Creating session-based authentication

A more advanced and interesting example is using `Url_PrefixInstall`, to provide a more complex authentication system for websites. HTTP provides an authentication mechanism; however it is only possible to authenticate users using HTTP's built-in mechanism—same as when using `.tclaccess` (described later). Our example will show how we can implement authentication, using cookies and session identifiers.

The code will work in the following way:

- If the user has already authenticated and has a valid cookie, we'll pass the request to a handler for getting files from document root.

- If the user has not authenticated yet or the cookie passed by the user is not valid, we provide the user with a page for logging in to the system.

- If the user has not authenticated yet, but is sending authentication information, it is processed—if the user is successfully authenticated, he / she can access all files.

We'll start by creating a namespace for this example, and loading the package uuid for generating unique session identifiers. We'll use a separate namespace as this example involves multiple procedures, and in such cases it is usually a good idea to put them in to a separate namespace.

The package uuid is used to generate universally unique identifiers for session identifiers. It generates identifiers conformant to the UUID version 4 standard, which is described in more detail at http://en.wikipedia.org/wiki/Universally_Unique_Identifier.

```
namespace eval customauth {}
package require uuid
```

The next step is to install a handler for our prefix. We set up our command to handle all requests coming to the /secure prefix.

We tell Tclhttpd to run the command customauth::handle and specify that the first argument should be secure, which tells it that all files should be prefixed with secure.

```
Url_PrefixInstall /secure \
    [list customauth::handle secure]
```

Specifying a prefix for the customauth::handle command allows requests pointing to one prefix to serve files that are in a different path — for example, requests for /secure can actually read files in the directory other/directory. For example, in such case the command would be:

```
Url_PrefixInstall /secure \
    [list customauth::handle other/directory]
```

We then create the procedure to handle requests for content. It takes the specified prefix as the first argument, followed by socket and suffix, which are appended by Tclhttpd.

```
proc customauth::handle {prefix sock suffix} {
```

First we specify that we want to use the global variable Config, which is needed later on for getting the docRoot parameter from the configuration, which is needed to find the actual file in the file system.

We also map a namespace specific variable called userid, which will be used to specify the user identifier in the context of the current request. This variable can then be referenced — for example, when using substify file handled, it can be put in HTML as <%=$customauth::userid%>.

```
    global Config
    variable userid
```

Then we map the HTTP state array as local array data, and use the `string trimleft` command to remove the leading slash from the `suffix` variable.

```
upvar #0 Httpd$sock data
set suffix [string trimleft $suffix /]
```

We then invoke the `getUserId` command that takes the socket, and works with cookies and / , or query data to determine the current user logged in. This command is described later in the example.

```
set userid [getUserId $sock]
```

If the user is not set, we enforce the return page to contain the contents of `login.thtml`, regardless of the actual request. Otherwise we allow any file to be processed.

```
if {$userid == ""} {
    set url $prefix/login.thtml
} else {
    set url $prefix/$suffix
}
```

The next step is to take the new URL and invoke the `DocDomain` command. This command is the handler for returning files based on the URL and document root.

The first step is to set the `pathlist` key in the HTTP state array to a list of elements in the new path. This is used by `DocDomain` to determine the file to load and needs to be overwritten with a path, which we redirect this request to.

The command `DocDomain` needs to be invoked with four arguments—the first one being the prefix for the request—we specify "/" because this is the way Tclhttpd invokes `DocDomain` in regular cases. The next argument is the path to the directory containing files—we take `Config(docRoot)`, which also points to the root directory for documents. The next parameters specify the socket the connection is using and the suffix for the connection. The last parameter is created to use the prefix passed to the command as well as the suffix for the request.

```
    set data(pathlist) [file split $url]
    DocDomain / $Config(docRoot) $sock $url
}
```

This causes the request to be handled as if our prefix was not installed, and the default handler for the files would receive the request.

The next step is to create the `customauth::getUserId` command that handles getting the current *userid* based on cookies, as well as using the query data to authenticate the user based on their username and password.

Cookies are compared against the `usersession` array that keeps track of all valid sessions. Each session is a different key in the array and the value is the user identifier. If the cookie `sessionid` exists then its value is read. If `usersession($sessionid)` exists, it is read and assumed to be the `userid`. Otherwise the session is assumed to be invalid.

If the user is not authorized, query data is checked for existence of both `username` and `password` fields. If both exist, it tries to authenticate the user. If it is a valid user and password, a new session identifier is created and stored in the `sessionid` cookie. The variable `usersession($sessionid)` is also set to identifier of the user. This way any subsequent requests with this cookie set would also be allowed to access all data.

We start by making the namespace-specific array `usersession` available, and mapping the HTTP state array as local array `data`. We also set the `userid` to be empty, which indicates a user that is not authenticated.

```
proc customauth::getUserId {sock} {
    variable usersession
    upvar #0 Httpd$sock data

    set userid ""
```

Next, we try to read the `sessionid` cookie. If it exists, we get the actual value as the first element of the list — this is needed since the `Cookie_Get` command returns a list of all values for that cookie.

```
    set sessionid [Cookie_Get "sessionid"]

    if {[llength $sessionid] > 0} {
        set sessionid [lindex $sessionid 0]
```

If a corresponding entry in the `usersession` array exists, we assume that this is a valid session, and take the value of the `usersession` array for this session to be the user identifier for this session.

```
        if {[info exists usersession($sessionid)]} {
            set userid $usersession($sessionid)
        }
    }
```

We then check if the user was not authenticated so far — either because of a lack of a *sessionid* cookie or the cookie value being invalid

```
    if {$userid == ""} {
```

If this is the case, we then try to authenticate the user based on the `username` and `password`.

We do this by first decoding the query and checking if both the `username` and `password` elements exist in the query:

```
array set query [Url_DecodeQuery $data(query)]
# check if both paremeters are set
if {[info exists query(username)] &&
    [info exists query(password)]} {
```

If the elements exist, we invoke another command that authenticates the user based on their `username` and `password`, and check if the returned value specifies the user identifier:

```
set userid [authenticateUser $query(username) \
    $query(password)]

if {$userid != ""} {
```

If the user identifier is not empty, it means that the user has been successfully authenticated. We will need to generate a new session identifier and store which user this session maps to:

```
set sessionid [uuid::uuid generate]
set usersession($sessionid) $userid
```

We'll then store this in a cookie as well. We then save all cookies in the HTTP headers to make sure they get sent to the client when a response is sent.

```
Cookie_Set \
    -name "sessionid" -value $sessionid
Cookie_Save $sock
```

Finally we close the braces for all of the conditions above, and return the final user identifier to `customauth::handle` command:

```
        }
    }
}

return $userid
}
```

A sample command for authenticating users can be as follows:

```
proc customauth::authenticateUser {username password} {
    if {$password == $username} {
        return $username
```

```
    }  else  {
        return ""
    }
}
```

This command will allow everyone whose username and password is set to the same value—for example, the user john with the password john. Of course, a real-life implementation would involve much more sophisticated authentication against the user's database, or LDAP—such as using the authenticateLDAP command from *LDAP* section of Chapter 8.

If you attempt to access for the first time any resource from the /secure domain (we choose the convention that physically the resource should be available in htdocs/secure directory), you will be prompted for the authentication:

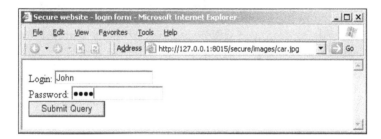

Once authenticated correctly, you will get a resource:

 Note that in this example, you can see how different features of TclHttpd works together—we requested the graphical file, which was also processed by our watermark code described earlier.

Using the TclHttpd template system

Another interesting feature offered by `TclHttpd` is the template system. Template files are all files stored in the `htdocs` directory with `.tml` as extension — for example, `test.tml` is treated by the server as template.

Imagine you have a normal HTML file named `test.htm` somewhere in your `htdocs` tree. When you request this file via the web browser, its contents will be returned — exactly as you would expect. The magic starts when you put an additional template file, named `test.tml`, in the same directory as `test.htm` resides.

The template may contain both normal HTML code, Tcl commands enclosed in square brackets, and Tcl variables with a *$* sign — the content of the template is used as the argument for Tcl `subst` command. When the client requests `test.htm`, the date of both files is checked. If `test.tml`'s last modification date is later, the HTML generated by that template is cached in the `test.htm` file returned. Otherwise, the content of `test.htm` is considered as up to date, and will be returned directly without processing of the template. Consider the following example content of `test.tml`:

```
<html>
    <body>
        <h3>The time is [clock format [clock seconds] -format
"%H:%M:%S"]</h3>
    </body>
</html>
```

When you request `test.htm` for the first time (even when it does not exist!), the corresponding `tml` file will be executed, its result written to `test.htm`, and returned, so the page will show you the current time:

```
<html>
    <body>
        <h3>The time is 18:58:12</h3>
    </body>
</html>
```

However, the consecutive requests will always return the same time value, as it was buffered in `test.htm`. You can skip this behavior in two ways:

- Request the `test.tml` file directly in the browser (for example, `http://127.0.0.1:8015/test.tml`), instead of `test.htm`. This will cause the template to be executed each time.

- Use the `Doc_Dynamic` command in your template. It will disable caching the content in `test.htm` file, and the template will be always executed. In this case the html file may not exist, and still both requests: `http://127.0.0.1:8015/test.htm` and `http://127.0.0.1:8015/test.tml` will be valid and return the output from the template.

Considering the second case, the template would be like:

```
[Doc_Dynamic]
<html>
    <body>
        <h3>The time is [clock format [clock seconds] -format
"%H:%M:%S"]</h3>
    </body>
</html>
```

Each subdirectory of your document root (`htdocs`) may contain a special 'per-directory' file named `.tml`. The content of this file should be normal Tcl code. Until now we stored all our code in `custom` directory. As an alternative, you may put it into `.tml` file. You may define here procedures that will be called in subsequent templates. You may also place here any other command, just as you do in *custom* scripts. The difference is that the code from the custom directory is executed once when the server is started, and the code from `.tml` is executed *every time*, but *only* when any template from that directory (containing `.tml`) is executed. Note that if you request static content such as an image or a HTML page that does not have a shadowing template, the `.tml` will not be executed.

Using `.tml` files may be useful at the time of development, later you will probably move more of its contents to a custom library (to improve performance). Normally you will store here definitions of your procedures, which you will later call in your template files. Of course you can use all other available commands as well — for example, from the `html` package which greatly facilitates the template's design.

Note that any procedure called in the template file should *return* the text, *not write* it to standard output. For example, the following template will not work as one might expect:

```
<h1>[puts "Welcome!"]</h1>
```

The resulting HTML will contain only `<h1></h1>`, and the welcome message will be written to the standard output.

As mentioned earlier, you may also refer to any existing Tcl variable:

```
<h2>The current document root directory is: $::Config(docRoot)</h2>
```

The preceding code will result in:

```
<h2>The current document root directory is: C:/tclhttpd/bin/../
htdocs</h2>
```

There is also a special variable—page array available for you to be used in your templates. The array contains some information about the query. The following template uses the command from the html package—html::tableFromArray—to display contents of that array:

```
<h2>The contents and values of <i>::page</i> array:</h2>
[::html::tableFromArray ::page border="1"]
```

The result is as follows:

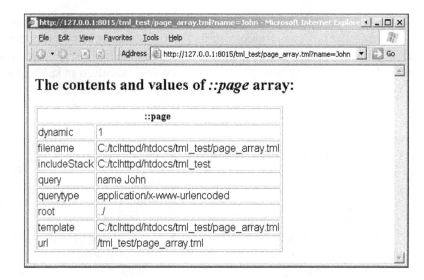

Most of keys of the array are self explanatory, for more details consult the server's manual.

The template system may be either your ally or your enemy. Mixing too much Tcl code with HTML will usually cause headaches, but when used wisely, the development of dynamic web pages will be quick and smooth.

Securing access to resources

TclHttpd offers two ways of securing resources—via .htaccess and .tclaccess files. The first one originates from Apache web server and TclHttpd supports a subset of the syntax related to authentication. For example, the following contents of the file will work:

```
AuthName "My Website"
AuthType Basic
AuthUserFile /path/to/htpasswd.users
require valid-user
```

This will cause all users specified in /path/to/htpasswd.users to be allowed access. Information on the syntax of the file and the creation of user files is outside the scope of this book.

We will focus on the .tclaccess method as it provides a more powerful authentication mechanism, and is better tied to TclHttpd.

The content of such a file is trivial:

```
set realm ".tclaccess test"
set callback checkAccess
```

It defines a realm name (that is displayed along with authorization request in the browser), and a Tcl procedure that will perform the check of privileges. In our example, this procedure is named checkAccess and you should define it in one of the files from the *custom* directory:

```
proc checkAccess {sock realm user pass} {
    if {[string compare $user John] == 0 &&
        [string compare $pass secret] == 0} {
        return 1
    }
    return 0
}
```

The interface of the procedure is simple:

- It is called with 4 parameters: The socket, realm name (the same that was defined in .tclaccess), user name, and password entered by the user.
- It has to return 1 if the user is allowed to access the protected content, or 0 otherwise.

Our procedure is not sophisticated — it accepts only the user *John* with password *secret*. In a real-world scenario, you could perform validation using for example, a database where all users of your application are registered.

The last thing to do is put .tclaccess in a secured directory — for example, htdocs/tclaccesstest and verify if it works:

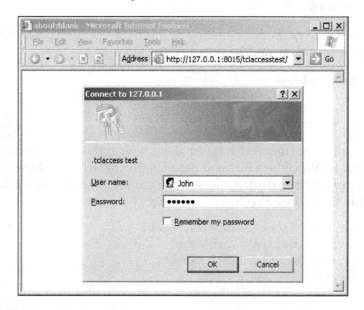

Debugging TclHttpd server

The server offers some debug facilities, available centrally under the /debug domain. In order to use them, you have to enter the password that is randomly generated at the start and printed in the console. For more details, go to http://127.0.0.1:8015/hacks.htm .It contains explanations how to use it. The most interesting feature is the ability to setup a remote debug session with TclPro debugger, by accessing the special URL:

```
http://tclhttpdHost:tclhttpdPort/debug/dbg?host=debuggerHost&port=deb
uggerPort
```

tclhttpdHost and tclhttpdPort define the socket where the web server is listening, and debuggerHost/debuggerPort — the listening socket of the debugger.

Assuming both the server and the debugger are launched on your *local* machine and will use the default port value (2576) for debugging, the URL would be:

```
http://127.0.0.1:8015/debug/dbg?host=127.0.0.1
```

Once you access it (and authorize with password, if you did not do this earlier), the debugging connection will be set up:

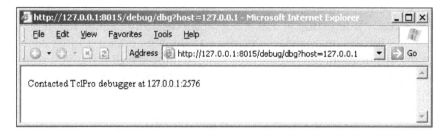

Next, accessing any resource hosted by `TclHttpd` will cause the start of debugging:

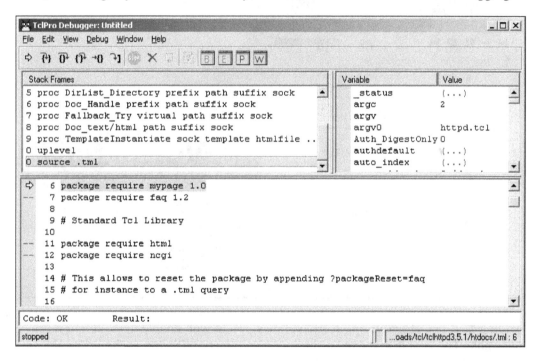

Embedding TclHttpd in your application

In this section, we will discuss how to enrich your new / existing application with a Web interface with the minimum effort. No surprise, we will use `TclHttpd` to do this task. What is really interesting is that it can be successfully packed into a Starpack one-binary `exe` file. If you wonder why you should even bother adding such a feature to the application, maybe the Snackamp example will bring you round to this idea — this mp3 player (written in Tcl, of course) is capable of being managed via the web browser:

Adding `TclHttpd` to your application allows you to web-enable it, making it more accessible. The goal is that even a single-`exe` application (*Starpack*) should be able to transparently expose the web interface to the user. The process may seem to be complicated at first glance, as the server's author does not refer to such a possibility directly. If you study the `httpd.tcl` file in detail, you will notice that it does some initialization tasks and start the server. Running the server embedded in our application will differ from standalone execution, so we have to rewrite the logic of `httpd.tcl` on our own.

To facilitate this task, we usually use our own package named `tclhttpdinit` that consists of a single script which does all the work related to `Tclhttpd` initialization, originally done by `httpd.tcl`.

The script has been created by extracting the `Tclhttpd` initialization scripts and embedding a minimal configuration. It initializes a minimal subset of `Tclhttpd` functionality in order to handle requests for files, as well as allow writing of handlers for URLs that our application supports. Note that this script does not aspire to be the most elegant and universal piece of code—on the contrary, you should consider it rather as an encouragement to develop it on your own.

In order to make it work, you have to copy all the content of the `tclhttpd/lib` directory as the separate package (there is already `pkgIndex.tcl` file existing)—we usually copy it to `tclhttpd.3.5.1`. You have to take care about TclLib, as it is required by TclHttpd. This eventually leads to the situation where the directory with packages (by convention named *lib*) has the following subdirectories:

Directory	Description
`tclhttpd.3.5.1`	Contains all the files from `tclhttpd/lib` directory. Provides all `httpd::*` packages
`tcllib`	Entire tcllib library
`tclhttpdinit`	Our initialization package
`WWW`	This is our `docroot` (hardcoded in `tclhttpdinit`). You can of course choose other name and location for this folder—it requires you to modify the `init` script.

All of these can be found in the examples that come with this book.

The script runs all commands in the global stack frame using the `uplevel #0` command. We start by loading `ncgi` and `md5` packages which are needed by `Tclhttpd`:

```
uplevel #0 {
    package require md5
    package require ncgi
```

Next we load the `Tclhttpd` packages—all of these packages start with `httpd`. The names of packages and their order have been taken from original `Tclhttpd` scripts:

```
package require httpd 1.6
package require httpd::version
package require httpd::utils
package require httpd::url
package require httpd::counter
package require httpd::doc
package require httpd::cgi
package require httpd::direct
package require httpd::redirect
package require httpd::mtype
```

Note that TclHttpd does not define the httpd:: namespace, even though package naming convention suggests it.

We then need to disable authentication at the HTTP level and load the package responsible for authentication:

```
set ::Config(Auth) {}
package require httpd::auth
```

Setting the ::Config(Auth) entry to be an empty variable prevents the httpd::auth code from generating a temporary password, and writing it to /tmp – our goal is that the embedded server should not write anything to disk without our permission.

Enabling authentication for particular folders can be done using .tclaccess scripts, or by manually authenticating connections in handler commands.

Next we need to read the mime.types file to provide Tclhttpd with mapping of file extensions to mime types (normally it is done in httpdthread.tcl that is loaded in httpd.tcl). We read the file from the same directory that our script is in:

```
Mtype_ReadTypes \
        [file join [file dirname [info script]] mime.types]
```

Note that it requires us to duplicate the mime.types (the original one is in tclhttpd3.5.1).

In order to prevent some Tclhttpd functionalities from throwing errors we create commands to tell Tclhttpd that threads have been disabled:

```
if {[info commands ::Thread_Enabled] == ""} {
    proc ::Thread_Enabled {} {return 0}
}
```

We also need to emulate a command to tell Tclhttpd which requests to handle in separate threads. It always returns 0, which tells Tclhttpd that all requests should be handled in the same thread as the current one:

```
if {[info commands ::Thread_Respond] == ""} {
    proc ::Thread_Respond {args} {return 0}
}
```

If our application needs to use threads at the Tclhttpd level, we can load the httpd::thread package and invoke the Thread_Init command, specifying the number of threads to use.

We do ignore the original logging command, as we do not want it to write anything to the filesystem, so we need to create our own implementation for logging `Tclhttpd` related events. In order to disable logging, we can create an empty one as follows:

```
proc ::Log {sock reason args} {
    switch -- $reason {
        Close {
        }
        Error {
        }
        Debug {
        }
        default {
        }
    }
}
```

In order to log `Tclhttpd` events, we can add handlers to particular types of logs — for example, for `Error` messages.

We can now initialize `Tclhttpd` components — we initialize the server itself and tell him that index files for a directory will be called `index.html`.

```
Httpd_Init
DirList_IndexFile "index.html"
```

We can change the default index file if our application will use a different file, or when creating custom handlers for specific types of files. `Tclhttpd` will take all dynamic handlers for file types into account when reading index files, similar to when reading any other file.

We also need to initialize counters:

```
Counter_Init
```

We also need to configure *docRoot* — the directory that contains our web page and / or static files. In our case, we set it statically to `../www` (making it effectively be the `lib/www` directory). The path is created by combining the current working directory with the path to the script, so that the path is valid even after the current directory is changed:

```
set ::Config(docRoot) [file normalize [file join \
    [pwd] [file dirname [info script]] .. WWW]]
Doc_AddRoot / $::Config(docRoot)
Doc_Root $::Config(docRoot)
```

We also tell `Tclhttpd` that the document root is stored in the same directory that we configured. Using additional `Doc_AddRoot` invocations we can have different parts of the website served from different directories.

```
}
```

Finally we mention that this file creates package `tclhttpdinit`.

```
package provide tclhttpdinit 1.0
```

We can also create `pkgIndex.tcl` file in the same directory that will tell Tcl that file `tclhttpdinit.tcl` provides package `tclhttpdinit`. Contents of the file would be as follows:

```
package ifneeded tclhttpdinit 1.0 [list source [file join $dir
tclhttpdinit.tcl]]
```

We can also use the `pkg_mkIndex` command from Tcl to create the package. In order to do this, simply go to the directory containing the `tclhttpdinit.tcl` script and run:

```
% pkg_mkIndex .
```

This will cause the `pkgIndex.tcl` file to be created and contain the preceding line, as well as additional comments created by the command.

In order to initialize the `Tclhttpd` package, we simply need to include the following code in our application:

```
package require tclhttpdinit
Httpd_Server 8081
```

The second line initializes a HTTP server on port 8081. In order to initialize SSL-enabled server we can run:

```
Httpd_SecureServer 8082
```

After that our server will listen on port 8081 and / or 8082, depending on which commands we ran.

 The source code of the examples presented in this section is located in the in the `05embeddedtclhttpd` directory in the source code examples for this chapter.

Summary

After this chapter, you should be familiar with the concepts of web programming, by which we understand a set of topics related to HTTP protocol and HTML language.

First we presented how to use Tcl code as legacy CGI scripts. This application can be significantly improved with `ncgi` package. We also presented a convenient way of generating HTML documents using the `html` package.

Having laid the basics, we focused on `TclHttpd`, a mature web server implemented entirely in Tcl. We discussed its various aspects, starting from serving the static content and cooperation with CGI scripts. Then we presented advanced concepts like creating handlers of a specific document type, which can alter the content returned to the client; mapping Tcl procedures to a URL, so that the HTTP query parameters are simultaneously the arguments for that procedure; and handling an entire sub-domain with delegated code. We also mentioned items related to security and debugging.

Finally, we presented how to use all described features in one-file standalone binaries made with *Starpack* technology. This is the moment where the full power of Tcl can be easily seen—just stop for a moment and reflect—how many languages do you know that offer you the possibility to freely embed a web server? And how many of them will let you easily pack your entire app into one `exe` file, for a wide set of platforms? And in how many cases the resulting file will be around 3 MB of size? Not many? Well, now there is one more.

Now that you have learned the solid basics of the TclHttpd, you are ready for the the next chapter, which will introduce you to the server in more detail, with a particular focus on client-server programming.

11
TclHttpd in Client-Server Applications

By now we have learned a lot about network communication, and HTTP in particular, along with setting up TclHttpd for providing files and responding to requests from Tcl. We also learned how Tcl uses VFS to provide both standalone applications and package multiple files, into a single deliverable file we can later on use. Now, we'll put this knowledge into practice and create a sample client-server application that uses these technologies.

Throughout this chapter, we'll create a simple application that consists of a client and server. The application will work over HTTP and will allow multiple clients to communicate with a single server. It will also offer a comm interface on the server to invoke commands on remote clients. We'll start off by creating a minimal client and server, which will be a good starting point for both understanding the model and its upsides and downsides. It will have a mechanism for running Tcl command a on client and sending results back to the server.

After this is done, an *automatic updates* feature will be added so that whenever the client application changes, it will automatically get updated. This is needed in case we want our application to be run on multiple systems, and a manual upgrade of each one is not possible.

We'll also add plugin capability to our application so that we can create multiple Tcl packages. Those can be deployed to certain clients so that client itself will be minimal, and packages will extend its functionality.

Of course, this is just a sample application and later on we'll reveal some of the shortcuts taken in its development, and what would need to be extended for production quality applications. We'll also mention better security models that could be used.

Creating HTTP-based applications

Client-server applications may use various ways to communicate. Some of them are:

- One way is to keep a permanent connection between the server and all clients. This approach requires creating protocol for sending messages both from the server to client and the other way around. While this approach is used by many applications, it is quite difficult to scale and can cause issues for long-running applications — such as detection of connections broken on one side, without proper end-of-file events received by other side.

- Another possibility is to use HTTP instead of a real time connection. HTTP based applications typically use a polling mechanism — that is they periodically query the server to determine if there is anything the client should perform. Using HTTP and timers simplifies implementation a lot, and fits very nicely into Tcl's event-driven programming.

Using HTTP means that our application can also use any HTTP proxy needed by location the client is in, and can be easily configured for majority of network configurations. HTTP on its own is stateless and each request is independent of the other. This means that application is responsible for keeping track of what needs to be sent — usually this is kept on both server and client-side.

All communication in our application will be using Tclhttpd for the server-side and the `http` package on client. Both packages have already been introduced in previous chapters.

Our application will initially have very small functionality — the client will periodically poll for new jobs to be performed. The server will provide a list of jobs to perform, if any:

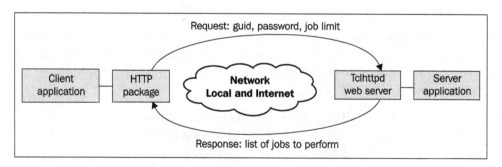

These operations will be done periodically. After this, whenever a job has been performed by the agent it sends results to the server as follows:

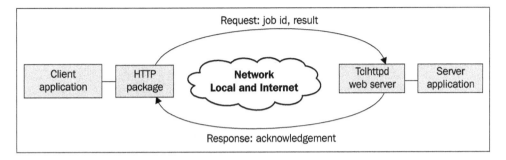

Preparing source code structure

Before implementing our applications, we need to set up our source code structure and build the system so that we can easily create multiple applications for multiple platforms—for this example only `win32` and `linux-x86`, but there could be more. The approach of creating a separate directory for the client or server on each of the platforms is not manageable in the long term; we would need to copy each change into multiple directories, which is difficult to do.

Even though this section provides a step by step introduction of what the preparations need to be, the code samples available along with this book provides a ready-to-use source code structure. Novice readers are advised to start by having a look at the sources provided for this chapter. This chapter also assumes the reader to be familiar with the content of the previous chapters—especially those related to Starkit technology, building standalone binaries, using databases, HTTP client, and TclHttpd.

Later in this section, we will introduce a building script to automate common tasks.

We want to create each of the binaries from a set of directories:

- Common libraries and packages for all platforms (pure Tcl)
- Common libraries and packages for specified platform
- Source code for specified binary

First let's create the following directories: `lib-common`, `lib-win32`, and `lib-linux-x86` for common packages. Let's also create `src-client` and `src-server` for sources for client and server applications.

The following is a complete file and directory tree of the project along with all scripts we'll create:

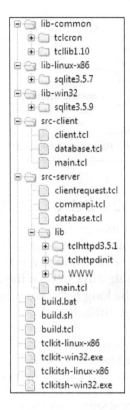

The image contains the results from next steps as well, such as build scripts, server and client code, as well as all libraries.

The next thing we need are binaries for each platform. We'll create both Tk and non-Tk versions of each UI. Even though we won't use Tk itself on Microsoft Windows, background processes should use the Tk version and withdraw its main window—otherwise they will have a console window shown to the user.

We can download all versions of Tclkit from:

- `http://www.patthoyts.tk/tclkit/win32-ix86/`
- `http://www.patthoyts.tk/tclkit/linux-ix86/`

The authors recommend using the latest version 8.5 of `tclkit` (with Tk) and `tclkitsh` (without Tk), and naming them `tclkit-<platform>` and `tclkitsh-<platform>` accordingly. For Microsoft Windows we also need a `.exe` extension for the binaries.

We also need to download and/or copy several packages that will be used by our csa application:

- We need to copy the tcllib package (available from: http://sourceforge.net/projects/tcllib/) as lib-common/tcllib

- We need to copy the lib subdirectory from the tclhttpd package available from: http://sourceforge.net/projects/tclhttpd/) as src-server/lib/tclhttpd

- We need to put the tclhttpdinit package (provided in *Chapter 10, Web Programming in Tcl*) in src-server/lib/tclhttpdinit

- We need to copy the Tcl sqlite package, all platforms (available from http://www.sqlite.org/) as lib-<platform>/sqlite

These packages are needed in order to initialize Tclhttpd web server and database storage. They have also been introduced in previous chapters.

Now we can finally create the script to build the binaries. First we need to iterate over each platform we want to build these binaries for, and binaries we want to build:

```
foreach {platform suffix} { win32 ".exe" linux-x86 "" } {
    foreach {binname appname dirname} {
        tclkitsh client-cli client tclkit client-ui client
        tclkitsh server-cli server tclkit server-ui server
    } {
```

Each platform also has a suffix we need to add to the filename, which is needed for Microsoft Windows platform. The list of binaries consists of three things— the type of Tclkit binary to use (tclkit or tclkitsh), the destination name of the binary, and the source directory to use.

We then create the filename we want to work on, which is copied to the binaries subdirectory:

```
set filename \
    [file join binaries $appname-$platform$suffix]
```

For example, when building a non-UI version of the client for Microsoft Windows the appname would be client-cli, the variable platform equal to win32 and the suffix set to .exe. The name of the target binary would be client-cli-win32.exe.

Then we copy the source binary as that particular file:

```
file copy -force $binname-$platform$suffix $filename
```

For the preceding `client-cli-win32.exe` example, `binname` would be set to `tclkitsh` and the source binary would be `tclkitsh-win32.exe`.

Then we mount it, copy appropriate directories, and unmount it:

```
vfs::mk4::Mount $filename $filename
docopy src-$dirname $filename
docopy lib-common [file join $filename lib]
docopy lib-$platform [file join $filename lib]
vfs::unmount $filename
```

In order to ease the automatic update feature, we will now calculate the MD5 checksum from the created binary and embed it in that binary. We create a script called `fileinfo.tcl` in the VFS that will set the `csa::applicationMD5` variable to value of the checksum. We'll also write that checksum to a separate file.

```
set md5 [md5::md5 -hex -file $filename]

vfs::mk4::Mount $filename $filename
set fh [open [file join $filename fileinfo.tcl] w]
puts $fh [list set csa::applicationMD5 $md5]
close $fh
vfs::unmount $filename
set fh [open $filename.md5 w]
puts -nonewline $fh $md5
close $fh
```

While the automatic updates are done later in this chapter, we introduce MD5 calculation earlier. An MD5 checksum is stored in the binary as well as separate file, so that the `csa` client will be able to easily check if an update is available. It would query the server for MD5 checksum of latest binary for specified platform, and compare it with the MD5 checksum of the local client application. If they are the same, the client is running the latest version. Otherwise, it can download the updated version and replace it.

Even though the actual binary will not have the same MD5 checksum as what we calculated, the checksum that was calculated before can be used to compare the binary that the client is running with the binary the server has, which can be read from the second file created, as the last step.

The `docopy` helper procedure mentioned earlier copies the contents of source directory to the target directory. It is similar to `file copy`, but handles the case where one or more files already exist. For example, if both `lib-common` and `src-client/lib` are copied to the `lib/` subdirectory of the target binary, the `file copy` command fails with the error that `lib/ already exists`. The `docopy` command handles this case properly.

It simply checks the file type and recursively copies directories while simply copying files:

```
proc docopy {from to} {
    foreach g [glob -directory $from -nocomplain -tails *] {
        set fromg [file join $from $g]
        set tog [file join $to $g]
        if {[file type $fromg] == "directory"} {
            file mkdir $tog
            docopy $fromg $tog
        } else {
            file copy -force $fromg $tog
        }
    }
}
```

Creating our applications

We now need to start creating code for our client and server applications — src-client/main.tcl and src-server/main.tcl. Both applications will start with the same code that initializes starkit, sets up a logger instance, and creates data directory to store configuration in:

```
package require starkit
starkit::startup

namespace eval csa {}
namespace eval csa::log {}

# initialize logging
package require logger
logger::init csa
logger::import -namespace csa::log csa

# set up directories
set csa::datadirectory [file join [pwd] data]
file mkdir $csa::datadirectory
```

Server-side

For our server application, besides the recently explained initialization, we'll need to initialize Tclhttpd and comm packages:

```
csa::log::debug "Initializing Tclhttpd"
package require tclhttpdinit
Httpd_Server 8981
csa::log::debug "Initializing comm interface"
package require comm
comm::comm configure -port 1991
```

This will cause the csa server to listen for HTTP connections on port 8981 and on comm connections on port 1991. The HTTP connection is used for communication with all clients, and the comm package is set up to allow adding requests from other applications and testing the application.

The next step is to load the additional scripts that initialize the database, set up the comm API and handle incoming HTTP requests:

```
csa::log::debug "Sourcing remaining files"
source [file join $starkit::topdir commapi.tcl]
source [file join $starkit::topdir database.tcl]
source [file join $starkit::topdir clientrequest.tcl]
```

The files we source are described later in the chapter. Finally we need to enter the main loop. If Tk is present, we'll show the UI that comes with Tclhttpd:

```
csa::log::debug "Entering main loop"

# Initialize Tk UI if possible
catch {package require Tk}
if {[info commands tk] != ""} {
    package require httpd::srvui
    SrvUI_Init "CSA server"
} else {
    puts "Server started"
    vwait forever
}
```

 The complete source code is located in the main.tcl in the 01clientserver/src-server directory in the source code examples for this chapter.

Client-side

For the client, after setting up the logger and the data directory, we'll accept the host name to connect to as argument, to print out an error if either one is not provided:

```
if {$argc < 1} {
    set error "Usage: client <hostname>"
    log::error $error
    puts stderr $error
    exit 1
}
lassign $argv csa::hostname

csa::log::info "Connecting to $csa::hostname"
```

We will now read the additional scripts — the initialization of local database, the client to communicate with the server, and read the local application's MD5 checksum:

```
source [file join $starkit::topdir database.tcl]
source [file join $starkit::topdir fileinfo.tcl]
source [file join $starkit::topdir client.tcl]
```

Then we'll schedule the csa client to request jobs to perform as soon as it is initialized:

```
after idle csa::requestJobs
```

The command csa::requestJobs is explained later in this chapter.

Finally we need to initialize the main loop. Similar to the server part, if Tk is present, we show a minimal UI with an exit button:

```
csa::log::debug "Entering main loop"

if {[info commands tk] != ""} {
    # basic UI
    wm title . "CSA Client"
    button .exit -text "Exit application" -command exit \
        -width 30 -height 3
    pack .exit -fill both -expand 1
} else {
    vwait forever
}
```

> The complete source code is located in the main.tcl in the 01clientserver/src-client directory in the source code examples for this chapter.

Communication and registration

While there is no silver bullet for all possible use cases, the authors of this book have decided to implement a simple solution. In order to simplify how our communication is done, everything that we send over HTTP will simply be dictionaries encoded as UTF-8. Since dictionaries can be converted from and to strings by Tcl, we do not need to perform any complex operations and everything seems to be transparent to our application.

Using Tcl's structures and format makes it easy to create both client and server in Tcl. It also makes it easier to access the data on server and client, and is much more efficient than using standards such as XML—which add the overhead of converting to and from XML, as well as require more code to send requests or get a response.

If our application needs to talk to other languages as well, it might be a good idea to provide communication using standards such as SOAP. These standards are shown in the next chapter.

Communication between the client and the server is done using the following steps:

- The client sends a HTTP POST request providing all data as query, encoded in UTF-8; fields guid and password should specify client's Globally Unique Identifier (**GUID**) and its password

- The server checks if guid and password are valid

- If client is authorized, server gets jobs to be performed by this agent and passes them as the response

- The client then performs these tasks, which are evaluated as Tcl scripts and sends back the results from each task

Authorization of guid and password is done against database of all agents. If an agent already exists in the database, its password has to match one that it provides. If an agent does not exist yet, its password is stored and compared upon the next communication. The client generates both GUID and password when it is first run.

Server-side

Let's start off with how our server would handle requests.

Our function to process a request would start off as follows:

```
proc csa::handleClientProtocol {sock suffix} {
    upvar #0 ::Httpd$sock s
    set req [dict create]
    set response [dict create]
    set ok 0
```

```
    if {[info exists s(query)]} {
        set req [dict create {*}[encoding \
            convertfrom utf-8 $s(query)]
    }
```

This would map the HTTP request data to the variable s, initialize default values for variables, and if a query was passed then store it in `req` variable. We also initialize the `ok` and `response` variables, to indicate that request was not correct and response to contain no data, which we'll add later.

After this, we'd check if a client is allowed to talk to our server by trying to authorize it, if `guid` and `password` keys were sent in the request:

```
    if {[dict exists $req guid]
        && [dict exists $req password]} {
        set guid [dict get $req guid]
        if {![authorizeClient $guid \
            [dict get $req password]]} {
            log::warn "handleClientProtocol: Access denied"
            unset guid
        }
    }
```

Our clients will send passwords as raw text. However, the password will be created as random string when client first connects, and applications requiring security should rely on more sophisticated algorithms for authorizing clients or users. such as SSL and signed certificates, described in *Chapter 13, SSL and Security*.

Authorization itself is done by `authorizeClient` command. If the authorization succeeds, the `guid` variable remains set. Otherwise we log an error and unset it.

Next, we can provide the client with additional data only if the user is authorized. For example, providing a list of jobs from `getJobs` command, providing at most the number of jobs client requests, or 10 by default:

```
    if {[info exists guid]} {
        set ok 1
        if {[dict exists $req joblimit]} {
            set joblimit [dict get $req joblimit]
        } else {
            set joblimit 10
        }

        dict set response jobs \
            [getJobs $guid $joblimit]
    }
```

We make sure that only valid clients get the data by checking if guid variable exists. If authorization fails, it is unset and server won't check for jobs to send to client.

Finally, we need to send the response back to the client, creating a list of ok and response variables values, and converting it into UTF-8:

```
    Httpd_ReturnData $sock application/x-csa-data \
        [encoding convertto utf-8 [list $ok $response]]
}
```

We've used our own MIME type of application/x-csa-data, but it is not required; the type application/octet-stream, which indicates any series of bytes, can also be used.

In order for a client to be able to send results from commands, we'll create an additional small handler. We'll start also by retrieving the query sent by client:

```
proc csa::handleClientResult {sock suffix} {
    upvar #0 ::Httpd$sock s
    set req [dict create]
    set ok 0

    if {[info exists s(query)]} {
        set req [encoding convertfrom utf-8 $s(query)]
    }
```

If both job and result keys are sent, we store the job's result in the database.

```
    if {[dict exists $req job]&&[dict exists $req result]} {
        setJobResult [dict get $req job] \
            [dict get $req result]
        set ok 1
    }
```

Finally we also send the result back to the client:

```
    Httpd_ReturnData $sock application/x-csa-data $ok
}
```

As the client needs to know a valid job identifier, we can assume that it is a valid client. Otherwise, the job identifier would probably be invalid, which setJobResult command needs to handle.

Last thing we need to do is to register handler for specified prefixes in our web server:

```
Url_PrefixInstall /client/protocol csa::handleClientProtocol
Url_PrefixInstall /client/result csa::handleClientResult
```

The code mentioned in this section is located in the `src-server/` `clientrequest.tcl` file in the `01clientserver` directory in the source code examples for this chapter.

Client-side

Implementation of the client for the communication is also not a very difficult task. We'll use a polling-based approach for communication, which means that the client will periodically poll the server for new tasks to be processed.

First thing to implement is command for requesting jobs to be performed from the server. We'll start off by defining the command that will periodically be called to get new jobs. It starts off by cancelling any other scheduled invocations of the check:

```
proc csa::requestJobs {} {
    variable hostname

    after cancel csa::requestJobs
```

We create URL to connect to, based on the hostname provided by the user. We also set the request's key `guid` and `password` in order to authenticate the request.

```
    set url "http://${hostname}:8981/client/protocol"
    set req [dict create]

    dict set req guid $::csa::guid
    dict set req password $::csa::password
```

Values for `guid` and `password` are stored in database and described later.

Next the command tries to send request to the server; we convert request to UTF-8, send it as `application/x-csa-request` MIME type and specify that `csa::requestJobsDone` command should be invoked whenever results are retrieved.

```
    if {[catch {
        http::geturl $url -timeout 30000 \
            -query [encoding convertto utf-8 $req] \
            -type application/x-csa-request \
            -command csa::requestJobsDone
    }]} {
        # try again in 1 minute
        after 60000 csa::requestJobs
    }
}
```

If the request has been successfully sent, then the next steps are followed using `requestJobsDone` command. Otherwise, we set up a retry in 60 seconds.

At the start, we'll set up another check for commands in 1 minute from now:

```
proc csa::requestJobsDone {token} {
    # schedule next communication in 1 minute from now
    after 60000 csa::requestJobs
```

Then we check if the response is valid and no error was encountered. In case of any error, we log it, clean up the HTTP token and return. Otherwise we convert the response from UTF-8 and proceed.

```
if {[http::status $token] != "ok"} {
    log::error "requestJobsDone: Invalid HTTP status"
    http::cleanup $token
    return
} elseif {[http::ncode $token] != 200} {
    log::error "requestJobsDone: Invalid HTTP code"
    http::cleanup $token
    return
} else {
    set response [encoding convertfrom utf-8 \
        [http::data $token]]
    log::debug "requestJobsDone: Response: $response"
}
```

As the first step, we assign `ok` and `response` variables to first and second element of the response, we retrieved from the server. If the server did not send a negative status as the `ok` variable, we check if the response contains key jobs—if it does, and it has any elements then we invoke the `runJobs` command to run each of the jobs.

```
lassign $response ok response

if {$ok} {
    if {[dict exists $response jobs]
        && ([llength [dict get $response jobs]] > 0)} {
        runJobs [dict get $response jobs]
    }
} else {
    log::error "requestJobsDone: Server returned error"
}
```

Finally we clean up the HTTP token.

```
    http::cleanup $token
}
```

Running the jobs themselves is done as evaluating them in the global stack frame using `uplevel #0` command. The `runJobs` command looks as follows:

```
proc csa::runJobs {jobs} {
    log::debug "runJobs: Running jobs"
    foreach {job command} $jobs {
        log::debug "runJobs: Running job $job"
        set result [uplevel #0 $command]
        log::debug "runJobs: Sending result"
        sendResult $job $result
    }
    log::debug "runJobs: Running jobs complete"
}
```

The command runs each of the commands and then submits its result to the server.

It uses `sendResult` to send a result for a job, which is shown as follows.

We first create a URL and a request, setting the keys job and result accordingly. Then the command sends a request to the server:

```
proc csa::sendResult {job result} {
    variable hostname

    set url "http://${hostname}:8981/client/result"
    set req [dict create job $job result $result]

    set token [http::geturl $url \
        -query [encoding convertto utf-8 $req]]
```

After finishing sending the HTTP request, we then check the response and whether the server has properly handled our request or not; if not, we log and throw an error:

```
    if {[http::status $token] != "ok"} {
        http::cleanup $token
        log::error "sendResult: Invalid HTTP status"
        error "Invalid HTTP status"
    } elseif {[http::ncode $token] != 200} {
        http::cleanup $token
        log::error "sendResult: Invalid HTTP code"
        error "Invalid HTTP code"
    }
```

Finally, the command cleans up HTTP token and exits.

```
    http::cleanup $token
}
```

This is a complete implementation of the client.

 The code mentioned in this section is located in the `src-client/client.tcl` file in the `01clientserver` directory in the source code examples for this chapter.

Storing information

For the purpose of this application we'll be using the SQLite database. Both the client and the server will use a database for storing their data; however each of them will use it for different types of information. Also, with the concept of modules that can be used in our applications, it is possible to store additional data by extensions.

Server side

For the server side, our application needs to keep at least two types of items—a list of clients and the list of jobs a client should perform, along with their results.

Database initialization code should go to `src-server/database.tcl`, which is read from the main script created earlier. We'll need to start off with loading packages and initializing the database:

```
package require sqlite3
package require uuid

sqlite csa::db [file join $csa::datadirectory csa-server.db]
```

After this, we'll create tables for storing clients and jobs. We'll start by checking if the tables already exist:

```
if {[catch {csa::db eval "SELECT COUNT(*) FROM clients"}]} {
```

If querying a number of items in clients table throws an error, this means that the table has not been created. In this case, we'll create both `clients` and `clientjobs` tables:

```
    csa::db transaction {
        csa::db eval {
            CREATE TABLE clients (
                guid CHAR(36) NOT NULL PRIMARY KEY,
                password VARCHAR(255) NOT NULL,
```

```
            status INTEGER NOT NULL DEFAULT 1,
            lastupdate INTEGER NOT NULL DEFAULT 0
        );
        CREATE TABLE clientjobs (
            job CHAR(36) NOT NULL PRIMARY KEY,
            client CHAR(36) NOT NULL,
            status INTEGER NOT NULL DEFAULT 0,
            lastupdate INTEGER NOT NULL DEFAULT 0,
            command TEXT,
            result TEXT
        );
    }
}
```

The first table stores the GUID and password of all clients, along with the time when they last queried the system. The field status defines current status of a client: 1 means enabled; 0 means disabled.

The table clientjobs stores jobs associated with a client. The field job is a GUID identifying the job and client is the GUID of the client that should run it. The field status defines whether the job has already been run or not: 0 means it has not run; 1 means it has already run. The field command keeps the command to run and result stores the result retrieved from the client.

Now we can create functions that other parts of the application will use.

Let's start with authorizing a client. Our csa::authorizeClient command would need to check if a client exists in the database, and add it if it does not. It would need to check if the password provided matches the one in the database and that the client's status is set to enabled. If not, it should return a message stating that the authentication failed. Otherwise, it should change the lastupdate field and return message that authentication succeeded:

```
proc csa::authorizeClient {guid password} {
    set now [clock seconds]
    set result [db eval {SELECT status, password
        FROM clients WHERE guid=$guid}]

    # if no entry found, add a new item to database
    # and assume the new agent is ok
    if {[llength $result] == 0} {
        db eval {INSERT INTO clients (guid, password)
            VALUES($guid, $password)}
        return true
    }
    lassign $result status dbpassword
```

```
        # check if passwords match
        if {![string equal $dbpassword $password]} {
            return false
        }

        # if client is not currently enabled, return false
        if {$status != 1} {
            return false
        }

        # if everything matched, it's a valid client
        db eval {UPDATE clients SET lastupdate=$now
            WHERE guid=$guid}
        return true
    }
```

Our application assumes that if we do not currently know a particular client, we'll silently add it to the database. While this assumption might not always be correct, in this case there is no danger as a client only accesses his own jobs, which need to be added for new clients explicitly. Also, such an assumption makes working with the examples much easier.

In the next step, we'll need to create functions for managing jobs:

- `csa::addJob` for creating new entries for a specified agent
- `csa::getJobs` to retrieve list of jobs for specified agent
- `csa::setJobResult` to set a result for specified entry when client provides it
- `csa::getJobResult` to retrieve a result after it has been provided

Let's start with the command for adding new entries:

```
proc csa::addJob {client command {callback ""}} {
    variable jobResultWait
```

First we'll check if a specified client exists and is active:

```
        # do not allow adding jobs for inactive clients
        if {[llength [db eval \
            {SELECT guid FROM clients WHERE guid=$client
                AND status=1}]] == 0} {
            return ""
        }
```

Now we'll create an identifier for the job and add it:

```
set job [uuid::uuid generate]
set now [clock seconds]
db eval {INSERT INTO clientjobs
    (job, client, lastupdate, command)
    VALUES($job, $client, $now, $command)}
```

If the callback script was provided, we store it:

```
if {$callback != ""} {
    set jobResultWait($job) $callback
}
```

Finally we return the job identifier.

```
    return $job
}
```

After we've added a job, clients need to be able to retrieve those using `getJobs` command, which is a simple query for jobs that were not yet run:

```
proc csa::getJobs {client limit} {
    return [db eval {SELECT job, command FROM clientjobs
        WHERE client=$client AND status=0 LIMIT $limit}]
}
```

The next step is being able to set a job's result:

```
proc csa::setJobResult {job result} {
    variable jobResultWait
    db eval {UPDATE clientjobs SET status=1,result=$result
        WHERE job=$job}
```

We also need to handle callback scripts that were passed to `addJob`; if it has to be set, we set it to be invoked by the event loop, and unset it:

```
    if {[info exists jobResultWait($job)]} {
        after idle [linsert $jobResultWait($job) end \
            $result]
        unset jobResultWait($job)
    }
}
```

Finally, retrieving a job's result is also a simple query:

```
proc csa::getJobResult {job} {
    return [db eval {SELECT status, result FROM clientjobs
        WHERE job=$job AND status=1}]
}
```

This provides us with all the database access functions needed for both clients and jobs.

The reason for creating callbacks for jobs is that for the comm interface, we will also provide a synchronous interface. This is an interface which from caller's perspective will return, once the client has finished processing the command. They are not stored in the database as whenever a server restarts, call-back scripts will no longer be valid.

 The code mentioned in this section is located in the src-server/ database.tcl file in the 01clientserver directory in the source code examples for this chapter.

Client side

The database for the client application is definitely smaller — all that we store in it is a single table with a single row, containing the guid and the password for connecting to server.

Similar to the server, we start by initializing the SQLite package and setting up a database object:

```
package require sqlite3
package require uuid

namespace eval csa {}

sqlite csa::db [file join $csa::datadirectory csa-client.db]
```

In the next step, we intialize the table if it was previously not there:

```
if {[catch {csa::db eval "SELECT COUNT(*) FROM
    configuration"}]} {
    csa::db transaction {
        csa::db eval {
            CREATE TABLE configuration (
                guid CHAR(36) NOT NULL PRIMARY KEY,
                password VARCHAR(255) NOT NULL
            );
        }
```

After setting up the table we also generate random `guid` and password strings, and insert them into the database:

```
        set guid [uuid::uuid generate]
        set password [uuid::uuid generate]

        # insert authentication data into database
        csa::db eval {INSERT INTO configuration
            VALUES($guid, $password)}
    }
}
```

Finally, regardless of the fact that the entries were just generated or were already stored in the database, we set `csa::guid` and `csa::password` to the values stored in the database:

```
lassign [csa::db eval {SELECT guid, password
    FROM configuration}] csa::guid csa::password

csa::log::info "Local client identifier: $csa::guid"
```

We also log the identifier that the client has assigned each time it is run, so that it is easier to test the application.

Although just these two values do not require a complete database, our application uses SQLite so that potential extensions could also benefit from a pre-initialized database.

 The code mentioned in this section is located in the `src-client/` `database.tcl` file in the `01clientserver` directory in the source code examples for this chapter.

Comm interface—spooling jobs

Now that both the client and the server code is complete, all that remains is to create a `comm` interface so we can send commands to the server to add jobs.

As `comm` interface is already initialized in a server's `main.tcl` file, all we need to create now is a handler that will limit the functions available and offer a synchronous mechanism for adding a job.

We'll start by creating a hook command for `comm`'s `eval` event:

```
comm::comm hook eval {
    return [csa::apihandle [lrange $buffer 0 end]]
}
```

We send each command to the `csa::apihandle` command, which then evaluates the command.

Let's create this command. We'll start off by checking the actual command that was sent, and creating a switch for handling various commands:

```
proc csa::apihandle {command} {
    set cmd [lindex $command 0]
    switch -- $cmd {
```

First we'll handle the `addJob` command — which simply accepts a client identifier and the command to evaluate, and returns the new job's identifier:

```
addJob {
    lassign $command cmd client command
    set job [csa::addJob $client $command]
    return $job
}
```

We'll also create a similar command, but one that waits for the command to be executed by the client and returns its result. We'll use `return_async` from `comm` and job callbacks for this:

```
addJobWait {
    lassign $command cmd client command
```

We'll now create a future object:

```
set future [comm::comm return_async]
```

We then pass this object as a callback when the new job is completed. This will cause the `comm`'s future object to be invoked with the actual result, as soon as the result has been submitted by a client.

```
set job [csa::addJob $client $command \
    [list $future return]]
```

In case a job was not created, we need to return an error to the user. This might be the case if the client identifier was invalid.

```
if {$job == ""} {
    # if no job was assigned because
    # specified client was not found
    $future return -code 1 "Unknown client"
}
}
```

The last method is getting a job's result, which maps directly to `getJobResult` command:

```
getJobResult {
    lassign $command cmd job
    return [getJobResult $job]
}
```

In case an unknown command was passed, we return an error:

```
    }
    error "Unknown command $cmd"
}
```

This concludes the `comm` API and was the last item of our server and client applications.

 The code mentioned in this section is located in the `src-server/commapi.tcl` file in the `01clientserver` directory in the source code examples for this chapter.

Testing our applications

Now that our application has been implemented, it is time to run it and see how it works.

Let's start with building our `01clientserver` code example. Depending on whether it is going to be run on a Linux or Windows system, we can run either `build.bat` or `build.sh` script.

After all the binaries have been created, which can take up to several minutes, we can now run them. Let's start by running the server in first console window:

```
C> binaries\server-cli-win32.exe
[Thu Nov 26 19:37:03 +0100 2009] [csa] [debug] 'Initializing Tclhttpd'
[Thu Nov 26 19:37:04 +0100 2009] [csa] [debug] 'Initializing comm
interface'
[Thu Nov 26 19:37:05 +0100 2009] [csa] [debug] 'Sourcing remaining files'
[Thu Nov 26 19:37:05 +0100 2009] [csa] [debug] 'Entering main loop'
Server started
```

For a Linux system the syntax would be slightly different, but the behaviour and logs would be the same.

We can now run the client. Assuming both are run on the same system we can simply run it with 127.0.0.1 as the hostname:

```
C> binaries\client-cli-win32.exe 127.0.0.1
[Thu Nov 26 19:38:23 +0100 2009] [csa] [info] 'Connecting to 127.0.0.1'
[Thu Nov 26 19:38:25 +0100 2009] [csa] [info] 'Local client identifier:
b5fac0c4-a2a6-439e-6eb1-b68b2d72e974'
[Thu Nov 26 19:38:25 +0100 2009] [csa] [debug] 'Entering main loop'
```

We now have our client and server set up. We also know that our client's identifier is `b5fac0c4-a2a6-439e-6eb1-b68b2d72e974`. Now we can run any other Tcl session and send the command to be evaluated by running:

```
% set cid "b5fac0c4-a2a6-439e-6eb1-b68b2d72e974"
% package require comm
% puts [comm::comm send 1991 addJobWait $cid {expr 1+1}]
2
% set job [comm::comm send 1991 addJob $cid {expr 1+2}]
% after 60000
% puts [lindex [comm::comm send 1991 getJobResult $job] 1]
1 3
```

We can see that both commands have been evaluated. The latter form returns both the status of the command and the value as a list, so we should in fact do the following:

```
% puts [lindex [comm::comm send 1991 getJobResult $job] 1]
3
```

In case of any problems with the commands, logs provided by both client and server on their standard outputs should provide additional information about what the problem might be.

Adding autoupdate to application

Very often we will want our clients to be able to update automatically, especially if clients are run on large number of computers and / or in different locations.

To make our application automatically update itself, we need to use a simple but efficient pattern for automatic updates. The approach is exactly the same as described in *Chapter 3, Tcl Standalone Binaries*.

All that is needed is to perform the following steps:

- Check if an updated version of the binary is available; if not, then download it
- Write the binary as a temporary file with the specified filename
- Run the temporary binary
- As the temporary binary, overwrite the actual binary and exit
- As the temporary binary, run the actual binary, which is now updated and exit
- As the actual binary, remove the temporary binary and perform normal actions

In order to be able to tell when we are running a temporary binary, we should always be able to know both file names. As our temporary binary will always be prefixed with `autoupdate-`, our file names are similar to `/path/to/client-cli-linux-x86` and `/path/to/autoupdate-client-cli-linux-x86` respectively. This way a simple check can be used to determine whether the application should work normally or should overwrite the actual binary, restart it and exit.

As for determining whether our version is up to date or not, we'll use the MD5 checksum calculated when binaries were built. This and the corresponding `.md5` files are enough to implement automatic updates.

 The complete code for automatic update is located in the `02autoupdate` directory in the source code examples for this chapter.

Server-side

For implementing automatic updates, server-side needs to be able to return information about the latest version of the application, and return the latest binary for each platform.

We need to make two changes in the `src-server/main.tcl` file, compared to previous example. The first one is that we need to store the directory where the binaries are kept:

```
set csa::binariesdirectory [file join [pwd] binaries]
```

Also, we'll load the additional `autoupdate.tcl` script that will be responsible for providing the client with the binaries.

```
source [file join $starkit::topdir autoupdate.tcl]
```

The script itself is relatively small. All it does is serve requests for binaries. It does this by getting whatever filename was supplied, and combining that with the path to the binaries that was previously initialized. If a specified file is not found, the `404` error is returned and an error is logged.

```
proc csa::handleClientBinary {sock suffix} {
    variable binariesdirectory

    set filename [file join $binariesdirectory \
        [file tail $suffix]]

    if {[file exists $filename]} {
        Httpd_ReturnFile $sock application/octet-stream \
            $filename
    } else {
        log::warn "handleClientBinary: $filename not found"
        Httpd_Error $sock 404
    }
}
```

We'll also bind a particular prefix so that all requests to the client/binary will be handled by our command.

```
Url_PrefixInstall /client/binary csa::handleClientBinary
```

It works in such a way that the request to `http://<host>:8981/client/binary/client-cli-linux-x86` will cause that file from the `binaries` subdirectory to be returned.

 The code mentioned in this section is located in the `src-server/autoupdate.tcl` file in the `02autoupdate` directory in the source code examples for this chapter.

Client-side

A lot more logic needs to be embedded in the client, though.

As many operating systems do not allow overwriting a binary that is currently running, our overwrite process is a bit more tricky and described earlier in the chapter.

In the client's `main.tcl` file we'll introduce some small changes—first we'll add loading `autoupdate.tcl` file, we'll also schedule `csa::checkAutoupdate` command immediately, but `csa::requestJobs` later. The purpose is to wait to get the jobs before making sure our binary is up to date.

```
source [file join $starkit::topdir autoupdate.tcl]

after idle csa::checkAutoupdate
after 60000 csa::requestJobs
```

The `autoupdate.tcl` script begins with checking the name of the binary we are running as. If it starts with the `autoupdate-` prefix, this means that our application should overwrite the actual binary, run it and exit:

```
if {[regexp -nocase \
    "autoupdate-(.*)" \
    [file tail [info nameofexecutable]] - binaryname]} {
    # wait for parent process to exit
    after 5000
```

We started by waiting 5 seconds for a parent process to exit. Then we determine target file name, which is the actual binary, such as /path/to/client-cli-linux-x86.

```
set dirname [file dirname [info nameofexecutable]]
set targetname [file join $dirname $binaryname]
```

Now we try to unmount the VFS of the executable, which is needed to copy the binary as a file from the Tcl level; otherwise Tcl will consider that path to be a directory.

Then we overwrite the target binary using our current binary, and try to change its permissions to being executable on Unix systems. Finally, we run the actual binary providing the same arguments that our autoupdate binary was run with.

```
catch {vfs::mk4::Unmount exe [info nameofexecutable]}
file copy -force [info nameofexecutable]  $targetname
catch {file attributes $targetname -permissions 0755}
exec $targetname {*}$argv &
exit 0
} else {
```

If our binary is not running in the `autoupdate` mode, we check if the `autoupdate-<binaryname>` file exists. If it does, this means that we have been just started the end of the automatic update process. In this case we wait for five seconds for the `autoupdate` binary to exit, and try to remove it from the filesystem.

```
set dirname [file dirname [info nameofexecutable]]
set targetname [file join $dirname \
    "autoupdate-[file tail [info nameofexecutable]]" \
    ]
```

```
        if {[file exists $targetname]} {
            after 5000
            catch {file delete -force $targetname}
        }
    }
```

This is a complete implementation of handling automatic updates themselves.

After this, we need to create a procedure that will periodically check for updates of the binary file, and if there is a newer version then download and run it.

Also, the command will set `csa::autoupdateInProgress` variable that can be used by other parts of the application to stop performing tasks, if we are expecting to be restarted.

We'll start off by cancelling any scheduled checks and building URL to the binary.

```
    proc csa::checkAutoupdate {} {
        variable hostname
        variable autoupdateInProgress

        after cancel csa::checkAutoupdate

        set url "http://${hostname}:8981/client/binary/"
        append url [file tail [info nameofexecutable]]
```

Next we'll try to download the `<binary>.md5` file, which is the MD5 checksum of the actual binary, and is generated as part of the build process. `csa::checkAutoupdateDone` command will be run when the request has been completed. If initializing the download fails, we try again in one minute from now:

```
        if {[catch {
            http::geturl "$url.md5" -timeout 30000 \
                -command [list csa::checkAutoupdateDone $url]
        }]} {
            log::error "checkAutoupdate: Unable to send request"
            # try again in 1 minute
            after 60000 csa::checkAutoupdate
        }
    }
```

After request for the MD5 checksum has been completed, we start off by setting up a next check for one hour from now, which is the default interval for checking for updates.

```
    proc csa::checkAutoupdateDone {url token} {
        variable autoupdateInProgress

        after 3600000 csa::checkAutoupdate
```

Next we check if the request has been successfully processed. Unlike many other examples so far, we also include support for error code 404 in this case—which means that the server does not have the appropriate file on its side.

```
if {[http::status $token] != "ok"} {
    log::error "checkAutoupdateDone: Invalid HTTP status"
    http::cleanup $token
    return
} elseif {[http::ncode $token] == 404} {
    log::warn "checkAutoupdateBinaryDone:\
        Server does not provide updates for this binary"
    http::cleanup $token
    return
} elseif {[http::ncode $token] != 200} {
    log::error "checkAutoupdateDone: Invalid HTTP code"
    http::cleanup $token
    return
} else {
```

If there was no error processing the request, we retrieve the checksum from the request and compare it with our local binary's checksum.

```
set checksum [http::data $token]
```

```
if {$checksum != $::csa::applicationMD5} {
```

If the checksums are different, we need to update our binary. We start off by cancelling the next scheduled automatic update and initialize a request to download the actual binary, which will invoke the `csa::checkAutoupdateBinaryDone` command when it completes.

```
after cancel csa::checkAutoupdate
if {[catch {
    http::geturl $url -timeout 900000 -binary 1 \
        -command csa::checkAutoupdateBinaryDone
}]} {
```

If an error has occurred, we set up the next attempt in one minute from now. We also log the error.

```
# an error occured;
# schedule next check in 1 minute from now
after 60000 csa::checkAutoupdate
log::error "checkAutoupdateDone: Unable to\
    download new binary"
} else {
```

If the download has started, we set the `csa::autoupdateInProgress` variable to true to indicate that an update is in progress.

```
            # if download has started, we set this
            # so no further requests for job are sent
            set autoupdateInProgress true
        }
    }
  }
}
```

When the download of the binary has finished, we start off by scheduling the next automatic update in case of problems. We also unset the `csa::autoupdateInProgress` variable for the same reason.

```
proc csa::checkAutoupdateBinaryDone {token} {
    variable autoupdateInProgress

    # just in case - schedule next check in 1 hour from now
    # and clear the autoupdate flag
    after 3600000 csa::checkAutoupdate
    catch {unset autoupdateInProgress}
    log::info "checkAutoupdateBinaryDone: Binary received"
```

The first thing we do is check whether the transfer has succeeded and no error was sent by the server—in case of any problems, we log them and exit the procedure. Next attempt will happen in an hour.

```
        # check status & HTTP code; return if error occurred
        if {[http::status $token] != "ok"} {
            log::error "checkAutoupdateBinaryDone:\
                Invalid HTTP status"
            http::cleanup $token
            return
        } elseif {[http::ncode $token] == 404} {
            log::warn "checkAutoupdateBinaryDone:\
                Server does not provide updates for this binary"
            http::cleanup $token
            return
        } elseif {[http::ncode $token] != 200} {
            log::error "checkAutoupdateBinaryDone:\
                Invalid HTTP code [http::ncode $token]"
            http::cleanup $token
            return
        } else {
```

In case the transfer succeeds, we create the `autoupdate-<binaryname>` filename as `aufilename` variable:

```
set aufilename [file join \
    [file dirname [info nameofexecutable]] \
    "autoupdate-[file tail [info nameofexecutable]]"]
log::debug "checkAutoupdateBinaryDone:\
    Writing to $aufilename"
```

We then try to write to that file and in case it fails we log an error.

```
if {[catch {
    set fh [open $aufilename w]
    fconfigure $fh -translation binary
    puts -nonewline $fh [http::data $token]
    close $fh
} error]} {
    log::error "checkAutoupdateBinaryDone:\
        Error writing autoupdate binary: $error"
} else {
```

If we were able to create the autoupdate binary, we now change its attributes to be able to run it. We run it with the same arguments that our binary was run with and exit:

```
    log::debug "checkAutoupdateBinaryDone:\
        Running $aufilename"
    catch {file attributes \
        $aufilename -permissions 0755}
    exec $aufilename {*}$::argv &
    exit 0
}

    http::cleanup $token

    }
}
```

 The code mentioned in this section is located in the `src-client/` `autoupdate.tcl` file in the `02autoupdate` directory in the source code examples for this chapter.

In addition to the automatic updates themselves, the new example also checks for automatic updates in progress when requesting jobs. The `csa::requestJobs` command now starts with the following check:

```
proc csa::requestJobs {} {
    variable hostname
    variable autoupdateInProgress

    after cancel csa::requestJobs

    if {[info exists autoupdateInProgress]} {
        log::info "requestJobs: Auto update in progress; \
            retrying in 1 minute"
        after 60000 csa::requestJobs
        return
    }
```

The changes in the code in this section are located in the `src-client/client.tcl` file in the `02autoupdate` directory, in the source code examples for this chapter.

Extending your applications

Very often applications need to be extended with additional functionalities. In many cases it is also necessary to run different code on various types of machines.

A good solution to this problem is to introduce extensibility to our application. We'll want to allow additional modules to be deployed to specified clients – this means delivering modules to clients, keeping them up to date, and handling loading and unloading of modules.

The following sections will introduce how Starkits and Tcl's VFS can be used to easily create modules for our application, and how these can be used to deploy additional code.

We'll also introduce a simple implementation of handling modules, both on server side and client side. This requires creating code for downloading modules themselves, loading them, and the mechanism for telling clients what actions they should be performing.

The server will be responsible for telling clients when they should load or unload any of the modules. They will also inform clients if any of the modules are out of date. Clients will use this information to make sure modules that are loaded are consistent, with what server expects.

The following steps will be performed by the client:

- The client sends a list of loaded modules and a list of all available modules along with their MD5 checksums to server
- The server responds with the list of modules to load, unload, and which need to be downloaded
- The client downloads modules that it needs to download; if the client already has downloaded all modules it needs, no action is taken
- The client unloads modules that it should unload and loads modules that it should load; if the client has already loaded all modules it should have, no action is taken

Handling security is an additional consideration when creating pluggable applications. Clients should check if files are authentic whenever they download any code, which will be run on the client. This can be achieved using SSL and Certificate Authorities, and such operations are described in more details in *Chapter 13*.

Starkits as extensions

One of the features Tcl offers is its VFS and using single file archives for staging entire archives. We've used these technologies to create our clients as single file executables.

Now we'll reuse similar mechanisms to create modules for our application. All modules will simply be a Starkit VFS—this will allow embedding all types of files, creating complex scripts, and easily manage whatever a module contains.

Our modules will have their MD5 checksum calculated, similar to the automatic update feature. This will allow the application to easily check whether a module needs to be updated or not. In order to deliver modules to a client, the server will allow downloading modules, similar to retrieving binaries for automatic update.

Building modules

Our modules will be built similar to how binaries were built, with a minor exception. Modules will have their MD5 checksum stored as the first 32 bytes of the file; this does not cause problems for MK4 VFS package and allows easy checking of whether a package is up to date or not.

The source code for each module will be stored in the mod-<modulename> directories. For the purpose of this implementation, clients will source the load.tcl script when loading the package and will source the unload.tcl script when unloading it. It will be up to the module to initialize and finalize itself properly.

The directory and file structure in the following screenshot show how files for modules are laid out.

It is based on previous example and only the `mod-comm` and `mod-helloworld` directories are new.

We'll need to modify the `build.tcl` script and the add code responsible for building of modules. We can do this after the initial binaries have been built.

First let's create the `modules` directory:

```
file mkdir modules
```

Then we'll iterate over each module to build and create name of the target file:

```
foreach module {helloworld comm} {
    set modfile [file join modules $module.kit]
```

We'll start off by creating a 32 byte file:

```
set fh [open $modfile w]
fconfigure $fh -translation binary
puts -nonewline $fh [string repeat "\0" 32]
close $fh
```

Next we'll create the VFS, copy the source code of the module, and unmount it:

```
vfs::mk4::Mount $modfile $modfile
docopy mod-$module $modfile
vfs::unmount $modfile
```

Now, calculate the MD5 checksum of the newly created module:

```
set md5 [md5::md5 -hex -file $modfile]
```

And set the first 32 bytes to the checksum:

```
    set fh [open $modfile r+]
    fconfigure $fh -translation binary
    seek $fh 0 start
    puts -nonewline $fh $md5
    close $fh
}
```

We'll create two modules—helloworld and comm. The first one will simply log "Hello world!" every 30 seconds. The second one will set up a comm interface that can be used for testing and debugging purposes.

Let's start with creating the mod-helloworld/load.tcl script which will be responsible for initializing the helloworld module:

```
csa::log::info "Loading helloworld module"

namespace eval helloworld {}

proc helloworld::hello {} {
    csa::log::info "Hello world!"
    after cancel helloworld::hello
    after 30000 helloworld::hello
}

helloworld::hello
```

Our module will log the information that it has been loaded ,and write out hello world to the log. The helloworld::hello command also schedules itself to be run every 30 seconds.

The mod-helloworld/unload.tcl script that cleans up the module looks like this:

```
csa::log::info "Unloading helloworld module"

after cancel helloworld::hello

namespace delete helloworld
```

This will log information about the unloading of a module, cancel the next invocation of the helloworld::hello command, and remove the entire helloworld namespace.

Implementing the comm module is also simple. The mod-comm/load.tcl script is as follows:

```
csa::log::info "Loading comm module"

package require comm

comm::comm configure -port 1992 -listen 1 -local 1
```

This script simply loads the comm package, sets it up to listen on port 1992, and only accepts connections on the local interface.

Unloading the package (in mod-comm/unload.tcl) will configure the comm interface not to listen for incoming connections:

```
csa::log::info "Unloading comm module"

comm::comm configure -listen 0
```

As the comm package cannot be simply unloaded, the best solution is for load.tcl to configure it to listen for connections and unload.tcl to disable listening.

Server side

The server side of extensibility needs to perform several activities. First of all we need to track which clients should be using which modules. The second function is providing clients with modules to download. The third functionality is telling clients which modules they need to fetch from the server, and which ones that they need to load or unload from the environment.

Let's start off with adding initialization of the modules directory to our server. We need to add it to src-server/main.tcl:

```
set csa::binariesdirectory [file join [pwd] binaries]
set csa::modulesdirectory [file join [pwd] modules]
set csa::datadirectory [file join [pwd] data]
```

We'll also need to load an additional script for handling this functionality:

```
csa::log::debug "Sourcing remaining files"
source [file join $starkit::topdir commapi.tcl]
source [file join $starkit::topdir database.tcl]
source [file join $starkit::topdir clientrequest.tcl]
source [file join $starkit::topdir autoupdate.tcl]
source [file join $starkit::topdir clientmodules.tcl]
```

Next we'll also need to modify `src-server/database.tcl` to add support for storing the modules list. We'll need to add a new table definition to script that creates all tables:

```
CREATE TABLE clientmodules (
    client CHAR(36) NOT NULL,
    module VARCHAR(255) NOT NULL
);
```

In order to work on the data we'll also need commands to add or remove a module for a specified client:

```
proc csa::setClientModule {client module enabled} {
    if {[llength [db eval \
        {SELECT guid FROM clients WHERE guid=$client
            AND status=1}]] == 0} {
        return false
    }

    db eval {DELETE FROM clientmodules WHERE
        client=$client AND module=$module}

    if {$enabled} {
        db eval {INSERT INTO clientmodules (client, module)
            VALUES($client, $module)}
    }

    return true
}
```

Our command starts off by checking if a client exists and returns immediately if it does not. In the next step, we delete any existing entries and insert a new row if we've been asked to enable a particular module for a specified client.

We'll also need to be able to list modules associated with a particular client, which means executing a simple SQL query to list modules:

```
proc csa::getClientModules {client} {
    return [lsort [db eval {SELECT module
        FROM clientmodules WHERE client=$client}]]
}
```

Then we'll need to create the `clientmodules.tcl` file that will have functionality related to handling modules, and providing them to clients.

The first thing required is a function to read MD5 checksums from modules. We'll first check if the file exists and return an empty string if it does not, otherwise we'll read and return the first 32 bytes of the file:

```
proc csa::getModuleMD5 {name} {
    variable modulesdirectory

    set filename [file join $modulesdirectory $name]

    if {![file exists $filename]} {
        return ""
    }
    set fh [open $filename r]
    fconfigure $fh -translation binary
    set md5 [read $fh 32]
    close $fh
    return $md5
}
```

Next we'll create a function that takes a client identifier, queries the database for modules for that client and returns a list of module-md5sum pairs, which can be treated as a dictionary – where the key is the module name and the value is its md5 checksum.

```
proc csa::getClientModulesMD5 {client} {
    set rc [list]
    foreach module [getClientModules $client] {
        lappend rc $module [getModuleMD5 $module]
    }
    return $rc
}
```

Another function will handle requests for a particular module. Similar to how it is implemented for automatic updates, we'll provide files only from a single directory and handle cases where a file does not exist, and register a prefix for the requests in TclHttpd:

```
proc csa::handleClientModule {sock suffix} {
    variable modulesdirectory
    set filename [file join $modulesdirectory \
        [file tail $suffix]]

    log::debug "handleClientModule: File name: $filename"
    if {[file exists $filename]} {
        Httpd_ReturnFile $sock application/octet-stream \
```

```
                $filename
        } else {
            log::warn "handleClientModule: $filename not found"
            Httpd_Error $sock 404
        }
    }
}


    Url_PrefixInstall /client/module csa::handleClientModule
```

For communication with the clients, we'll reuse the protocol for requesting jobs.

We also need a function that given a client identifier, request dictionary, and name of the response variable will provide information to the client. It will also return whether a client should be provided with a list of jobs or not. If a client will need to download new or updated modules first, we do not need to provide a list of jobs as the client will need to have updated modules first.

Let's start by making sure that both the modules available on the client and the list of loaded modules has been sent to the client:

```
    proc csa::csaHandleClientModules {guid req responsevar} {
        upvar 1 $responsevar response

        set ok true

        if {[dict exists $req availableModules]
            && [dict exists $req loadedModules]} {
```

Then we copy the values to local variables for convenience, and get a list of modules that a client should have along with their MD5 checksums.

```
            set rAvailable [dict get $req availableModules]
            set rLoaded [dict get $req loadedModules]
            set lAvailable [getClientModulesMD5 $guid]
```

We'll also create a list of actions we want to pass back to the client— the list of modules it needs to download and the list of modules to load and unload. By default, all lists are empty and we'll add items only if we detect that the client should perform actions:

```
            set downloadList [list]
            set loadList [list]
            set unloadList [list]
```

As the first step, we'll iterate over the modules that the client should have and check if it has them — if the client either does not have a module or its checksum differs, we'll tell the client to download it.

```
foreach {module md5} $lAvailable {
    if {(![dict exists $rAvailable $module]) ||
    ([dict get $rAvailable $module] != $md5)} {
        lappend downloadList $module
    }
```

After this we check if the client has already loaded this module. If not, we'll tell him to load the module.

```
    if {[lsearch -exact $rLoaded $module] < 0} {
        lappend loadList $module
    }
}
```

We'll also iterate over the modules that the client currently has loaded and if any of them should not be loaded according to our list, we'll tell the client to unload it.

```
foreach module $rLoaded {
    if {![dict exists $lAvailable $module]} {
        lappend unloadList $module
    }
}
```

Once we've conducted our comparison, we tell the agent what should be done. If he needs to download any modules, we only return this information and return that there is no point in providing the list of jobs to perform:

```
if {[llength $downloadList] > 0} {
    dict set response moduleDownload \
        $downloadList
    set ok false
} else {
```

Otherwise if all modules on the client are updated, we provide a list of modules to load or unload if this is needed.

```
    if {[llength $loadList] > 0} {
        dict set response moduleLoad \
            $loadList
    }

    if {[llength $unloadList] > 0} {
        dict set response moduleUnload \
            $unloadList
    }
}
```

Finally, we return whether or not we should provide the client with a list of jobs to perform or not:

```
    }

    return $ok
}
```

Now we'll need to modify the `csa::handleClientProtocol` command in the `src-server/clientrequest.tcl` file to invoke our newly created `csa::csaHandleClientModules` command:

```
if {[csaHandleClientModules \
    $guid $req response]} {
    # only specify jobs if client
    # has all the modules

    if {[dict exists $req joblimit]} {
        set joblimit [dict get $req joblimit]
    } else {
        set joblimit 10
    }

    dict set response jobs \
        [getJobs $guid $joblimit]
    log::debug "handleClientProtocol: Jobs:\
        [llength [dict get $response jobs]]"
}
```

This will cause jobs to be added only if the `csaHandleClientModules` command returned true.

We can also modify the `csa::apihandle` command in the `src-server/commapi.tcl` file to allow adding or removing a module from a client. The following needs to be added inside the main switch responsible for handling commands:

```
switch -- $cmd {
    addClientModule {
        lassign $command cmd client module
        return [setClientModule $client $module 1]
    }
    removeClientModule {
        lassign $command cmd client module
        return [setClientModule $client $module 0]
    }
```

These commands simply invoke the `csa::setClientModule` command created earlier.

 All changes are located in the `src-server` directory in the `03extensions` directory in the source code examples for this chapter.

Handling modules on client

The first thing that we'll need to implement on the client is support for handling modules—storage, loading and unloading, and keeping the state of the currently loaded modules.

Let's start off with adding initialization of the `modules` directory to our server. We need to add it to `src-client/main.tcl`:

```
set csa::datadirectory [file join [pwd] data]
set csa::modulesdirectory [file join [pwd] data modules]

file mkdir $csa::datadirectory
file mkdir $csa::modulesdirectory
```

Next we'll need to add loading of `clientmodules.tcl`, which will hold all scripts related to handling modules:

```
source [file join $starkit::topdir fileinfo.tcl]
source [file join $starkit::topdir autoupdate.tcl]
source [file join $starkit::topdir database.tcl]
source [file join $starkit::topdir client.tcl]
source [file join $starkit::topdir clientmodules.tcl]
```

The `clientmodules.tcl` file will hold all scripts related to modules. We'll start off by creating the code for getting the MD5 checksum of a module. Implementation on the client will use the `modulemd5cache` array for caching checksums of a module.

Caching checksums is needed because of the way that VFS is implemented, reading MD5 checksum is not possible for currently loaded modules. Also, this will speed up operations and as the client will download updates on its own, it is safe to keep MD5 checksums cached here.

```
proc csa::getModuleMD5 {module} {
    variable modulesdirectory
    variable modulemd5cache
    if {![info exists modulemd5cache($module)]} {
```

If we don't know the checksum of the requested module we'll initialize it. If the file exists, then read the first 32 bytes and store it in the cache. If the file does not exist, we set it to an empty string:

```
        set filename [file join $modulesdirectory $module]
        if {[file exists $filename]} {
            set fh [open $filename r]
            fconfigure $fh -translation binary
            set modulemd5cache($module) [read $fh 32]
            close $fh
        } else {
            set modulemd5cache($module) ""
        }
    }
    return $modulemd5cache($module)
}
```

We'll also need a procedure that removes the MD5 cache for a specified module:

```
proc csa::cleanModuleCache {module} {
    variable modulemd5cache

    catch {unset modulemd5cache($module)}
}
```

This will be needed in case we download a new version as we need to make sure our client does not use an older version of the checksum.

Now, we'll create a function to list all modules that are available locally to this client. We'll simply use the `glob` command to list items in the `modules` directory matching `*.kit`:

```
proc csa::getAvailableModules {} {
    variable modulesdirectory

    return [lsort [glob -nocomplain -tails \
        -directory $modulesdirectory *.kit]]
}
```

Similar to the server-side implementation, we'll also create a function that returns all local modules along with their MD5 checksums.

```
proc csa::getAvailableModulesMD5 {} {
    set rc [list]
    foreach module [getAvailableModules] {
        lappend rc $module [getModuleMD5 $module]
    }
    return $rc
}
```

Let's implement the loading of a particular module. The command returns whether the package has been successfully loaded or not.

We'll store all currently loaded modules in the `loadedmodule` array — loading package first checks if the specified package has currently been loaded. If it has been, we return the following code immediately:

```
proc csa::loadModule {module} {
    variable loadedmodule
    variable modulesdirectory

    set filename [file join $modulesdirectory $module]

    if {[info exists loadedmodule($module)]} {
        return true
    }
}
```

Then we check if a module exists. If it does not, its checksum is empty. In this case, too, we exit:

```
if {[getModuleMD5 $module] == ""} {
    return false
}
```

Assuming the module exists we'll now mount it as read only and initialize the `loadedmodule` value for the specified module to the output of mounting the VFS, and source the VFS's `load.tcl` script:

```
set loadedmodule($module) \
    [vfs::mk4::Mount $filename $filename -readonly]

if {[catch {
    uplevel #0 [list \
        source [file join $filename load.tcl] \
        ]
} error]} {
```

If sourcing the script fails, we log an error and unload the module. We'll also

```
        log::error "Error loading module $module: $error"
        unloadModule $module true
        return false
    }


    return true
}
```

Now let's create the command to unload a module. It returns whether the package needed to be unloaded or not. Unloading a package works in similar way to loading it. We start off by checking if it is currently loaded:

```
proc csa::unloadModule {module} {
    variable loadedmodule
    variable modulesdirectory

    set filename [file join $modulesdirectory $module]

    if {![info exists loadedmodule($module)]} {
        return false
    }
```

If a package is currently loaded, we source the `unload.tcl` script. If it fails, we log an error, but continue anyway.

```
    if {[catch {
        uplevel #0 [list \
            source [file join $filename unload.tcl] \
            ]
    } error]} {
        log::error "Error unloading module $module: $error"
    }
```

Then we try to unmount the VFS. If that fails, we again log an error:

```
    if {[catch {
        vfs::unmount $filename
    } error]} {
        log::error "Error unloading module $module: $error"
    }
```

Finally, we unset `loadedmodule` for a specified module and return:

```
unset loadedmodule($module)

return true
}
```

We can also create a function to list all currently loaded modules:

```
proc csa::getLoadedModules {} {
    variable loadedmodule
    return [lsort [array names loadedmodule]]
}
```

We simply return keys for the `loadedmodule` array since they correspond to the currently loaded modules.

Communication with server

Now that the `csa` client can handle modules, we'll need to implement retrieving information about them from the server.

It will need to send a list of all available modules, along with their checksums, and a list of currently loaded ones. Then the server will tell it which modules to download, load, and unload.

In order to do that we'll need to modify the `csa::requestJobs`, and `csa::requestJobsDone` commands in the `src-client/client.tcl` file.

The first thing is that in `csa::requestJobs` we need to add a feature for sending the list of modules:

```
set url "http://${hostname}:8981/client/protocol"
set req [dict create]

dict set req guid $::csa::guid
dict set req password $::csa::password

dict set req availableModules \
    [getAvailableModulesMD5]

dict set req loadedModules \
    [getLoadedModules]
```

This will cause information about modules to be sent.

Next, in the `csa::requestJobsDone` command we need to handle the processing of the response related to modules:

```
if {$ok} {
    if {![processModulesResponse $response]} {
        after cancel csa::requestJobs
        after 3600000 csa::requestJobs
        log::info "requestJobsDone: Rescheduling next\
            communications for in 1 hour from now"
    }

    # evaluate jobs to perform if any are available
    if {[dict exists $response jobs]
        && ([llength [dict get $response jobs]] > 0)} {
        runJobs [dict get $response jobs]
    }
} else {
    log::error "requestJobsDone: Server returned error"
}
```

What we do is invoke the `csa::processModulesResponse` command with the response. If it returns false, we schedule the next communication for after one hour from now. The command will return false if new modules need to be downloaded — in this case, we schedule the next communication in one hour in case downloading the modules fails.

We now need to write the procedure for handling part of the response related to modules.

We start by checking if a list of modules to download has been returned. If it has, we initialize the download of all modules and return.

```
proc csa::processModulesResponse {response} {
    if {[dict exists $response moduleDownload]} {
        downloadModules [dict get $response moduleDownload]
        return false
    }
```

Now we check if there are any modules to load or unload. We then iterate over the lists and load or unload the modules appropriately:

```
if {[dict exists $response moduleLoad]} {
    foreach module [dict get $response moduleLoad] {
        log::info "Loading module $module"
        loadModule $module
    }
}
if {[dict exists $response moduleUnload]} {
```

```
        foreach module [dict get $response moduleUnload] {
            log::info "Unloading module $module"
            unloadModule $module
        }
    }

    return true
}
```

We'll implement downloading one or more modules asynchronously. The idea is that the `csa::downloadModules` command will start the download of the first module in the list, and pass any remaining modules as arguments to the `csa::downloadModulesDone` callback, which will be invoked when HTTP request is done. Then we'll write the module to disk and if there are any other modules pending for download, we'll invoke the `csa::downloadModules` command again with remaining modules. This will then be done until all modules have been downloaded.

Let's start by creating the `csa::downloadModules` command. It gets the first module from the list and stores any remaining modules. Next we create the URL to the module and unload this module, if it is currently loaded. Unloading will allow us to write to that module later on.

```
proc csa::downloadModules {modules} {
    variable hostname

    set module [lindex $modules 0]
    set modules [lrange $modules 1 end]

    log::debug "downloadModules: Downloading $module; \
        [llength $modules] modules remaining"

    set url http://${hostname}:8981/client/module/$module
    unloadModule $module
```

Next we try to initialize an HTTP request to specified URL. We provide the callback command that gets both current module and list of remaining modules passed as arguments.

In case of any errors, we log them and initialize the next communication with the server in one minute.

```
    if {[catch {
        http::geturl $url \
            -timeout 900000 -binary 1 -command [list \
```

```
                csa::downloadModulesDone $module $modules]
    }]} {
        log::error "downloadModules: Unable to \
            download module $module"

        # set up next request for jobs sooner
        after cancel csa::requestJobs
        after 60000 csa::requestJobs
    }
}
```

Once the download of a module has been completed, our callback is invoked. We start off by checking for errors in the HTTP transaction.

```
proc csa::downloadModulesDone {module modules token} {
    variable modulesdirectory

    if {[http::status $token] != "ok"} {
        log::error "downloadModulesDone: Invalid HTTP status"
    } elseif {[http::ncode $token] == 404} {
        log::warn "downloadModulesDone:\
            Server does not provide module $module"
    } elseif {[http::ncode $token] != 200} {
        log::error "downloadModulesDone: Invalid HTTP code"
    } else {
```

If no error has occurred, we write the module to disk. We then clear the cache of this module's checksum and clean up the HTTP token.

```
        log::info "downloadModulesDone: Module $module \
            downloaded"
        set filename [file join $modulesdirectory $module]
        set fh [open $filename w]
        fconfigure $fh -translation binary
        puts -nonewline $fh [http::data $token]
        close $fh

        cleanModuleCache $module

        http::cleanup $token
```

Finally, we check if there are any additional modules to download. If there are, we retrieve them. If there are no more modules to download, we initialize the next communication as soon as possible to request which modules to load and get jobs to perform.

```
if {[llength $modules] > 0} {
    downloadModules $modules
} else {
    log::info "downloadModulesDone: All modules \
        have been downloaded"
    after cancel csa::requestJobs
    after idle csa::requestJobs
}
return
}
```

Regardless of the presence of any additional modules, we also return from the procedure here.

The following code will get run if we ran into any problems. It will clean up the HTTP token and set up the next communication for one minute from now.

```
http::cleanup $token
after cancel csa::requestJobs
after 60000 csa::requestJobs
return
}
```

 The source code for both module handling and communication related to modules is located in the src-client/clientmodules.tcl file in the 03extensions directory in the source code examples for this chapter.

Improving scalability and performance

The preceding example shows a simple application that uses a local SQLite database, and performs all operations on a single machine. However, as the number of clients we need to support grows, our application would need to change part of the approach in order to support a large number of clients.

In most small and medium sized cases it is sufficient to create an application that works on a single system, in some cases it is worth considering how to make our application scale better.

One or more of the following steps can be done to gain better scalability and improve its performance:

- Create multiple systems for managing subsets of clients and create an application that works on top of servers, and points clients to the appropriate servers. Clients could initially ask for the actual server to communicate with, and then contact this server. The comm API would then also be handled in a similar case — a single interface could be exposed that would query the server manager for the actual server managing a particular client. That API would then proxy the command to the actual server and pass the result back to the caller. The approach is similar to load balancing, but instead of simply redirecting the requests we also split database — a server responsible for a subset of clients will only store data related to these clients.

- Split where parts of the application are carried out. For example, a different system can provide clients with updates to binaries and offer download of modules. Other systems could serve only requests for jobs and module information. In addition to this, static files such as binaries, modules, and their checksums can be served by a dedicated web server which does not even have to be Tclhttpd based

- Optimize when agents connect to spread the load of handling requests over time. This can be done by providing agents the exact times to query the data, so that server would always add new clients into slots that have least load. An alternate approach is to allow server to tell clients to try again in specified amount of time, and use this when server is overloaded with requests to process.

- Use a more scalable database, and set up a dedicated system just for the database that our application would then access remotely.

All of the items recently mentioned are independent, and can be implemented separately or combined to get better performance.

Summary

Throughout this chapter we've created a complete solution for creating a client-server application in Tcl.

In this chapter we learned to:

- Create a client-server application based on HTTP protocol and Tclhttpd as an embedded web server packed into Starkit technology for easy deployment
- Build a polling-based application for performing tasks on clients and sending their results back to server, as well as provide comm interface to invoke tasks using server
- Create support for automatic update of clients based on Starkit technology
- Create extensible applications using Tcl-based modules and an automated model, for managing and automatic update of modules

This chapter does not focus on the security aspects of our application. We have only used a trivial mechanism of validating clients by using passwords, which are sent using clear text. Chapter 13 introduces SSL based security, and shows how similar example can be extended to use SSL and Certificate Authority for authentication.

The next chapter shows how to create web services from Tcl. It shows how to use XML-RPC and SOAP based services, and how to build your own SOAP-based web service.

12
SOAP and XML-RPC

By now, we have learned about invoking commands remotely in Tcl. We have used the `comm` package, deployed debugger remotely, connected using TclDevKit Inspector, and provided other interfaces with which to run Tcl commands. While all these solutions have their uses, their disadvantage is that they are limited to the Tcl language only.

Often, we need our applications to talk to or export services to other parts of our company's IT infrastructure. The problem, that applications written in different languages need to be able to communicate with each other, has been known for a long time. Fortunately, there are standards that describe how to export methods in a cross-language manner. In this chapter, we'll learn about two of them which are in common use.

We'll start by learning about **XML-RPC**, which is a protocol for invoking remote methods based on XML and HTTP. This protocol defines how sending simple and complex data types can be done, as well as sending single items and lists of elements. The standard also provides a means of delivering errors.

XML-RPC is designed so that requests are fairly simple and basically require passing the name of the method to invoke along with all parameters, and specifying their name and data type. The standard does not define a means for querying available methods and / or their parameters. This means that in order to use a service over XML-RPC, we need to know the names of the methods and parameters they accept.

Another standard is **SOAP**, which stands for Simple Object Access Protocol. It is a much more complex standard based on XML and also used over HTTP protocol. It specifies how to send both simple and complex data types, similar to XML-RPC. It also defines means for providing errors.

In addition to this, SOAP defines a standard for describing all available methods, their parameters and the data types used in a service. The standard is called **WSDL**, which stands for Web Service Definition Language. Usually all that is needed to use a SOAP based service is to either know the URL of the WSDL definition or have the WSDL definition itself. It provides applications with definitions of all methods used along with their parameters, and is used by the majority of languages to build commands to be invoked.

Tcl and standards for remote procedure calls

Tcl offers packages for both clients and servers of various standards. Even though this book focuses on XML-RPC and SOAP, Tcl also supports other standards, such as JSON-RPC, SOAP over SMTP, and can easily be used for REST interfaces — using JSON, XML, and other formats for passing data.

The previous chapter shows how to implement such an interface using Tcl's dictionaries. Using XML would only require using the tDOM package, which was described in Chapter 5. JSON, which stands for JavaScript Object Notation is an open standards based, widely used web application which is derived from JavaScript. Currently, the Tcl package json only offers functionality for mapping JSON to Tcl dictionaries. Creating json responses requires us to create our own code for writing to JSON data.

For XML-RPC we'll be using the Tcl package XMLRPC available from http://tclsoap. sourceforge.net/. These packages are also available in the ActiveTcl distribution so all the packages you need will already be available if you are using ActiveTcl.

This package offers an easy to use XML-RPC client and server, which we can use to communicate with other websites. It provides an intuitive way to invoke APIs, and requires very little knowledge of either XML-RPC or its internals to use it.

XML-RPC has been designed as a fairly simple protocol. It supports various data types, but does not provide a way to describe the service as part of the protocol itself. An opposite approach has been introduced in SOAP. It is a service that is more complex than XML-RPC, and offers a language (WSDL) for describing web services that can be parsed by SOAP client libraries.

For SOAP communication we'll be using a different package than for XML-RPC. We'll use the Web Services for Tcl package available from http://code.google. com/p/tclws/. Even though the SOAP package also provides SOAP support, tclws has better support for SOAP itself as well as the WSDL standard. It also has more active development and support.

This package provides full support for WSDL, which means that in order to invoke an existing SOAP API all we need to do is point to the URL to WSDL, and we can then instantly use all remote methods. It also supports complex data types.

The Web Services for Tcl package allows exporting of APIs. It uses `Tclhttpd` as the web server for providing APIs over HTTP (non-SSL) and HTTPS (encrypted using SSL). The package uses the `/service` URL prefix for providing various SOAP services. Aside from that, that Tclhttpd instance can be shared with other parts of the application—so we can use one Tclhttpd instance and same TCP port, for both SOAP features and other functionality exposed by our application.

When creating a web service, Web Services for Tcl generates a WSDL for it automatically. This can be used by any SOAP application to use methods exposed by our application, and makes using our services much easier for any external developer. In addition to this, the package also generates a user-friendly HTML page that documents the entire API. It shows all methods, data types, and additional information.

The Web Services for Tcl package requires the `tDOM` package for accessing XML and DOM inside SOAP. This package is available from `http://www.tdom.org/`. It is also part of the ActiveTcl distribution so running tclws package from ActiveTcl should work smoothly.

The following table summarizes protocols:

Protocol	Tcl package (link)	Functionality covered
XML-RPC	XMLRPC (`http://tclsoap.sourceforge.net/`)	Client
SOAP	tclws (`http://code.google.com/p/tclws/`)	Server, Client

Connecting to XML-RPC services

Using XML-RPC to call commands remotely from Tcl is trivial. A new Tcl command will be created for each method, which makes invoking remote functions almost the same as invoking local commands.

As mentioned earlier, invoking any XML-RPC command requires knowing the available remote methods and their definitions. We also need to know the address of the remote service.

Invoking a command using XML-RPC will look similar to:

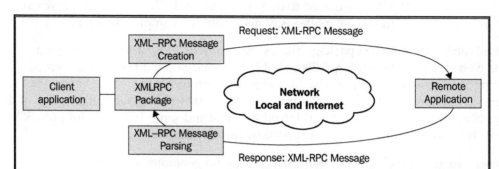

All requests are sent over HTTP or HTTPS to the remote application, building an XML-RPC message and sending it in the request. The response is also XML-RPC content and is then parsed by the XMLRPC package.

Defining available methods

In order to perform any XML-RPC operations in Tcl, we first need to load the XMLRPC package:

```
package require XMLRPC
```

Invoking commands over XML-RPC requires us to define the names of functions, which we want to invoke as well as list all the input parameters that they take. The XMLRPC package will then create a Tcl command that we can invoke directly.

We can use the XMLRPC::create function to create new methods that we will invoke remotely. It takes the Tcl command name to create as the first argument and additional options as name-value pairs.

The option -proxy is used to specify URL to the remote XML-RPC handler and has to be specified. Another mandatory option -params specifies parameters that should be passed to the application, specified as name-datatype pairs list. We can also specify the option -name, which indicates the method name to invoke. If not specified, the XML-RPC method name is the same as the name of the Tcl command to create.

For example, in order to create a simple command to invoke XML-RPC we can do:

```
XMLRPC::create "someMethod" -proxy http://localhost/xmlrpc \
    -params {firstname string lastname string}
```

This describes the someMethod method which should be passed to http://localhost/xmlrpc. It will pass the firstname and lastname arguments as strings.

This will create a Tcl command called someMethod . Then, invoking it is as simple as:

```
set result [someMethod "John" "Doe"]
```

Specifying data types

There are two kinds of data type in XML-RPC—simple and complex. Simple data types are scalar values such as strings, numbers, or dates. Complex data types are composed of one or more other data types, such as a structure describing a person which includes information such as first name and last name.

XML-RPC allows the following simple data types:

Data type	Description	Example
string	Any text	Sample text
i4, int	32-bit integer; i4 indicates integer stored over 4 bytes in memory	15360
double	Floating point value	6.25
boolean	Boolean value	1
dateTime.iso8601	Date and time	2009-12-06T23:34:45
base64	base64-encoded binary	U2FtcGxlIHRleHQ=

The XMLRPC package does not transform values in any way; so it is the responsibility of the application calling the methods to prepare values for all fields in the appropriate way.

The date time data type needs to be formatted in accordance with ISO-8601. Usually it is sufficient to specify it in the YYYY-MM-DDTHH:MM:SS format. An example might be 2009-12-06T23:34:45. We can use Tcl's clock command to format and / or scan values. The command clock scan will handle converting any value properly. The command clock format using %Y-%m-%dT%H:%M:%S as formatting string can be used to convert a timestamp back to a conforming date and time representation. For example:

```
% set time [clock scan "2009-12-06T23:34:45"]
1260117285
% puts [clock format $time -format "%Y-%m-%dT%H:%M:%S"]
2009-12-06T17:34:45
```

Complex data types are defined using the rpcvar::typedef command. It takes two arguments— the definition of a data type as the first parameter and the name of data type as the second.

For example, to create a person data type that consists of the strings `firstname` and `lastname` we can do the following:

```
::rpcvar::typedef {
    firstname string
    lastname string
} person
```

Next we can use this as a definition of the data type for parameters to commands:

```
::XMLRPC::create getUserId -proxy $url -params \
    [list person person]
```

The complex data type is built by specifying a list of name-value pairs where names are fields within a data type, and values are the values of the corresponding fields. This means that values can be built as lists, taken from the `array get` command or passed as dictionary objects.

For example, we can use the latter method in the following way:

```
set id [getUserId [list firstname John lastname Doe]]
```

The XML-RPC standard also covers arrays of elements, which are zero or more items of specified type. Not to be confused with Tcl arrays, arrays in XML-RPC are the equivalent of Tcl lists.

In order to specify an array of a specified data type as an input parameter we need to append `()` to data type; `integer()` means an array of integers.

For example, we can specify that a method accepts a list of integers by doing the following:

```
::XMLRPC::create getUsers -proxy $url -params \
    [list ids integer()]
```

In order to specify an array as an argument, we need to provide a Tcl list with all of the items that should be put in the array. For example, we can invoke the `getUsers` method to get information about users with an id of 1, 2, and 3 by doing:

```
set userInfo [getUsers [list 1 2 3]]
```

Similarly, we can specify an array of complex data types. For example, person() specifies an array of `person` objects:

```
::XMLRPC::create lookupUsers -proxy $url -params \
    [list people person()]
```

Specifying an array of complex data type requires us to create a Tcl list, where each element is a name-value pairs list that specifies a particular item.

For example, we can invoke preceding method as follows:

```
set idList [lookupUsers [list \
    [list firstname John lastname Doe] \
    [list firstname James lastname Smith] \
    ]
```

This will pass two items to the method.

While it is required to specify data types for parameters passed as input for methods, output from methods is handled automatically by the XMLRPC package. The following table shows how various return types are mapped to Tcl:

Return type	Mapping to Tcl	Example
Simple type, one element	As value	`2009-12-06T23:34:45`
Complex type, one element	As name-value pairs list	`{Firstname John lastname Doe}`
Array of simple types	As list of values	`{John James}`
Array of complex types	As list of name-value pairs lists	`{{firstname John lastname Doe} {firstname James lastname Smith}}`

An example of retrieving complex data types is shown in next section of this chapter.

Using XML-RPC

We can now move on to a more practical example of XML-RPC usage. Nowadays many websites, blogs, and CMS systems offer an XML-RPC based mechanism for managing them. They either offer standard APIs or custom APIs that are described in manuals.

A good example can be using XML-RPC to post blogs. Many websites offer one or more standard API sets:

- Blogger API — described at `http://www.blogger.com/developers/api/1_docs/`

- Movable Type API — described at `http://www.sixapart.com/developers/xmlrpc/movable_type_api/`

- MetaWeblog API — described at `http://www.xmlrpc.com/metaWeblogApi`

Even though the majority of these standards have been created by commercial companies, they are in wide use in multiple products such as Joomla, WordPress, and Blogger from Google.

For example, the following is a definition of the Blogger API's `blogger.newPost` method:

```
XMLRPC::create "blogger.newPost" \
    -proxy "http://www.yoursite.com/xmlrpc.php" \
    -params {appkey string blogid string
        username string password string
        content string publish boolean}
```

For our example we'll use blogger API. While this has been tested on a WordPress installation, all these methods are available in majority of blogging engines. We'll create a function to create all XML-RPC invocations so that we can easily attach it to more blogs.

When posting to applications over the Internet, there are multiple ways to authenticate. The most commonly used is to provide username and password, which usually is the same as the one used for accessing the administrative panel.

Another idea is to use application keys, which are unique identifiers assigned to each application or generated for each website. They are usually provided along with a secret key, and are used instead of providing the username and password. This allows different credentials to be used for real users and applications. Application keys can also be used in addition to the username and password, in which case the user needs to provide their usual username and password and also provide an application ID.

The blogger API is an example of an API that used to use application keys. Even though the blogger API requires specifying `appkey`, this is no longer used by the majority of blogging engines. It is recommended that you specify the value `0123456789ABCDEF` for `appkey` unless your blog specifies a key to use.

In this example we'll do the following:

- Initialize a namespace `initblogger` for our command that initializes blog API in a separate namespace
- Create the command `initblogger::initBlogger` that creates commands from the blogger API in a specified namespace; it will accept a Tcl namespace name as the first argument and the URL to the actual blog as the second arugment

- Set up our sample blog's functions as the `::myblog` Tcl namespace
- Post a sample entry to the blog

First let's create the namespace `initblogger` for our command:

```
namespace eval initblogger {}
```

Next, we'll create the `initBlogger` command, which takes new a namespace name and the URL to the blog's XML-RPC interface.

```
proc initblogger::initBlogger {namespace url} {
```

Now we'll create the target namespace.

```
namespace eval $namespace {}
```

Then, we'll iterate over the list of methods and the parameters they take. These are blogger API methods, and the field definition is as described in its documentation. The inside `foreach` loop will create a command in specified namespace, using the URL specified. The command name and argument are taken from the list we iterate over.

```
foreach {command parameters} {
    blogger.getUsersBlogs {
        appkey string
        username string password string
    }
    blogger.newPost {
        appkey string blogid string
        username string password string
        content string publish boolean
    }
    blogger.editPost {
        appkey string postid string
        username string password
        string content string publish boolean
    }
} {

    ::XMLRPC::create ${namespace}::$command -proxy $url \
        -params $parameters -name $command
}
}
```

After this, we can configure our blog's authentication details and URL; this needs to be replaced by real information, obviously.

```
set blogAppkey "0123456789ABCDEF"
set blogUsername "YourUsername"
set blogPassword "YourPassword"
set blogURL "http://www.yoursite.com/xmlrpc.php"
```

And then we can set up our blog's XML-RPC methods in the `myblog` namespace:

```
initblogger::initBlogger ::myblog $blogURL
```

We are specifying the namespace as `::myblog` so that it does not get created relative to the `initblogger` namespace.

Now, we can create some sample text for our blog. The text itself can be any valid HTML. We'll set up some text consisting of the current time and the text *"This is an automated blog entry"*:

```
set text "It is <b>"
append text [clock format [clock seconds] -format "%H:%M"]
append text "</b> now."
append text "<br /><br /><i>"
append text "This is an automated blog entry."
append text "</i>"\1
```

Next we'll use the `blogger.getUsersBlogs` method to list all the blogs our user can post to.

Many people are allowed to post information on multiple blogs, which is why the blogger API uses a blog identifier to specify all blogs. We can use this similarly to find a blog matching specified criteria instead of posting on all available blogs.

```
foreach blog [::myblog::blogger.getUsersBlogs \
    $blogAppkey $blogUsername $blogPassword] {
```

This method returns an array of complex type. In order to access particular fields, we can treat the value as dictionary. In order to get the blog's identifier, we need to get the value of the `blogid` attribute:

```
set blogid [dict get $blog blogid]
puts "Adding entry to [dict get $blog url]"
```

The next step is to actually post to the blog. In this case we can post to it right away.

```
myblog::blogger.newPost \
    $blogAppkey $blogid $blogUsername $blogPassword \
    $text 1
```

Usually, especially when testing on your own blog, set the `publish` attribute to `0`. This will cause the post to be saved as draft and it should not be publicly visible.

In general it is a good idea to set up your own test blog if you want to experiment with using APIs for automating content creation. Testing on a website that contains live posts is not a good idea.

As the final step we exit after iteration through all blogs has been finished.

```
}

exit 0
```

After running the example our blog should have a new post that would state the current time and the text *"This is an automated entry"*.

The previous example is placed in the `blogger-post.tcl` file in the `01xmlrpc` directory in the source code samples for this chapter. It comes with all the libraries needed to run the code.

Using SOAP protocol

Another protocol that is a standard for invoking methods remotely over the web is SOAP. The standard itself is modular, which means that both way in which machines communicate and how content is sent can be implemented in any way. However, most implementations use XML for sending content and the HTTP / HTTPS protocol for sending information.

One of the major features of this protocol is that it is self-descriptive, which means that all that a client needs is WSDL. It specifies the available data types, methods, what arguments they accept, what is the result type. It also specifies address of host that we should use.

Usually applications first download the WSDL file from a remote server, which looks as follows:

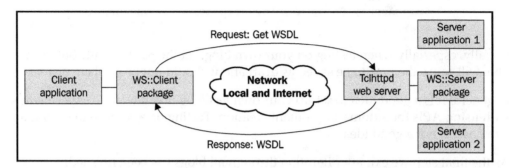

WSDL can also be sent using other means, such as a file on a disk as it includes the URL of the application. The client will be able to determine how to connect to the remote service regardless of how the service definition was provided.

Web Services for Tcl supports both retrieving WSDL over network and loading it locally. It uses the `http` package for all network communication, and supports both the HTTP and HTTPS protocols.

The server side of the `tclws` package uses Tclhttpd as a web server and can be used by more than one web service at a time. Each web service needs to have a different name. The URL to the service itself is generated based on the name and takes the form of `http://<host>:<port>/service/<serviceName>`.

After the client learns the methods and data types of server side from WSDL, it can communicate with it. This is done over the HTTP or HTTPS protocols. All requests are sent as SOAP messages that can be parsed by any of the sides. Request provides a message with the method name to invoke as well as all parameters and response provides the output from the command. This is very similar to XML-RPC.

Below is a sample communication flow in SOAP protocol:

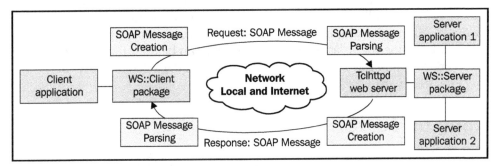

Creating Web Services

The Web Services for Tcl package allows us to create a SOAP web service that will export functionality of our application.

The package is pure Tcl and can be downloaded from `http://code.google.com/p/tclws/`. In order to install it, simply copy the contents of the folder to your Tcl distribution's `lib` directory. For example, `C:/Tcl/lib` on Microsoft Windows or `/opt/ActiveTcl-8.5/lib` on Unix systems.

In the majority of cases SOAP is used to integrate applications in a language independent way. It is also used as standardized way of providing public API access across a network, either in different parts of single application or across applications. This is different from using the `comm` package described in *Chapter 8, Using Additional Internet Services* which is used only in Tcl.

When planning a public API to our application it is a good idea to start off with designing it, and making sure it will not introduce incompatibility over time.

It is a good idea to make our application backward-compatible. For example, if we ever need to change functions or data type definition, our code should handle the case that some attributes or parameters are not specified. This can happen if the application was created against an earlier version of our API. A similar issue applies to data type definitions—if we ever add new parameters, it is a good idea to handle the case that they could be skipped and handle reasonable default values properly.

Since SOAP does not check the actual values passed by applications, we also have to keep in mind that data sent to our application needs to be checked. It can pose a security risk, especially if this information is passed "as is" to other parts of the application. A typical example is assuming that integers are always passed as integers and passing them "as is" to database - this can be used to perform an SQL injection attack. More information about this type of attack can be found at: `http://en.wikipedia.org/wiki/SQL_injection`

Setting up server

Exporting SOAP interfaces can be done using `WS::Server` package, which is part of Web Services for Tcl project. It allows defining services over Tclhttpd web server by using several commands.

Before creating any services, we need to initialize the Tclhttpd server and set up a listening connection.

For setting up Tclhttpd we'll use `tclhttpdinit` package described in *Chapter 9, Learning SNMP*. We'll also load the `WS::Server` package for setting up web services.

```
package require tclhttpdinit
package require WS::Server
```

In order to listen for HTTP connections on port 8001, we can do the following:

```
Httpd_Server 8001
```

We can also set up listening for HTTPS connections. In this case, we'll need to start by initializing the `tls` package:

```
package require tls
```

We can also generate a self-signed SSL certificate if it is not present directly from Tcl:

```
set keyfile server.key
set certfile server.pem

if {![file exists $keyfile]} {
    tls::misc req 1024 $keyfile $certfile \
        [list CN "localhost" days 7300]
}
```

This will create an SSL key which will be valid for 20 years and specified as valid for the `localhost` host name.

Next we can configure `tls` to use the newly generated certificate by doing:

```
tls::init -keyfile $keyfile -certfile $certfile
```

Finally we can set up a listening connection on port 8002:

```
Httpd_SecureServer $port
```

Creating a service

First thing that needs to be done in order to expose an API as web service is to create the service itself. The command `WS::Server::Service` can be used to define services. It accepts one or more options as arguments. The first mandatory option is `-service` which specifies the name of the service. It is used for identifying the web service inside Tcl.

The option `-host` also needs to be specified, and it specifies the host (and optionally port) that should be passed in the web service definition as a URL to invoke methods. This needs to be defined as an actual IP address, or a host name and port – such as `192.168.2.1:8001`.

When defining a service we should also specify the description option, which specifies the HTML description of the service. As part of creating a service, the `WS::Server` package also creates a HTML page describing all methods and data types, so it is a good practice to provide a description for all elements of the web service. It also serves as a good starting point for documenting our API.

The option `-mode` specifies the mode for supporting a web server; currently only Tclhttpd is supported, but in the future additional servers such as AOLserver, Wub or embedded HTTP server will be supported. Therefore it is a good practice to provide the `-mode tclhttpd` flag.

For example, our service definition can be as follows:

```
WS::Server::Service -service Myservice \
    -host "127.0.0.1:8001" \
    -description "My sample service" \
    -mode tclhttpd
```

The `WS::Server::Service` command also accepts additional options that can be used for more advanced features such as header and / or IP address authorization, or logging invocations of web services. More details can be found in the `WS::Server` documentation at `http://code.google.com/p/tclws/wiki/WSServer`.

All services are available using standard URLs. Each service has a prefix of `/service/<serviceName>`; for example, `/service/Myservice`.

In order to access this service from the local machine listening on port 8001 the URL is `http://127.0.0.1:8001/service/Myservice`. That URL always points to the HTML documentation of a web service. Here is a sample screenshot of the web page:

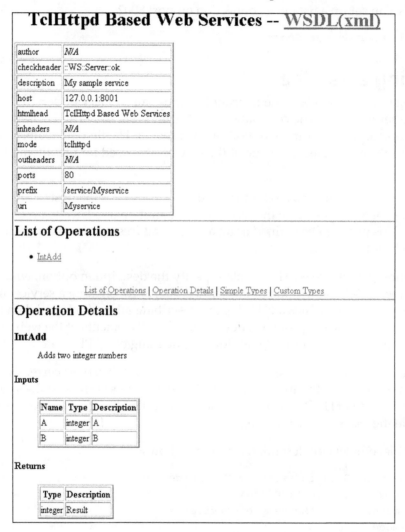

The actual WSDL for each of the services is available from the `/service/<serviceName>/wsdl` address. Actual invocations of the web service are done via `/service/<serviceName>/op` address. For our previous example, the URLs would be `http://127.0.0.1:8001/service/Myservice/wsdl` and `http://127.0.0.1:8001/service/Myservice/op` respectively.

Specifying data types

The Web Services for Tcl package specifies all data types in the same way — for all input, output, and complex structures. Information on all fields is specified as name-value pairs list. The following information should be provided:

- `type` specifies data type
- `comment` describes what a particular value provides

The first item specifies the data type and should refer to either standard data types or types defined for this service. Available types as well as how to create our own types are described later in this chapter.

The second item should be human readable information about data type. This is used for generating the HTML page that describes web service in more details. This page is generated for all web services by `tclws` package and is described later in this chapter.

The following example specifies a string type which comments `Resulting string`:

```
{type string comment {Resulting string}}
```

It is also possible to specify a list of zero or more elements by adding `[]` to data type. For example:

```
{type string[] comment {List of strings}}
```

This way our type is a list of strings. Despite having a different meaning in Tcl terms, such lists are also often referred to as arrays. Using lists in web services is shown further in the examples for both client and server applications.

Creating service methods

Now that our service is defined, we can define methods that can be invoked. The command `WS::Server::ServiceProc` can be used for this. It accepts five arguments — service name, method information, arguments list, documentation and body. Service name is the name specified as service option to `WS::Server::Service` command.

For example, a simple method for adding two integers would look as follows:

```
WS::Server::ServiceProc Myservice \
    {IntAdd {type integer comment {Result}}} \
    {
        A          {type integer comment {A}}
        B          {type integer comment {B}}
    } \
```

```
        {Adds two integer numbers} \
    {

        return [list IntAddResult [expr {$A + $B}]]

    }
```

Method information is a list of three elements that describe the operation. The first is the method name (`IntAdd` in last example), the second is the definition of the data type of the returned data.

The third parameter is a HTML description of the value returned by the method. As mentioned earlier, it is a name-value pairs list and should contain `type` and `comment` keys.

The arguments list is specified as pairs of elements, where the first item is the name of the argument, and the second item is the data type definition; `type` and `comment` also need to be specified.

The description is a HTML description of the method. It should describe what the method is doing and / or provide information about when it is ok to invoke it, similar to the usual API documentation.

Body is the Tcl code to be invoked. It is similar to creating a typical Tcl procedure. The body is evaluated in a separate stack frame as in with normal procedures. All arguments that have been specified as input can be accessed as normal variables.

The return value of the command is passed as a result to the caller, but requires specifying it in a specified format. It needs to be a dictionary or a name-value pair list, containing `<methodName>Result` as name of the only key and the actual value stored as value of that key.

From the last example, arguments `A` and `B` are simply referenced as variables, similar to how procedures are created in Tcl. As mentioned before, the result is formed as a name-value pair where the name is `IntAddResult`, which corresponds to the `IntAdd` method name and the value is actual value is an integer.

An example of a simple server is located in the `soap-server-http.tcl` and `soap-server-https.tcl` files, in the `02soap-basics` directory in the source code examples for this chapter. It comes with all the libraries needed to run the example.

Defining data types

When creating web services using the WS::Server package, there are many places where we need to define data types. One example might be when specifying arguments to a method and its return value. Another example is defining additional data types, which can then be used when creating methods.

Similar to XML-RPC, SOAP defines two types of data types: simple and complex. **Simple data types** are values of specified type such as text, integer, and date. **Complex data types** are composed of one or more values. They are also represented as dictionaries when passing complex data types to or from Tcl code.

Using simple data types

The first kind of data type is simple data types that the SOAP standard defines. These include the following types:

Data type	Description	Example
string	Textual values	Sample text
integer	Numeric values	15360
dateTime, time, date	Date and/or time representation	2009-12-06T23:34:45
boolean	Boolean value; can be 1 or 0	1
float, double	Floating point values	6.25

For more information about data types in SOAP and a complete list of data types supported by SOAP, please refer to the XML Schema documentation at http://www. w3.org/TR/2001/REC-xmlschema-2-20010502/#built-in-datatypes. From a Tcl perspective, information about the data type is not used in any way and values are passed the way they were provided by the remote peer.

When specifying dateTime, date, or time data type values we need to follow a specified pattern. A date needs to be specified as YYYY-MM-DD and time as HH:MM:SS. Specifying a value for dateTime field requires formatting it in the form of YYYY-MM-DDTHH:MM:SS, where T is the letter T. An example might be 2009-12-06T23:34:45 for dateTime, 2009-12-06 for date, and 23:34:45 for time.

Similarly to XML-RPC we can use Tcl's clock command to format and / or scan any date and / or time. The command clock scan will handle converting any value properly. The command clock format using %Y-%m-%dT%H:%M:%S, %Y-%m-%d or %H:%M:%S as formatting string can be used to convert a timestamp back to a conforming date and/or time representation.

For example:

```
% set time [clock scan "2009-12-06T23:34:45"]
1260117285
% puts [clock format $time -format "%Y-%m-%dT%H:%M:%S"]
2009-12-06T17:34:45
% puts [clock format $time -format "%Y-%m-%dT"]
2009-12-06T
% puts [clock format $time -format "%Y-%m-%d"]
2009-12-06
% puts [clock format $time -format "%H:%M:%S"]
17:34:45
```

As mentioned earlier, it is also possible to specify an array of zero or more elements as a data type by specifying data type followed by brackets, that is, `string[]`. Arrays in SOAP are equivalent of lists in Tcl.

Arrays are specified as a list of items, where each item is of the specified type. For example, an array of integers could be constructed as follows:

```
set listOfIntegers [list 12 34 56]
```

Creating complex data types

In addition to simple data types it is also possible to create complex data types; these are items that consist of one or more attributes. Each of the attributes has to be specified when creating a complex data type, and can be of any other data type. For example, the data type `Person` could be composed of two string elements: `Firstname` and `Lastname`.

Complex data types are created using `WS::Utils::ServiceTypeDef` command. It takes four arguments: mode, service name, data type name, and data type definition. The first argument specifies whether the data type is connected with the client or server definition.

When defining data types for exported services we should specify `Server` as the value for this argument. The second value is the same as the service type passed when creating a service with the `WS::Server::Service` command. The data type name is the name of the data type to be defined. It should be unique within a specified service. Multiple services can define data types with the same names, and this does not create any conflicts.

The data type definition is a list of one or more name-value pairs, which describe the attributes of a complex data type. Name should be the name of the attribute and value is the data type definition. As before, we need to specify the `type` and `comment` need to be specified. Type can be any other simple or complex data type, and comment is the HTML comment to be used when generating HTML documentation of the service.

For the purpose of showing how to create and use data types, we will create another service called `Rentbook` that will provide a service of managing users, books, and borrowing / returning books by users.

For example, in order to define a `Book` data type in `Rentbook` service which keeps track of book's identifier, its ISBN symbol, title, current status, and user owning the book:

```
WS::Utils::ServiceTypeDef Server Rentbook Book {
     id              {type integer comment {User identifier}}
     isbn            {type string comment {ISBN number}}
     title           {type string comment {Title}}
     status          {type string comment {Book status}}
     user            {type User comment {User owning book}}
}
```

The attribute `user` uses another complex data type to describe the user owning the book. The definition of this data type is as follows:

```
WS::Utils::ServiceTypeDef Server Rentbook User {
     id              {type integer comment {User identifier}}
     username        {type string comment {User name}}
     fullname        {type string comment {Full name}}
     status          {type string comment {User status}}
     books           {type Book[] comment {Books owned by user}}
}
```

We can see that the `User` data type also has a reference to the `Book` data type; each user can be supplied along with list of books he/she currently owns.

Providing attributes to a complex type is optional. When we return user information for the user currently owning a book, we do not need to specify that user's `books` attribute.

Similarly when specifying books owned by a user, we do not need to specify the `user` attribute for each of the books, as we already are specifying the user owning these books.

Using data types inside service

Now that we have set up our service and defined the data types, we can move on to creating methods themselves. Our methods will invoke the database API that is responsible for storing this information.

 While these commands are not shown in this chapter, they are included in the soap-server-db.tcl file located in the 03soap-complex directory in the source code examples for this chapter.

We'll start by creating the method for adding new books. It takes an array of Book type objects and adds each book to the database. It returns an array of integers which are identifiers of each book in the database:

```
WS::Server::ServiceProc Rentbook \
    {AddBooks {type integer() comment {New book ids}}} \
    {
        books {type Book[] comment {Books to add}}
    } \
    {Add new books and return their identifiers} \
{
    set rc [list]
    foreach book $books {
        lappend rc [dbAddBook \
            [dict get $book isbn] \
            [dict get $book title] \
            ]
    }
    return [list AddBooksResult $rc]
}
```

Using an array of complex types is quite straightforward — the array itself is converted to a list. Each element of that list is in fact a dictionary we can access using the dict command. The resulting list, which is an array of simple types, is created by adding each value to the list. Both the input and output from the method is automatically converted.

Similarly we can create a method for adding new users to the system. It will take an array of User type objects, add them to the database and return their identifier:

```
WS::Server::ServiceProc Rentbook \
    {AddUsers {type integer() comment {New user ids}}} \
    {
        users {type User[] comment {Users to add}}
    } \
    {Add new users and return their identifiers} \
{
```

```
        set rc [list]
        foreach user $users {
            lappend rc [dbAddUser \
                [dict get $user username] \
                [dict get $user fullname] \
                ]
        }
        return [list AddUsersResult $rc]
    }
```

Next, we'll create methods for listing all users and books in the system:

```
    WS::Server::ServiceProc Rentbook \
        {ListAllUsers {type User[] comment {All users}}} \
        {
        } \
        {List all users in the system and their books} \
    {
        return [list ListAllUsersResult [dbListAllUsers]]
    }

    WS::Server::ServiceProc Rentbook \
        {ListAllBooks {type Book[] comment {All books}}} \
        {
        } \
        {List all books in the system and current owner} \
    {
        return [list ListAllBooksResult [dbListAllBooks]]
    }
```

The methods define an array of User and Book type items, respectively. Internally each of the result is created as a list. Each element is a dictionary that defines attributes specific to the data type.

For example, the code for listing books that uses SQLite database as storage, which is defined as the dbListBooks procedure, and is invoked from within the dbListAllBooks command is as follows:

```
        set rc [list]

        foreach {id isbn title user_id} [db eval \
            "SELECT id, isbn, title, user_id FROM books"] {
```

We start off by setting up an rc variable which will hold resulting list. Then we iterate through the entries by running an SQL query to retrieve specific fields.

After this, we create a dictionary that stores the `id`, `isbn`, and `title` keys using values retrieved from the database:

```
set item [dict create id $id isbn $isbn \
    title $title]
```

Next we check if the `user_id` is non-zero. This means that a book is currently borrowed:

```
if {$user_id !=0} {
```

If a book is currently borrowed, we set its status to `unavailable` and retrieve information about the user that owns it. In order to do this we call a command that lists users matching specific criteria and take the first element from the list:

```
dict set item status "unavailable"
dict set item user [lindex \
    [dbListUsers " WHERE id=$user_id"] 0]
} else {
```

If the book is not currently borrowed we set its status to `available` and do not retrieve the user information.

```
dict set item status "available"
}
```

Next we add this dictionary to list of all items.

```
lappend rc $item
}
```

The command `dbListUsers` is similar to `dbListBooks` which we've just described. It also lists items from the database and creates a dictionary for each of the items in the database.

Next we'll create a command to borrow and return a book. This is also a wrapper around database APIs. They take a book and user identification and return whether the operation has succeeded.

```
WS::Server::ServiceProc Rentbook \
    {BorrowBook {type boolean comment {Success status}}} \
    {
        bookid {type integer comment {Book identifier}}
        userid {type integer comment {User identifier}}
    } \
    {Marks book as borrowed by specified user} \
{
    return [list BorrowBookResult \
```

```
        [dbBookBorrow $bookid $userid]]
}

WS::Server::ServiceProc Rentbook \
    {ReturnBook {type boolean comment {Success status}}} \
    {
        bookid {type integer comment {Book identifier}}
        userid {type integer comment {User identifier}}
    } \
    {Marks book as returned by specified user} \
{
    return [list ReturnBookResult \
        [dbBookReturn $bookid $userid]]
}
```

It is a good idea to create SOAP methods in such a way that they are only small wrappers around other commands. This makes it much easier to test the backend that retrieves information, both using manual and automated tests.

> An example of a simple server is located in `soap-server-http.tcl` file in `03soap-complex` directory in the source code examples for this chapter. It comes with all libraries needed to run the example.
>
> Implementation functions for storing a user and book information using SQLite 3 database are located in `soap-server-db.tcl` file in `03soap-complex` directory in the source code examples for this chapter.

Connecting to SOAP based services

Now that we know how to create web services from Tcl we can move on to the other side of the process: accessing and using web services. Since SOAP is a wide standard we can use the SOAP client from the Web Services from Tcl package, to access Tcl services as well as any other type of web services available.

In order to use SOAP based services we need to use the `WS::Client` package from Web Services from Tcl:

```
package require WS::Client
```

Now that we have loaded the package to access web services, we can move on.

In order to use a web service, it's best to start off by downloading and parsing WSDL that describes all methods and data types. This can be done using the `WS::Client::GetAndParseWsdl` command. It requires that we specifying the URL to WSDL. We can also specify a list of HTTP headers for sending request and service name to use.

The headers list is a name-value pairs list, where each name is a HTTP header name and the value is its value. This is passed as the `-headers` option to the http package when retrieving the WSDL. For more information please refer to *Chapter 7, Using Common Internet Services* or the documentation available at `http://www.tcl.tk/man/tcl8.5/TclCmd/http.htm#M19`.

Similar to the WS::Server package, service name is used to reference a particular service across API calls. It is also the name of the namespace used to create commands that map to remote invocations, which is described later in the chapter. If a service name is specified then it is used. Otherwise it defaults to the name specified in WSDL. For Tcl based services, the service name exported in WSDL is the service name used for creating the service.

To parse a WSDL for a previously created `Myservice` hosted on the same machine we can invoke the following command:

```
WS::Client::GetAndParseWsdl \
    "https://127.0.0.1:8002/service/Myservice/wsdl"
```

In order to access the HTTPS version, we can invoke the following command:

```
WS::Client::GetAndParseWsdl \
    "https://127.0.0.1:8002/service/Myservice/wsdl"
```

This command will download the WSDL from specified URL, parse it, and register a client web service named `Myservice`.

We can also specify `file://` scheme URL to load WSDL from a file. The format is `file://localhost:<path>`. For example:

- On Unix systems the URL would be `file://localhost:/tmp/myservice.wsdl` for `/tmp/wyservice.wsdl` file
- The URL for Microsoft Windows is `file://localhost:C:/myservice.wsdl` if path to file is `C:/myservice.wsdl`

Web Services for Tcl uses the `uri` package to handle URLs. More information about `file` URI scheme can be found in the `uri` package documentation available from `http://tcllib.sourceforge.net/doc/uri.html`.

Invoking methods via commands

We can now use other commands to access remote APIs. Most often we'll want to invoke methods remotely. Web Services for Tcl package offers two ways to invoke methods:

- Creating Tcl commands that invoke remote interfaces internally; this is similar to approach in XMLRPC package
- Using a generic command to invoke methods

Let's start with creating Tcl commands that map to SOAP methods. These are called **stub commands**. While this approach is easier to use, we need to remember that list of arguments that the command is created by taking all items as input for the method and sorting them. This means that if the definition for the method changes, the order of parameters accepted by the Tcl command will also be changed. While usually parameters for a method do not change over time, it is worth keeping in mind, especially when developing a service.

In order to create stub commands we need to invoke the WS::Client::CreateStubs command. It requires a service name as its only argument.

For example, in order to create stubs for Myservice we can invoke the following command:

```
WS::Client::CreateStubs Myservice
```

We can now access the IntAdd method as the Myservice::IntAdd command.

We can then use it in a fashion similar to a regular command:

```
set result [Myservice::IntAdd 1 2]
```

The result variable will contain a dictionary result, where the only key is IntAddResult. In order to access the actual result we need to get it using the dict command, for example:

```
puts "1 + 2 = [dict get $result IntAddResult]"
```

Whenever an error occurs when invoking a web service, this error is thrown back to caller of the method. This means that if the server side of our application throws an error that parameters are invalid, the same error is then thrown by a command invoked on the client.

If a timeout occurs when connecting to a web service, this also causes a Tcl error to be thrown. Therefore it is a good idea to wrap all calls to remote methods inside catch command calls.

[The last code is located in `soap-server-http-client-stubs.tcl` files in `02soap-basics` directory in the source code examples for this chapter.]

In addition to using just our web service, we can also use public services list available at `http://www.xmethods.net/ve2/Directory.po`. This site provides a list of SOAP web services along with details and link to WSDL.

Invoking methods API using DoCall commands

Another way to access remote methods from `WS::Client` package is to use a generic command for invoking methods. These commands are generic and accept all parameters as a dictionary, where the key is name of the parameter and the value is its value.

The benefit of this approach is that even if parameters, change it does not cause our client code to be invalid. On the other hand, manually coding all invocations is a bit more difficult. We recommend whichever method is easier for everyone, unless a particular service API is bound to change often — then it is best to use generic commands for invoking methods.

In order to invoke a remote method, we can use `WS::Client::DoCall` command. It accepts 3 parameters: service name, method name, and dictionary of parameters.

For example, to call the `IntAdd` method from `Myservice` service we can do the following:

```
Set result [WS::Client::DoCall Myservice IntAdd \
    [dict create A 2 B 3]]
```

This will invoke the `IntAdd` method providing the value 2 for `A` and 3 for `B` parameters. The result is also a dictionary result, where the only key is `IntAddResult`. Similarly, to print out a result from our method we can do:

```
puts "2 + 3 = [dict get $result IntAddResult]"
```

This should print `2 + 3 = 5` text assuming a Tclhttpd server with `Myservice` set up is running.

Command `WS::Client::DoCall` as well stub commands operate in synchronous way; which means that commands return after result from remote method have been retrieved, or an error has occurred.

In many cases it is better to invoke methods asynchronously. This makes sense, especially if we want our application to be more responsive. It also allows us to invoke APIs when we do not need to wait for results for the application to proceed, such as when only notifying other systems of an event without actually expecting any results.

Asynchronous calls to web services can be done using the `WS::Client::DoCallAsync` command. It accepts five arguments: service name, method name, arguments, command to run on successful call, and command to run in case on error. The first three arguments are provided in the same way as for `WS::Client::DoCall` command.

After a successful response has been received, the command provided as the fourth argument is run with the result dictionary appended.

If there is an error the command provided as the fifth argument is run. It is provided with the error code and any error information as two additional arguments.

For example, in order to invoke the `IntAdd` method from `Myservice` asynchronously, we can do the following:

```
WS::Client::DoAsyncCall Myservice IntAdd \
    [dict create A 3 B 4] \
    IntAddDone IntAddError
```

This will cause the command `IntAddDone` to be invoked in the case of a successful request and response. Otherwise, `IntAddError` will be called.

If a web service call succeeds the command is invoked with just the result dictionary as only argument. In the case of errors both the `errorCode` and `errorInfo` are passed. If the problem occurred on the remote side, these should contain error information as thrown by remote peer. In the case of local problems this will contain information about any connectivity errors, such as a timeout or connection refused.

These commands are defined as follows:

```
proc IntAddDone {result} {
    puts "3 + 4 = [dict get $result IntAddResult]"
}

proc IntAddError {errorCode errorInfo} {
    puts "Error during remote API invocation: $errorInfo"
}
```

This will cause the `IntAddDone` command to be run and the text `3 + 4 = 7` to be printed out in case of success. If there is an error detailed information about it will be printed out.

 The previously mentioned code is located in the `soap-server-http-client-call.tcl` file in the `02soap-basics` directory in the source code examples for this chapter.

Using complex data types

When accessing remote APIs we will often need to pass or receive complex data types and / or arrays of elements. The ws::Client package handles them in the same way as server part. Arrays of elements are converted to Tcl lists and complex types are read, and created as dictionaries. Throughout this section, we will use methods from our previously created Rentbook service. We'll use stub commands to make the examples easier to read.

Let's start by adding a few books to our database using the AddBooks method:

```
set result [Rentbook::AddBooks [list \
    [dict create isbn "12-34" title "Book 1"] \
    [dict create isbn "12-35" title "Book 2"] \
    ]]

set b1 [lindex [dict get $result AddBooksResult] 0]
set b2 [lindex [dict get $result AddBooksResult] 1]
```

Each of the books to be added is created as a dictionary containing isbn and title elements, matching the Book data type definition. We create a list of these dictionaries and pass that to the method.

Next, we process the result—get the AddBooksResult key which holds the results, and then take first and second element from that list; these are identifiers of the books we have just added to the system.

Similarly, we'll add new users using the AddUsers method and store their identifiers:

```
set result [Rentbook::AddUsers [list \
    [dict create username "User1" fullname "User 1"] \
    [dict create username "User2" fullname "User 2"] \
    ]]

set u1 [lindex [dict get $result AddUsersResult] 0]
set u2 [lindex [dict get $result AddUsersResult] 1]
```

This will cause our application to have books and users in the database that we can use.

We can then use these to try booking and returning books we have just created. First let's borrow book 1 as user 2:

```
Rentbook::BorrowBook $b1 $u2
```

We'll also borrow book 2 as user 1:

```
Rentbook::BorrowBook $b2 $u1
```

This way we have a set of borrowed books. Now we can try to list information about all users by using the `ListAllUsers` method:

```
foreach user [dict get [Rentbook::ListAllUsers] \
    ListAllUsersResult] {
    puts "User [dict get $user fullname]:"
    puts " Status: [dict get $user status]"
    foreach book [dict get $user books] {
        puts "  Book [dict get $book title] \
            ([dict get $book isbn])"
    }
}
```

The preceding example first iterates over each element retrieved as the result. It then prints out information about the user along with all the books they own. Listing the books is done by iterating over the `books` key. The result would be similar to following:

```
User User 1:
 Status: active
  Book Book 2 (12-35)
User User 2:
 Status: active
  Book Book 1 (12-34)
```

Similarly, we can list all books along with the user that owns them if this is the case. We can use the `ListAllBooks` method, iterate over the elements and print out the details. If the `userkey` is present, this means that a particular book is currently borrowed by this user. In this case, we can access this element and print out the details of that person.

```
foreach book [dict get [Rentbook::ListAllBooks] \
    ListAllBooksResult] {
    puts "[dict get $book title] ([dict get $book isbn]):"
    puts " Status: [dict get $book status]"
    if {[dict exists $book user]} {
        puts "  Owned by [dict get $book user fullname]"
    }
}
```

And the output from this command would be:

```
Book 1 (12-34):
 Status: unavailable
  Owned by User 2
Book 2 (12-35):
 Status: unavailable
  Owned by User 1
```

Examples of using the `Rentbook` service is located in the `soap-server-http-client.tcl` file in the `03soap-complex` directory in the source code examples for this chapter.

Summary

Tcl offers support for a wide range of standards for remote method invocations. We can use it for accessing APIs available from other applications or services. We can also export our own functionality.

We can interact with other applications using XML-RPC, which is widely used by websites as it is easier to implement and lightweight. All that is needed is to know the methods and arguments they take; we can then easily access methods from other applications. Our application can also benefit from SOAP. Similar to XML-RPC we can invoke commands over SOAP. In this case we only need to know the URL of the WSDL file, which is a definition of the web service, the methods it offers and all data types related to it.

Despite the advantages of easy integration with different languages and technologies, the SOAP standard has a major drawback. As it is uses XML and is designed to be self-descriptive, the overhead of metadata in each request is very high and SOAP should not be used for communication where network bandwidth or CPU / memory resources are crucial.

In this chapter we have learned:

- How to connect to XML-RPC services and issue methods remotely
- How XML-RPC can be used to easily integrate with major blogging engines
- How to create SOAP services using Tclhttpd and Web Services for Tcl; define complex data types for storing structured information
- How to invoke methods remotely in SOAP based web services

In the next chapter, we'll learn more details about security in networked applications, how to build public key infrastructure into our application and how to use Tcl's safe interpreter feature to reduce the risks related to running code from an unknown source.

13
SSL and Security

Previous chapters of this book have presented how to write networked applications in Tcl. However, they did not cover any of the security aspects in detail. While security on its own is a subject large enough for a separate book, we will focus only on some aspects of it.

Security is a very important aspect of any application, especially if it communicates over a network. When communication is made, we need to be sure that we know who the other peer is; this is called **authentication**. This can be achieved using usernames and passwords, authenticating using public / private key based encryption, and many other aspects. We also need to check that a specified user can perform specific actions. For example, only the administrator can maintain a system. This is called **authorization**.

The terms authentication and authorization are often confused, as from a user perspective, these usually mean the same. When checking our e-mail, providing a valid username and password causes both authentication and authorization. However, it is important to be able to differentiate between these terms:

- Authentication is the ability to verify the peer we are talking to
- Authorization is the ability to verify whether this peer can perform specified operation

Whenever we receive any information, we also need to be sure that it has not been modified in any way during the transmission, which is called the **integrity** of our data. When sending data over public networks, if our application is not protected against it, information might be modified on its path by malicious users. Securing such communication can be achieved by sending data over an encrypted, secure connection channel where it is not possible to modify the transmitted data.

In many cases, we also need to be certain that the data we send over the network cannot be intercepted on its route; for example, that sensitive information cannot be read by anyone except for recipient(s) of the message. Intercepting and listening to a communication by an unauthorized user and / or application is called **eavesdropping**.

It is very easy to ensure authentication and authorization using **Secure Socket Layer (SSL)**. This is a standard for encrypted network connections that works on top of regular sockets and provides an encryption layer on top of it. SSL uses public keys for authenticating peers and making sure only authorized users and / or computers can communicate with each other. In this chapter, we'll learn how to use encrypted connections from Tcl and how to make sure we know the other side our application is communicating with.

This chapter also shows the basics of authorizing users, dealing with issues of roles and access to various functions. We'll show how to map this to public-key based authentication.

We'll also learn how to use Tcl's safe interpreter feature. This can come in handy in order to hide some of Tcl's features or limit access to an operating system's resources—for example, to disallow accessing file system. You will learn how to limit commands or the time an interpreter can spend running. The Tcl safe feature can also be used for creating a sandbox that will allow / disallow specific features based on access level.

Learning Secure Socket Layer

SSL offers a security layer for communications over networks. SSL itself is a very generic standard for encrypting any form of communication. It is usually used for securing network connections to prevent messages from being modified and / or eavesdropped. We'll use it for securing TCP sockets, and show how applications can become SSL-enabled and switch to a secure model of communication.

SSL is the most popular standard for encrypted network communication and is used for almost all protocols, such as WWW, e-mail, FTP, and Jabber. It has multiple implementations, including open source ones such as OpenSSL, available from http:// www.openssl.org/.

SSL offers end-to-end encryption of communication. It uses private and public key pairs for each of the peers communicating over the network. Public keys may be signed by a **certificate authority (CA)**. Usually it is an application and / or machine in the network that deals with signing keys, and is trusted by other elements of the infrastructure. Signed public keys are called **certificates**. They are signed by certificate authority and can be used for authenticating remote peers in a communication.

Certificates and CAs allow the remote peer to be securely identified — remote peer needs to provide a valid certificate, which is signed by a trusted element of the network (CA). All systems within a network have a certificate for CA itself. Upon any connection a certificate is checked as to whether it is signed by a valid CA. The certificate also provides information about the identity of remote peers, and because it is signed by CA, this data can be trusted.

There are different types of certificate authorities:

- The first type of CAs are publicly available certificate authorities called root CAs. These are organizations that verify and sign certificates for other companies for use in the Internet. An example is secure HTTPS websites, whose certificates are signed by such root CAs.

- Many companies and / or IT applications also use their own certificate authorities that are trusted by an entire infrastructure. Each part of the system can then use that system's CA certificate(s) to check if a certificate of a remote peer is valid. This concept is discussed in more detail later in this chapter.

SSL provides two ways in which communication and authentication is carried out:

- The first one is that only the server provides a valid and signed certificate, in which case the server can be authenticated, but the client remains anonymous

- The second possibility is for both the server and client to provide a valid certificate

Server-only authentication is used for web browsing and many client-server applications. This means that only validity of the server is checked — the client checks if the server certificate is valid, but there is no key-based check performed for the client. In this case, additional authentication is made at application level, for example, by providing an additional username / password over the encrypted channel to authorize the user using the application.

Authenticating both the client and server is often used for applications that only communicate with trusted peers. This is used in client-server applications that use certificates for authentication. This is the model that the remaining part of this chapter will focus on, as a majority of our examples are applications that need to communicate in a secure manner.

Using SSL from Tcl

In order to create an SSL-enabled client or server from Tcl, we need to use `tls` package. It provides SSL support over TCP connections as well as any other type of connection, such as Unix pipes. For the purposes of this book, we'll focus on TCP connections only.

Package `tls` is an open source project built on top of the `OpenSSL` package, and it's available from `https://sourceforge.net/projects/tls/`. The page provides both binary and source code distribution of the package. The package is also provided with ActiveTcl distributions, so using any of the examples from ActiveTcl will work without additional dependencies.

SSL-enabled TCP sockets in Tcl work in the same way as any other kind of connections. The only difference is that the `tls::socket` command needs to be used instead of `socket`. The command can be used to set up both client and server connections. Syntax of the command is the same as that of the `socket` command. The command also accepts additional options related to SSL keys and options, which are described later in this chapter.

For example, in order to connect to host `192.168.2.1` port `443` using SSL, we can do the following:

```
package require tls

set channel [tls::socket 192.168.2.1 443]
```

We can then use commands such as `puts`, `gets`, or `read` for accessing data.

SSL sessions begin with a handshake. At that point, encryption of algorithms along with certificate exchange takes place. From a Tcl perspective, this happens when we first try to write to a channel for a client or after a first read for a server. If an SSL handshake fails, then a read or write will fail. Those commands will also fail if the connection is terminated, which is the same as that for regular TCP sockets.

Setting up an SSL-enabled server is also the same as that with regular TCP sockets. All we need to run is:

```
package require tls

tls::socket -server mycommand 8992
```

The preceding code will cause Tcl to listen for incoming SSL connections and invoke the `mycommand` command, just the same as for regular TCP connections. It will be passed a new channel name as the first argument, followed by a remote IP address and remote port.

The `tls` package accepts various parameters as name-value pairs that specify items such as key and certificate files, supported protocols, and authentication policies. There are two possibilities to specify SSL-related parameters:

- We can specify them globally using `tls::init` command.
- Another possibility is to specify them directly in `tls::socket` command. In this case, options will only apply to the specified socket. In case of server connections, those options will apply to all incoming connections on the specified port. Options provided to `tls::socket` always overwrite options specified using `tls::init`.

The most important options are `-keyfile` and `-certfile`, which are used to specify key and certificate files accordingly. These files are created either using the `tls` package itself or using additional tools such as the `openssl` command-line utility. Private key file usually has `.key` extension and certificate usually has `.pem` extension.

For example, in order to specify a globally used SSL key and certificate files, we can run the following:

```
tls::init -keyfile "/path/to/server.key" \
    -certfile "/path/to/server.pem"
```

We can also specify and / or overwrite these for specific connections by running:

```
tls::socket –server mycommand -keyfile "/path/to/other.key" \
    -certfile "/path/to/other.pem" 8992
```

This will cause connections for this particular port to use specified keys regardless of the ones specified in `init` command.

When passing options using both `tls::init` and `tls::socket`, options provided to `tls::socket` overwrite ones passed to `tls::init`.

The options `-cadir` and `-cafile` allow for specifying a file or directory that contains information about certificate authorities (CAs). The first option specifies a directory that holds one or more CA certificates. The second option can be used to specify a single CA certificate to use. CA certificate files usually have `.crt` extension.

We can also specify whether to ask the remote peer for a certificate, and whether to only accept valid SSL certificates during handshake or not. The option `-request` is used to specify whether to request a certificate from remote peer during SSL handshake and it defaults to true.

The option -require, if enabled (that is, when specifying -require true), forces accepting only valid SSL certificates. It defaults to false. A valid certificate is a certificate signed by one or more trusted CAs. All connections not having a certificate signed by a trusted CA will be closed. Enabling this option also requires enabling the -request option and specifying either -cadir or -cafile.

The package tls also supports using password protected SSL keys. This is commonly used to improve security. The option -password can be used to specify a command to be run whenever OpenSSL will need to get a password. The command is run without additional parameters and should return a string that is then passed back to OpenSSL.

For example, to pass a pre-defined password we can do the following:

```
proc gettlspassword {} {
    return "hardcodedpassword"
}

tls::init -keyfile $keyfile -certfile $certfile \
    -password [gettlspassword]
```

Options set using the tls::init command are combined with any other options passed when the socket is created. Note that the tls::init command should be called first. This is especially important for server sockets; for example, the following code will not work:

```
package require tls

tls::socket -server mycommand 8992

tls::init -keyfile "/path/to/server.key" \
    -certfile "/path/to/server.pem"
```

When creating the server socket, tls did not have any key and certificate specified. Even though this is specified later, tls did pick up the values at the time tls::socket was invoked. The next example is correct:

```
package require tls

tls::init -keyfile "/path/to/server.key" \
    -certfile "/path/to/server.pem"

tls::socket -server mycommand 8992
```

The preceding code differs by setting the `tls` default parameter before initializing the socket. At the time the server socket is created, key and certificate filenames are already set.

Generating self-signed certificates

As stated earlier, SSL needs to have a valid certificate either at just server, or at both the server and client. We will need to tell the `tls` package where a valid key and certificate is located.

There are multiple possibilities for creating and signing a certificate, which are described later in this chapter. For test purposes, it is enough to generate a **self-signed** certificate; this is a certificate that is signed by its own key.

The package `tls` offers a command for generating a self-signed key and certificate quickly. It is done using the `tls::misc` command and its `req` subcommand. It requires four parameters. The first one is the size of the key, in bits. It is recommended to use at least 1024 bits or 2048 bits, as a smaller amount of bits can be considered insecure. The second argument specifies a path to the private key file and the third specifies a path to the certificate file. The last argument is a list of name-value pairs that specify information included in the certificate.

Certificate information can contain one or more elements. The `days` attribute specifies the number of days a certificate should be valid; it defaults to 365. The `serial` attribute specifies the key's serial number and defaults to 0. Additional details about the key's validity period, expiration, and serial numbers are described in more detail later in this chapter.

Certificate information can also include one or more of the following attributes, which map to SSL certificate fields:

Attribute name	Description
C	Country; should be specified as two-letter country code; for example, US for United States of America, UK for United Kingdom, and PL for Poland
ST	State or province name, specified as full name; potential values for this field vary across countries
L	Locality name; for example, city
O	Organization name; for example, company name
OU	Organization Unit Name; for example, section / department name
CN	Common Name, varies depending on type of certificate
Email	E-mail address of system or application administrator

The field common name is often used to identify resource that owns the certificate. For example, for the majority of Internet applications, the common name is set to the hostname of the host we are connecting to, such as www.packtpub.com.

For many applications, the common name can be used to uniquely name a resource or client; for systems that use **Globally Unique Identifier (GUID)** for identifying resources, the common name can be the GUID of the system. This way, SSL-based authorization can be used to map a connection to a particular resource, application, or agent.

For example, in order to create a sample SSL key and certificate we can do the following:

```
set keyfile server.key
set certfile server.pem

if {![file exists $keyfile]} {
    tls::misc req 1024 $keyfile $certfile \
        [list CN "localhost" days 7300]
}
```

Now, we configure tls to use the newly generated certificate by calling:

```
tls::init -keyfile $keyfile -certfile $certfile
```

We can use the tls::status command to get SSL-specific information about a socket. The result is a list of key-value pairs that describe the remote peer. If an SSL handshake has not been done yet, the command returns an empty list. Otherwise, the following keys are returned:

Attribute name	Description
issuer	Information about certificate issuer
subject	Information about certificate subject
notBefore	Begin date for validity of this certificate
notAfter	Expiry date for this certificate
serial	Serial number of this certificate
cipher	Encryption used for communication
sbits	Number of bits used for session key

The fields `issuer` and `subject` are in the form of `attribute=value`, separated by comma(s). They contain the same fields as ones used for SSL certificate generation, except that `emailAddress` is used instead of `Email`. An example value for `subject` or `issuer` is:

```
emailAddress=root@localhost,CN=CertificateAuthority,O=Tcl Network
Programming Book,L=Krakow,ST=Malopolskie,C=PL
```

 A complete example of using SSL-enabled sockets is located in the `01sockets` directory in the source code examples for this chapter.

Setting up and using public key infrastructure

As our applications grow and include larger numbers of applications or devices that communicate within the system, we will need a consistent way to identify and trust other nodes in the system.

A very common solution is to use SSL certificates. The idea is that we create a trusted entity that is responsible for authenticating everyone else in the system.

We start off with a commonly trusted entity that is only used for signing other entities' certificates. This way any certificate that is signed by this entity is considered secure, and we trust whatever identity is stored in the certificate itself. This is what certificate authority is.

Identity is usually equal to the common name contained in the certificate itself. Naming for certificates is up to either the administrator or creator of the application. In the following examples, we're using identifiers of clients as the common name. For web applications, it has to be the hostname of the website. As a trusted entity is signing certificates, we assume that information in the certificate that is also signed can be trusted.

Throughout our example, we'll be performing the following steps:

- Creating a key and self-signed certificate for certificate authority, which will be the trusted entity for entire infrastructure
- Creating a key and certificate request for a sample server
- Generating a certificate for the newly created server key — this step uses the certificate request from the previous step
- Creating a key and certificate request for a sample client
- Generating a certificate for the newly created client key — this step uses the certificate request from previous step

In order to create additional server and client keys, only the steps for generating the key and the request, as well as generating the certificates themselves, have to be performed. The key and self-signed certificate for certificate authority should be generated only once.

Each of the entities in the system will also need their own key and certificate. Each certificate should be signed by the certificate authority. We will need to generate certificate authority, keys and certificates signed by a previously created CA. We'll use openssl command from OpenSSL package for these actions. Its documentation can be found at http://www.openssl.org/docs/apps/openssl.html.

Easy RSA is a very good open source package for managing keys using certificate authority. It can be used to set up a CA infrastructure and can be found at http://openvpn.net/easyrsa.html. Even though we will not use the package itself, we'll be using an OpenSSL configuration file based on the one from Easy RSA package.

Setting up certificates manually

The first thing we need to do is to set up directories for our keys. We'll store all keys in a keys subdirectory. We'll also need an empty index.txt file and serial file with contents of 01, which is used by OpenSSL.

To do this, let's invoke the following commands:

```
root@ubuntu:/private/ssl/keys# mkdir keys

root@ubuntu:/private/ssl/keys# touch keys/index.txt

root@ubuntu:/private/ssl/keys# echo 01 >keys/serial
```

> The configuration file openssl.cnf should also be put in the main directory. It is located in the 02opensslconfig directory in the source code examples for this chapter.

Examples show these commands run as the administrative user, but all commands can be run as any user. The same applies to Microsoft Windows and MacOSX. It also applies to all examples for running openssl command, both automatically and manually.

The following shows the layout of files and directories:

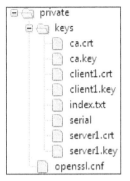

The files `ca.crt`, `ca.key`, `client1.crt`, `client1.key`, `server1.crt`, `server1.key` are files that are created by commands shown in the following section.

Creating certificate authority

After creating the directory structure, we need to create a key and certificate for certificate authority. We'll use `openssl` and its `req` subcommand, which is used for creating and managing certificates.

For example, we can invoke the following command:

```
root@ubuntu:/private/ssl/keys# openssl req -days 3650 \
    -nodes -new -x509 -config openssl.cnf \
    -keyout keys/ca.key -out keys/ca.crt
Generating a 1024 bit RSA private key
..................+++++
..........+++++
writing new private key to 'keys/ca.key'
-----
(...)
-----
Country Name (2 letter code) [PL]: <Enter>
State or Province Name (full name) [Malopolskie]: <Enter>
Locality Name (eg, city) [Krakow]: <Enter>
Organization Name (eg, company) [Tcl Network Programming Book]:
<Enter>
Organizational Unit Name (eg, section) [SSL]: <Enter>
Common Name (eg, your name or your server's hostname) []:
CertificateAuthority
Email Address []:
```

The same can be made in silent, non-interactive mode. For this purpose, it's necessary to create properly built `openssl.cnf` in which all listed parameters will be specified. Automating this process is described later in the chapter.

Parts of command output were omitted and are marked with (...) in command output. Commands and output we have entered are marked in bold. Whenever the `openssl` command asked for input and just leaving the value empty was required, an `<Enter>` text has been added.

The preceding command is invoked with various flags:

- Specifying `-days 3650` tells OpenSSL that the CA should be valid for 3650 days, which is roughly 10 years. The option `-nodes` disables DES encryption and also disables password protection of the CA certificate.

- The option `-new` combined with `-x509` causes OpenSSL to generate a new key and certificate. Without the latter option, it will generate a key along with certificate request.

- The option `-config` specifies which configuration file to use. The options `-keyout` and `-out` specify paths of CA private key file and CA certificate file respectively.

All functionality of the `openssl req` command is documented at: http://www.openssl.org/docs/apps/req.html

As a result, the `openssl req` command invoked will create `keys/ca.key` containing private key, used by CA for signing additional keys. This file should be kept secret and users should not have access to it. The file `keys/ca.crt` is the certificate for this CA. It can be passed to users in order to verify the signature of additional keys.

We can also skip using the `-nodes` option and create a CA key that is password protected. This increases security of the CA key, but for the purposes of this chapter and ease of automation, we will not use password protected CA or keys.

Generating the CA key and certificate needs to be done only once regardless of the number of keys we want to generate.

Generating and signing keys

Now, we can create one or more keys for clients or other servers in the network. We will also sign these keys using the CA done in previous step.

Command for creating the key itself is similar to previous one:

```
root@ubuntu:/private/ssl/keys# openssl req -days 3650 \
    -nodes -new -config openssl.cnf \
    -keyout keys/server1.key -out keys/server1.csr
```

```
Generating a 1024 bit RSA private key
..........................++++++
.................................................++++++
writing new private key to 'keys/server1.key'
-----
(...)
-----
Country Name (2 letter code) [PL]: <Enter>
State or Province Name (full name) [Malopolskie]: <Enter>
Locality Name (eg, city) [Krakow]: <Enter>
Organization Name (eg, company) [Tcl Network Programming Book]:
<Enter>
Organizational Unit Name (eg, section) [SSL]: <Enter>
Common Name (eg, your name or your server's hostname) []:server1
Email Address []:<Enter>

Please enter the following 'extra' attributes
to be sent with your certificate request
A challenge password []: <Enter>
An optional company name []: <Enter>
```

This will create a key and its certificate. Similar to previous example, parts of text were omitted and text we entered is marked in bold.

Options specified for the openssl req command are very similar to ones provided for generating the CA key and certificate. The only difference is that in this case we do not specify the -x509 option. This creates a certificate request instead of generating a certificate. This is needed, as the request is then signed by CA to create a properly signed certificate.

Now our new private key is created as keys/server1.key and an unsigned request in keys/server1.csr. The private key should be kept secret, similar to the ca.key file. The file server1.csr can be made public.

The next step is to sign the certificate as Certificate Authority. We will use the ca subcommand from openssl for this purpose.

The following is an example of signing a certificate:

```
root@ubunturouter:/private/ssl/keys# openssl ca \
    -days 3650 -config openssl.cnf \
    -extensions server \
    -in keys/server1.csr -out keys/server1.crt
Using configuration from openssl.cnf
Check that the request matches the signature
Signature ok
```

```
The Subject's Distinguished Name is as follows
countryName              :PRINTABLE:'PL'
stateOrProvinceName      :PRINTABLE:'Malopolskie'
localityName             :PRINTABLE:'Krakow'
organizationName         :PRINTABLE:'Tcl Network Programming Book'
organizationalUnitName:PRINTABLE:'SSL'
commonName               :PRINTABLE:'server1'
Certificate is to be certified until Dec 28 14:17:48 2019 GMT (3650
days)
Sign the certificate? [y/n]:y
1 out of 1 certificate requests certified, commit? [y/n]y
Write out database with 1 new entries
Data Base Updated
```

Similar to previous examples, we have chosen a few of the options available using `openssl` command:

- The option `-days 3650` tells OpenSSL that the certificate should be valid for 3650 days.
- The option `-config` specifies configuration file to use.
- `-in` and `-out` specify paths of certificate request and output certificate respectively.
- The option `-extensions server` specifies that the certificate should indicate that it can be used as a server. This is used whenever a client connects to verify if the remote peer is actually signed as a server.

Even though options do not specify a path to CA key and certificate, OpenSSL knows this as it is hardcoded in the `openssl.cnf` file.

All functionality of the `openssl ca` command is documented at: http://www.openssl.org/docs/apps/ca.html

Now a signed certificate has been created as `keys/server1.crt`. The file `keys/server1.csr` can now be deleted. After this, we can use it from within Tcl as follows:

```
tls::init -cafile keys/ca.crt \
    -keyfile keys/server1.key -certfile keys/server1.pem
```

The text `server1` in filenames should be replaced with the actual name of the key to use. All servers and clients should also include the `-cafile` option to allow for checking the certificate signature.

We can also add the `-require` true option to require a valid certificate from remote peers. This will require all peers to have a signed certificate in order to communicate with other systems.

The previous example created a server key and certificate using the `-extensions server` option. The procedure for creating certificates for a client is exactly the same, but signing a certificate should be done without this flag. For example:

```
root@ubuntu:/private/ssl/keys# openssl req -days 3650 \
    -nodes -new -config openssl.cnf \
    -keyout keys/client1.key -out keys/client1.csr
Generating a 1024 bit RSA private key
.........................++++++
.................................................++++++
writing new private key to 'keys/server1.key'
-----
(...)
-----
Common Name (eg, your name or your server's hostname) []:client1
Email Address []: <Enter>
(...)
```

Creating the key is exactly the same as before. The command for signing this key is the same except for removing `-extensions server` option:

```
root@ubunturouter:/private/ssl/keys# openssl ca \
    -days 3650 -config openssl.cnf \
    -in keys/client1.csr -out keys/client1.crt
(...)
Sign the certificate? [y/n]:y
1 out of 1 certificate requests certified, commit? [y/n]y
Write out database with 1 new entries
Data Base Updated
```

 The configuration file used in preceding examples is located in the `02opensslconfig` directory in the source code examples for this chapter.

In this example, we have created all keys and certificates from the same machine and in same directory. It is also possible to perform these steps on multiple machines. In this case, generation of CA keys and the certificate and the signing of all keys needs to be done on one machine. Generation of all other keys can be done on other machines. Then, the unsigned keys (files with `.csr` extension) should be passed to the machine where the CA key and certificate is kept. After signing and creating the certificate file (files with `.crt` extension), it should be passed back to the machine where the key was generated. There is no need to transfer private keys (files with `.key` extension) at any point so transfers of (`.csr` and `.crt` files) can be made using unencrypted channels.

An implementation of a safe mechanism for generating and signing certificates is shown later in this chapter.

Automating certificates from Tcl

The package `tls` does not offer functionality for creating anything other than self-signed certificates. However, we can automate invocations of `openssl` command from within Tcl in order to manage certificates automatically from within Tcl.

We'll use the configuration file from the previous example with slight modifications. We'll be using a feature of passing environment variables to specify data for OpenSSL. This way we can automatically generate certificates with specified information, without any interaction on standard input or standard output.

The command `openssl` accepts the `-batch` option that causes it to use default values from configuration, instead of reading them from standard input.

OpenSSL also allows values to be specified for some fields using environment variables by specifying `$ENV::<variableName>` in the `openssl.cnf` file, where `<variableName>` is the name variable and maps to `$::env(<variableName>)` in Tcl. We will use this mechanism to pass parameters for certificate information from Tcl.

This will allow us to automate certificate creation and and customize the information contained in each certificate. This is needed for new nodes in the system or when a certificate expires and a new one needs to be generated. Automating this will allow us to add in new clients to our network without any manual effort from the administrator, such as adding new computers to a managed system. It will also help if we decide that automated certificate creation and signing from Tcl takes a few steps to complete. First let's initialize the namespace and variables for keeping the configuration:

```
namespace eval sslkeys {}

set sslkeys::keydirectory "keys"
set sslkeys::confdirectory "conf"
set sslkeys::keysize 1024
set sslkeys::expires 3650
set sslkeys::openssl "openssl"
```

The variables `keydirectory` and `confdirectory` store paths to keys and the configuration directory, respectively. The `keysize` variable specifies the number of bits to use for each key, `expires` specifies the expiration period in days, and the `openssl` variable specifies the path to `openssl` binary.

Next we'll set up defaults for each certificate. It is a list of name-value pairs:

```
set sslkeys::defaults {
    COUNTRY         "PL"
    PROVINCE        "Malopolskie"
    CITY            "Krakow"
    ORG             "Tcl Network Programming Book"
    OU              "SSL"
    CN              "TBD"
    EMAIL           "root@localhost"
}
```

Attributes are similar to the ones used for generating certificates in Tcl.

For each key, we'll merge preceding defaults with additional information provided when generating a key. We can create a helper procedure to merge values and copy information to the environment variable:

```
proc sslkeys::_initArray {argslist} {
    variable keydirectory
    variable keysize
    variable defaults
```

We'll map the `ar` array to the same variable in the previous stack frame. This can be implemented to use the `ar` array directly in commands that generate keys. We'll also combine defaults with arguments provided to the procedure using `array set`:

```
    upvar 1 ar ar

    array set ar $defaults
    array set ar $argslist
```

Now we'll copy required values to environment variables. We'll also set up a key directory as well as key size.

```
    foreach k {COUNTRY PROVINCE CITY ORG OU CN EMAIL} {
        set ::env(KEY_$k) $ar($k)
    }
    set ::env(KEY_DIR) $keydirectory
    set ::env(KEY_SIZE) $keysize
}
```

These environment variables are later used by the `openssl` binary to access information about the key and directories to use. Tcl variable `::env` represents the operating system's environment variables.

We'll also create a helper function to clean up environment variables, which can be used after invoking OpenSSL. It will also remove *.old files, which are created as part of the signing certificates process and do not need to be kept.

```
proc sslkeys::_finiArray {} {
    variable keydirectory

    foreach k {
        COUNTRY PROVINCE CITY ORG OU CN EMAIL DIR SIZE
    } {
        unset ::env(KEY_$k)
    }

    foreach g [glob -nocomplain -directory $keydirectory \
        *.old *.OLD] {
        catch {file delete -force $g}
    }
}
```

We can now move to functions that will invoke openssl binary to perform actions.

The procedure we'll need to write is initializing certificate authority files if they are not there. We'll start by mapping needed namespace variables, and initializing the ar variable using the helper procedure recently mentioned. The command accepts any number of arguments, which are passed to _initArray command.

```
proc sslkeys::initialize {args} {
    variable keydirectory
    variable confdirectory
    variable keysize
    variable expires
    variable openssl

    _initArray $args
```

The first thing we check is whether the key directory exists at all. If it does not, we create it:

```
if {![file exists $keydirectory]} {
    file mkdir $keydirectory
}
```

After this, we'll check if the file ca.key exists in the keys directory. If it exists, it means that CA has already been set up and there is no need to create those files:

```
if {![file exists [file join $keydirectory ca.key]]} {
```

If the file does not exist, we'll need to create the serial and index.txt files as before. These are used by OpenSSL to keep information about signed certificates.

```
set fh [open [file join $keydirectory serial] w]
puts $fh 01
close $fh

set fh [open [file join $keydirectory index.txt] w]
close $fh
```

Now we'll create a Tcl command that will run the openssl binary to create a CA key and certificate. We'll first build it as a Tcl list and evaluate it as the next step. This approach allows for logging and debugging which command will be run.

```
set command [list exec $openssl req -batch \
    -days $expires -nodes -new -x509 \
    -keyout [file join $keydirectory ca.key] \
    -out [file join $keydirectory ca.crt] \
    -config [file join $confdirectory openssl.cnf] \
    2>@1]

set result [eval $command]
```

We're using the exec command to run the openssl binary. We're also redirecting standard error to standard output using 2>@1 statement. This is because openssl writes additional information to standard error, and without this statement Tcl will throw an error that information was written to standard output.

Finally, we need to unset environment variables.

```
    }

    _finiArray
}
```

The final procedure is creating and signing a new certificate. It accepts the type of certificate—either client or server, the filename for keys, and arguments for certificate information. Certificate type is used to determine whether -extensions server should be passed to the openssl binary when signing the certificate. Filename is the base name for the key and certificate file to create.

We start by mapping the required namespace variables and initializing the ar array:

```
proc sslkeys::createAndSign {type filename args} {
    variable keydirectory
    variable confdirectory
    variable expires
    variable openssl

    _initArray $args
```

Now we build a Tcl list for running the openssl binary to create the key and run it:

```
set command [list exec $openssl req -batch \
    -days $expires -nodes -new \
    -keyout [file join $keydirectory $filename.key] \
    -out [file join $keydirectory $filename.csr] \
    -config [file join $confdirectory openssl.cnf] \
    2>@1]

set result [eval $command]
```

We then create a Tcl command for signing the new certificate.

```
set command [list exec $openssl ca -batch \
    -days $expires \
    -in [file join $keydirectory $filename.csr] \
    -out [file join $keydirectory $filename.crt] \
    -config [file join $confdirectory openssl.cnf] \
    ]
```

Next, if the certificate type is server, we also append the -extensions server option.

```
if {$type == "server"} {
    lappend command -extensions server
}
```

We then append the 2>@1 statement and run the command:

```
lappend command 2>@1

set result [eval $command]
```

Finally, we remove the `.csr` file which was used to sign the certificate and clean up the environment variables:

```
file delete \
    [file join $keydirectory $filename.csr]

_finiArray
}
```

This code can now be used to create a complete set of certificates for our system — starting with the CA certificate and providing both client and server keys. This can be used to create a communication system, which can authenticate each of the peers and ensure the security and integrity of communication.

In order to create a CA, server, and certificate key all we need to do is invoke the following commands:

```
sslkeys::initialize CN "CertificateAuthority"
```

The previous command will create our CA's key and certificate. Now we can create a certificate for a client which can only be used for outgoing connections:

```
sslkeys::createAndSign client client1 CN "client1"
```

We can also create a server certificate:

```
sslkeys::createAndSign server server1 CN "server1"
```

Now our client will have the `client1.key` and `client.crt` files ready. Our server will have `server1.key` and `server1.crt` available. These can now be used directly from the `tls` package.

It is always better to specify a meaningful value for the common name. Usually it'll also work in such way that the common name will be the system's identifier, which will also be the filename of the key. For examples in this chapter, we decided to use GUIDs and the common name was the same as the GUID generated by the client.

Using the code to generate SSL certificates is shown in more detail in the next section, which also shows how to automate the process of generating and assigning certificates to other parts of the system.

Managing certificates from Tcl

Now that we can create and sign certificates, the next step is to create a simple solution that would allow us to build an infrastructure using these keys. We'll create a server that handles creating certificates for clients and exports a simple service over HTTPS.

The following is a diagram of how communication from the client will look like:

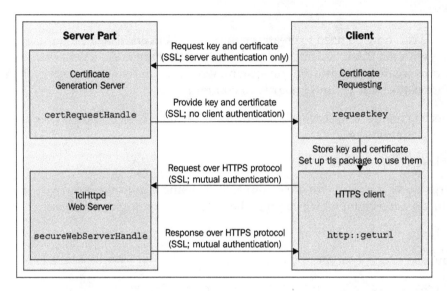

Our example will be performing the following steps:

1. The client requests a new key and certificate from the server; the client will check if the other side is valid by comparing the server's certificate against certificate authority's certificate, which the client needs to already have

2. The server provides the client with new key and certificate

3. The client can request information over HTTPS using newly created key and certificate

4. The server will be able to authenticate the other side by checking if the certificate is signed by certificate authority

All further communication can use HTTPS as a proper key has been provided to the client.

Our example will have a server that can create a complete certificate authority, create, and sign its own key. It will also offer a HTTPS server that will only accept requests from clients using a valid certificate. We will use the recently mentioned code for managing CA and server / client keys.

Additionally, our server will provide an SSL-enabled server for clients to request certificates. This server will not require a valid certificate. This would allow any client to request a certificate that would then be used for communicating over HTTPS. This is needed because the HTTPS server will not allow any incoming connections without a valid certificate. We'll create a dedicated service just for creating the key and a signed certificate that accepts connections without a valid certificate.

While the server will not be able to authenticate clients at this point, client will be able to use CA certificate to verify that a server can be trusted.

In a typical application, the client would start by requesting a new certificate if it does not have it. The HTTPS server would be used for communication, once the certificate has been issued. It could export services similar to those described in *Chapter 11, TclHttpd in Client-Server Applications,* or any other type of service.

In order to simplify the example, the protocol for requesting a certificate is very simple. A client connects over the SSL-encrypted socket. At this point the client does not have a valid certificate yet, so this will not be checked. It sends a single line specifying the command, common name, and e-mail address for the certificate. The server generates it and sends a response. It sends a single line containing a result, which is true or false, followed by the size of the key and certificate file in bytes. Next the key and certificate are sent as binary data. Since the client knows their sizes, it reads this back to key and certificate files. After retrieving a valid certificate, the client can now connect over HTTPS using a valid certificate and issue other commands.

In many cases, the infrastructure could also be extended to provide multiple servers. In this case, only one server would offer certificate creation — for both clients and servers. From then on communication could be made with all servers.

Server side

Let's start by creating server side of our sample application. It will be built up from two things — a server for issuing certificates and the HTTPS server for invoking commands for clients with valid certificates. The server side of the application will store all keys and certificates in the keys subdirectory. It will keep CA key and certificate, its own key and certificate, and certificates of all other systems in the network. Although keeping all certificates is not necessary, it is used as a mechanism for detecting whether a specified client has already had its key generated or not.

First we'll set up our server name, create a Certificate Authority, and create this server's certificate, if it does not exist yet:

```
set server "server1"

sslkeys::initialize CN "CertificateAuthority"

set sslkey [file join $sslkeys::keydirectory $server.key]
set sslcert [file join $sslkeys::keydirectory $server.crt]
if {![file exists $sslkey]} {
    sslkeys::createAndSign server $server CN $server
}
```

Next, we'll set up a `tls` package to use these keys and that requires a valid certificate:

```
tls::init -keyfile $sslkey -certfile $sslcert \
    -cafile [file join $sslkeys::keydirectory ca.crt] \
    -require true
```

Now let's set up the HTTPS server along with a very small application serving all requests:

```
package require tclhttpdinit
Httpd_SecureServer 9902

proc secureWebServerHandle {sock suffix} {
    set certinfo [dict get [tls::status $sock] subject]
    set client ""
    foreach item [split $certinfo ,/] {
        if {[regexp "^CN=(.*)\$" $item - client]} {
            break
        }
    }
    set text "Clock: [clock seconds]; Client: $client"
    Httpd_ReturnData $sock text/plain $text}

Url_PrefixInstall / secureWebServerHandle
```

Our server will listen for HTTPS requests on port 9902 and return information about the current time and client identifier, extracted from the SSL certificate. Since we require the certificate to be signed by a valid CA, we can assume that we can trust its value.

We can now proceed to creating code for requesting certificates. We'll start by setting up an SSL-enabled server socket that, as an exception from the `tls::init` invocation shown in the preceding code, does not require a valid SSL certificate. It will listen on port 9901 and run the `certRequestAccept` command for each new connection:

```
tls::socket -require false -server certRequestAccept \
    9901
```

Whenever a connection comes in, we configure the channel as non-blocking, set up binary translation, and set up an event each time it is readable:

```
proc certRequestAccept {chan host port} {
    fconfigure $chan -blocking 0 -buffering none -translation binary
    fileevent $chan readable [list certRequestHandle $chan]
}
```

Every time a channel is readable, our command will try to read a line from it. If it fails, we close the channel and do nothing:

```
proc certRequestHandle {chan} {
    if {[catch {gets $chan line} rc]} {
        catch {close $chan}
    } else {
```

If reading a line did not produce an error, we proceed with checking whether the end of the file has been reached for this channel or not. If it has, we also close it:

```
        set eof 1
        catch {set eof [eof $chan]}
        if {$eof} {
            catch {close $chan}
        } else {
```

Otherwise we check if a line has been read successfully. The variable `rc` stores whatever the `gets` command returned; if a complete line has been read, it will contain the number of characters read. Otherwise it will be set to 1:

```
            if {$rc < 0} {
                return
            }
```

If reading the line succeeds, we split the text on each white space to a list and assign each element of the list to variables. The first one is the command, only certificate being supported, followed by the common name and e-mail values to be used in certificate.

```
set line [split $line]
lassign $line command commonName email
if {$command != "certificate"} {
    close $chan
    return
}
```

We'll also use the common name as the filename for the keys. Usually common names would be identifiers used throughout the system, such as GUIDs.

The next step is to create a full path to the destination key and certificate files, and check if the certificate file exists:

```
set keyfile [file join \
    $sslkeys::keydirectory $commonName.key]
set certfile [file join \
    $sslkeys::keydirectory $commonName.crt]

if {[file exists $certfile]} {
```

If it exists, a client with this identifier has already requested this certificate. In this case, we send information that we refused to create a certificate and close the channel.

```
if {[catch {
    puts $chan "false 0 0"
    flush $chan
    close $chan
}]} {
    catch {close $chan}
}
} else {
```

If a certificate has not been created yet, we create it and get the size of both files.

```
sslkeys::createAndSign client $commonName \
    CN $commonName EMAIL $email
set keysize [file size $keyfile]
set certsize [file size $certfile]
```

Then, we send a response to the client specifying that a certificate has been generated and the size of both files.

```
if {[catch {
        puts $chan "true $keysize $certsize"
```

The next step is to send the contents of both files and flush the channel to make sure it gets sent:

```
set fh [open $keyfile r]
fconfigure $fh -translation binary
fcopy $fh $chan
close $fh
unset fh

set fh [open $certfile r]
fconfigure $fh -translation binary
fcopy $fh $chan
close $fh
unset fh

flush $chan
```

If writing the response produced an error, we assume that unless all data was sent, an error might have occurred. We close the socket and remove both keys and the certificate file.

```
}]} {
        catch {close $fh}
        catch {close $chan}
        catch {file delete -force $keyfile}
        catch {file delete -force $certfile}
} else {
```

We also try to close the `file handle` first—if an operation such as `fcopy` failed, the handle might have been left open and we need to close the file handle in order to delete it.

If the operation succeeds, we close the connection and only remove the private key. The certificate is left on the server for reference purposes, and for checking if it has already been passed to a client.

```
        catch {close $chan}
        file delete -force $keyfile
    }
}
}
}
}
```

Finally we need to enter Tcl's event loop:

```
vwait forever
```

We now have a complete server that allows the creation of SSL keys and certificates, and offers functionality over HTTPS protocol only to authenticated peers.

 The server code for this example is located in the `server.tcl` file in the `04keymgmt` directory in the source code examples for this chapter.

Client side

The next step is to create a client side of our application. It will contain two parts – a client for requesting a certificate and a test of whether issuing HTTPS requests using a valid certificate works afterwards. In order to make it easier to run both the server and client from the same directory and / or on the same computer, client stores all of its keys in the `keys-client` subdirectory. If both the server and client are run on the same computer, the client will copy the `ca.crt` file from the `keys` subdirectory. If not, it is needed to copy `ca.crt` from the `keys` directory on the machine where the server is running to the `keys-client` subdirectory on the machine where the client will be run.

We'll start creating client code by creating a command to retrieve a certificate. It accepts the hostname to connect to and the common name, and the e-mail to send.

First we will open a connection, set it to blocking and binary mode, and send a request to the server.

```
proc requestKey {hostname name email} {
    set chan [tls::socket $hostname 9901]
    fconfigure $chan -blocking 1 -translation binary
    puts $chan "certificate $name $email"
    flush $chan
```

Now, we read the result from the server and assign results to variables. If the server refused to create a certificate, we show an error.

```
gets $chan result
lassign [split $result] result keysize certsize
if {!$result} {
    close $chan
    error "Request to generate certificate denied"
} else {
```

If the server has created keys and certificates, we copy and save them in the keys-client directory. The common name is used as a base for the key and certificate filename. After that we close the connection to the server and return.

```
        set fh [open [file join keys-client $name.key] w]
        fconfigure $fh -translation binary
        fcopy $chan $fh -size $keysize
        close $fh

        set fh [open [file join keys-client $name.crt] w]
        fconfigure $fh -translation binary
        fcopy $chan $fh -size $certsize
        close $fh

        close $chan
    }
}
```

We can now move to initializing our client. We start by loading the tls and http packages, then set up the https protocol for http package and assign arguments passed to script as variables.

```
package require tls
package require http
http::register https 443 tls::socket

lassign $argv host name email
```

After this we check arguments that were passed. If either host or name is empty, we print out usage information on standard error and exit.

If only email is empty, we set it to $name@localhost, where $name is the common name passed as argument.

```
if {($host == "") || ($name == "")} {
    puts stderr "Usage: [info script] host name ?email?"
    exit 1
}

if {$email == ""} {
    set email "$name@localhost"
}
```

Now we create filenames of the key and certificate, and check if a certificate file exists:

```
set keyfile [file join "keys-client" "$name.key"]
set certfile [file join "keys-client" "$name.crt"]

if {![file exists $certfile]} {
```

If it does not exist, we set up `tls` to use the CA certificate and require a valid certificate from the remote peer. Next, we invoke the previously created `requestKey` function, passing the host to connect to, the common name and e-mail.

We also print the status—either that we've successfully requested the keys or that the keys were already present on the filesystem.

```
    tls::init \
        -cafile "keys-client/ca.crt" \
        -require true

    requestKey $host $name $email
    puts "SSL keys retrieved"
} else {
    puts "SSL keys already present"
}
```

We now initialize `tls` again, using key, certificate and CA information, requiring the remote peer to have a valid certificate.

```
tls::init \
    -cafile "keys-client/ca.crt" \
    -keyfile $keyfile \
    -certfile $certfile \
    -require true
```

Now we send an HTTPS request to the remote host. This connection will leverage the newly retrieved key and certificate:

```
set token [http::geturl "https://${host}:9902/test"]
```

Finally we check the result from the HTTPS request. If it is an `error` or `eof` status, we print out the information. If the request succeeds, we print out information about response.

```
switch -- [http::status $token] {
    error {
        puts "  ERROR: [http::error $token]"
    }
    eof {
```

```
        puts "  EOF reading response"
    }
    ok {
        puts "  OK; HTTP code: [http::ncode $token]"
        puts "  Response size: [http::size $token] bytes"
        puts "  Response:      [http::data $token]"
    }
}
http::cleanup $token
```

This concludes the code for a test client.

 The *Code of client* part of this example is located in the client.tcl file in the 04keymgmt directory in the source code examples for this chapter.

Testing our solution

Now that we have both client and server applications, we can run them in order to check if everything works. In order to run our example, we need to be sure that the openssl command can be run from the command line. A good test would be to run the version subcommand:

```
zoro@ubuntu:~$ openssl version
OpenSSL 0.9.8g 19 Oct 2007
```

If we have not received an error, we can continue. Otherwise we need to make sure openssl libraries and openssl command are installed in our system, and that the directory containing the openssl command is present in our shell's path.

This is usually the case on Unix systems. On Windows machines, it might be necessary to add a directory such as C:\Program Files\OpenSSL\bin to your path. For example, you can do this by running:

```
path "  C:\Program Files\OpenSSL\bin;%PATH%"
```

Of course, you will need to verify paths to your OpenSSL distribution first. After setting the path, you can verify if it is correct by running the openssl version command.

Assuming everything went fine we can move on to running the server. We can run it by using tclsh. For example:

```
zoro@ubuntu:~/tcl$ tclsh8.5 server.tcl
```

Then we can run the client. We need to specify the hostname and common name for the client:

```
zoro@ubuntu:~/tcl$ tclsh8.5 client.tcl 127.0.0.1 client1
```

Sample output from the client should be as follows:

```
OK; HTTP code: 200
Response size: 34 bytes
Response:       Clock: 1262879775; Client: client1
```

For the purpose of this example, we'll assume we're running both on the same machine. If this is not the case, we need to copy keys/ca.crt from the machine where the server is run as keys-client/ca.crt on the machine where the client will be run. We also need to specify actual server IP address or a hostname instead of 127.0.0.1.

Also, in real world scenarios, a request for a new certificate might be queued in the system, and require system administrator to confirm that a new certificate should be created. In these cases, the additional step of checking those permissions should be done on the server for each request. The client would need to periodically check if the certificate has been generated and then retrieve it.

Another feature omitted from this example is handling expiration of certificates. While for this example all certificates are generated to expire in 10 years, usually CA is generated for a very long period of time; all other certificates should expire much faster, such as in one year. In these cases clients would need to keep track of when their certificate expires, and request a new one either before that happens or as soon as this has happened.

SSL and performance issues

While SSL seems like a very good solution to all security aspects, we have to remember that it also introduces some drawbacks that we might need to take into account when creating software.

Using encrypted connections produces overhead. While it might seem minimal, it is worth remembering a few things about how using SSL for communication impacts it.

SSL generates a large overhead on both the client and server when a connection is established. This is usually a problem for the server side if a lot of connections are made; in these cases, it is a good idea to limit the number of connections.

One way to do this is to combine multiple requests into one, such as querying server for new tasks, if an update is available, and which modules should be loaded at once. Another option is to use the HTTP keep alive feature by using the -keepalive flag from the http package on the clients.

Encrypted communication itself also generates overhead; transferring things such as large files over an encrypted connection might be a bit slower than unencrypted files. Any modern computer will be able to keep up a transfer of several megabytes per second over SSL connections.

When a server is providing data over encrypted connection to multiple clients, the transfer rate might be much slower due to SSL overhead. This issue mainly applies to large environments, where big volumes of information need to be shared over encrypted networks. In many cases, it is also possible to create an instance of a web server just for providing files; either Tclhttpd or Apache configured for SSL handling.

Authorization and roles

Key-based authentication offers functionality to securely associate connections with peers within an infrastructure. Very often it is enough to make sure that only authenticated systems can communicate. There are also cases where we need to allow / disallow certain operations based on the remote peer issuing the command. The process of verifying whether a peer is allowed to issue a certain command or not is called authorization, as mentioned earlier in the chapter.

Very often we associate one or more roles to specified users or systems in the infrastructure. An example is that IT administrators need to perform different operations from regular users of a system. It could also be different from operations performed by an automated backup system.

Also, defining what each of the users or applications in the system is allowed to perform can be very time consuming. If our application offers a large number of features and supports hundreds of users or systems, it is a tedious process to define a set of features for each user.

A typical approach to standardizing this is to define roles, which can be a set of allowed and disallowed operations. It can also be additional information for these operations. A good example is distinguishing between users with limited permissions, normal users, and administrators. All these are roles and define sets of allowed operations.

Securing your application

Very often we will want our application to run Tcl code provided from a trusted or untrusted source. In these cases, it makes sense to run such scripts in environments with limited access to operating system and / or limited resources. In some cases, we can use this to provide an additional security layer. In other cases, it can be used as additional layer for securing ourselves against badly written code.

Typical examples of such cases include running code retrieved over the network. Our application may choose to limit access to an operating system for code written by sources we do not fully trust. An example is a data processing system using multiple computers; commands received from science units might be run in different environment than commands received from system administrators.

Slave interpreters, functionality offers creating a Tcl sandbox for running commands, which we might not want to have full access to our main application's code and / or provide additional security to limit the potential dangers of running these scripts. It works in such a way that we can create an additional Tcl interpreter, called the **slave interpreter**, which we can evaluate commands in. From our slave interpreter's perspective, the interpreter that created it is called the **master interpreter**.

In addition we might impose limits on some operations, such as terminating after a specified amount of time. This can be used to detect and terminate scripts that are taking too long to complete. It can also be used as a typical feature of an application, allowing users to specify if a command should be terminated after a specified time.

Safe interpreters are based on a more generic concept of slave interpreters, which allow for creating additional Tcl interpreters, exporting commands and channels as needed. This can be used to both provide security and provide a separate interpreter, which can't directly access data in other interpreters.

Slave interpreters

All slave interpreters are managed from the `interp` command. It is used to create normal and safe slave interpreters. All of its functionality is accessed using the command's subcommands. All slave interpreters are referenced by name and all interpreters are also accessible via an additional command, which is the same as interpreter name.

Each interpreter is a completely separated from other Tcl interpreters by default—it has different namespaces, variables, commands, and channels. This allows things such as running legacy code that uses same command or variable names as other parts of our application; names will not collide and all that is needed is additional code to use remote commands from an interpreter. We can also use information from different interpreters and details on how to do this are described later in this chapter.

Complete documentation of the `interp` command and all of its subcommands can be found at: `http://www.tcl.tk/man/tcl/TclCmd/interp.htm`

Using slave interpreters

Command `interp create` can be used to create a slave interpreter. It can be run without parameters, in which case it creates a unique interpreter name or one with the interpreter name as an argument. In the latter case, that name is used for the interpreter. The command also accepts the optional flag `-safe` as first argument. In most cases it is better to use a name provided by `interp create` command. This will not cause problems with the same interpreter name being used by multiple parts of an application, and is generally a better approach, especially in reusable code.

For example, we can create a slave interpreter by doing:

```
set childInterp [interp create]
```

This will set the `childInterp` variable to the name of a newly created interpreter. We can access slave interpreters functionality either by using the `interp` command's subcommands or by using the interpreter's own command. The name of the interpreter is the same as the name of the command created.

Slave interpreters are run in the same thread as the current interpreter; therefore, entering event loop in any of the interpreters will cause all interpreters to process events.

We can now evaluate Tcl commands in this interpreter using the `eval` subcommand. It can be run either from generic `interp` command or from the interpreter's own command.

Running `eval` from the interpreter's own command requires specifying command(s) to evaluate as arguments. For example:

```
puts "1 + 1 = [$childInterp eval {expr { 1 + 1 }}]"
```

This will cause the `expr 1+1` command to be evaluated in slave interpreter and result from that printed from master interpreter.

We can also use a generic `interp` command, which requires specifying the interpreter name followed by the command(s) to evaluate. For example:

```
set result [interp eval $childInterp {string repeat "Test " 10}]
```

The preceding code will evaluate the `string repeat` statement in the slave interpreter, and set the `result` variable in the master interpreter to the result of that command.

Commands passed to `eval` can be created as multiple arguments, but it is always a safer approach to specify all commands to evaluate as one argument.

We can also create commands using Tcl lists that will be evaluated in the slave interpreter. This can be used to pass arguments from local variables or for dynamically creating a command to run.

For example, we can set variables in the slave interpreter from a local value by doing:

```
$childInterp eval [list string repeat $someString 10]
```

This will cause a value of the variable `someString` in the master interpreter to be repeated 10 times, but using string repeat from the slave interpreter. This can be used to pass values from variables in the master as parameters to commands in the slave interpreter.

Sharing information with the slave interpreter

Tcl does not offer any way to map variables between the master and slave interpreter. Therefore, this is very often the most convenient way to set variables in slave interpreters.

For example, we can set variables in the slave interpreter from a local value by doing:

```
$childInterp eval [list set value $value]
```

This will set the variable in the slave interpreter to a current value from the master interpreter. However, if either the master or slave changes the value of a variable, this information will not be propagated.

Tcl channels are also not shared across interpreters by default. This means that a file opened in the master interpreter cannot be read from slave one without additional steps.

In order to use a channel from the master interpreter in the slave, we need to invoke the `interp share` or `interp transfer` commands. The first command makes a channel available in target interpreter without removing it from the source interpreter. The second command makes the channel available in the target interpreter, and removes it from the source interpreter. Both commands accept the source interpreter as the first argument, followed by the channel name and target interpreter.

For example, to make the `stdout` channel available in a slave interpreter we can do the following:

```
interp share {} stdout $childInterp
```

The channels `stdin`, `stdout`, and `stderr` are available in regular slave interpreters by default. They are not available in safe interpreters; if we want our safe interpreter to write to a standard output channel, we need to explicitly share the channel.

Channels shared between interpreters require both interpreters to close the channel for the underlying channel to be cleaned up. For example, if a file handle is shared across interpreters, unless all interpreters close it, the file will remain open. Channels transferred from one interpreter to another only need to be closed in the target interpreter.

Channel sharing and transferring can also be used to pass file handles or network connections to slave interpreters. For example, if we want to make code responsible for communication more secure, it can be run in a separate and safe interpreter.

Commands themselves cannot be shared, but the master interpreter can create commands in a slave interpreter by invoking the `eval` subcommand and running the `proc` command in the slave interpreter. Aliases also allow mapping of commands from the master interpreter to the slave interpreter. They are described in more detail in the next section.

The following table summarizes what information can be shared across interpreters:

Type	Command	Comments
Variables	N/A	Cannot be automatically shared; although variables in slave can be set from master
Channels	`interp share` `interp transfer`	Channels can be shared and / or transferred between interpreters
Commands	`interp alias`	Commands from any interpreter can be run in any other interpreter

Creating and managing aliases

Slave interpreters can create commands that invoke other commands in any other interpreters. It can be used to have a slave interpreter call command in master interpreter. It can be used to expose functionality to slave interpreters, create wrappers for safe interpreters that limit functionality. This functionality is called **aliases**.

Aliases can be created between any interpreters, but usually a master creates an alias that is accessible in a slave interpreter. Creating or retrieving aliases can be done using an alias command. Invoked as the `interp alias` command, it requires specifying a target interpreter as the first argument, the source interpreter the command should be run in, and the name of the command to run.

When creating an alias by running the `alias` subcommand of the interpreter's command, it only requires specifying the target command name and source command name. The target interpreter is the interpreter passed as a command name, and the source interpreter is the current interpreter.

This will create a command in the target interpreter; the name will be the target command name, specified as a first argument. When invoked, it will cause the source command to be invoked in the source interpreter.

We can create a command to increase the value of a global variable and print it out in the master interpreter:

```
proc incrCounter {variable} {
    global $variable
    set v [incr $variable]
    puts "Current value of \"$variable\" is $v"
}
```

It is worth noting that the preceding code is evaluated in the master interpreter, and we have to be careful with handling data passed by slave interpreters. For example, it is always a bad idea to pass values passed by users to commands such as `eval`. As we assume code run in the slave interpreter is not trusted, we also should not assume values passed by it are valid.

We also define an alias that will cause this command to be accessible from the slave interpreter under the same name.

```
interp alias $childInterp incrCounter {} incrCounter
```

An alias can be also created by invoking the interpreter command. The following command is equivalent to the previous code:

```
$childInterp alias incrCounter incrCounter
```

We can now invoke our command by doing:

```
set value 12
$childInterp eval {incrCounter value}
```

This will cause the `Current value of "value" is 13` to be printed on standard output. As the `incrCounter` command is actually evaluated in the master interpreter, no variables are passed to the slave interpreter and the variable itself is not fully accessible.

We can also add arguments to pass to this command, before arguments provided when invoked as target command after source command name.

For example:

```
interp alias $childInterp incrCounterValue {} incrCounter value
```

Next, we can invoke the following command:

```
$childInterp eval {incrCounterValue}
```

This will cause the `incrCounter` command to be invoked in the master interpreter with `value` as its argument. The output would be similar to `Current value of "value" is 14`.

Another example is creating commands for things like HTTP or POP3 protocols. We can then pass a token or any other information as part of the alias; for example:

```
set handle [pop3::open $hostname $username $password]
interp alias $childInterp emailRetrieve {} pop3::retrieve $handle
interp alias $childInterp emailList {} pop3::list $handle
```

This will cause commands `emailRetrieve` and `emailList` in the slave interpreter to access a valid POP3 session from the master interpreter. POP3 protocol and related commands are described in more detail in *Chapter 7, Using Common Internet Services*.

Typically aliases are used for two types of things. The first use is to export specific functions to the slave interpreter. This is then used to run scripts provided by users or different parts of the infrastructure; scripts themselves won't have access to an application's private data, but will be able to perform many operations remotely.

The second functionality is limiting the scope of a command. This is mainly used for safe interpreters. We can overwrite a command and check whether a specified operation is valid. For example, we can overwrite the `socket` command to only allow outgoing connections and only to specified hosts and / or ports. This method is described in more detail later in this chapter.

The Tcl slave interpreter's mechanism offers functionality for listing and getting definitions of aliases for a specified slave interpreter. This can be done using the aliases subcommand, either running the `interp aliases <interpName>` or `<interpName> aliases` command, where `<interpName>` is the name of the interpreter.

Retrieving the definition of an individual alias is done by invoking the `alias` subcommand with just alias name as argument. When invoking as an `interp alias` command, this needs to be prefixed by a target interpreter name — for example, `interp alias <interpName> <commandName>` or `<interpName> alias <commandName>`.

For example, we can list and print all aliases by doing:

```
foreach alias [interp aliases $childInterp] {
    puts "$alias is \"[$childInterp alias $alias]\""
}
```

Deleting interpreters

Deleting a slave interpreter can be done using the `interp delete` command. It accepts a single argument, which is the name of the interpreter to delete. For example, we can delete our previously deleted interpreter by doing:

```
interp delete $childInterp
```

Tcl automatically removes all information and objects related to this interpreter, such as timers, variables, commands, and channels.

 Examples of using slave interpreters, described in this and previous sections, is located in the `interp.tcl` file in `05slaveinterp` directory in the source code examples for this chapter.

Imposing limits on interpreters

Very often we need to limit time or the number of commands that can be run. In many cases it can serve as simply a mechanism for detecting infinite loops and / or other errors in the code sent to clients. This can be very useful mostly for scripts that are written and sent to clients ad hoc — often they will contain errors that can cause things such as infinite loops, or performing operations over a long period of time. Slave interpreter limits can be used to detect and prevent these issues.

Limits are checked before each command is run. If either number of commands run or time limit has been reached, an error is shown. If script has been run from the master interpreter, this error is then received by the master interpreter.

All limits are set using the `interp limit <interpName>` or `<interpName> limit` commands. The first argument is limit type, which can be either `time` or `commands`. It can be specified by one or more options for this limit. Options depend on limit type and are described further in the section.

When not specifying any additional option, it returns a list of name-value pairs containing all options and their current values. When specifying only the option name, its current value is returned. Specifying one or more options and corresponding values causes those options to be set.

There are two types of interpreter limits. We can set up a limit on the number of commands that can be run, specified as limit type `commands`. It accepts the `-value` option that specifies the number of commands, after which a limit should be reached.

Running the following command will cause an interpreter to limit it to only running 10000 commands:

```
$childInterp limit commands -value 10000
```

We can also set it in the following way:

```
interp limit $childInterp commands -value 10000
```

We can then run the following command:

```
set value 0
proc increaseValue {} {
    global value
    incr value
}
interp alias $childInterp increaseValue {} increaseValue

$childInterp eval {
    while {true} {increaseValue}
}
```

It will show after 10000 `increaseValue` command executions. At that point the `value` variable should be set to 10001 or a similar value. The actual number might differ depending on the Tcl version, and how limits are internally handled. It is not a good idea to depend on an exact value; instead use a reasonable limit.

The current number of commands run can be retrieved using the `info cmdcount` command. This is the same value that limits are compared to.

For example, setting the limit to allow 10000 more operations to be performed can be done as follows:

```
interp limit $childInterp commands -value \
    [expr {[$childInterp eval {info cmdcount}] + 10000}]
```

A time-based limit is another type of limit. It is defined as a time limit type and accepts two options -seconds and -milliseconds. The first option defines the Unix timestamp at which a limit for the interpreter should be triggered. This can be output from the clock scan command, but can be any Unix timestamp. The option -milliseconds defines the number of milliseconds after a specified Unix timestamp has been reached, at which point a limit should be triggered. This option should only be specified along with the -seconds option.

For example, in order to cause an interpreter to reach a limit after three seconds we can do the following:

```
$childInterp limit time -seconds [clock scan "+3 seconds"]
```

All types of limits also accept two additional options – -command and -granularity. Both options are set independently for each limit type.

The first option specifies a Tcl script to be executed in the interpreter that the interp limit command is currently run from. It can modify limits of the interpreter if it wants the interpreter to continue executing.

We can also modify how often a check is made by using the -granularity option. This option specifies how frequently a check is made; usually the check is done before any command invocation. Setting the value to a greater value will cause a check to be made less often, which increases performance, especially in the case of a time limit type. Usually it is not necessary to change the default values of this option, but if your application needs more exact limit checking, it is advised to set the -granularity option to 1 for all limit types.

An additional limit can be set on recursion, that is, how many times one command can invoke another inside it, either itself or any other procedure. We can specify after how many levels of recursion an error should be thrown by using interp recursionlimit <interpName> or <interpName> recursionlimit. If run without arguments, it returns the current limit. If run with a single argument, it sets the value of the recursion limit. For Tcl 8.4 and 8.5, the default value for all interpreters is 1000.

For example, we can test it in the following way:

```
$childInterp recursionlimit 16

$childInterp eval {
```

```
proc test {} {
    global recursecount
    incr recursecount
    test
}
test
}
```

This will give an error about the recursion limit being hit. The value of the `recursecount` variable in the slave interpreter should be set to 15 or similar. Similar to limits on a command count, it is not a good to depend on an exact value; instead use a reasonable limit.

 Examples of slave interpreter limits is located in the `limits.tcl` file in the `05slaveinterp` directory in the source code examples for this chapter.

Working with safe interpreters

As mentioned earlier, Tcl offers a mechanism for creating safe interpreters. These can be created using the `interp create` command with the `-safe` option provided. For example:

```
set childInterp [interp create -safe]
```

This will cause a safe Tcl interpreter to be created. It can be used in the same way as a regular slave interpreter. The main difference is that many commands are not accessible. For example, the command `socket` is not available by default. Default limitations and command hiding and exposing is explained later in this chapter.

One of the limitations is that such an interpreter cannot access any of Tcl's libraries, as source and other commands are not available by default. For example, the following will fail:

```
package require http
```

The ability to load packages and provide limited access to the filesystem using the Safe Base mechanism is described later in this chapter.

Another difference between safe and normal interpreters is how binary extensions, such as Tcl package for SQLite3, are loaded. Binary extensions have two different mechanisms for initialization, and when creating an extension its author can choose to limit functionality of an extension in safe interpreters. For example, the `sqlite3` package does not offer any functions in safe interpreters. The package `Tclx` only offers limited functionality in safe interpreters.

As mentioned earlier, safe interpreters do not have access to `stdin`, `stdout`, and `stderr` channels by default. The reason for this is that a safe interpreter is created with minimum resources available by default. We can use the `interp share` or `interp transfer` command to make some of the channels available in a safe interpreter.

Hiding and exposing commands

Slave interpreters do not offer a full set of Tcl commands so that commands such as `exit` could not be invoked, which would cause our application to exit completely. Instead of simply removing the commands, which would make any attempt of invoking them again impossible, slave interpreters allow hiding particular commands. This means that they can't be accessed directly (that is, invoking `exit` will not work), but can be invoked from the master interpreter.

This is often used in conjunction with an alias running in master interpreter that checks whether a particular operation can be performed; for example, before reading a file, a check can be made as to whether the interpreter should be allowed to read it.

Hiding a command can be done using the `interp hide <interpPath>` or `<interpPath> hide` commands. The command accepts the name of the command to hide as its argument. For example, in order to hide the command `after` we can do the following:

```
interp hide $childInterp after
```

The command `interp expose` can be used to make hidden commands available again. Similar to hide, it can be invoked as `interp expose <interpPath>` or `<interpPath> expose`. It takes one argument—the name of the hidden command. It can be used for commands hidden by both our code as well as by Tcl itself, such as `open` command for safe interpreters.

In order to make the `after` command available in the interpreter again, we can do the following:

```
$childInterp expose after
```

Commands that are hidden in a specified interpreter can be called using the `interp invokehidden` command; either invoked as `interp invokehidden <interpPath>` or `<interpPath> invokehidden`. It accepts the hidden command name as the first argument, followed by arguments to pass to the command.

Typically this is done so that a slave interpreter's command is hidden, then an alias is created that runs in the master interpreter and checks whether an operation can be allowed. If it is ok to continue, `invokehidden` is called to invoke the hidden command.

For example, let's consider modifying a socket command so that it only allows outgoing connections and only to specific hosts. We'll need to start by hiding the original `socket` command. The command `socket` is hidden by default for safe interpreters. For regular slave interpreters though, we can hide it using the following command:

```
$childInterp hide socket
```

Afer this, we need to create a procedure in the master interpreter that checks permissions and invokes the hidden `socket` command of the slave interpreter, only if it is ok to continue:

```
proc interpSocket {childInterp args} {
```

We accept any number of arguments since the `socket` command also accepts multiple switches.

We'll start by searching for the `-server` switch; if it is present, we show an error:

```
if {[lsearch $args "-server"] >= 0} {
    error "Server sockets not allowed"
}
```

Now let's retrieve the host name specified for the command. Usually it is the argument preceding the port, which is the last argument:

```
set host [lindex $args end-1]
```

After this we check whether the host is either www.google.com or 127.0.0.1. If it is we invoke the command. If not, we give out an error:

```
if {$host == "www.google.com"} {
    interp invokehidden $childInterp socket {*}$args
}   elseif {$host == "127.0.0.1"} {
    $childInterp invokehidden socket {*}$args
}   else  {
    error "Connections to $host not allowed"

}
}
```

Finally, we need to make an alias that maps the `socket` command in the slave interpreter to the `interpSocket` command in the master interpreter.

```
interp alias $childInterp socket {} interpSocket $childInterp
```

After that, we can test our code by running the following code:

```
$childInterp eval {
    set chan [socket www.google.com 80]
    set chan [socket malicious-server 80]
}
```

It should terminate with error `Connections to malicious-server not allowed` or a similar error.

 The preceding example is located in the `socket.tcl` file in the `06safetcl` directory in the source code examples for this chapter.

Default safe interpreter setup

Safe interpreters come with limited functionality by default. Many commands are hidden by default. Commands that allow network or filesystem access are disabled. They also cannot access environment variables via global `env` array; giving untrusted code access to a user's environment variables is not considered safe.

Safe interpreters can't also access standard channels—`stdin`, `stdout`, and `stderr`. We can share any of these channels using the `interp share` command, but by default they are not accessible.

Interpreters do not also have the possibility of loading additional packages by default; as commands such as open and source·are unavailable, Tcl has no way to load any additional package.

Even though safe interpreters have access to the `interp` command, this command also has limited functionality. Safe interpreters can only create other safe slave interpreters, even if the `-safe` switch is not specified when using `interp create`, a new interpreter is created as safe anyway. Safe interpreters can't also change the limits (commands, time, and recursion limits) of its own interpreter. It is also not possible to call the `interp invokehidden` command, as safe interpreters can't get access to hidden commands.

Detailed information about commands available by default in safe interpreters, as well as what are additional limitations of safe interpreters, can be found at `http://www.tcl.tk/man/tcl8.5/TclCmd/interp.htm#M42`.

Using Safe Base

Safe interpreters cannot load any packages by default and their use is very limited. Tcl also comes with a Safe Base package that extends safe interpreter functionality to allow limited filesystem access as well as other additions that aid in package loading.

Safe Base uses safe interpreters created with the `interp create -safe` command. Safe Base creates additional commands, described further in this section, that allow more functionality while retaining the safety of the interpreter. Such interpreters can load basic Tcl packages, but cannot access parts of the filesystem other than the Tcl libraries that are included in Tcl itself.

We can create a safe interpreter using Safe Base by invoking the `safe::interpCreate` command. It accepts an optional interpreter name. It also accepts one or more options. These options are described later in this section.

```
set childInterp [safe::interpCreate]
```

This creates a safe Tcl interpreter that can only access the part of the filesystem that contains Tcl libraries. We can now safely load packages such as `http`, but trying to source any file outside of Tcl's libraries fails. For example:

```
$childInterp eval {source /tmp/myscript.tcl}
```

The preceding code will give a `permission denied` error.

We can also initialize any existing safe interpreter to offer Safe Base's extended functionality using the `safe::interpInit` command. It accepts the slave interpreter and options for the interpreter. For example:

```
set childInterp [interp create -safe]
safe::interpInit $childInterp
```

Safe Base supports the options `-accessPath`, `-deleteHook`, `-statics`, and `-nested`. The first option specifies a list of paths that the interpreter is allowed to access. Adding and removing directories from the list allows for managing paths where the interpreter can source and load files from.

The option `-deleteHook` defines the command to run just before this interpreter is deleted. This command will be run with the interpreter's name specified as an additional argument. This can be used for retrieving values or cleaning up data kept outside of the specified interpreter.

The option -statics specifies whether a package is allowed to load statically defined packages. The option -nested specifies whether this slave interpreter will be allowed to load packages into its own slave interpreters. These options are mainly meant for dealing with packages created in C, and can be left as they are for the majority of Safe Base uses.

These options can be changed or read at any time using the safe::interpConfigure command, followed by the slave interpreter name. If invoked with no additional arguments, it returns a name-value pair's list with all available options and their current values. Specifying just the option name returns the current value for that option. Specifying one or more name-value pairs sets these options to new values.

For example:

```
interp::safeConfigure $childInterp -accessPath \
    [linsert \
        [interp::safeConfigure $childInterp -accessPath] 0 \
        "/path/to/libraries"]
```

This command will read the current -accessPath option's value and insert /path/to/libraries as the first item in the path list.

Deleting an interpreter created using Safe Base can be done using the safe::interpDelete command. For example:

```
safe::interpDelete $childInterp
```

This will cause the delete hook to be run and the interpreter to be deleted.

Complete documentation for Safe Base and Safe Tcl functionality can be found at: http://www.tcl.tk/man/tcl/TclCmd/safe.htm

Safe Base and filesystem access

In order to provide loading of packages, Safe Base provides a few additional commands in addition to the ones safe interpreters offer. These are source, load, file, glob, encoding, and exit. The first two commands limit filesystem to only access packages in specified paths.

The scope of the glob command has been limited to only access directories in the interpreter's path. The command file is limited to dirname, join, extension, root, tail, pathname, and split subcommands. The command encoding cannot change system encoding or access / change paths where encodings are looked up. Finally, exit causes only the interpreter to be deleted, but the Tcl process and master interpreter is left intact.

More details about commands available in Safe Base-created safe interpreters can be found at `http://www.tcl.tk/man/tcl/TclCmd/safe.htm#M21`.

Unlike default slave interpreters, Safe Base offers limited file system access. By default only `source` and `load` command are available for accessing files. These allow for loading packages without providing direct access to a file system.

In addition, the list of directories that can be accessed is limited. The configuration option `-accessPath` provides a list of directories that can be accessed from within the interpreter. We can retrieve the current value, modify, and set it using `safe::interpConfigure` command.

We can also use the `safe::interpAddToAccessPath` command to add additional directories to the access list. It accepts the interpreter name and directory to add to the list. This is a helper function that checks if a path exists, and adds it if it does not exist. If the path is already in the access list, an error is produced.

For example, in order to add `/tmp` to the list of accessible directories, we can do:

```
safe:: interpAddToAccessPath $childInterp /tmp
```

Another feature of Safe Base is the ability to obscure actual directory names. In many cases, finding out the path to where an application or user's directory is set up can be sensitive information; for example, providing a path to the home directory can specify a user's name, which might not always be what the script should be able to access.

For this purpose, Safe Base Tcl has provided a mechanism for translating paths to obscure original paths.

The `safe::interpFindInAccessPath` command can be used to find a path in an interpreter and convert it into a safe representation. It accepts the interpreter name followed by the directory name.

For example, we can map the Tcl library directory to a safe representation by doing:

```
set safepath [safe::interpFindInAccessPath \
    $childInterp $tcl_library]

puts "Directory $tcl_library is mapped to $safetcldir"
```

The variable `tcl_library` is defined by Tcl and specifies the directory used for Tcl base functionality. The output from this would be something similar to `/opt/ActiveTcl-8.5/lib/tcl8.5` is mapped to `$p(:0:)`.

We can then use this for commands such as source or load from within a Safe Base interpreter. For example, to manually load parray.tcl from the Tcl library directory we can do:

```
$childInterp eval [list source \
    [file join $safetcldir parray.tcl]]
```

This will invoke a command similar to source $p(:0:)/parray.tcl. Implementation of the source command in Safe Base will map this to actual path.

Examples of using the safe interpreter and accessing the file system can be found in the safebase_filesystem.tcl file in the 06safetcl directory, in the source code examples for this chapter.

We can also extend the approach taken from source command and create an open command wrapper that only allows files specified in the -accessPath option to be opened

We can start by creating a wrapper that checks whether a path can be accessed or not. It accepts the slave interpreter name and directory name:

```
proc safeCheckAccessPath {childInterp dirname} {
    if {[catch {
        set path [safe::TranslatePath $childInterp $dirname]
        safe::DirInAccessPath $childInterp $path
    }]} {
        return ""
    } else {
        return $path
    }
}
```

The directory name is translated first, which expands obscured paths and a check is made as to whether it can be accessed or not. If any of these operations fail, an empty string is returned. Otherwise a valid path is returned.

This command uses Safe Base's internal commands safe::TranslatePath and safe::DirInAccessPath. The first command translates path; expanding obscured paths such as $p(:0:) and making sure it does not contain dangerous items. Second command checks if a path can be accessed and returns an error if it cannot be accessed.

Now we can create a safe open command wrapper. It takes the interpreter name, a list of allowed open modes, and any additional arguments. Open modes can be those such as r, w, r+, w+, and all others supported by the open command. Please see *Chapter 2, Advanced Tcl Features* for more details about open modes.

The command first splits the path and checks whether the directory can be accessed or not, and if specified, the access mode is in the list of allowed open modes. We also check if `allowedModes` is not set to *; this causes all modes to be available. If either directory is not in the allowed path or the mode is not allowed, an error occurs. Otherwise, the `hidden` open command is invoked in the slave interpreter, and a file handle is returned.

```
proc safeOpen {childInterp allowedModes name {access r} args} {
    set dirname [safeCheckAccessPath $childInterp \
        [file dirname $name]]
    set filetail [file tail $name]

    if {($dirname == "") ||
        (([lsearch $allowedModes $access] < 0) &&
        ($allowedModes != "*"))} {
        return -code error "Permission denied"
    }
    return [interp invokehidden $childInterp open \
        [file join $dirname $filetail] $access {*}$args]
}
```

We can now create an alias that only allows reading files for reading by doing:

```
$childInterp alias open safeOpen $childInterp {r}
```

We can then test opening various files. The following command will succeed as, by default, the Tcl library directory is accessible:

```
$childInterp eval [list open $tcl_library/tclConfig.sh]
```

However, trying to read a file outside it will fail:

```
$childInterp eval [list open /etc/passwd]
```

We can also use an obscured filename using the `safetcldir` variable set earlier:

```
$childInterp eval [list open $safetcldir/tclConfig.sh]
```

In addition to this, any attempt to open a file for writing will fail, even if the file itself can be accessed for reading:

```
$childInterp eval [list open $tcl_library/tclConfig.sh w]
```

 Safe implementation of the `open` command is located in the `safebase_open.tcl` file in the `06safetcl` directory in the source code examples for this chapter.

Role-based authorization and interpreters

Safe Base and safe interpreters can also be used to create role-based authorization to functionality. We can use it to create sandboxes based on what roles the user is able to access.

We'll also modify the concept a bit—instead of defining a role, we'll define levels for various items. For example, let's consider file access; we can think of cases where limited and read-only access is enough. Other tasks (such as system maintenance) might need to have full access to the entire filesystem.

Similarly for network functionality and limits, in some cases it is good to disable connectivity and set up a one minute limit on execution. In other cases it might be a good idea not to impose limits on any of these, especially for network-related activities, which can also take time due to lagged networks or hosts being down.

We'll use separate Tcl namespaces for defining various roles and a list of acceptable values. Commands for applying roles will be put in the `roles` namespace. Each role is defined as a child namespace; for example, `roles::limits`.

Each role will define the `values` variable in its namespace that will specify acceptable values. The default value for the role will be the first value in the list of acceptable values. For example:

```
set roles::limits::values [list none 5s 10s 60s 300s]
```

This defines that acceptable values for the `limits` role are `none`, `5s`, `10s`, `60s`, and `300s`. The value of `none` is the default value if not specified.

Applying roles to an interpreter is also simple. We'll create a command for applying any acceptable value for each of the roles. Its name will be in the form of `<value>Apply`, and it will be defined in the namespace for this role. A command to apply `none` value to the `limits` role would be defined as the `roles::limits::noneApply` command.

This way, creation of an interpreter will simply require getting values for all available roles and applying them.

Creating interpreters using roles

We can create a procedure that creates a safe interpreter based on name-value pairs of roles. Each role is defined by the role name (such as file access) and value (such as read-only).

Let's start with procedure definition:

```
proc roles::safeInterpCreate {roles} {
```

We'll create a list containing the actual `roles` definition, based on provided values and default values for roles not specified in the `roles` argument.

The procedure will start by listing all existing roles and setting the value to the default value.

```
    set allroles [list]
    # map current role definitions to all available roles
    # and create a complete list of values for each role
    foreach ns [namespace children ::roles] {
        set role [namespace tail $ns]
        set values [set ${ns}::values]
        set value [lindex $values 0]
```

If a value of a current role is specified in the input list of roles, we check if it is any of acceptable values. If this is the case, we set the value to what was specified as the value for this role.

```
        if {[dict exists $roles $role]} {
            set v [dict get $roles $role]
            if {[lsearch -exact $values $v] >= 0} {
                set value $v
            }
        }
```

Finally we add the role name and value, either the default or that provided by the user, to the list of all roles and their values.

```
        lappend allroles $role $value
    }
```

The next step is to create an interpreter using Safe Base and apply all of the roles.

```
    set childInterp [safe::interpCreate]

    foreach {role value} $allroles {
        ::roles::${role}::${value}Apply $childInterp
    }

    return $childInterp
}
```

For many of the roles we might want to expose a command, assuming it has not already been exposed. For this reason, we also create a helper procedure `roles::exposeCommand`:

```
proc roles::exposeCommand {childInterp command} {
    if {[lsearch -exact [$childInterp hidden] $command] >= 0} {
        $childInterp expose $command
    }
}
```

It checks whether a command is hidden or not and if it is, exposes it. This will cause hidden commands to be exposed and commands already available to be skipped.

Sample role definitions

Roles will usually depend on the types of tasks that scripts run in a sandbox would be performing. However, some roles such as managing access to the filesystem and network can be considered common.

One of the common roles could be managing file access, which can be set to:

- no file access
- read-only
- read-write access to limited set of directories
- full access to entire filesystem

Let's start by defining this role's namespace and `values` variable:

```
namespace eval roles::files {}
```

```
set roles::files::values [list none readonly readwrite full]
```

Now we need to implement a method to apply any of these values to an interpreter.

The filesystem access does not perform any operations at all, but needs to be created:

```
proc roles::files::noneApply {childInterp} {
}
```

Read-only access and read-write access use `safeOpen`, which was implemented earlier in this chapter. For this example, it has been moved to the `roles::files` namespace. Read-only access specifies `r` as the only mode available. Read-write does not limit open access modes.

Both read-only and read-write modes also expose the fconfigure command to allow specification of encoding, translation, and other parameters needed for reading from and/or writing to files.

```
proc roles::files::readonlyApply {childInterp} {
    # create an alias for open to allow any operation
    # within limited paths only
    $childInterp alias ::open \
        ::roles::files::safeOpen $childInterp "r"
    roles::exposeCommand $childInterp fconfigure
}

proc roles::files::readwriteApply {childInterp} {
    # create an alias for open to allow any operation
    # within limited paths only
    $childInterp alias ::open \
        ::roles::files::safeOpen $childInterp "*"
    roles::exposeCommand $childInterp fconfigure
}
```

Full access to the filesystem exposes open, fconfigure, and file commands in their full functionality.

The alias for the file command needs to be removed prior to exposing the original file command.

```
proc roles::files::fullApply {childInterp} {
    roles::exposeCommand $childInterp open
    roles::exposeCommand $childInterp fconfigure

    $childInterp alias file {}
    roles::exposeCommand $childInterp file
}
```

Defining the time limits roles is very similar. We define available values, which correspond to time limits that will be imposed on the interpreter.

```
namespace eval roles::limits {}

set roles::limits::values [list none 5s 10s 60s 300s]
```

Applying no limits simply does nothing:

```
proc roles::limits::noneApply {childInterp} {
}
```

Any other limit requires specifying an appropriate value for the -seconds option to the interp limit command and time limit type. We'll use the clock scan command for this:

```
proc roles::limits::5sApply {childInterp} {
    $childInterp limit time -seconds [clock scan "+5 seconds"]
}

proc roles::limits::10sApply {childInterp} {
    $childInterp limit time -seconds [clock scan "+10 seconds"]
}

proc roles::limits::60sApply {childInterp} {
    $childInterp limit time -seconds [clock scan "+60 seconds"]
}

proc roles::limits::300sApply {childInterp} {
    $childInterp limit time -seconds [clock scan "+300 seconds"]
}
```

Using role-based interpreters

We can now create a sample interpreter that can access all files, has limited network connectivity, and has a five-second time limit.

```
set childInterp [roles::safeInterpCreate [list \
    files full \
    network local \
    limits 5s \
    ]]
```

We can now test if our new interpreter can connect to the www.packtpub.com port 80 by running:

```
if {[catch {
    $childInterp eval {socket www.packtpub.com 80}
} error]} {
    puts "Remote connection failed: $error"
} else {
    puts "Remote connection succeeded"
}
```

The result should be a message saying `Remote connection failed: Connection to www.packtpub.com disallowed` or something similar.

We can also try to run an infinite loop, which should also fail:

```
$childInterp eval {set j 0; while {true} {incr j}}
```

 A complete example is located in the `07roles` directory in the source code examples for this chapter.

The `roles.tcl` file is the main file, while `role_file.tcl`, `roles_limit.tcl` and `roles_network.tcl` files define sample roles for file, network access, and limits.

Summary

Security is a very important aspect of creating an application. It should be considered when creating a complex application; for example, how to securely communicate, establish a system for authenticating and authorizing users, and many other aspects.

In this chapter, we have learned how to:

- Use SSL to create client and server applications.
- Set up our own Public Key Infrastructure using the OpenSSL package. This can be used to set up a set of SSL keys and certificates, which all components of our system can use to authenticate themselves.
- Create a secure communication system, and make sure all certificates can be generated and transferred securely to remote systems before they can be fully authenticated within the infrastructure.
- Use Tcl slave interpreters as parts of the application and / or provide a sandbox for running potentially untrusted code.
- Tcl mechanisms for securing evaluation of such code, as well as ways of limiting resources that such code could use.
- Apply role-based authorization to providing functionality in slave interpreters.
- Use safe Tcl interpreters, authentication, and roles to provide an efficient and easy-to-manage way to create interpreters customized for a particular user, and / or operation's privileges and access rights.

While this chapter focused on the security aspects of creating a networked application, this is far from covering all possible aspects of security that we should have in mind. Whenever designing or writing a networked application and / or an application that takes input from users, it is always a good idea to think about how the user input could either cause unwanted effects, gain access to information that should not be exposed or even damage the system itself. Creating a proper security model is a large issue and should be dealt with for obtaining each solution separately.

This chapter concludes this book. You are encouraged to run examples that were shown throughout the book as well as experiment on your own with Tcl, how it can be used to build networked applications. We hope that you have found Tcl's unique ability to create standalone binaries useful. We also hope that this book will be the beginning of your journey into the world of Tcl, networking, and creating solutions using technologies presented throughout this book.

Index

T

Tcl
about 8, 9, 46
channel 73
databases, using 184
data types 49
default channels 73
e-mail, handling 248
event-driven programming 90
extensions 12
features 46
file operations 73
files, accessing 73
files, transfering 271
global variable 54
installation 13
internationalization 176
local variable 54
modules 89
multithreaded applications 98
namespace variable 54
object-oriented programming 62
object types 49
package, creating 88
package, loading 87
packages 87
raw values, storing 204, 205
Scotty 334
SQL, using 183
stack frames 56
TCP sockets, using 208
Tk 12
time and date manipulation 46-48
time package 298
UDP sockets, using 234
variables, types 54
XMl, handling 195-204

Tcl, as CGI scripts
html package, used 362
ncgi package, used 357, 358
using 355-357

Tcl-ers 107

TclApp 132

Tcl applications
commands, limiting 314-316
commands, performing asynchronously 310, 311
comm client and server 307-309
comm package, using 307
communicating with 307
debugging 157
logging 136
security 528
security aspects 311-314
troubleshooting 135

Tcl commands documentation syntax 22

Tclcron
about 97
manual package 97

tclcron::schedule command 97

Tcl Dev Kit Debugger
about 162
features 169
local debugging 162-163
remote debugging 167

Tcl Dev Kit Inspector 158-161

Tcl events
-command option 95
-size option 95

Tcl event types
file/channel events 90
GUI events 91
idle events 91
time events 90

TclHttpd
about 367
configuring 372
default directory structure 371
documentation 368
homepage link 367
installing 367
performance 373
running 369, 370
startup parameters 371

Tclhttpd 465

TclHttpd server
CGI, using 374
debugging 402, 403
document type handlers, creating 379
domain handlers 386
embedding, in application 404-408
programming 373

Thank you for buying
Tcl 8.5 Network Programming

About Packt Publishing

Packt, pronounced 'packed', published its first book "*Mastering phpMyAdmin for Effective MySQL Management*" in April 2004 and subsequently continued to specialize in publishing highly focused books on specific technologies and solutions.

Our books and publications share the experiences of your fellow IT professionals in adapting and customizing today's systems, applications, and frameworks. Our solution based books give you the knowledge and power to customize the software and technologies you're using to get the job done. Packt books are more specific and less general than the IT books you have seen in the past. Our unique business model allows us to bring you more focused information, giving you more of what you need to know, and less of what you don't.

Packt is a modern, yet unique publishing company, which focuses on producing quality, cutting-edge books for communities of developers, administrators, and newbies alike. For more information, please visit our website: www.packtpub.com.

About Packt Open Source

In 2010, Packt launched two new brands, Packt Open Source and Packt Enterprise, in order to continue its focus on specialization. This book is part of the Packt Open Source brand, home to books published on software built around Open Source licences, and offering information to anybody from advanced developers to budding web designers. The Open Source brand also runs Packt's Open Source Royalty Scheme, by which Packt gives a royalty to each Open Source project about whose software a book is sold.

Writing for Packt

We welcome all inquiries from people who are interested in authoring. Book proposals should be sent to author@packtpub.com. If your book idea is still at an early stage and you would like to discuss it first before writing a formal book proposal, contact us; one of our commissioning editors will get in touch with you.

We're not just looking for published authors; if you have strong technical skills but no writing experience, our experienced editors can help you develop a writing career, or simply get some additional reward for your expertise.

open source
community experience distilled

Drupal 6 Social Networking

ISBN: 978-1-847196-10-1   Paperback: 312 pages

Build a social or community web site, with friends lists, groups, custom user profiles, and much more

1. Step-by-step instructions for putting together a social networking site with Drupal 6

2. Customize your Drupal installation with modules and themes to match the needs of almost any social networking site

3. Allow users to collaborate and interact with each other on your site

4. Requires no prior knowledge of Drupal or PHP; but even experienced Drupal users will find this useful to modify an existing installation into a social web site

Zabbix 1.8 Network Monitoring

ISBN: 978-1-847197-68-9   Paperback: 428 pages

Monitor your network hardware, servers, and web performance effectively and efficiently

1. Start with the very basics of Zabbix, an enterprise-class open source network monitoring solution, and move up to more advanced tasks later

2. Efficiently manage your hosts, users, and permissions

3. Get alerts and react to changes in monitored parameters by sending out e-mails, SMSs, or even execute commands on remote machines

4. In-depth coverage for both beginners and advanced users with plenty of practical, working examples and clear explanations

Please check **www.PacktPub.com** for information on our titles

Drools JBoss Rules 5.0
Developer's Guide

ISBN: 978-1-847195-64-7   Paperback: 320 pages

Develop rules-based business logic using the
Drools platform

1. Discover the power of Drools as a platform for
   developing business rules

2. Build a custom engine to provide real-time
   capability and reduce the complexity in
   implementing rules

3. Explore Drools modules such as Drools Expert,
   Drools Fusion, and Drools Flow, which adds
   event processing capabilities to the platform

4. Execute intelligent business logic with ease
   using JBoss/Drools, a stronger business-rules
   solution

GlassFish Security

ISBN: 978-1-847199-38-6   Paperback: 296 pages

Secure your GlassFish installation, Web applications,
EJB applications, Application Client modules, and
Web services

1. Secure your GlassFish installation and J2EE
   applications

2. Develop secure Java EE applications including
   Web, EJB, and Application Client modules

3. Secure web services using GlassFish and
   OpenSSO web service security features

4. Support SSL in GlassFish including Mutual
   Authentication and Certificate Realm with this
   practical guide

Please check **www.PacktPub.com** for information on our titles